T0206975

Electronics Projects with the ESP8266 and ESP32

Building Web Pages, Applications, and WiFi Enabled Devices

Neil Cameron

Apress®

Electronics Projects with the ESP8266 and ESP32: Building Web Pages, Applications, and WiFi Enabled Devices

Neil Cameron
Edinburgh, UK

ISBN-13 (pbk): 978-1-4842-6335-8   ISBN-13 (electronic): 978-1-4842-6336-5
https://doi.org/10.1007/978-1-4842-6336-5

Managing Director, Apress Media LLC: Welmoed Spahr
Acquisitions Editor: Natalie Pao
Development Editor: James Markham
Coordinating Editor: Jessica Vakili

Distributed to the book trade worldwide by Springer Science+Business Media New York, 1 NY Plaza, New York, NY 10004. Phone 1-800-SPRINGER, fax (201) 348-4505, e-mail orders-ny@springer-sbm.com, or visit www.springeronline.com. Apress Media, LLC is a California LLC and the sole member (owner) is Springer Science + Business Media Finance Inc (SSBM Finance Inc). SSBM Finance Inc is a **Delaware** corporation.

For information on translations, please e-mail booktranslations@springernature.com; for reprint, paperback, or audio rights, please e-mail bookpermissions@springernature.com.

Apress titles may be purchased in bulk for academic, corporate, or promotional use. eBook versions and licenses are also available for most titles. For more information, reference our Print and eBook Bulk Sales web page at http://www.apress.com/bulk-sales.

Any source code or other supplementary material referenced by the author in this book is available to readers on GitHub via the book's product page, located at www.apress.com/978-1-4842-6335-8. For more detailed information, please visit http://www.apress.com/source-code.

Printed on acid-free paper

Table of Contents

About the Author

Neil Cameron is an experienced analyst and programmer with a deep interest in understanding the application of electronics. Neil wrote the book *Arduino Applied: Comprehensive Projects for Everyday Electronics* by Apress. He was a research scientist and has previously taught at the University of Edinburgh and Cornell University.

About the Technical Reviewer

Mike McRoberts is the author of *Beginning Arduino* by Apress. He is winner of Pi Wars 2018 and member of Medway Makers. He is an Arduino and Raspberry Pi enthusiast.

C/C++, Arduino, Python, Processing, JS, Node-Red, NodeJS, Lua.

Preface

It's never been so easy and practical to access information over the Internet, develop web pages to update sensor information, build mobile apps to remotely control devices with speech recognition, or incorporate *Google Maps* in a GPS route tracking app. The combination of Wi-Fi functionality, high computing power, and low cost of the ESP8266 and ESP32 development boards extends the range of opportunities for microcontrollers. Communicating with devices and accessing information over the Internet with the ESP8266 and ESP32 microcontrollers is the focus of *Electronics Projects with the ESP8266 and ESP32.*

The first section (Chapters 1 to 6) of the book demonstrates the ease of use and the power of the ESP8266 and ESP32 microcontrollers to access and display information on the Internet. Projects include building an Internet radio, an Internet-based clock, and an international weather station and a project with the ESP32-CAM camera to upload pictures to a web page.

The book's second section (Chapters 7 to 9) covers web page design projects for updating your web page with sensor information using real-time graphics or controlling a remote device through a web page. You'll learn about AJAX (Asynchronous JavaScript and XML), which combines XML (eXtensible Markup Language) HTTP (Hypertext Transfer Protocol) requests for updating a web page with JavaScript to manage those requests, JSON (JavaScript Object Notation) to combine information transmitted by a server to the client, the two-way fast communication WebSocket protocol, MQTT brokers, and IFTTT (If This, Then That) for communication between devices on different networks. The practical projects include uploading information to the Internet and controlling devices from anywhere in the world with the ESP8266 and ESP32 microcontrollers.

Mobile apps are now ubiquitous, making the app build projects in the book's third section (Chapters 10 to 13) very relevant. An app to control remotely located motors connected to an ESP8266 or ESP32 development board mimics robotics used in the automotive industry; a speech recognition app controls devices; and a GPS tracking app, incorporating *Google Maps*, displays the current position and route information. Each project with the ESP8266 and ESP32 microcontrollers is fully described, as no previous experience in mobile app design and build is required.

Communication between ESP8266 and ESP32 microcontrollers is described in the fourth section (Chapters 14 to 18) of the book. The built-in *ESP-NOW* communication system, LoRa (long range), and RF (Radio Frequency) communication are applied to controlling remotely located devices with the device information updated on a web page by the ESP8266 and ESP32 microcontrollers. Communication protocols are extended to signal generation with the ESP8266 and ESP32 microcontrollers transmitting alphanumeric text or signals to produce sounds, as used in electronic music. Signal generation without a microcontroller is illustrated with an electronic piano, a motor control project, and an alarm system including an MP3 player with a movement detector. The book's fourth section spans the built-in communication protocol of the ESP8266 and ESP32 microcontrollers to communication with back-to-basics electronics. A chapter on measuring electricity with an ESP8266 or ESP32 microcontroller, applied to a solar panel project, continues the electronics theme to understand the methodology behind sensors.

The ESP32 microcontroller is more powerful than the ESP8266 microcontroller and also includes Bluetooth and Bluetooth Low Energy (BLE) communication. Chapters on practical differences between the ESP8266 and ESP32 microcontrollers and on specific features of the ESP32 microcontroller form the last section (Chapters 21 and 22) of the book.

Throughout the book, all differences in libraries or instructions for the ESP8266 and ESP32 microcontrollers are described, as each project is compatible with both microcontrollers.

All sections of the book are stand-alone, so you can delve into a section of the book rather than having to start from the beginning. Several chapters build on information from earlier chapters. For example, Chapter 12 (*GPS tracking app with Google Maps*) incorporates mobile app design, Bluetooth communication, sourcing information from the Internet, and updating a web page. Some programming experience with the Arduino IDE is assumed, although all sketches are completely described and comprehensively commented. The book *Arduino Applied: Comprehensive Projects for Everyday Electronics* is recommended as an introduction to microcontrollers ranging from blinking an LED to building a robot car. Schematic diagrams were produced with *Fritzing* software (`www.fritzing.org`), with an emphasis on maximizing the clarity of component layout and minimizing overlapping connections. Authors of libraries used in the book are acknowledged in each chapter, with library details included in the Appendix. All the Arduino IDE sketches and MIT App Inventor source code for the apps are available to download at *GitHub* (`github.com/Apress/ESP8266-and-ESP32`). The Arduino programming environment and libraries are constantly being updated, so information on consequences of the updates is also available on the *GitHub* website.

CHAPTER 1

Internet radio

Internet radio is the continuous streaming of digital audio over the Internet. Digital audio, in MP3 format, is received by the ESP8266 or ESP32 microcontroller through a Wi-Fi connection. The ESP8266 or ESP32 microcontroller communicates with a VS1053 audio decoder by Serial Peripheral Interface (SPI), and the MP3-formatted data is decoded by an 18-bit digital to analog converter (DAC) to an audio signal that is amplified for a loudspeaker. ESP8266 and ESP32 microcontrollers have Wi-Fi functionality and sufficient processor speed for an Internet radio. Connection to the wireless local area network (WLAN) requires the Wi-Fi network SSID (Service Set Identifier) and password.

© Neil Cameron 2021
N. Cameron, *Electronics Projects with the ESP8266 and ESP32*,
https://doi.org/10.1007/978-1-4842-6336-5_1

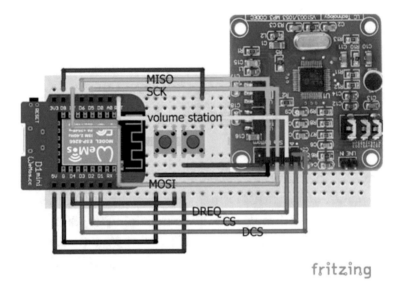

Figure 1-1. *Internet radio with volume and station switches and a LOLIN (WeMos) D1 mini*

Connections for the ESP8266 development board and the VS1053 audio decoder are shown in Figure 1-1, with a detail in Figure 1-2, and listed in Table 1-1. Connections for SPI communication are indicated in green, with data connections in blue. Two switches, attached to interrupts, control the volume and Internet radio station selection. For the ESP8266 development board, the volume and station switches on pins *D4* and *D8* are connected to GND and 5V, as pins *D4* and *D8* are connected to internal pull-up and pull-down resistors, respectively. Connections for an ESP32 development board are also given in Table 1-1. When using an ESP32 development board, the volume and station switches are both connected to GND.

An amplifier and loudspeaker, or a mini-loudspeaker as used with a mobile phone, are connected to the VS1053 audio decoder by plugging into the audio jack socket of the VS1053 audio decoder.

Figure 1-2. *VS1053 connections*

Table 1-1. *Internet radio and switches*

Component	Connect to ESP8266	Connect to ESP32
VS1053 5V	5V	VIN or V5
VS1053 DGND	GND	GND
VS1053 MOSI	(MOSI) D7	(MOSI) GPIO 23
VS1053 DREQ (data request)	D1	GPIO 4
VS1053 XCS (chip select)	D2	GPIO 0
VS1053 MISO	(MISO) D6	(MISO) GPIO 19
VS1053 SCK	(SCK) D5	(CLK) GPIO 18
VS1053 XRST (reset)	RST	GPIO EN
VS1053 XDCS (data chip select)	D3	GPIO 2
Switch volume left	GND	GND
Switch volume right	D4	GPIO 26
Switch station left	5V	GND
Switch station right	D8	GPIO 27

3

The URL (Uniform Resource Locator) or web address of an Internet radio station is obtained from the website www.radio.de. Search for the required station, click the *play* button, and select *View Page Source*. In the displayed HTML (HyperText Markup Language) file, search for *streams*, which precedes the radio station URL. The URL is formatted as *host:port/path*. For example, *The UK 1940s Radio Station* has URL 1940sradio1.co.uk:8100/stream/1/ with *host* equal to the text before the first backslash: 1940sradio1.co.uk – and *path* equal to the remaining text: stream/1/. If the *port* is not equal to default value of 80, which is the web browsing port, then it follows the colon after *host*, such as *8100*.

The sketch for an Internet radio with an ESP8266 development board (see Listing 1-1) uses the *VS1053* library by Ed Smallenburg and James Coliz that is downloaded as a *.zip* file from github.com/baldram/ESP_VS1053_Library. The first section of the sketch defines the number of Internet radio stations and URLs, initializes the audio decoder, establishes a Wi-Fi connection, and defines the interrupts. The variables *newStation* and *newVolume* are defined as volatile, as they are accessed by both the main sketch and the interrupts. With an ESP32 development board, the station change switch pin is set *HIGH* with an internal pull-up resistor using the instruction pinMode(statPin, INPUT_PULLUP), and the interrupt attached to the station switch is set to *FALLING*. The ESP8266 and ESP32 microcontrollers store compiled code in internal RAM (IRAM), rather than in the slower flash memory, by prefixing code with the *IRAM_ATTR* attribute. The interrupt ISR (Interrupt Service Routine) is defined as IRAM_ATTR void ISR() rather than void ISR().

In the *loop* function, a connection is made to an Internet radio station website, and the VS1053 audio decoder processes data in 32-byte batches. The two interrupt service routines, *chan* and *vol*, move to the next radio station and increase the volume, respectively. The volume scale is from 0 to 100%. The *VS1053* library references the *SPI* library, and the #include <SPI.h> instruction is not required.

Connection to the Internet radio station server with the instruction connect(host[station], port[station]) is followed by an HTTP (Hypertext Transfer Protocol) request. The *VS1053* library uses HTTP for communication between the client, which is the web browser, and the Internet radio station server. The client submits an HTTP request to the server for audio data, and the server sends a response to the client with the required data. The HTTP request instructions "GET pathname HTTP/1.1" and "Host: hostname" are followed by an instruction to close the connection "Connection: close". Using the example of *"The UK 1940s Radio Station,"* the request instructions are

```
GET stream/1/HTTP/1.1
Host: 1940sradio1.co.uk
Connection: close
<\r\n>
```

Note that the fourth instruction of carriage return, \r, and new line, \n, is required, which is equivalent to a println() instruction.

Listing 1-1. Internet radio with volume and station switches and an ESP8266 board

```
#include <VS1053.h>              // include VS1053 library
#include <ESP8266WiFi.h>         // include ESP8266WiFi library
int CS = D2;
int DCS = D3;                    // define VS1053 decoder pins
int DREQ = D1;
VS1053 decoder(CS, DCS, DREQ);   // associate decoder with VS1053
int statPin = D8;                // define switch pins for
int volPin = D4;                 // station and volume
WiFiClient client;               // associate client and library
char ssid[] = "xxxx";            // change xxxx to Wi-Fi ssid
char password[] = "xxxx";        // change xxxx to Wi-Fi password
```

```
const int maxStat = 4;              // number of radio stations
String stationName[] = {"1940 UK", "Bayern3", "ClassicFM", "BBC4"};
char * host[maxStat] = {"1940sradio1.co.uk",    // station host
                        "streams.br.de",
                        "media-ice.musicradio.com",
                        "bbcmedia.ic.llnwd.net"};
char * path[maxStat] = {"/stream/1/",            // station path
                        "/bayern3_2.m3u",
                        "/ClassicFMMP3",
                        "/stream/bbcmedia_radio4fm_mf_q"};
int port[] = {8100,80,80,80};   // default station port is 80
unsigned char mp3buff[32];      // VS1053 loads data in 32 bytes
int station = 0;
int volume = 0;                 // volume level 0-100
volatile int newStation = 2;    // station number at start up
volatile int newVolume = 80;    // volume at start up

void setup ()
{
  Serial.begin(115200);         // Serial Monitor baud rate
  SPI.begin();                  // initialise SPI bus
  decoder.begin();              // initialise VS1053 decoder
  decoder.switchToMp3Mode();    // MP3 format mode
  decoder.setVolume(volume);    // set decoder volume
  WiFi.begin(ssid, password);   // initialise Wi-Fi
  while (WiFi.status() != WL_CONNECTED) delay(500);
  Serial.println("WiFi connected"); // wait for Wi-Fi connection
  pinMode(volPin, INPUT_PULLUP);    // switch pin uses internal
                                    // pull-up resistor
  attachInterrupt(digitalPinToInterrupt(statPin), chan, RISING);
  attachInterrupt(digitalPinToInterrupt(volPin), vol, FALLING);
}            // define interrupts for changing station and volume
```

```
void loop()
{
  if(station != newStation)        // new station selected
  {
    station = newStation;          // display updated station name
    Serial.print("connecting to CH"); Serial.print(station);
    Serial.print(" ");Serial.println(stationName[station]);
    if(client.connect(host[station], port[station]))
    {                              // connect to radio station URL
      client.println(String("GET ")+ path[station] + " HTTP/1.1");
      client.println(String("Host: ") + host[station]);
      client.println("Connection: close");
      client.println();           // new line is required
    }
  }
  if(volume != newVolume)          // change volume selected
  {
    volume = newVolume;            // display updated volume
    Serial.print("volume ");Serial.println(volume);
    decoder.setVolume(volume);     // set decoder volume
  }
  if(client.available() > 0)       // when audio data available
  {                                // decode data 32 bytes at a time
    uint8_t bytesread = client.read(mp3buff, 32);
    decoder.playChunk(mp3buff, bytesread);
  }
}
```

```
IRAM_ATTR void chan()            // ISR to increment station number
{
  newStation++;
  if(newStation > maxStat-1) newStation = 0;
}              // stations numbered 0, 1, 2...

IRAM_ATTR void vol()             // ISR to increase volume
{
  newVolume = newVolume + 5;
  if(newVolume > 101) newVolume = 50;
}                                // maximum volume is 100
```

Connections for the ESP32 development board and to the VS1053 audio decoder are shown in Figures 1-3 and 1-2, respectively, and given in Table 1-1. Both switch pins are connected to internal pull-up resistors, so both interrupts are activated by a *FALLING* signal. The only changes to Listing 1-1, other than defining the decoder, station, and volume control pins, are inclusion of the *WiFi* library rather than the *ESP8266WiFi* library and the instruction pinMode(statPin, INPUT_PULLUP) to change the interrupt on the station switch pin from *RISING* to *FALLING*.

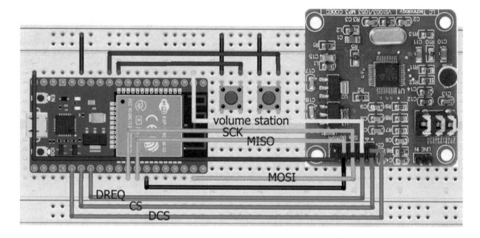

Figure 1-3. *Internet radio with volume and station switches and an ESP32 board*

Station display and selection

In Listing 1-1, station selection and volume control are activated by switches, with station and volume information displayed on the Serial Monitor. For a portable Internet radio, station and volume information is displayed on an ST7735 TFT LCD (Thin-Film Transistor Liquid Crystal Display) screen, and a station is selected or the volume is controlled with a rotary encoder (see Figures 1-4 and 1-5 with connections in Table 1-2). Note that both the rotary encoder and ST7735 TFT LCD screen are connected to 3.3V, with only the VS1053 audio decoder connected to 5V. The ESP32 microcontroller communicates with both the VS1053 audio decoder and ST7735 TFT LCD screen by SPI, so the microcontroller has the same MOSI (Main-Out Secondary-In) and SCK (Serial Clock) connections to the audio decoder and screen, but the CS (Chip Select) connections are device specific.

Figure 1-4. *Internet radio screenshots*

The sketch uses the *ESP32 vs1053_ext* library by Wolle that is downloaded as a *.zip* file from github.com/schreibfaul1/ESP32-vs1053_ext. The *ESP32 vs1053_ext* library is for the ESP32 microcontroller, while the *VS1053* library by Ed Smallenburg and James Coliz is compatible with both the ESP8266 and ESP32 microcontrollers. The *ESP32 vs1053_ext* library provides station and track information, such as the streamed track title. The instruction to connect to an Internet radio station server is connecttohost("host:port/stream"), for example, connecttohost("1940sradio1.co.uk:8100/stream/1/"). The port number is only required when it does not equal the default value of 80. The functions *vs1053_showstation, vs1053_icyurl, vs1053_bitrate,* and *vs1053_showstreamtitle* hold the Internet radio station name and homepage URL, the bit rate, and the streamed track title. When a new track is streamed, the *vs1053_showstreamtitle* function is automatically updated. The *volume* variable has 22 levels of 0,50,60,65,70,75,80,82...90,91...100%, with volume level 10 equal to 88%, as volume level 0 has value 0%.

Listing 1-2 demonstrates the output of the *ESP32 vs1053_ext* library functions that are used in Listing 1-3 to display information about the Internet radio station and the streamed track.

Listing 1-2. ESP32 vs1053_ext library functions

```
#include <vs1053_ext.h>        // include ESP32 VS1053_ext lib
#include <WiFi.h>              // include Wi-Fi library
int CS = 0;
int DCS = 2;                   // define VS1053 decoder pins
int DREQ = 4;
VS1053 decoder(CS, DCS, DREQ); // associate decoder with VS1053
char ssid[] = "xxxx";          // change xxxx to Wi-Fi ssid
char password[] = "xxxx";      // change xxxx to Wi-Fi password
int volume = 10;               // volume level

void setup()
{
  Serial.begin(115200);        // Serial Monitor baud rate
  SPI.begin();                 // initialise SPI bus
  WiFi.begin(ssid, password);  // initialise Wi-Fi
  while (WiFi.status() != WL_CONNECTED) delay(500);
  decoder.begin();             // initialise VS0153 decoder
  decoder.setVolume(volume);   // set decoder volume level
  decoder.connecttohost
  ("media-ice.musicradio.com:80/ClassicFMMP3");
}

void loop()
{
  decoder.loop();
}
void vs1053_showstation(const char * info)
{                                // display radio station name
  Serial.print("Station:     ");
  Serial.println(info);
}
```

```
void vs1053_bitrate(const char * info)
{                                      // display streaming bit rate
  Serial.print("Bit rate:     ");
  Serial.println(String(info)+"kBit/s");
}
void vs1053_icyurl(const char * info)
{                                      // display radio station URL
  Serial.print("Homepage:     ");
  Serial.println(info);
}
void vs1053_showstreamtitle(const char * info)
{                                      // title of streamed track
  Serial.print("Stream title: ");
  Serial.println(info);
}
```

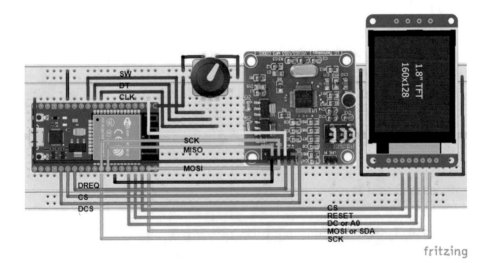

Figure 1-5. *Internet radio with screen and rotary encoder and an ESP32 board*

Table 1-2. *Internet radio with screen and rotary encoder and an ESP32 board*

Component	Connect to ESP32
VS1053 audio decoder	See Table 1-1
Rotary encoder CLK	GPIO 25
Rotary encoder DT	GPIO 26
Rotary encoder SW	GPIO 27
Rotary encoder VCC	3V3
Rotary encoder GND	GND
ST7735 TFT LCD GND	GND
ST7735 TFT LCD CS	GPIO 22
ST7735 TFT LCD RESET	GPIO 1
ST7735 TFT LCD DC or A0	GPIO 3
ST7735 TFT LCD SDA	GPIO 23
ST7735 TFT LCD SCK	GPIO 18
ST7735 TFT LCD LED	3V3

The sketch for a portable Internet radio is given in Listing 1-3. Pressing the rotary encoder switch once displays the menu of available radio stations, with volume control as the first menu item. Turning the rotary encoder moves the menu of radio stations up or down the ST7735 TFT LCD screen. The mid-screen station, which is highlighted in *RED*, is selected by pressing the rotary encoder for a second time; and an HTTP request is made to the Internet radio station server for audio data. When *Volume* is selected on the menu, the current volume level is displayed and turning the rotary encoder decreases or increases the volume level, which is selected by pressing the rotary encoder switch. The ST7735 TFT LCD screen is refreshed with the current radio station information and the updated volume level displayed, but the station menu is still positioned at the current radio station.

The sketch in Listing 1-3 consists of several functions to compartmentalize the instructions. The lengthy first section of the sketch defines the libraries, the Internet radio station URLs, pin numbers for the VS1053 audio decoder, the ST7735 TFT LCD screen, and the rotary encoder, with initial values for the station and volume level and the rotary encoder parameters. The *Adafruit ST7735* library is available in the Arduino IDE. The *ESP32 vs1053_ext* and *Adafruit ST7735* libraries reference the *SPI* and *Adafruit GFX* libraries, so the #include <SPI.h> and #include <Adafruit_GFX.h> instructions are not required. The *setup* function establishes the Wi-Fi connection, initializes the VS1053 audio decoder and the ST7735 TFT LCD screen, attaches internal pull-up resistors to the rotary encoder, and defines interrupts for the rotary encoder. The direction and number of turns of the rotary encoder are determined by the *change* interrupt, as described in Chapter 19 (Rotary encoder control).

On pressing the rotary encoder switch, the *loop* function calls the *screen* function to display the volume and station menu, the *readMenu* function to determine the selected radio station or the *readValue* function function to obtain the new volume level, and then the *radio* function. The *radio* function either connects to the selected radio station server or changes the volume on the VS1053 audio decoder. The *readMenu* and *readValue* functions determine the selected row number of the menu, which is a list of stations, and the selected volume level, when the rotary encoder is turned. The *vs1053_icyurl* function obtains a string, starting with *https://* and followed by the station URL, and extracts a substring starting two positions after the location of the first backslash. The *vs1053_showstation* and *vs1053_showstreamtitle* functions obtain the radio station name and the title of the streamed track and then call the *showStation* function, which displays the station name, streamed track title, volume value, and station URL information on the ST7735 TFT LCD screen. Some text, such as the station name or title of the streamed track, will be longer than the width of the ST7735 TFT LCD screen, so the *lines* function splits the station name or title into screen-sized substrings for display. The *encoder* and *swPress* functions count the direction and number of turns of the rotary encoder and the number of presses of the rotary encoder switch.

Listing 1-3. Internet radio with screen and rotary encoder and an ESP32 board

```
#include <vs1053_ext.h>          // include ESP32 VS1053_ext,
#include <WiFi.h>                // WiFi and
#include <Adafruit_ST7735.h>     // Adafruit_ST7735 libraries
int CS = 0;
int DCS = 2;                     // define VS1053 decoder pins
int DREQ = 4;
VS1053 decoder(CS, DCS, DREQ);   // associate decoder with VS1053
char ssid[] = "xxxx";            // change xxxx to Wi-Fi ssid
char password[] = "xxxx";        // change xxxx to Wi-Fi password
const int maxStation = 11;       // number of radio stations
String stationName[] = {"Volume",   // first item on menu
"1940 UK", "Berlin", "Bayern3", "Classic", "BBC4",
"Vermont", "Ketchikan", "Kathmandu", "Ithaca", "Trondeim",
"Virgin"};
char * URL[maxStation] = {            // radio station URLs
"1940sradio1.co.uk:8100/1",
"streambbr.ir-media-tec.com/berlin/mp3-128/vtuner_web_mp3/",
"streams.br.de/bayern3_2.m3u",
"media-ice.musicradio.com:80/ClassicFMMP3",
```

```
"bbcmedia.ic.llnwd.net/stream/bbcmedia_radio4fm_mf_q",
"vpr.streamguys.net/vpr64.mp3",
"96.31.83.94:8082/stream",
"streaming.softnep.net:8037/stream.nsv",
"17993.live.streamtheworld.com/WITHFM.mp3",
"stream.radiometro.no/metro128.mp3",
"radio.virginradio.co.uk/stream"
};
int TFT_CS = 22;
int DCpin = 3;                  // define ST7735 TFT screen pins
int RSTpin = 1;                 // associate tft with Adafruit ST7735
Adafruit_ST7735 tft = Adafruit_ST7735(TFT_CS, DCpin, RSTpin);
int CLKpin = 25;
int DTpin = 26;
int SWpin = 27;                 // define rotary encoder pins
int oldRow = 0;
int newRow = 1;
int menuItem, val, upLimit;
int displayVol[] =             // define volume values for 22 levels
{0,50,60,65,70,75,80,82,84,86,88,90,91,92,93,94,95,96,97,98,
99,100};
int volume = 0;
int newVolume = 10;            // volume level at start up
int station = 0;
int newStation = 3;            // station level at start up
int textlen, textrows;
String showstatn, showtitle, showurl, text, text1, text2;
volatile int change = 0;   // rotary encoder variables
volatile int pressed = 0;
volatile int vals[] = {0,-1,1,0,1,0,0,-1,-1,0,0,1,0,1,0,-1,0};
volatile int score = 0;
```

```
volatile int oldState = 0;
volatile int turn;

void setup()
{
  SPI.begin();                         // initialise SPI bus
  WiFi.begin(ssid, password);          // initialise Wi-Fi
  while (WiFi.status() != WL_CONNECTED) delay(500);
  decoder.begin();                     // initialise VS0153 decoder
  decoder.setVolume(volume);           //  set decoder volume level
  tft.initR(INITR_BLACKTAB);           // initialise screen
  tft.fillScreen(ST7735_BLACK);        // clear screen
  tft.setRotation(1);                  // orientate ST7735 screen
  tft.setTextSize(2);                  // set screen text size
  tft.drawRect(0,0,158,126,ST7735_WHITE);  // draw white frame line
  tft.drawRect(2,2,154,122,ST7735_RED);  // and second frame line
  pinMode(CLKpin, INPUT_PULLUP);
  pinMode(DTpin, INPUT_PULLUP);        // rotary encoder uses
  pinMode(SWpin, INPUT_PULLUP);        // internal pull-up resistors
  attachInterrupt(CLKpin, encoder, CHANGE);
  attachInterrupt(DTpin, encoder, CHANGE);
                                 // attach rotary encoder interrupts
  attachInterrupt(SWpin, swPress, CHANGE);
}

void loop()
{
  if(pressed == 1)               // switch pin pressed first time
  {                              // to change station or volume
    clearScreen();               // call clearScreen function
```

```
    screen();                           // call screen function
    menuItem = readMenu(maxStation);      // selected row in menu
  }
  else if (pressed == 2)              // switch pin pressed second time
  {                                   // to select station
    if(menuItem > 0)                  // station selected
    {
      newStation = menuItem-1;        // selected station in menu
      clearScreen();                  // call clearScreen function
      showStation(volume, showstatn, showtitle);
                                      // call showStation function
      if(newStation == station) showStation(volume, showstatn,
      showtitle);
    }                                 // volume change selected
    else if(menuItem== 0) newVolume = readValue("volume: ",
    volume, 21, 1);
    pressed = 0;                      // reset variable
  }
  else if(pressed > 2) pressed = 0;     // volume changed
  radio();                            // call radio function
}

void radio()                          // function to connect to
{                                     // selected radio station server
  if(station != newStation)           // new station selected
  {
    clearScreen();                    // call clearScreen function
    station = newStation;
    showurl = "";
    decoder.connecttohost(URL[station]);
  }                                   // connect to radio station server
```

```
  if(volume != newVolume)          // new volume level selected
  {
    volume = newVolume;
    newRow = station+1;            // retain station number on menu
    decoder.setVolume(volume);     // update VS1053 volume
    clearScreen();                 // call clearScreen function
    showStation(volume, showstatn, showtitle);
  }                                // call showStation function
  decoder.loop();
}

int readMenu (int rows)            // function to obtain station
{                                  // number on menu
  while(pressed < 2)               // while station not selected
  {
    if(change != 0)                // rotary encoder turned
    {
      newRow = oldRow + change;    // retain row number on menu
      newRow = constrain(newRow, 0, rows);
      clearScreen();               // call clearScreen function
      screen();                    // call screen function
      oldRow = newRow;
      change = 0;
    }
    delay(10);
  }
  return newRow;                   // return row number on menu
}
                                   // function to obtain volume level
```

```
int readValue(String text, int current, int upLimit, int gain)
{
  val = current;                     // current volume level
  clearScreen();                     // call clearScreen function
  tft.setTextColor(ST7735_WHITE);
  tft.setTextSize(2);
  tft.setCursor(10, 50);
  tft.print(text);                   // display text and
  tft.print(displayVol[val]);        // current volume value
  while(pressed < 3)            // while switch pin is not pressed
  {
    if(change != 0)              // rotary encoded turned
    {
      val = val + change * gain; // increment volume level
      val = constrain(val, 0, upLimit);
                                     // constrain volume level
      clearScreen();                 // call clearScreen function
      tft.setCursor(10, 50);
      tft.print(text);               // display text and
      tft.print(displayVol[val]);    // new volume value
      change = 0;
    }
    delay(10);
  }
  return val;                        // return new volume level
}
void vs1053_showstation(const char * info)
{                                    // function to obtain station name
  showstatn = String(info);    // station name
  showtitle = "";
}
```

```
  if(showstatn == "No Name") showstatn = stationName[station+1];
  clearScreen();
  showStation(volume, showstatn, showtitle);
}                                    // call showStation function

void vs1053_showstreamtitle(const char * info)
{                                    // function to obtain streamed title
  showtitle = String(info);
  clearScreen();
  showStation(volume, showstatn, showtitle);
}

void vs1053_icyurl(const char * info)
{                                    // function to obtain station URL
  showurl = String(info);
  int i = showurl.indexOf("/");   // position of first / in string
  showurl = showurl.substring(i+2); // station URL as substring
  clearScreen();
  showStation(volume, showstatn, showtitle);
}

void showStation(int volume, String showstatn, String showtitle)
{          // function to display station name, streamed title
           // and station URL on screen
    tft.setTextColor(ST7735_GREEN);
    tft.setTextSize(1);
    lines(showstatn, 10);    // lines function to display station
    tft.setTextColor(ST7735_YELLOW);
    lines(showtitle, 40);    // lines function to display title
    tft.setTextColor(ST7735_GREEN);
```

```
    tft.setCursor(80, 100);    // display volume value
    tft.print("volume: ");tft.print(displayVol[volume]);
    tft.setCursor(5, 110);
    tft.print(showurl);        // display URL
}

void lines(String text, int line)
{        // function to split string into screen sized substrings
  textlen = text.length();    // get string length
  textrows = 1+textlen/23;     // required number of screen rows
  for(int i=0; i<textrows; i++)
  {
    tft.setCursor(10, line + i*10);   // move cursor to next row
    tft.println(text.substring(i*23, (i+1)*23));
  }                                // display substring
}

void screen()                      // function to display station menu
{
  tft.setTextSize(2);
  tft.setTextColor(ST7735_RED);        // selected station in RED
  tft.setCursor(20, 55);
  tft.print
  (stationName[newRow]);               // display station name
  tft.setTextSize(1);
  tft.setTextColor(ST7735_WHITE);   // all other stations in WHITE
  for (int i=1; i<4; i++)            // display other station names
  {
    tft.setCursor(30, 50 - i*12);    // above selected station
    if(newRow-i >=0) tft.print(stationName[newRow-i]);
    tft.setCursor(30, 65 + i*12);   // below selected station
```

```
    if(newRow+i < maxStation+1) tft.print(stationName
    [newRow+i]);
  }
}

void clearScreen()              // function to clear screen
{                               // by displaying a BLACK rectangle
  tft.fillRect(3,3,152,120,ST7735_BLACK);
}

IRAM_ATTR void encoder()        // function to count rotary
{                               // encoder turns
  int newState = (oldState<<2)+(digitalRead(CLKpin)<<1)
  +digitalRead(DTpin);
  score = score + vals[newState];   // allocate score from array
  oldState = newState % 4;    //  remainder to leave new CLK and DT
  if(score == 2 || score == -2)   // 2 steps for complete rotation
  {
    change = score/2;             // unit change per two steps
    score = 0;                    // reset score
  }
}

IRAM_ATTR void swPress()        // function to count switch presses
{                               // pressed = 1, 2, 3 to change station,
                                // station selected, volume changed
  if(digitalRead(SWpin) == HIGH) pressed = pressed + 1;
}
```

Minimal Internet radio

The sketch in Listing 1-3 that included an ST7735 TFT LCD screen to
display radio station name and URL, streamed track title, and volume level
with a rotary encoder for station selection and volume control consisted
of 250 lines of code. In contrast, Listing 1-4 for a minimal Internet radio
preset to one radio station with one volume value has only 21 lines of code.
Just change the Internet radio station URL to the required URL!

Listing 1-4. Minimal Internet radio

```
#include <vs1053_ext.h>        // include ESP32 VS1053_ext
#include <WiFi.h>              // and WiFi libraries
int CS = 0;
int DCS = 2;                   // define VS1053 decoder pins
int DREQ = 4;
VS1053 decoder(CS, DCS, DREQ);   // associate decoder with VS1053
char ssid[] = "xxxx";          // change xxxx to Wi-Fi ssid
char password[] = "xxxx";      // change xxxx to Wi-Fi password

void setup()
{
  SPI.begin();                        // initialise SPI bus
  WiFi.begin(ssid, password);    // initialise Wi-Fi
  while (WiFi.status() != WL_CONNECTED) delay(500);
  decoder.begin();                    // initialise VS0153 decoder
  decoder.setVolume(10);              // pre-set decoder volume level
  decoder.connecttohost
  ("media-ice.musicradio.com:80/ClassicFMMP3");
}                      // connect to pre-set radio station server
```

```
void loop()
{
  decoder.loop();
}
```

Summary

An Internet radio was built with a VS1053 audio decoder and an ESP8266 or ESP32 microcontroller, with radio station selection and volume controlled using tactile switches. A portable Internet radio consisted of the VS1053 audio decoder, an ESP32 development board, and an ST7735 TFT LCD screen to display the radio station details, the title of the streamed track, and the volume level, with a rotary encoder to control station selection and volume. The sketch for a minimal Internet radio consisted of only 21 lines of code.

Components List

- ESP8266 microcontroller: LOLIN (WeMos) D1 mini or NodeMCU board

- ESP32 microcontroller: ESP32 DEVKIT DOIT or NodeMCU board

- VS1053 audio decoder module

- Mini-loudspeaker

- Tactile switch: 2×

- Rotary encoder: KY-040

- TFT LCD screen: ST7735, 1.8 inches

CHAPTER 2

Intranet camera

The ESP32-CAM module is based on the ESP32-S microcontroller and includes a 2M-pixel OV2640 camera and a micro-SD (Secure Digital) card slot. JPEG files of images are stored on the micro-SD card or loaded to a web page or streamed to a web page on a computer, Android tablet, or mobile phone.

The ESP32-CAM module (see Figure 2-1) contains serial TX and RX pins, six pins associated with the micro-SD card, and a COB (Chip on Board) LED, which flashes when taking a photo, and a red LED, which is active *LOW*, accessed with GPIO (General-Purpose Input-Output) 4 and 33 pins, respectively. A COB LED includes many LED chips bonded directly to a substrate to form a single module. There are three GND pins, a 3.3V and a 5V input pin, and the VCC pin outputs 3.3V or 5V with the jumper closed. GPIO 0 pin determines the flashing mode of the ESP32-CAM microcontroller, with the pin connected to GND when loading a sketch as the pin has a built-in pull-up resistor. GPIO pins 2, 4, 12, 13, 14, and 15 are associated with the micro-SD card functionality. When the micro-SD card is not in use, the GPIO pins are available as output pins. The pin layout of the ESP32-CAM module is shown in Figure 2-1 with *Rup* indicating the built-in pull-up resistor.

© Neil Cameron 2021
N. Cameron, *Electronics Projects with the ESP8266 and ESP32*,
https://doi.org/10.1007/978-1-4842-6336-5_2

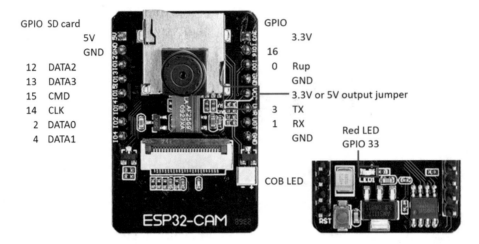

Figure 2-1. *ESP32-CAM module pins*

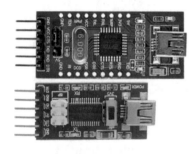
The ESP32-CAM module does not have a USB connector, and the module is connected to a computer or laptop with a USB to serial UART (Universal Asynchronous Receiver-Transmitter) interface, such as an FT232RL FTDI USB to TTL Serial converter module. The Serial communication voltage of the USB to serial UART interface must be set at 3.3 V, with USB to serial UART interface RX and TX pins connected to the ESP32-CAM module TX and RX pins, respectively (see Figure 2-2 with connections in Table 2-1). The USB to serial UART interface 5V pin is connected to the ESP32-CAM module 5V pin. Details on installing the CP210x USB to UART Bridge driver for the ESP32 microcontroller, with the additional Boards Manager URLs and libraries for ESP32, are included in Chapter 21 (Microcontrollers). The camera module is attached to the ESP32-CAM module by lifting the black tab on the ESP32-CAM module, sliding the camera module into the connector, and closing the black tab.

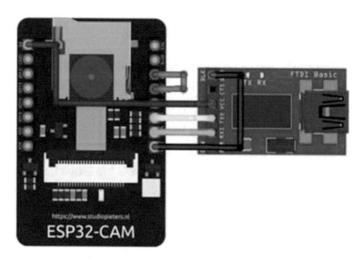

Figure 2-2. *USB to serial UART interface with the ESP32-CAM module*

Table 2-1. *USB to serial UART interface with the ESP32-CAM module*

Component	Connect to	
USB to serial UART RXD	ESP32-CAM TX pin	
USB to serial UART TXD	ESP32-CAM RX pin	
USB to serial UART VCC	ESP32-CAM 5V	
USB to serial UART GND	ESP32-CAM GND	ESP32-CAM GPIO 0 pin

In the Arduino IDE, from the *Tools* ➤ *Board* drop-down list, select *ESP32 Wrover Module*; in *Tools* ➤ *Partition Scheme,* select *Huge APP (3MB no OTA/1MB SPIFFS);* and in *Tools* ➤ *Port,* select the appropriate *COM* port.

Prior to loading a sketch onto the ESP32-CAM module, the module GPIO 0 pin is connected to the module GND pin, and then the module *RESET* button is pressed. After the sketch is uploaded, the GPIO 0 pin of the ESP32-CAM module is disconnected from the module GND pin, and then the module *RESET* button is pressed.

Save images to the SD card

With the sketch in Listing 2-1, the ESP32-CAM module takes a photo every two seconds, and the resulting JPEG file is stored on the micro-SD card. The number of photos taken is held in EEPROM (Electrically Erasable Programmable Read-Only Memory) to sequentially number the JPEG files as */pictureN.jpg* for the Nth photo. When the sketch is rerun, JPEG files of images are numbered from with the last JPEG file stored, rather than from */picture0.jpg,* which would overwrite existing JPEG files stored in the micro-SD card. Saving data on EEPROM is described in Chapter 20 (OTA and saving data to EEPROM, SPIFFS, and Excel). Pressing the ESP32-CAM module *RESET* button, after uploading a sketch, causes vibration to the camera module, so a two-second delay allows the camera module time to stabilize. The number of photos to take is entered on the Serial Monitor, and after the camera and micro-SD card are initialized, the camera takes the required number of photos. The Arduino IDE built-in *SD-MMC* library uses the faster ESP32 SDMMC hardware bus instead of SPI, as used by the SD library. Note that the ESP32-CAM module supports a baud rate of 115200 Bd.

The JPEG files, in *UXGA* format with 1200×1600 pixels, have an average size of 100 kB; and a 4 GB micro-SD card, in FAT32 format, stores thousands of images. A 16 GB micro-SD card was used in this chapter. Time-lapse photography is possible with the ESP32-CAM module by storing JPEG images on the micro-SD card with intervals of 2–30 s between photographs. In Listing 2-1, setting the variable *maxPhoto* to 3000 will generate sufficient images for a two-minute video with a 25 FPS (frames per second) frame rate, which only requires 300 MB of the micro-SD card storage.

The ESP32-CAM camera configuration instructions are included in the *config_pins.h* tab rather than in the main sketch, to make the sketch easier to interpret. The additional tab is created in the Arduino IDE by selecting the triangle below the *Serial Monitor* button, on the right side of the IDE, and choosing *New Tab* from the drop-down menu. The *New Tab* is titled *config_pins.h*.

The sketch in Listing 2-1 loads the libraries for the ESP32-CAM, with the *config_pins.h* tab (see Listing 2-2) including instructions to configure the ESP32-CAM camera with the *configCamera* function. The micro-SD card is initialized with the *initSDcard* function, which determines the SD card type. After the required time interval between photos has elapsed, the *takePhoto* function is called. A JPEG file of the image is saved to the micro-SD card with the file name incremented after each photo and the image number written to EEPROM. The *takePhoto* function uses the ampersand, &, and asterisk, *, characters to relate to the memory address of a variable, with spacing to emphasize the characters. In Chapter 14 (ESP-NOW and LoRa communication), Listing 14-3 illustrates use of a memory address pointer.

Listing 2-1. Taking a photo and saving to the micro-SD card

```
#include <esp_camera.h>       // include esp_camera library
#include <SD_MMC.h>           // include SD_MMC library
#include <EEPROM.h>           // include EEPROM
#include "config_pins.h"      // configure instructions tab
uint8_t SDtype;
int SDpics;                   // number of pictures on SD card
int maxPhoto = 0;             // maximum number of photos
int Nphoto = 0;               // number of photos taken
int photoTime = 2000;         // delay (ms) between photos
```

```
String filename;
unsigned long nowTime, lastTime = 0;

void setup()
{
  Serial.begin(115200);            // baud rate for Serial Monitor
  Serial.println("\n\nenter number of required photos");
  Serial.println("\n\nsettling down for 2s");
                                   // time to settle vibration
  delay(2000);
  Serial.println("initialising camera, then take photos");
  configCamera();                  // functions to configure camera
  initSDcard();                    // and to initialise micro-SD card
  EEPROM.begin(1);                 // EEPROM with one record
  SDpics = EEPROM.read(0);         // number of saved pictures
}

void loop()
{
  while (Serial.available()>0)
  {                                // maximum photo number
    maxPhoto = Serial.parseInt();  // parsed from Serial buffer
    Nphoto = 0;
  }                                // if photo number < maximum
                                   // photo number
  nowTime = millis();              // take photo after photoTime ms
  if((nowTime - lastTime > photoTime) && (Nphoto < maxPhoto))
  {
    Nphoto++;                      // increment photo number
    takePhoto();                   // call function to take photo
```

```
    lastTime = millis();            // update time of photo
  }
}

void initSDcard()                   // function to initialise SD card
{
  if(!SD_MMC.begin())               // check SD card in position
  {
    Serial.println("error loading SD card");
    return;
  }
  SDtype = SD_MMC.cardType();    // obtain SD card type
  if(SDtype == CARD_NONE)
  {
    Serial.println("insert SD Card");
    return;
  }
  Serial.print("SD card type: ");
  if(SDtype == CARD_MMC) Serial.println("MMC");
  else if(SDtype == CARD_SD) Serial.println("SDSC");
  else if(SDtype == CARD_SDHC) Serial.println("SDHC");
  else Serial.println("UNKNOWN");
}

void takePhoto()                    // function to take and save photo
{
  camera_fb_t * frame = NULL;    // associate fb with esp_camera
  frame = esp_camera_fb_get();   // take photo with camera
```

```
if(!frame)
{
  Serial.println("photo capture error");
  return;
}
SDpics ++;                          // increase picture number
filename = "/picture" + String(SDpics) +".jpg";
                                    // generate JPEG filename
fs::FS & fs = SD_MMC;
File file = fs.open(filename.c_str(), FILE_WRITE);
                                    // access SD card
if(!file) Serial.println("file save error");
else
{
  file.write(frame->buf, frame->len);      // save file to SD card
  Serial.print("Picture filename: ");
  Serial.println(filename);
  EEPROM.write(0, SDpics);        // update EEPROM
  EEPROM.commit();                // with picture number
}
file.close();                     // close file on SD card
esp_camera_fb_return(frame);      // return frame buffer to driver for
}                                 // reuse
```

The ESP32-CAM camera configuration instructions are included in the *config_pins.h* tab rather than in the main sketch (see Listing 2-2). The JPEG pixel format is selected from the available options of *YUV422, GRAYSCALE, RGB565,* and *JPEG.* If a microcontroller does not support PSRAM (pseudostatic RAM), which is dynamic RAM that behaves like static RAM, then a lower picture frame size; lower JPEG quality, with a value between to either 0 and 63; and lower frame count must be set.

Listing 2-2. Camera configuration instructions tab

```
camera_config_t config;        // store camera configuration parameters
void configCamera()
{
  config.ledc_channel = LEDC_CHANNEL_0;
  config.ledc_timer = LEDC_TIMER_0;
  config.pin_d0 = 5;
  config.pin_d1 = 18;
  config.pin_d2 = 19;                    // GPIO pin numbers
  config.pin_d3 = 21;
  config.pin_d4 = 36;
  config.pin_d5 = 39;
  config.pin_d6 = 34;
  config.pin_d7 = 35;
  config.pin_xclk = 0;
  config.pin_pclk = 22;
  config.pin_vsync = 25;
  config.pin_href = 23;
  config.pin_sscb_sda = 26;
  config.pin_sscb_scl = 27;
  config.pin_pwdn = 32;
  config.pin_reset = -1;
  config.xclk_freq_hz = 20000000;        // clock speed of 20MHz
  config.pixel_format = PIXFORMAT_JPEG;  // JPEG file format
  config.frame_size = FRAMESIZE_SVGA;    // 800x600 pixels
  config.jpeg_quality = 10;              // image quality index
  config.fb_count = 1;                   // frame buffer count
  esp_err_t err = esp_camera_init(&config);   // initialize camera
```

```
if (err != ESP_OK)
{
  Serial.print("Camera initialise failed with error");
  Serial.println(err);
  return;
}
}
```

Load images on a web page

A photo taken by the ESP32-CAM module is uploaded to a web page using an HTTP request. Once the Wi-Fi connection is made and the WLAN web page loaded, clicking the *New photo* button calls the *newPhoto* function, which initiates a client HTTP request with the /photoURL URL for the server camera to take a photo and send the JPEG image to the client. The web page is reloaded with the location.reload() instruction to update the web page with the new photo. Clicking the *Rotate* button rotates the image on the web page through 90°. Rotating the image covers the buttons, so the button positions are redefined if the image is portrait (rotation of 90° or 270°) or landscape. Loading an ESP32-CAM image directly to a webpage is based on the method of Nuno Santos (techtutorialsx.com).

The sketch in Listing 2-3 includes HTTP GET requests, with corresponding URLs, and references the *buildpage.h* tab containing the HTML code for the web page (see Listing 2-4). The *underscore P* in the instruction request->send_P identifies that the JPG image is stored in PROGMEM, as flash (or program) memory has more capacity than RAM.

The photo size is displayed on the Serial Monitor, for information only. The *ESPAsyncWebServer* and *AsyncTCP* libraries by Hristo Gochkov are required, and *.zip* files containing the libraries are downloaded from github.com/me-no-dev/ESPAsyncWebServer and github.com/me-no-dev/AsyncTCP, respectively. The *ESPAsyncWebServer* library references the *AsyncTCP* and *WiFi* libraries, so the instructions #include <AsyncTCP.h> and #include <WiFi.h> are not required. The *WiFi* library is included in the Arduino IDE when the ESP32 driver is installed. There is no change to the content of the *config_pins.h* tab (see Listing 2-2).

Listing 2-3. Taking a photo and loading to a web page

```
#include <esp_camera.h>            // include esp_camera,
#include <ESPAsyncWebServer.h>     // ESPAsyncWebServer libraries
AsyncWebServer server(80);         // associate server with library
#include "config_pins.h"           // configure instructions tab
#include "buildpage.h"             // HTML code for webpage
char ssid[] = "xxxx";              // change xxxx to Wi-Fi ssid
char password[] = "xxxx";          // change xxxx to Wi-Fi password
String pSize;                      // photo size (bytes)

void setup()
{
  Serial.begin(115200);            // Serial Monitor baud rate
  Serial.println("\n\nsettling down for 2s");
                                   // time to settle vibration
  delay(2000);
  Serial.println("initialising camera, then take photos");
  configCamera();                  // function to configure camera
  WiFi.begin(ssid, password);      // initialise Wi-Fi
  while (WiFi.status() != WL_CONNECTED) delay(500);
  Serial.print("IP Address: ");
```

```
Serial.println(WiFi.localIP());          // display WLAN IP address
server.begin();                          // initialise server
server.on("/",  HTTP_GET, [](AsyncWebServerRequest * request)
{  request->send_P(200, "text/html", page);});
server.on("/photoURL", HTTP_GET, [](AsyncWebServerRequest *
request)
{
  camera_fb_t * frame = NULL;
  frame = esp_camera_fb_get();           // take photo as JPEG
  request->send_P(200, "image/jpeg",    // send JPEG image to client
          (const uint8_t *)frame->buf, frame->len);
  esp_camera_fb_return(frame);           // clear photo buffer
  pSize = String(frame->len);            // display photo size
  Serial.print("pSize ");Serial.println(pSize);
});
}

void loop()                              // nothing in loop function
{}
```

The HTML code for the web page, stored as a *string literal*, is contained
in the *buildpage.h* tab (see Listing 2-4). HTML instructions for XML HTTP
requests are described in Chapter 8 (Updating a web page). The location.
reload() instruction reloads the web page, exactly as the reload button
in a browser. An image is rotated through *N* degrees with the instruction
rotate(Ndeg) with the transform attribute.

The HTML code displays the two buttons in a table row and allocates
functions to each button. In the AJAX code, the *newPhoto* function makes
an XML HTTP request with the */photoURL* URL to initiate taking a photo
and then reloading the web page.

Listing 2-4. AJAX code for the web page with a ESP32-CAM photo

```
char page[] PROGMEM = R"(
<!DOCTYPE HTML><html><head>
<title>ESP32-CAM</title>
<style>
body {text-align:center; font-size: 25px;}
.vert {margin-bottom: 10%}
.hori {margin-bottom: 0%}
.btn {background-color:White; font-size: 25px}
table {margin: auto}
td {padding: 10px}
</style></head>
<body>
<h2>ESP32-CAM</h2>
<div id='buttons'>
<table><tr>
<td><button onclick='newPhoto()' class='btn'>New photo
</button></td>
<td><button onclick='turn()' class='btn'>Rotate</button></td>
</tr></table></div>
<img src='/photoURL' id='photo' width='80%'>
<script>
function newPhoto()
{
  var xhr = new XMLHttpRequest();
  xhr.open('GET', '/photoURL', true);
  xhr.send();
  location.reload();
}
var deg = 0;
function turn()
```

```
{
  deg = deg + 90;
  var img = document.getElementById('photo');
  img.style.transform = 'rotate(' + deg + 'deg)';
  if((deg/90)%2 == 1)
  document.getElementById('buttons').className = 'vert';
  else document.getElementById('buttons').className = 'hori';
}
</script>
</body></html>
)";
```

Including the instruction var rpt = setInterval(newPhoto, 5000) in the <script> section of Listing 2-4 calls the *newPhoto* function every five seconds, which is a very basic form of streaming images. The next section streams images to a web page.

Stream images to a web page

The ESP32-CAM module streams images to a web page, and the streaming frame rate ranges from 3 FPS (frames per second) with UXGA (1600 × 1200 pixels) format to 30 FPS with QQVGA (160 × 120 pixels) format. Several image formats are shown in Table 2-2. The smaller the image size, the faster the frame rate. The *CameraWebServer* sketch, accessed in the Arduino IDE by *File* ➤ *Examples* ➤ *ESP32* ➤ *Camera*, includes face recognition and face detection functions, with options to change numerous image characteristics.

Table 2-2. *Image pixel size options*

Frame	UXGA	SXGA	XGA	SVGA	VGA	CIF	QVGA	HQVGA	QQVGA
Width	1600	1280	1024	800	640	400	320	240	160
Height	1200	1024	768	600	480	296	240	176	120

The sketch in Listing 2-5 manages streaming of images to a web page. The sketch loads the required libraries, which are available in the ESP32 Arduino IDE, establishes a Wi-Fi connection, configures the camera in the *config_pins.h* tab (see Listing 2-2), and calls the startCameraServer function, which accesses the *stream_handler* function (see Listing 2-6) in the *stream_handler* tab. The delay() instruction in the loop function may be required to prevent the watchdog timer from initiating a software reset.

Listing 2-5. Real-time viewing on a web page

```
#include <esp_http_server.h>        // include esp http_server,
#include <esp_camera.h>             // camera and Wi-Fi libraries
#include <WiFi.h>
#include "config_pins.h"            // configure instructions tab
#include "stream_handler.h"         // code to stream images
char ssid[] = "xxxx";               // change xxxx to Wi-Fi ssid
char password[] = "xxxx";           // change xxxx to Wi-Fi password

void setup()
{
  Serial.begin(115200);            // Serial Monitor baud rate
  Serial.setDebugOutput(false);    // no debug information
  WiFi.begin(ssid, password);      // initialise Wi-Fi
  while (WiFi.status() != WL_CONNECTED) delay(500);
  Serial.print("IP Address: ");
  Serial.println(WiFi.localIP()); // display WLAN IP address
  configCamera();
```

```
sensor_t * s = esp_camera_sensor_get();   // reduce frame size
s->set_framesize(s, FRAMESIZE_VGA);        // to 640x480 pixels
startCameraServer();
}

void startCameraServer()                    // function to start camera server
{
  httpd_handle_t stream_httpd = NULL;
  httpd_config_t config = HTTPD_DEFAULT_CONFIG();
  config.server_port = 80;
  httpd_uri_t index_uri = {.uri="/", .method=HTTP_GET,
                           .handler=stream_handler,
                           .user_ctx=NULL};
  if (httpd_start(&stream_httpd, &config) == ESP_OK)
      httpd_register_uri_handler(stream_httpd, &index_uri);
}

void loop()                                 // nothing in loop function
{}
```

Listing 2-6 is derived from sections of the *CameraWebServer*
sketch which specifically manage streaming images to a web page. The
instruction httpd_resp_send_chunk() returns the JPEG buffer as 64-bit
sections in response to the client HTTP request, with the instruction
snprintf((char *)part_buf, 64,...) generating the 64-bit sections
of the JPEG buffer. The static keyword creates a variable specific to a
function, and the value of the variable is maintained between repeated
calls to the function. Several instructions in Listing 2-6 are identical
to those in the *takePhoto* function of Listing 2-1, as indicated by the
comments for Listing 2-6.

Listing 2-6. Streaming real-time images

```
#define Boundary "1234567890000000000000987654321"
static const char* ContentType =
"multipart/x-mixed-replace;boundary=" Boundary;
static const char* StreamBound = "\r\n--" Boundary "\r\n";
static const char* StreamContent =
"Content-Type: image/jpeg\r\nContent-Length: %u\r\n\r\n";
static esp_err_t stream_handler(httpd_req_t *req)
{
  camera_fb_t * frame = NULL;          // as in Listing 2-1
  esp_err_t res = ESP_OK;              // error status
  uint8_t * jpgBuffer = NULL;          // JPEG buffer
  size_t jpgLength = 0;                // length of JPEG buffer
  char * part_buf[64];
  res = httpd_resp_set_type(req, ContentType);
  if(res != ESP_OK) return res;

  while(true)
  {
    frame = esp_camera_fb_get();       // as in Listing 2-1
    if (!frame)                        // as in Listing 2-1
    {
      Serial.println("Camera capture failed");
                                       // as in Listing 2-1
      res = ESP_FAIL;
    } else {
      if(frame->width > 400)
      {
        jpgLength = frame->len;        // set JPEG buffer length
        jpgBuffer = frame->buf;        // set JPEG buffer
      }
    }
```

```
    if(res == ESP_OK)                         // no error, stream image
    {
      size_t hlen = snprintf((char *)part_buf, 64,
      StreamContent, jpgLength);
      res = httpd_resp_send_chunk(req, (const char *)
      part_buf, hlen);
    }
    if(res == ESP_OK) res =
    httpd_resp_send_chunk(req, (const char *)jpgBuffer,
    jpgLength);
    if(res == ESP_OK) res =
    httpd_resp_send_chunk(req, StreamBound,
    strlen (StreamBound));
    if(frame)
    {
      esp_camera_fb_return(frame);        // as in Listing 2-1
      frame = NULL;
      jpgBuffer = NULL;                        // reset to NULL value
    } else
    if(jpgBuffer)
    {
      free(jpgBuffer);                         // reset to NULL value
      jpgBuffer = NULL;
    }
    if(res != ESP_OK) break;
  }
  return res;
}
```

PIR trigger to stream images to a web page

The ESP32-CAM module requires 130 mA to stream images to a web page, which rapidly drains a battery. If the ESP32-CAM module is in sleep mode, when not streaming images, and a PIR (passive infrared) sensor on the HC-SR501 PIR module triggers the ESP32-CAM module from sleep mode to start taking photos and stream images to a web page, then a battery-powered module is feasible (see Figure 2-3 with connections in Table 2-3). The ESP32 sleep mode is described in Chapter 22 (ESP32 microcontroller features); and a *HIGH* or *LOW* signal on a GPIO pin wakes the microcontroller from sleep mode, with the instruction esp_sleep_enable_ext0_wakeup(pin, state), when the state of *pin* is equal to *state*. When no movement is detected by the PIR sensor, the value of *state* is zero, as the PIR pin is pulled down by an ESP32 microcontroller pull-down resistor. ESP32 microcontroller pull-down resistors are disabled during sleep, so the instruction rtc_gpio_pulldown_en(pin) enables a pull-down resistor on the GPIO pin connected to the PIR sensor pin. When the PIR sensor is activated by infrared radiation, such as a person moving in the range of the sensor, the signal pin of the PIR sensor module is set *HIGH*, which wakes the microcontroller from sleep mode. After the ESP32-CAM module has streamed images to a web page for the required time, the microcontroller is moved to sleep mode, with the instruction esp_deep_sleep_start().

An HC-SR501 or HC-SR505 PIR module requires up to 50 s to stabilize, particularly the HC-SR505 module. If the PIR module triggers with no movement after the stabilization period, then the PIR module should be powered independently from the ESP32-CAM, but with a common GND.

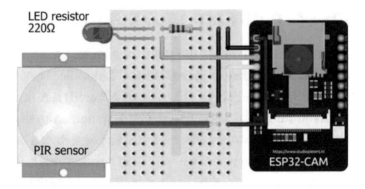

Figure 2-3. *PIR trigger to stream ESP32-CAM images to a web page*

Table 2-3. *PIR trigger to stream images to a web page*

Component	Connect to	And to
ESP32-CAM 5V	HC-SR501 5V	
ESP32-CAM GND	HC-SR501 GND	
ESP32-CAM GPIO 12	LED long leg	
ESP32-CAM GPIO 13	HC-SR501 OUT	
LED short leg	220 Ω resistor	GND

In the sketch in Listing 2-7, the ESP32-CAM is triggered by the PIR sensor, the LED is flashed to indicate detected movement, the Wi-Fi connection is established, and the ESP32-CAM camera is configured. The LED is again flashed to indicate the start of image streaming, images are streamed to the web page for *camTime* seconds, and the LED is again flashed to indicate the end of image streaming. The sketch in Listing 2-7 is based on Listing 2-5, with only the addition of the real-time clock (RTC) input-output (*rtc_io*) library, the *flash* function to flash the LED, the *esp_sleep* instructions, and the *loop* function, which determines the elapsed time since image streaming started. There is no change to the content of the *config_pins.h* and *stream_handler.h* tabs. Only the additional instructions to Listing 2-5 are annotated in Listing 2-7, to emphasize the few changes required to the sketch.

Listing 2-7. PIR trigger to stream images to a web page

```
#include <esp_http_server.h>
#include <esp_camera.h>
#include <WiFi.h>
#include "config_pins.h"
#include "stream_handler.h"
#include <driver/rtc_io.h>          // include rtc input-output library
int PIRpin = 13;                    // define PIR and LED pins
int LEDpin = 12;
unsigned long startTime,
lastTime = 0;                       // timer variables
int camTime = 10;                   // define image streaming time (s)
int count = 0;                      // counter for steaming time
char ssid[] = "xxxx";
char password[] = "xxxx";

void setup()
{
  pinMode(LEDpin, OUTPUT);          // LED pin as output
  flash();                          // call function to flash LEDs
  Serial.begin(115200);
  Serial.setDebugOutput(false);
  WiFi.begin(ssid, password);
  while (WiFi.status() != WL_CONNECTED) delay(500);
  Serial.print("IP Address: ");
  Serial.println(WiFi.localIP());
  configCamera();
```

```
  sensor_t * s = esp_camera_sensor_get();
  s->set_framesize(s, FRAMESIZE_VGA);
  startCameraServer();
  rtc_gpio_pulldown_en
  ((gpio_num_t)PIRpin);                   // pull-down PIR pin
  esp_sleep_enable_ext0_wakeup((gpio_num_t)PIRpin, 1);
}                                         // wakeup on PIR pin with state 1

void startCameraServer()
{
  httpd_handle_t stream_httpd = NULL;
  httpd_config_t config = HTTPD_DEFAULT_CONFIG();
  config.server_port = 80;
  httpd_uri_t index_uri = {.uri="/", .method=HTTP_GET,
                           .handler=stream_handler,
                           .user_ctx=NULL};
  if (httpd_start(&stream_httpd, &config) == ESP_OK)
    httpd_register_uri_handler(stream_httpd, &index_uri);
}

void loop()
{
  if(count < 1) flash();              // call function to flash LEDs
  startTime = millis();               // start of image streaming time
  if(startTime - lastTime > 1000 && count < camTime)
  {                                   // display seconds elapsed
    Serial.print("camera ");Serial.println(count);
    count++;                          // update counter
    lastTime = startTime;            // reset image streaming time
  }
  if(count == camTime)                // defined streaming time elapsed
```

```
  {
    flash();
    Serial.print("sleep mode on PIR pin ");
    Serial.println(PIRpin);
    esp_deep_sleep_start();                 // ESP32 in sleep mode
  }
}

void flash()                                // function to flash LEDs
{
  for (int i=0; i<3; i++)                   // flash LED three times
  {
    digitalWrite(LEDpin, HIGH);             // turn on LED
    delay(200);
    digitalWrite(LEDpin, LOW);              // turn off LED
    delay(100);
  }
}
```

When the sketches in Listings 2-1 and 2-7 are combined, the ESP32-CAM is triggered by the PIR sensor to take photos and store the image JPEG files on the micro-SD card.

Summary

The ESP32-CAM module includes an ESP32-S microcontroller, a 2M-pixel OV2640 camera, and a micro-SD card slot. Images are stored on the micro-SD card, loaded to a web page, or streamed to a web page on a computer, Android tablet, or mobile phone. Images are stored on the micro-SD card at timed intervals, for use with time-lapse photography.

Images are remotely uploaded to a web page on an Android tablet or mobile phone, where the image is rotated and also saved to the Android tablet or mobile phone. Real-time images are streamed from the ESP32-CAM module to a web page, with frame rates of up to 30 FPS. A PIR sensor is used to wake the microcontroller from sleep mode, which then streams images to a web page for a defined time period. The ESP32-CAM module is then returned to the energy-saving sleep mode.

Components List

- ESP32-CAM module

- USB to serial UART interface: FT232RL FTDI USB to TTL Serial converter module

- Passive infrared (PIR) sensor: HC-SR501 or HC-SR505

- LED

- Resistor: 220 Ω

CHAPTER 3

International weather station

International weather information is displayed on a touch screen where the user selects weather information for different cities and chooses between two screens of displayed information. Initially, this chapter describes displaying text and shapes on the screen, calibrating the touch function of the screen, and creating images by pressing the touch screen. Once sketches are developed to display information and utilize the touch function of the touch screen, the focus shifts to accessing international weather data from OpenWeatherMap.org and the reformatting of the *OpenWeatherMap* data to display on a touch screen.

Displaying text and shapes on a touch screen or creating images by pressing the touch screen does not require Internet access. An Arduino Uno or Nano is sufficient to run the sketches, but a logic-level converter is required to reduce the voltage to the touch screen to 3.3 V, as the Arduino Uno and Nano operate at 5 V. Accessing *OpenWeatherMap* data requires connection to the local Wi-Fi network, which is provided by an ESP8266 or ESP32 microcontroller.

© Neil Cameron 2021
N. Cameron, *Electronics Projects with the ESP8266 and ESP32*,
https://doi.org/10.1007/978-1-4842-6336-5_3

ILI9341 SPI TFT LCD touch screen

The 2.4-inch ILI9341 SPI TFT LCD touch screen with 240 × 320 pixels has touch screen functionality for displaying text and drawing shapes with different colors on the screen. The acronyms SPI, TFT, and LCD represent Serial Peripheral Interface, Thin-Film Transistor, and Liquid Crystal Display, respectively. The ILI9341 SPI TFT LCD screen and the ESP8266 and ESP32 microcontrollers operate at 3.3 V, so a logic-level converter is not required. Connections for the ILI9341 SPI TFT LCD screen with the ESP8266 and ESP32 development boards are shown in Figures 3-1 and 3-2 and given in Table 3-1. Note that the microcontroller SPI MOSI, MISO (Main-In Secondary-Out), and serial clock (SCL) pins are connected to both the display and the *touch* function pins of the ILI9341 SPI TFT LCD screen.

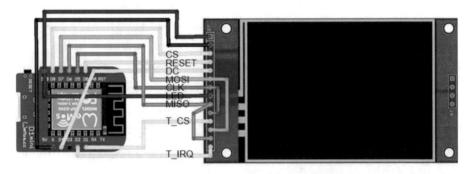

Figure 3-1. *ILI9341 SPI TFT LCD screen and the LOLIN (WeMos) D1 mini development board*

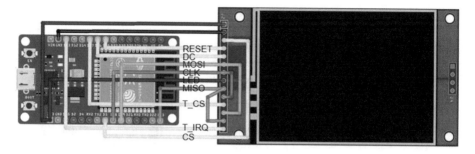

RESET
DC
MOSI
CLK
LED
MISO
T_CS
T_IRQ
CS

Figure 3-2. *ILI9341 SPI TFT LCD screen and the ESP32 DEVKIT DOIT development board*

Table 3-1. *ILI9341 SPI TFT LCD screen and ESP8266 and ESP32 development boards*

Component	Pin Function	ESP8266 Pin	ESP32 Pin
ILI9341 TFT screen VCC 3.3V		3V3	3V3
ILI9341 TFT screen GND		GND	GND
ILI9341 TFT screen CS	Chip select	D8	GPIO 5
ILI9341 TFT screen RESET		D0	GPIO 25
ILI9341 TFT screen DC	Data command	D4	GPIO 26
ILI9341 TFT screen SDA (MOSI)	Serial data in (DI)	D7	GPIO 23
ILI9341 TFT screen SCL (CLK)	Serial clock	D5	GPIO 18
ILI9341 TFT screen LED		3V3	3V3
ILI9341 TFT screen SDO (MISO)	Serial data out	D6	GPIO 19
"touch"			
ILI9341 TFT screen T_CLK	Serial clock	D5	GPIO 18
ILI9341 TFT screen T_CS	Chip select	D1	GPIO 27

(continued)

Table 3-1. (*continued*)

Component	Pin Function	ESP8266 Pin	ESP32 Pin
ILI9341 TFT screen T_DIN	Data input	D7	GPIO 23
ILI9341 TFT screen T_DO	Data output	D6	GPIO 19
ILI9341 TFT screen T_IRQ	Interrupt	D2	GPIO 13

Listing 3-1 demonstrates displaying text and drawing shapes on the ILI9341 SPI TFT LCD screen. The *Adafruit ILI9341* and *Adafruit GFX* libraries are installed within the Arduino IDE. The *Adafruit GFX* and *SPI* libraries are referenced by the *Adafruit ILI9341* library, so are not explicitly included in the sketch. Color codes are available within the *Adafruit ILI9341* library, so HEX codes for colors are not defined in the sketch. The screen orientation is set as portrait or landscape with the instruction setRotation(N) with value of 0 or 1, respectively, or the value of 2 or 3 to rotate the screen image by 180° for portrait or landscape, respectively. For example, portrait orientation with pin connections at the top of the ILI9341 SPI TFT LCS screen is set with setRotation(2). The default font size is 5 × 8 pixels per character that is increased to 5N × 8N pixels with the setTextSize(N) instruction.

Listing 3-1. Display text and shapes

```
#include <Adafruit_ILI9341.h>      // include ILI9341 library
int tftCS = D8;                     // screen chip select pin
int tftDC = D4;                     // data command select pin
int tftRST = D0;                    // reset pin
                                    // associate tft with ILI9341 lib
Adafruit_ILI9341 tft = Adafruit_ILI9341(tftCS, tftDC, tftRST);
String texts[] =                    // color names
  {"BLUE","RED","GREEN","CYAN","MAGENTA","YELLOW","WHITE","GREY"};
```

```
unsigned int colors[ ] =                  // color codes
  {ILI9341_BLUE, ILI9341_RED, ILI9341_GREEN, ILI9341_CYAN,
   ILI9341_MAGENTA, ILI9341_YELLOW, ILI9341_WHITE,
   ILI9341_LIGHTGREY};
String text;
unsigned int color, chkTime;

void setup()
{
  tft.begin();                            // initialise screen
  tft.setRotation(2);                     // portrait, connections at top
  tft.fillScreen(ILI9341_BLACK);              // fill screen in black
  tft.drawRect(0,0,239,319,ILI9341_WHITE);    // draw white frame line
  tft.drawRect(1,1,237,317,ILI9341_WHITE);    // and second frame line
  tft.setTextSize(4);                         // set text size
}

void loop()
{                                       // clear screen apart from frame
  tft.fillRect(2,2,235,314,ILI9341_ BLACK);
  for (int i=0; i<8; i++)               // for each color
  {
    color = colors[i];                 // set color
    text = texts[i];                   // set text for color
    tft.setTextColor(color);           // set text color
    tft.setCursor(20,40*i+2);          // position cursor
    tft.print(text);                   // print color text (name)
    delay(250);                        // delay 250ms between colors
  }
```

```
for (int i=0; i<8; i++)                 // for each color
{
  color = colors[i];
  text = texts[i];
  tft.fillRect(2,2,235,314,ILI9341_BLACK);
  tft.setCursor(20,25);                   // cursor to position (20, 25)
  tft.setTextColor(color);
  tft.print(text);                        // draw filled-in triangle
  if ((i+1) % 3 == 0) tft.fillTriangle(20,134,64,55,107,134,color);
                                          // draw open rectangle
  else if ((i+1) % 2 == 0) tft.drawRect(20,55,88,80,color);
  else tft.fillCircle(64,95,39,color);    // draw filled-in circle
  delay(250);
}
tft.fillRect(2,2,235,314,ILI9341_BLACK);
tft.drawLine(2,158,236,158,ILI9341_RED);
                                          // draw horizontal RED line
delay(250);
}
```

In Listing 3-1, SPI pins are defined for an ESP8266 development board, which must be changed for an ESP32 development board. Alternatively, the instructions in Listing 3-2 can be included at the start of a sketch. See Chapter 21 (Microcontrollers) for more information.

Listing 3-2. Pin definitions for ESP8266 and ESP32 development boards

```
#ifdef ESP32
  int tftCS = 5;                // screen chip select pin
  int tftDC = 26;               // data command select pin
  int tftRST = 25;              // reset pin
```

```
#elif ESP8266
   int tftCS = D8;
   int tftDC = D4;
   int tftRST = D0;
#else                                    // Arduino IDE error message
   #error "ESP8266 or ESP32 microcontroller only"
#endif
```

Touch screen calibration

A library for the touch screen function with the ESP8266 and ESP32 microcontrollers, *TFT_eSPI* by Bodmer, is available within the Arduino IDE. Prior to using the *TFT_eSPI* library in sketches, the touch screen driver, pin connections to the ESP8266 or ESP32 development board, and SPI frequencies must be defined in the file *User_Setup.h*, which is located in the *TFT-eSPI* library folder. Listing 3-3 includes the settings used in this chapter for ESP8266 and ESP32 microcontrollers, with the settings for the ESP32 microcontroller commented out. Note that default pin connections for the ESP8266 SPI MOSI, MISO, and CLK are not required, but pin numbers for the ESP8266 development board are preceded with *PIN_*, while the ESP32 microcontroller GPIO numbers are sufficient.

Listing 3-3. TFT-eSPI library User_Setup settings for ESP8266 and ESP32 development boards

```
#define TFT_CS   PIN_D8              // ESP8266 SPI and touch screen
#define TFT_DC   PIN_D4
#define TFT_RST  PIN_D0
#define TOUCH_CS PIN_D1

/*                        // lines between /* and */ are commented out
#define TFT_MISO 19       // ESP32 SPI and touch screen
```

```
#define TFT_MOSI 23
#define TFT_SCLK 18
#define TFT_CS    5
#define TFT_DC    26
#define TFT_RST   25
#define TOUCH_CS 27
*/
```

```
#define ILI9341_DRIVER               // ILI9341 SPI TFT LCD screen
#define TFT_RGB_ORDER TFT_BGR        // color order Blue-Green-Red
#define LOAD_GLCD                    // font 1: Adafruit 8-pixel high
#define LOAD_FONT2                   // font 2: small 16-pixel high
#define LOAD_FONT4                   // font 4: medium 26-pixel high
#define SPI_FREQUENCY 40000000          // SPI 40MHz
#define SPI_READ_FREQUENCY 20000000     // SPI read 20MHz
#define SPI_TOUCH_FREQUENCY 2500000     // SPI touch 2.5MHz
```

Before using the touch screen facility of the ILI9341 SPI TFT LCD screen, the screen must be calibrated (see Listing 3-4). Arrows are displayed on the ILI9341 SPI TFT LCD screen, which the user presses with a screen pen. Five calibration parameters are displayed on the ILI9341 SPI TFT LCD screen, which are included in the *calData* array of subsequent sketches. The *SPI* library is referenced by the *TFT_eSPI* library, so is not explicitly included in the sketch. Listing 3-4 is adapted from the *Touch_calibrate* sketch in the *TFT-eSPI* ➤ *Generic* library.

Listing 3-4. Calibration of the ILI9341 SPI TFT LCD screen

```
#include <TFT_eSPI.h>          // include TFT_eSPI library
TFT_eSPI tft = TFT_eSPI();     // associate tft with TFT-eSPI lib
uint16_t calData[5];           // calibration parameters
String str;
```

```
void setup()
{
  tft.init();                          // initialise ILI9341 TFT screen
  tft.setRotation(1);                  // landscape, connections on right
  tft.setTextFont(1);                  // set text font and size
  tft.setTextSize(1);
  calibrate();                         // call calibration function
}

void calibrate()        // function to calibrate ILI9341 TFT screen
{
  tft.fillScreen(TFT_BLACK);           // fill screen in black
  tft.setTextColor(TFT_WHITE, TFT_BLACK);
                                       // set text color, white on black
  tft.setCursor(30, 0);                // move cursor to position (0, 30)
  tft.println("Touch corners as indicated");
  tft.calibrateTouch(calData, TFT_RED, TFT_BLACK, 15);
                                       // calibrate screen
  tft.fillScreen(TFT_BLACK);
  tft.setCursor(0, 50);
  tft.setTextSize(2);
  tft.print("Calibration parameters");
  str = "";                    // display calibration parameters
  for (int i=0; i<4; i++) str = str + String(calData[i])+",";
  str = str + String(calData[4]);
  tft.setCursor(0, 90);
  tft.print(str);
}
void loop()                            // nothing in loop function
{}
```

For example, the calibration parameters for the ILI9341 SPI TFT LCD screen used in this chapter of *450, 3400, 390, 3320,* and *3* are copied into the *calDat* array of the instruction uint16_t calData[] = {450, 3400, 390, 3320, 3} of subsequent sketches. However, the calibration parameters for your ILI9341 SPI TFT LCD screen would be included in the sketches.

Painting on-screen

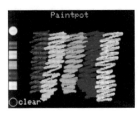

The sketch in Listing 3-5 draws images on the ILI9341 SPI TFT LCD screen when the screen is pressed with a screen pen, with colors selected from a color palette. The first section of the sketch installs libraries and defines the touch screen pins and the paintbrush size. The *setup* function sets the touch screen orientation and incorporates the touch screen calibration parameters obtained in Listing 3-4. When a screen press is detected, the touch position is identified; and if the *x* co-ordinate is less than 20, then the screen was pressed on the color palette and the selected color, mapped to the *y* co-ordinate, is subsequently used for drawing on the screen. Color codes are available in the file *TFT_eSPI.h* of the *TFT_eSPI* library. The *clear* function resets the screen, displays the title, and redraws the color palette. Have fun painting!

Listing 3-5. Paintpot with TFT-eSPI library

```
#include <TFT_eSPI.h>              // include TFT-eSPI library
TFT_eSPI tft = TFT_eSPI();         // associate tft with TFT-eSPI lib
uint16_t calData[] = {450, 3400, 390, 3320, 3};
                                   // calibration parameters
```

```
uint16_t x = 0, y = 0;
int radius = 2;                         // define paintbrush radius
unsigned int color;

void setup()
{
  tft.init();                           // initialise ILI9341 TFT screen
  tft.setRotation(1);                   // landscape, connections on right
  tft.setTouch(calData);                // include calibration parameters
  clear();                              // call function to reset screen
}

void loop()
{
  if (tft.getTouch(&x, &y)>0)     // if screen pressed
  {
    if(x>20) tft.fillCircle(x, y, radius, color); // draw point
    if(x>0 && x<20)                     // select color from color palette
    {
          if(y>75 && y<95)   color = TFT_RED;
        else if(y>100 && y<120) color = TFT_YELLOW;
        else if(y>125 && y<145) color = TFT_GREEN;
        else if(y>150 && y<170) color = TFT_BLUE;
        else if(y>175 && y<195) color = TFT_WHITE;
                                  // display selected color
        if(y>75 && y<195) tft.fillCircle(10, 50, 10, color);
        else if(y>215) clear();         // clear screen
    }
  }
}
```

```
void clear()                              // function to reset screen

{
  tft.fillScreen(TFT_BLACK);              // fill screen
  tft.setTextColor(TFT_GREEN);            // set text color
  tft.setTextSize(2);                     // set text size
  tft.setCursor(110,5);                   // position cursor
  tft.print("Paintpot");                  // screen title
  tft.fillRect(0,75,20,20, TFT_RED);
  tft.fillRect(0,100,20,20,TFT_YELLOW);
  tft.fillRect(0,125,20,20,TFT_GREEN);    // build color palette
  tft.fillRect(0,150,20,20, TFT_BLUE);
  tft.fillRect(0,175,20,20, TFT_WHITE);
  tft.drawCircle(10,225,10, TFT_WHITE);   // select to clear screen
  tft.setCursor(25,217);
  tft.setTextColor(TFT_WHITE);
  tft.print("clear");
  color = TFT_WHITE;
}
```

ESP8266-specific touch screen calibration and paint

The advantage of the *TFT-eSPI* library is that one library incorporates screen display and touch functionality, with the applicability to both ESP8266 and ESP32 microcontrollers in conjunction with the ILI9341 SPI TFT LCD screen. The *Adafruit_ILI9341esp* library, adapted specifically for the ESP8266 microcontroller, has an excellent touch screen painting function. The *Adafruit_ILI9341esp* library by NailBuster Software is contained in the *tft28esp.zip* file that is downloaded from nailbuster.com/?page_id=341. The *Adafruit_ILI9341esp* library requires the *XPT2046* library by Spiros Papadimitriou, which is downloaded from github.com/spapadim/XPT2046.

Calibration for the ILI9341 SPI TFT LCD screen with the *XPT2046* library differs from calibration with the *TFT-eSPI* library. In the calibration sketch (see Listing 3-6), two crosses, at 20-pixel margins from the screen edges, are displayed on the ILI9341 SPI TFT LCD screen, which the user presses with a screen pen. Four calibration parameters are then displayed on the ILI9341 SPI TFT LCD screen, that are included in the touch.setCalibration instruction of subsequent sketches.

The *getPoints* function determines the touched screen position, with the & parameter referencing a pointer to a whole array, rather than a pointer to the first element of the array. A touched position, *(p, q)*, is mapped to a display position, *(np, nq)*, of the 240 × 320–pixel ILI9341 SPI TFT LCD screen. For the screen used in this chapter, the regression equations, $np = (150 - p) \times 240/145$ and $nq = (115 - q) \times 320/100$, were determined from a series of marked positions on the ILI9341 SPI TFT LCD screen and the corresponding touched positions identified by the *XPT2046* library.

Listing 3-6. Calibration of the ILI9341 SPI TFT LCD screen for the XPT2046 library

```
#include <Adafruit_ILI9341esp.h>    // include ILI9341esp and
#include <XPT2046.h>                // XPT2046 libraries
int tftCS = D8;
int tftDC = D4;
int tftRST = D0;                    // define screen and touch pins
int touchCS = D1;
int touchIRQ = D2;                  // associate tft with ILI9341 lib
Adafruit_ILI9341 tft = Adafruit_ILI9341(tftCS, tftDC, tftRST);
XPT2046 touch(touchCS, touchIRQ);   // associate touch with XPT2046
uint16_t p,q, np, nq;               // co-ordinates of touched point
String str;
```

```
void setup()
{
  tft.begin();                        // initialise ILI9341 screen
  tft.setRotation(0);                 // portrait connections at bottom
  touch.begin(tft.height(), tft.width());
                                      // XPT2046 orientated y, x
  touch.setRotation(XPT2046::ROT0);   // no screen rotation
  tft.fillScreen(ILI9341_BLACK);      // fill screen
  tft.setTextColor(ILI9341_WHITE);    // set text color
  tft.setTextSize(1);                 // set text size
  tft.setCursor(0, 100);              // position cursor
  str = "width: "+String(tft.width())+", height:"
  +String(tft.height());
  tft.print(str);
  calibrate();                        // calibrate touch screen
}

void calibrate()                      // function to calibrate screen
{
  uint16_t x1,y1,x2,y2,i1,j1,i2,j2;   // uint16_t is unsigned integer
  tft.setCursor(0, 50);               // position cursor
  tft.print("press screen on crosses");
  touch.getCalibrationPoints(x1, y1, x2, y2);
                                      // values pre-set in library at 20
  getPoints(x1, y1, i1, j1);          // function to get touch position
  delay(500);
  getPoints(x2, y2, i2, j2);          // get second touch position
  touch.setCalibration(i1, j1, i2, j2);   // string with parameters
  str = String(i1)+","+String(j1)+","+String(i2)+","+String(j2);
  tft.setTextColor(ILI9341_WHITE);
  tft.setCursor(0, 175);
```

```
  tft.print("calibration parameters");
  tft.setCursor(0, 200);
  tft.setTextSize(2);                    // reset text size
  tft.print(str);                        // display calibration parameters
}

void getPoints(uint16_t x, uint16_t y, uint16_t &i, uint16_t &j)
{
  marker(y, x, ILI9341_WHITE);       // draw white cross on screen
  while (!touch.isTouching()>0) delay(10);      // wait for screen touch
  touch.getRaw(i, j);
  marker(y, x, ILI9341_BLACK);          // over-write cross
  touch.getPosition(p, q);              // get position of screen touch
  np = (150.0-p)*240.0/145.0;           // transform from touch to tft
  nq = (115.0-q)*320.0/100.0;
  tft.fillCircle(np, nq, 2, ILI9341_GREEN);
}                                        // indicated touch position

void marker(unsigned short x, uint16_t y, int col)
{
  tft.setTextColor(col);                  // set marker color
  tft.drawLine(x-8, y, x+8, y, col);     // draw horizontal line
  tft.drawLine(x, y-8, x, y+8, col);     // draw vertical line
}

void loop()                              // nothing in loop function
{}
```

The sketch in Listing 3-7 has the same structure as Listing 3-5, which uses the *TFT_eSPI* library. The differences between the sketches are that screen pins, touch pins, and rotation parameters are defined in the sketch, rather than in an external file with the *TFT_eSPI* library, and that

colors are referenced to the *Adafruit_ILI9341* and *TFT_eSPI* libraries. The
paint function with the *XPT2046* library is more responsive than with the
TFT-eSPI library, which is more suited for a screen pointer. The sketch in
Listing 3-7 operates with any screen rotation position, but either landscape
orientation is recommended.

Listing 3-7. Paintpot with the XPT2046 library

```
#include <Adafruit_ILI9341esp.h>   // include ILI9341esp and
#include <XPT2046.h>               // XPT2046 libraries
int tftCS = D8;
int tftDC = D4;
int tftRST = D0;                   // define screen and touch pins
int touchCS = D1;
int touchIRQ = D2;                 // associate tft with ILI9341 lib
Adafruit_ILI9341 tft = Adafruit_ILI9341(tftCS, tftDC, tftRST);
XPT2046 touch(touchCS, touchIRQ); // associate touch with XPT2046
String str;
uint16_t x, y;
int radius = 2;                    // define paintbrush radius
unsigned int color;                // rotation: 0, 1, 2 or 3 refers to
int rotate = 1;                    // rotation of 0, 90, 180 or 270°

void setup()
{
  tft.begin();                     // initialise ILI9341 screen
  setRotation();                   // function for rotation parameters
  touch.setCalibration(1850,1800,320,300);
                                   // calibration parameters
  clear();                         // call function to reset screen
}
```

```
void loop()
{
  if (touch.isTouching()>0)         // if screen pressed
  {
    touch.getPosition(x, y);
    if(x>20) tft.fillCircle(x, y, radius, color);  // draw point
    if(x>0 && x<20)                 // select color from color palette
    {
          if(y>75 && y<95)   color = ILI9341_RED;
      else if(y>100 && y<120) color = ILI9341_YELLOW;
      else if(y>125 && y<145) color = ILI9341_GREEN;
      else if(y>150 && y<170) color = ILI9341_BLUE;
      else if(y>175 && y<195) color = ILI9341_WHITE;
                                       // display selected color
      if(y>75 && y<195) tft.fillCircle(10, 50, 10, color);
      else if(y>215) clear();          // clear screen
    }
  }
}

void clear()                             // function to reset screen
{
  tft.fillScreen(ILI9341_BLACK);         // fill screen
  tft.setTextColor(ILI9341_GREEN);       // set text color
  tft.setTextSize(2);                    // set text size
  tft.setCursor(110,5);                  // position cursor
  tft.print("Paintpot");                 // screen title
  tft.fillRect(0,75,20,20, ILI9341_RED);
  tft.fillRect(0,100,20,20,ILI9341_YELLOW);
  tft.fillRect(0,125,20,20,ILI9341_GREEN);    // build color palette
  tft.fillRect(0,150,20,20, ILI9341_BLUE);
  tft.fillRect(0,175,20,20, ILI9341_WHITE);
```

```
  tft.drawCircle(10,225,10, ILI9341_WHITE);    // select to clear screen
  tft.setCursor(25,217);
  tft.setTextColor(ILI9341_WHITE);
  tft.print("clear");
  color = ILI9341_WHITE;
}

void setRotation()                  // function to set rotation parameters
{
  tft.setRotation(rotate);
  switch (rotate)
  {
    case 0:                                         // no rotation
       touch.begin(tft.width(), tft.height());      // portrait
       touch.setRotation(XPT2046::ROT0);      // connections at bottom
       break;
    case 1:                                   // rotation through 90°
       touch.begin(tft.height(), tft.width());      // landscape
       touch.setRotation(XPT2046::ROT90);      // connections on right
    break;
    case 2:                                   // rotation through 180°
       touch.begin(tft.width(), tft.height());      // portrait
       touch.setRotation(XPT2046::ROT180);      // connections at top
    break;
    case 3:                                   // rotation through 270°
       touch.begin(tft.height(), tft.width());      // landscape
       touch.setRotation(XPT2046::ROT270);      // connections on left
    break;
  }
}
```

Weather data for several cities

Another example of using the ILI9341 SPI TFT LCD touch screen displays detailed weather information for several cities, with weather data from OpenWeatherMap.org. *OpenWeatherMap* data is free to access within limits defined on the website. The *OpenWeatherMap* data requires a username, a password, an API (Application Programming Interface) key, and the city identity (ID) code. Details on opening an account and obtaining an API key for *OpenWeatherMap* are available at openweathermap.org/appid. The API key identifies the client to the web server. The city ID is obtained, from the OpenWeatherMap.org website, by entering the city name in the *Your city name search* box. Select the relevant city, and the city ID is the number at the end of the URL. For example, the Berlin URL is openweathermap.org/city/2950159.

The *ESP8266WiFi or WiFi, ArduinoJson,* and *Time* libraries are required for Wi-Fi communication, interpreting JSON (JavaScript Object Notation) formatted data, and calculating the date and time. Both the *ArduinoJson* library by Benoît Blanchon and the *TimeLib* library by Michael Margolis are available in the Arduino IDE, with the latter listed under *Time*. Several data providers format the date and time as the number of seconds since January 1, 1970, the Unix epoch time. The *Time* library converts the Unix epoch time to the corresponding minute, hour, day, month, and so on.

An example sketch (see Listing 3-8) obtains and displays the ultraviolet (UV) index for Edinburgh from *OpenWeatherMap* data. If there are problems with the Wi-Fi connection, HTTP request, or data receipt, then a message is displayed. The message instructions are optional and not incorporated in the *connect* function of Listing 3-9, but the client instructions in **bold** must be retained. If the instructions

```
if (!client.find("\r\n\r\n"))
{
  Serial.println("Received data not complete");
  return;
}
```

regarding a data error are deleted, then they must be replaced with the instruction `client.find("\r\n\r\n")`.

The URL is `api.openweathermap.org/data/2.5/uvi?lat=55.95&` `lon=-3.19&appid="+APIkey` which displays the following data:

lat	55.95	// latitude
lon	- 3.19	// longitude
date_iso	"2020-06-13T12:00:00Z"	// date
date	1592049600	// Unix epoch time
value	6.94	// UV index

The JSON formatted data consists of the name and value pairs, such as *lat* and *55.95*, that form the JSON document, which is defined as the character array, `jsonDoc[]`, in the sketch. The *value* of a name and value pair is identified by the name and extracted with the instruction `jsonDoc['name'].as<x>()`, where x refers to `float`, `long`, or `char*` for a real number, an integer, or a string, respectively. For example, `latitude = jsonDoc['lat'].as<float>()`.

In Listing 3-8, the libraries are installed, a Wi-Fi connection is established, and an HTTP request is sent to the *OpenWeatherMap* server for the Edinburgh UV index. The latitude, longitude, date, and UV index are extracted from the JSON document, received in response to the HTTP request. A comprehensive set of error checks are made regarding establishing the Wi-Fi connection, the HTTP request, the response to the HTTP request, the receipt of the JSON document in the HTTP response, and the extraction of the JSON document.

Listing 3-8. OpenWeatherMap data example

```
#include <ESP8266WiFi.h>        // library to connect to Wi-Fi network
#include <ArduinoJson.h>
WiFiClient client;             // create client to connect to IP address
char ssid[] = "xxxx";          // change xxxx to your Wi-Fi SSID
char password[] = "xxxx";      // change xxxx to your Wi-Fi password
String APIkey = "xxxx";        // and xxx to openweathermap API key
char server[]="api.openweathermap.org";
String output;

void setup()
{
  Serial.begin(115200);                // Serial Monitor baud rate
  WiFi.begin(ssid, password);          // initialise Wi-Fi and wait
  while (WiFi.status() != WL_CONNECTED) delay(500);
                                       // for Wi-Fi connection
  Serial.print("IP address: ");
  Serial.println(WiFi.localIP());   // Wi-Fi network IP address
  Serial.println("Connecting...");
  client.connect(server, 80);          // connect to server on port 80
  if (!client.connect(server, 80)) // connection error message
  {
    Serial.println("Connection failed");
    return;
  }
  Serial.println("Connected!");
  client.println("GET /data/2.5/uvi?lat=55.95&lon=-3.19&"
  "appid="+APIkey+" HTTP/1.1");        // send HTTP request
  client.println("Host: api.openweathermap.org");
  client.println("User-Agent: ESP8266/0.1");
  client.println("Connection: close");
```

```
client.println();
if (client.println() == 0)        // HTTP request error message
{
  Serial.println("HTTP request failed");
  return;
}
char status[32] = {0};
client.readBytesUntil('\r', status, sizeof(status));
if (strcmp(status, "HTTP/1.1 200 OK") != 0)
{                                   // HTTP status error message
  Serial.print("Response not valid: ");
  Serial.println(status);
  return;
}
else Serial.println("HTTP status OK");
if (!client.find("\r\n\r\n"))   // received data error request
{
  Serial.println("Received data not complete");
  return;
}
//  client.find("\r\n\r\n");
DynamicJsonDocument jsonDoc(1024);
DeserializationError error =
deserializeJson(jsonDoc, client);
if (error)
{                                   // JSON error message
  Serial.print("deserializeJson() failed: ");
  Serial.println(error.c_str());
  return;
}
```

```
serializeJson(jsonDoc, output);                    // display all data
Serial.print("data length: ");Serial.println(output.length());
Serial.println(output);
Serial.println("extracted text");
Serial.println(jsonDoc["lon"].as<float>(), 2);
                                                   // display specific data
Serial.println(jsonDoc["lat"].as<float>(), 2);
Serial.println(jsonDoc["date_iso"].as<char*>());
Serial.println(jsonDoc["date"].as<long>());
Serial.print("UV ");
Serial.println(jsonDoc["value"].as<float>(), 2);
}

void loop()                                        // nothing in loop function
{}
```

Listing 3-9 displays *OpenWeatherMap* data for a selected city with weather information displayed on different screens. The first screen displays the current minimum and maximum temperature and the forecasted weather, with the current humidity and pressure. The second screen displays cloud cover, the wind speed and direction, and more details on forecasted weather, with sunrise and sunset times. A city is selected from the city abbreviations on the right of the screen, and the screen displays are alternated by touching the ⊕ symbol on the left of the screen. The sketch is lengthy, due to processing the comprehensive weather data, and is split into functions to make the sketch more readily interpretable. The weather information is reduced by deleting the *secondScreen* function and the reference to it in the *getWeather* function.

The first section of the sketch includes the libraries and defines the screen and touch pins, *OpenWeatherMap* API key, and city identity codes. The first element of the *days* and *mths* arrays is a blank, so that *days[1]* and *mths[1]* correspond to *Sunday* and *January*, respectively. The *setup* function establishes the Wi-Fi connection, initializes the touch screen,

and incorporates the touch screen calibration parameters obtained in
Listing 3-4. The *loop* function calls the *checkTime* function to determine
if the required time has elapsed since the screen was last refreshed and
the selected city. The *connect* function sends a GET HTTP request to the
OpenWeatherMap server, incorporating the API key, and downloads the
JSON-formatted data for display on the ILI9341 SPI TFT LCD screen.
The JSON-formatted data from *OpenWeatherMap* is displayed with the
following instructions:

```
String output
serializeJson(jsonDoc, output)
Serial.println(output.length())
Serial.println(output)
```

An example of *OpenWeatherMap* JSON-formatted data is

{"coord":{"lon":-3.2,"lat":55.95},
"weather":[{"id":803,"main":"Clouds", "description":"broken
clouds", "icon":"04d"}],
"base":"stations",
"main":{"temp":14.38,"feels_like":7.99,"temp_min":12.78,
*   "temp_max":15.56, "pressure":1024,"humidity":62},*
"visibility":10000,"wind":{"speed":8.2,"deg":80},"clouds":{"all":68},
"dt":1591882710,
"sys":{"type":1,"id":1442,"country":"GB", "sunrise":1591846048,
"sunset":1591909066},
"timezone":3600,"id":2650225,"name":"Edinburgh", "cod":200}

Values are referenced according to the class outside the curly brackets,
{}, the category within the curly brackets, and the variable name, with each
term enclosed by square brackets, *[ ]*. For example, the humidity value
of 62 is referenced as *["main"]["humidity"]*. The weather class may have

two levels, referenced as *[0]* and *[1]*. Times are expressed in Unix epoch time. For example, the sunrise value of *1591846048*, referenced as *["sys"]* *["sunrise"]*, is 04:27 GMT on June 11, 2020.

JSON-formatted data is equated to a *string, float,* or *unsigned long,* such as

```
String weather = jsonDoc["weather"][0]["main"]
float temp = jsonDoc["main"]["temp"]
unsigned long srise = jsonDoc["sys"]["sunrise"]
```

and displayed with a print instruction, for example, `Serial.` `println(weather)`. JSON-formatted data is displayed directly by including the data reference and the output format in the print instruction, for example

```
Serial.println(jsonDoc["weather"][0]["main"].as<char*>())
Serial.println(jsonDoc["main"]["temp"].as<float>(), 2)   // for 2 DP
Serial.println(jsonDoc ["sys"]["sunrise"].as<long>())
```

The structures of the *firstScreen* and *secondScreen* functions are the same (see Figure 3-3). The *citySquare* function clears the screen; displays the list of city abbreviations, using the *screen* function that positions and displays strings; and draws a rectangle around the selected city abbreviation. The Unix epoch time for the weather update is converted to day, date, and time and displayed on the screen. Weather data is extracted from the JSON document, and the *screen* function positions and displays the string in the required color. To maintain text positioning, text is padded with blanks using the *addb* function. To make the functions in Listing 3-9 more readily interpretable, the first part of the instruction `screen("variable"` is in bold.

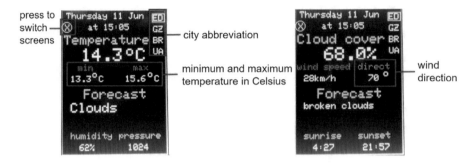

Figure 3-3. OpenWeatherMap information by screen

Listing 3-9. OpenWeatherMap information

```
#include <ESP8266WiFi.h>      // include ESP8266WiFi library
#include <ArduinoJson.h>      // include JSON library
#include <TimeLib.h>          // include TimeLib library
#include <TFT_eSPI.h>         // include TFT_eSPI library
TFT_eSPI tft = TFT_eSPI();    // associate tft with TFT-eSPI lib
uint16_t calData[] = {450, 3400, 390, 3320, 3};
                              // calibration parameters
uint16_t x = 0, y = 0;
WiFiClient client;            // create client to connect to IP address
char ssid[] = "xxxx";         // change xxxx to your Wi-Fi SSID
char password[] = "xxxx";     // change xxxx to your Wi-Fi password
String APIkey = "xxxx";       // change xxxx to weathermap API key
String city[] = {"ED","GZ","BR","UA"};
                              // Edinburgh, Günzburg, Brisbane, Ushuaia
                              // openweathermap city identity codes
String cityID[] = {"2650225","2913555","2174003","3833367"};
int Ncity = 4;                // number of cities
int cityNow = 0;              // current city, initially set at 0
int count = 99;               // run getWeather function at start
```

```
char server[] = "api.openweathermap.org";
int screenFlag = 0;              // flag for first or second screen
int touchFlag = 0;               // to indicate screen pressed
String days[] = {"",
"Sunday","Monday","Tuesday","Wednesday","Thursday","Friday",
"Saturday"};
String mths[] = {"",
"Jan","Feb","Mar","Apr","May","Jun","Jul","Aug","Sep","Oct",
"Nov","Dec"};
String wkdy, mth, addb, text;
int sunriseh, sunrisem, sunseth, sunsetm, dy, hr, mn;
unsigned int chkTime;
DynamicJsonDocument jsonDoc(1024);        // JSON formatted data

void setup()
{
  WiFi.begin(ssid, password); // initialise Wi-Fi and wait
  while (WiFi.status() != WL_CONNECTED) delay(500);
                                     // for WiFi connection
  tft.init();                        // initialise screen for graphics
  tft.setTouch(calData);             // calibration parameters
  tft.setRotation(2);                // portrait, connections on top
  tft.fillScreen(TFT_BLACK);         // fill screen in black
  tft.drawRect(0,0,239,319,TFT_WHITE);     // draw white frame line
  tft.drawRect(1,1,237,317,TFT_WHITE);     // and second frame
}

void loop()
{
  checkTime();                            // check if time to refresh screen
  if(tft.getTouch(&x, &y)>0 && touchFlag == 0)
                                  // if screen pressed
```

```
  {
    touchFlag = 1;
    if(y > 290)                          // city to be selected
    {
      screenFlag = 0;                    // start with first screen
            if(x > 215)          cityNow = 0;
      else if(x > 195 && x<216) cityNow = 1;
      else if(x > 175 && x<196) cityNow = 2;       // select city
      else if(x > 155 && x<176) cityNow = 3;
    }
    if(y < 20) screenFlag = 1-screenFlag;          // change screen
    count = 99;                    // run getWeather function immediately
  }
}

void checkTime()                         // check for screen refresh
{
  if(count > 4)                          // update screen every 5 minutes
  {
    getWeather();                        // call weather report function
    count = 0;                           // reset counter
  }
  else if(millis()-chkTime>60000)        // increment counter after 60s
  {
    chkTime = millis();                  // reset timer
    count++;                             // increment counter
  }
}

void getWeather()                        // function to get weather data
{
  connect();                             // call Wi-Fi connection function
  if(screenFlag == 0) firstScreen();   // select screen to be displayed
```

```
  else secondScreen();
  touchFlag = 0;                          // reset touch indicator
}

void connect()                     // function for Wi-Fi connection
{
  client.connect(server, 80);   // connect to server on port 80
  client.println("GET /data/2.5/weather?id="+cityID[cityNow]+
  "&units=metric&appid="+APIkey+" HTTP/1.1");   // send HTTP
                                                // request
  client.println("Host: api.openweathermap.org");
  client.println("User-Agent: ESP8266/0.1");
  client.println("Connection: close");
  client.println();
  client.find("\r\n\r\n");        // essential instruction
  DeserializationError error = deserializeJson(jsonDoc, client);
}

void firstScreen()                 // weather data for first screen
{
  citySquare();                    // call function to display header
  String weather = jsonDoc["weather"][0]["main"];
  String weather2 = jsonDoc["weather"][1]["main"];
  String id1 = jsonDoc["weather"][1]["id"];
  float temp = jsonDoc["main"]["temp"];
  float pres = jsonDoc["main"]["pressure"];
                                   // convert JavaScript objects
  float humid = jsonDoc["main"]["humidity"];
                                   // to strings or real numbers
  float tempMin = jsonDoc["main"]["temp_min"];
  float tempMax = jsonDoc["main"]["temp_max"];
  if(id1.length()<1) weather2 = " ";
```

```
screen("Temperature",TFT_GREEN,5,55,3);
                                      // display weather variable name
text = String(temp,1);                // convert value to string
if(temp<9.95) text = " "+text;        // add space if less than 10
screen(text,TFT_WHITE,45,85,4);       // display string on screen
screen("o", TFT_WHITE,148,80,3);      // add °symbol
screen("C", TFT_WHITE,170,85,4);      // add C for Celsius
screen("min",TFT_BLUE,37,120,2);      // minimum temperature
text = String(tempMin,1);
if(tempMin<10) text = " "+text;
screen(text,TFT_WHITE,20,145,2);
screen("o",TFT_WHITE,70,135,2);
screen("C",TFT_WHITE,85,145,2);
screen("max",TFT_RED,163,120,2);             // maximum temperature
text = String(tempMax,1);
if(tempMax<10) text = " "+text;
screen(text,TFT_WHITE,145,145,2);
screen("o",TFT_WHITE,197,135,2);
screen("C",TFT_WHITE,212,145,2);
screen("Forecast",TFT_GREEN,50,175,3); // forecast weather
addb = blank(weather);                       // add spaces after text
weather=weather+addb;
screen(weather,TFT_WHITE,20,205,3);
if(weather2 == "null") weather2="";
addb = blank(weather2);
weather2=weather2+addb;
screen(weather2,TFT_WHITE,20,235,3);       // forecast weather detail
screen("humidity",TFT_GREEN,20,270,2);  // humidity
text = String(humid,0)+"% ";
screen(text,TFT_WHITE,40,295,2);
screen("pressure",TFT_GREEN,130,270,2);   // pressure
text = String(pres,0);
```

```
  if(pres<1000) text = " "+text;
  screen(text,TFT_WHITE,150,295,2);
}

void secondScreen()                    // weather data for second screen
{
  citySquare();                        // call function to display header
  String desc = jsonDoc["weather"][0]["description"];
  String desc2 = jsonDoc["weather"][1]["description"];
  String id1 = jsonDoc["weather"][1]["id"];
                                       // convert JavaScript objects
  float windspd = jsonDoc["wind"]["speed"];
                                       // to strings or real numbers
  float winddeg = jsonDoc["wind"]["deg"];
  float cloud = jsonDoc["clouds"]["all"];
  unsigned long srise = jsonDoc["sys"]["sunrise"];
  unsigned long sset = jsonDoc["sys"]["sunset"];
  if(id1.length()<1) desc2 = " ";
  screen("Cloud cover",TFT_GREEN,5,55,3);              // cloud cover
  text = String(cloud,1)+"%";
  screen(text,TFT_WHITE,65,85,4);
  screen("wind speed",TFT_BLUE,5,120,2);               // wind speed
  windspd = windspd*3.6;               // convert m/s to km/h
  text = String(windspd,0)+"km/h";
  screen(text,TFT_WHITE,20,145,2);
  screen("direct",TFT_RED,140,120,2);   // wind direction
  text = String(winddeg,0);
  if(winddeg<10) text = " "+text;
  if(winddeg<100) text = " "+text;
  screen(text,TFT_WHITE,152,145,2);
  screen("o",TFT_WHITE,197,135,2);
  screen("Forecast",TFT_GREEN,50,175,3);   // weather forecast (2)
```

```
  addb = blank(desc);
  desc=desc+addb;
  if(desc.length()<13) screen(desc,TFT_WHITE,20,205,3);
  else screen(desc,TFT_WHITE,20,205,2);
                                        // font size depends on text length
  if(desc2 == "null") desc2="";
  addb = blank(desc2);
  desc2=desc2+addb;
  if(desc.length()<13 && desc2.length()<13)
          screen(desc2,TFT_WHITE,5,235,3);
  else screen(desc2,TFT_WHITE,5,235,2);
  screen("sunrise",TFT_GREEN,20,270,2);   // sunrise time
  text = String(minute(srise));
  if(minute(srise)<10) text = "0"+text;
  text = String(hour(srise)+1)+":"+text;
  screen(text,TFT_WHITE,40,295,2);
  screen("sunset",TFT_GREEN,140,270,2);   // sunset time
  text = String(minute(sset));
  if(minute(sset)<10) text = "0"+text;
  text = String(hour(sset)+1)+":"+text;
  screen(text,TFT_WHITE,150,295,2);
}

void citySquare()       // display header and city abbreviations
{
  tft.fillRect(2,2,235,315,TFT_BLACK);
                                      // clear screen apart from frame
                                      // display city abbreviations
  for (int i=0; i<Ncity; i++) screen(city[i],
  TFT_YELLOW,210,10+i*25,2);
```

```
for (int i=0; i<Ncity; i++) tft.drawRect(208,8+i*25,29,19,
TFT_BLACK);
                                      // draw rectangle for selected city
tft.drawRect(208,8+cityNow*25,29,19,TFT_WHITE);
screen("X",TFT_YELLOW,7,31,2);          // draw X with circle
tft.drawCircle(11,37,11,TFT_WHITE);
unsigned long stime = jsonDoc["dt"];  // time in secs since 1 Jan 1970
hr = hour(stime)+1;
mn = minute(stime);
dy = day(stime);                        // convert time
wkdy = days[weekday(stime)];
mth = mths[month(stime)];
text = wkdy+" "+String(dy)+" "+mth;   // display day, date and time
screen(text,TFT_YELLOW,10,5,2);
text = "at "+String(hr)+":"+String(mn);
if(mn<10) text = "at "+String(hr)+":0"+String(mn);
screen(text,TFT_YELLOW,60,30,2);
}
                  // function to position and display strings
void screen(String text, unsigned int color, int x, int y,
int size)
{
  tft.setCursor(x, y);                  // position cursor
  tft.setTextColor(color,TFT_BLACK);    // background color: black
  tft.setTextSize(size);
  tft.print(text);
}
```

```
String blank(String txt)         // function to add spaces to text
{
  String addb = "";
  int len = 12-txt.length();   // add up to 11 spaces
  for (int i=0;i<len;i++) addb=addb+" ";
  return addb;
}
```

Summary

The Wi-Fi functionality of the ESP8266 and ESP32 microcontrollers enabled Internet access to weather data from *OpenWeatherMap*. The ILI9341 SPI TFT LCD touch screen function enabled a city to be selected from the touch screen menu. The JSON-formatted weather data was extracted and displayed on the ILI9341 SPI TFT LCD screen. Use of the *TFT-eSPI* and *XPT2046* libraries illustrated two screen calibration processes and differences in ILI9341 SPI TFT LCD touch screen function applied to a screen painting example.

Components List

- ESP8266 microcontroller: LOLIN (WeMos) D1 mini or NodeMCU board

- ESP32 microcontroller: DEVKIT DOIT or NodeMCU board

- SPI TFT LCD touch screen: ILI9341, 2.4 inches, 240 × 320 pixels

CHAPTER 4

Internet clock

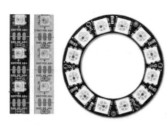
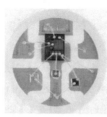

Each LED (Light-Emitting Diode) in an RGB (Red Green Blue) LED strip or ring is individually addressed using only one microcontroller pin for all the LEDs in the strip or ring. The term WS2812 5050 RGB LED refers to a strip or ring consisting of RGB LEDs with a WS2812 controller chip incorporated in each LED, and *5050* refers to the LED dimensions of 5.0 × 5.0 mm. *NeoPixel* is the Adafruit brand name for individually addressable RGB LEDs.

The *Adafruit NeoPixel* library is applicable to WS2812 RGB LED strips and rings as well as *NeoPixel* products. The number of RGB LEDs in the strip or ring, *LEDnumber*, and the microcontroller pin, *LEDpin*, are defined with the instruction

```
Adafruit_NeoPixel strip(LEDnumber, LEDpin, NEO_GRB + NEO_KHZ800)
```

which associates *strip* with the *Adafruit NeoPixel* library, as the WS2812 RGB LED strips and rings are wired for a GRB (Green Red Blue) 800 kHz bit stream. Alternatively, the *NEO_RGB + NEO_KHZ800* settings may be required. RGB LED display instructions are followed with the show() instruction to activate display instructions.

© Neil Cameron 2021
N. Cameron, *Electronics Projects with the ESP8266 and ESP32*,
https://doi.org/10.1007/978-1-4842-6336-5_4

The RGB LED brightness is defined in the *setup* function, but not in the *loop* function, by the brightness(N) instruction with the parameter between 1 and 255, for low to full brightness. The instruction unsigned long col = strip.Color(R, G, B) converts the three 8-bit red (R), green (G), and blue (B) components of a color into a 32-bit number, as required by the *Adafruit NeoPixel* library with RGB values for each color stored in arrays. The RGB color is calculated as $16^4R + 16^2G + B$, with the instruction pow(16,4)*R + pow(16,2)*G + B. The RGB LEDs in a strip or ring are numbered from zero, and the instruction strip.setPixelColor(n, col) sets the color of the $(n + 1)^{th}$ RGB LED. The color of *number* sequential RGB LEDs is set with the instruction strip.fill(col, n, number), starting at the $(n + 1)^{th}$ RGB LED. If the number of LEDs is not included in the fill instruction, then all RGB LEDs from the $(n + 1)^{th}$ RGB LED to the end of the strip or ring are set. Likewise, if the starting RGB LED is omitted, then the whole strip or ring is set. The instruction strip.clear() turns off all RGB LEDs in a strip or ring.

An RGB LED uses up to 60 mA with all three LEDs at full brightness. When an ESP8266 development board is powered by USB, the 5V pin supplies 400 mA, so an absolute maximum of six RGB LEDs at full brightness are powered by the ESP8266 development board 5V pin. An RGB LED strip should be powered by an external 5V, as shown in Figure 4-1 with connections in Table 4-1. To protect the RGB LEDs from a current surge, when the power supply is switched on, a 100 µF capacitor is fitted across the power supply 5V and GND pins. Fitting a 470 Ω resistor between the *data in* pin of the RGB LED strip or ring and the ESP8266 development board *data* pin prevents voltage spikes on the data line that could damage the first RGB LED on the strip or ring. Connections to the RGB LED strip should be checked with a multimeter continuity function, as the data and GND wires may be green and white, respectively.

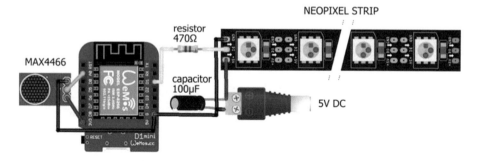

Figure 4-1. *WS2812 RGB LED strip and microphone*

Table 4-1. *WS2812 RGB LED strip and MAX4466 microphone with the ESP8266 development board*

Component	Connect to	And to	And to
LED strip VCC	External power 5V		100 µF capacitor positive
LED strip GND	External power GND	ESP8266 GND	100 µF capacitor negative
LED strip DI (data in)	470 Ω resistor	ESP8266 D1	
MAX4466 VCC	ESP8266 3V3		
MAX4466 OUT	ESP8266 A0		
MAX4466 GND	ESP8266 GND		

The only change to Listing 4-1 for an ESP32 microcontroller, rather than an ESP8266 microcontroller, is the definition of the ESP32 development board *data* pin int LEDpin = x.

The sketch in Listing 4-1 demonstrates sweeping colors along a RGB LED strip.

87

Listing 4-1. Sweeping colors along an RGB LED strip

```
#include <Adafruit_NeoPixel.h>   // include Adafruit NeoPixel library
int LEDpin = D1;                 // define data pin
int LEDnumber = 30;              // number of LEDS in strip
                                 // associate strip with NeoPixel library
Adafruit_NeoPixel strip(LEDnumber, LEDpin, NEO_GRB + NEO_KHZ800);
// color white, red, lime, blue, yellow, cyan, magenta,
// grey, maroon, olive, green, purple, teal, navy
int R[ ] = {255,255,  0,  0,255,  0,255,128,128,128,  0,128,  0,  0};
int G[ ] = {255,  0,255,  0,255,255,  0,128,  0,128,128,  0,128,  0};
int B[ ] = {255,  0,  0,255,  0,255,255,128,  0,  0,  0,128,128,128};
uint32_t color;                  // color is 32-bit or unsigned long

void setup()
{
  strip.begin();                 // initialise LED strip
  strip.setBrightness(10);       // define LED brightness (1 to 255)
  strip.show();                  // sets all pixels to "off" as no color set
}

void loop()
{
  for (int i=0; i<14; i++)       // cycle through the RGB colors
  {                              // convert RGB values to 32-bit number
    color = strip.Color(R[i],G[i],B[i]);
    sweep(color, 40);            // sweep color through the LED strip
  }
  rainbow(3, 10);                // rainbow colors for three cycles
}                                // with a 10ms time lag for each color
```

```
void sweep(uint32_t color, int lag)              // color sweep function
{
  for (int i=0; i<strip.numPixels(); i++)   // for each LED in strip
  {
    strip.setPixelColor(i, color);               // set the LED color
//   strip.setPixelColor
//   (strip.numPixels()-i-1, color);             // reverse direction
    strip.show();                        // update LED strip
    delay(lag);                          // time lag between color changes
  }
}

void rainbow(int cycle, int lag)
{                                        // from Adafruit NeoPixel>strandtest
  for (long Pixel1Hue = 0; Pixel1Hue < cycle*65536;
  Pixel1Hue += 256)
  {
    for (int i=0; i<strip.numPixels(); i++)
    {
      int pixelHue = Pixel1Hue + (i * 65536L / strip.numPixels());
      strip.setPixelColor(i,
      strip.gamma32(strip.ColorHSV(pixelHue)));
    }
    strip.show();                        // update LED states and colors
    delay(lag);
  }
}
```

WS2812 RGB LEDs responsive to sound

Controlling the WS2812 RGB LED strip with a MAX4466 electret microphone amplifier module produces a light display responsive to sounds, such as speech or music. The sound level detected by the microphone determines the number of WS2812 RGB LEDs to turn on with the LED color dependent on the sound level (see Figure 4-1). The MAX4466 electret microphone amplifier module is powered with 3.3 V and not 5 V. Sound or peak-to-peak values for the MAX4466 electret microphone amplifier module are defined as the difference between the maximum and minimum sound values recorded during the sample time.

The MAX4466 electret microphone amplifier module, used in this chapter, detected noise, particularly when the sketch included instructions to control the RGB LED strip. On the left side of Figure 4-2, there was minimal sound for the MAX4466 electret microphone amplifier module to detect, while the right side of Figure 4-2 reflected music being played. In both cases, the noise was obvious, and a median filter excluded the noise values from the sound sample. The median filter selects the median value of a sample in contrast to a circular buffer, which selects the mean value of a sample. For example, if three sample sequences with five values per sample are 3, 4, 5, 6, 80; 4, 5, 6, 80, 7; and 5, 6, 80, 7, 8, then the three median values are 5, 6, and 7, respectively. Median filtering may lag behind the actual sample sequence, but extreme values are excluded. Figure 4-2 illustrates that median filtering effectively removed the noise, both at low and medium sound volumes. Median filtering is used in Listing 4-2, with the *RunningMedian* library by Rob Tillaart, which is available within the Arduino IDE.

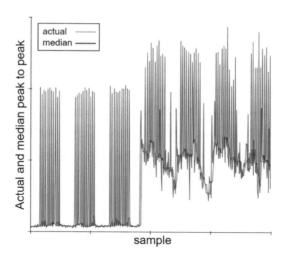

Figure 4-2. *Median filter of peak-to-peak values*

For the sketch in Listing 4-2, the MAX4466 electret microphone amplifier module samples sound over a 50 ms time period, corresponding to a sampling frequency of 20 Hz, to determine the number of RGB LEDs to turn on. A median filter with sample size of seven removed noise. The sensitivity of the electret microphone is adjusted with the *adjustVol* variable, to increase or decrease the number of RGB LEDs to turn on. Changing the sensitivity results in a number of RGB LEDs being permanently turned on, which is adjusted to zero with the *baseline* variable. The *adjustVol* and *baseline* variables are entered on the Serial Monitor with the Serial buffer string converted to two integers by the parseInt() instruction. For a strip containing 30 RGB LEDs, seven colors were selected with four RGB LEDs for each color. The RGB values for each color are stored in arrays with the RGB LED color set by the instructions strip.color() and strip.setPixelColor().

In Listing 4-2, the ESP32 development board *data* and analog input pins are defined, by updating the instructions int LEDpin = D1 and sound = analogRead(A0). The ESP32 microcontroller has a 12-bit ADC (analog to digital converter), in contrast to the 10-bit ADC of the ESP8266 microcontroller. For the ESP32 microcontroller, the instructions soundMin = 1024 and peak2peak = soundMax - soundMin are changed to soundMin = 4096 and peak2peak = (soundMax - soundMin)/4.

The noise experienced with the ESP8266 microcontroller was not evident with the ESP32 microcontroller, so median filtering was not required. The number of LEDs to turn on or off was determined directly from the *peak2peak* variable with the instruction LEDs = adjustVol*(peak2peak/1024.0)*LEDnumber-baseline.

Listing 4-2. RGB LED strip and sound

```
#include <Adafruit_NeoPixel.h>   // include Adafruit NeoPixel lib
int LEDpin = D1;                  // define data pin
int LEDnumber = 30;              // number of LEDS in strip
                                 // associate strip with NeoPixel lib
Adafruit_NeoPixel strip(LEDnumber, LEDpin, NEO_GRB + NEO_KHZ800);
     // colors red, orange, yellow, green, blue, indigo, violet
int R[ ] = {255, 255, 255,   0,   0,  75, 238};
int G[ ] = {  0, 102, 153, 255,   0,   0, 130};
int B[ ] = {  0,   0,   0,   0, 255, 130, 238};
uint32_t color;                  // color is 32-bit or unsigned long
#include <RunningMedian.h>       // include Running Median lib
RunningMedian samples = RunningMedian(7);
                                 // median filter sample size of 7
int sound, soundMax, soundMin, peak2peak, median, LEDs, val;
int adjustVol = 1;               // initial volume and baseline
int baseline = 0;
int soundTime = 50;              // sample sound time (ms)
unsigned long startTime;

void setup()
{
  Serial.begin(115200);          // Serial Monitor baud rate
  Serial.println("\nenter volume adjustment , baseline");
```

```
  strip.begin();                    // initialise LED strip
  strip.setBrightness(10);          // define LED brightness (1 - 255)
  strip.show();                     // sets all pixels to "off" as no color set
}

void loop()
{
  while(Serial.available()>0)          // adjust volume and baseline
  {
    adjustVol = Serial.parseInt();   // convert Serial buffer to integers
    baseline = Serial.parseInt();
    Serial.print("\nVolume ");Serial.print(adjustVol);
    Serial.print("\tBaseline ");Serial.println(baseline);
  }                                  // get new peak to peak value
  getSound();                        // number of LEDs to turn on
  LEDs = adjustVol*(median/1024.0)*LEDnumber-baseline;
  strip.clear();                     // turn all LEDs off
  delay(10);                         // allow time to switch off LEDs
  for (int i=0; i<LEDs; i++)
  {
    val = i/4;                       // four LEDs have the same color
    color = strip.Color(R[val],G[val],B[val]);
                                     // convert RGB values to color
    strip.setPixelColor(i, color);              // set the LED color
  }
  strip.show();                      // update LED states and colors
}

void getSound()                      // function for peak to peak value
{
  soundMax = 0;                          // initial values for minimum and
  soundMin = 1024;                       // maximum sound values
  startTime = millis();                  // start of sampling period
```

```
while(millis() - startTime < soundTime)
                                      // during sampling period
{                                     // determine minimum and
   sound = analogRead(A0);            // maximum sound values
   if(sound > soundMax) soundMax = sound;
   else if(sound < soundMin) soundMin = sound;
}
peak2peak = soundMax - soundMin; // peak to peak value
samples.add(peak2peak);
median = samples.getMedian();      // median peak to peak value
}
```

For a portable RGB LED strip display, values of the *adjustVol* and *baseline* variables are determined by the output voltage from two potentiometers, instead of entering the *adjustVol* and *baseline* variables on the Serial Monitor. The ESP32 microcontroller has several analog input pins, but the ESP8266 microcontroller has only one analog input pin, which is resolved by connecting a multiplexer.

ESP8266 and multiplexer

The ESP8266 microcontroller has one analog pin, which limits the number of analog input devices simultaneously connected to the ESP8266 development board. The 74HC4051 eight-channel analog multiplexer enables connection, to the ESP8266 development board, of up to eight analog input devices. Signals from analog input devices are routed through the multiplexer output channel, which is managed by three switch pins on the multiplexer, and the switch pin states are controlled by the ESP8266 microcontroller. Three switch pins are required to manage eight channels, as $8 = 2^3$.

The 74HC4051 multiplexer pins are numbered 1–16, with the cut-out or dot at the end of the multiplexer indicating the end with pins 1 and 16. Connections to the 74HC4051 multiplexer are shown in Table 4-2, with the over-line on $\overline{E}$ (input enabled) indicating that the pin is active *LOW*. The 5V pin of the ESP8266 development board powers the 74HC4051 multiplexer, which has an operating voltage of 2–10 V. Voltage of the input channel signals is between VCC and VEE, with the latter connected to GND. Analog input devices connected to the 74HC4051 multiplexer cannot be powered at 5 V, as the ESP8266 microcontroller pins are not 5 V tolerant. In Figure 4-3, the potentiometers are supplied by the 3.3V output pin of the ESP8266 microcontroller, so the maximum voltage on the microcontroller analog input pin will also be 3.3 V.

Table 4-2. *74HC4051 multiplexer and ESP8266 development board*

Component	Connect to
74HC4051 pin 3 output	ESP8266 A0
74HC4051 pin 6 $\overline{E}$ (input enable)	ESP8266 GND
74HC4051 pin 7 VEE	
74HC4051 pin 8 GND	ESP8266 GND
74HC4051 pin 9 switch S2	ESP8266 D2
74HC4051 pin 10 switch S1	ESP8266 D1
74HC4051 pin 11 switch S0	ESP8266 D0
74HC4051 pin 16 VCC	ESP8266 5V
Potentiometer left pin	ESP8266 GND
Potentiometer signal pins	74HC4051 pins 13, 14, 15
Potentiometer right pin	ESP8266 3V3

Figure 4-3. *74HC4051 multiplexer and LOLIN (WeMos) D1 mini*

The three switch pins, 13, 14, and 15, of the multiplexer enable signals of up to eight analog input devices to be routed through the multiplexer output channel. If only two input devices are connected to the multiplexer, then switch pins 14 and 15 are connected to GND. Similarly, if at most four input devices are connected to the multiplexer, then switch pin 15 is connected to GND. Noise on multiplexer input channels that are not connected to an analog input device is significantly reduced by a delay of 10 ms between setting the multiplexer switch pins and reading the multiplexer output channel. If the 10 ms delay is not included in the sketch, then the multiplexer VEE pin must be connected to GND, but there will still be substantial noise.

A multiplexer input channel is routed to the multiplexer output channel, when the switch settings equal the binary representation of the multiplexer input channel number. For example, an analog input signal on multiplexer input channel 3 is output by the multiplexer with switch settings of 011. Multiplexer input channels 0–7 correspond to multiplexer pins 13, 14, 15, 12, 1, 5, 2, and 4, respectively.

Connection of three potentiometers to an ESP8266 development board demonstrates use of the 74HC4051 multiplexer (see Figure 4-3). The sketch in Listing 4-3 sets the multiplexer switch pin states to the corresponding binary representation of the multiplexer input channel for routing to the multiplexer output channel. The bitRead(number, j) instruction reads the jth bit of *number*, starting with the least significant bit (LSB), which is bit zero. A bit value of one corresponds to a *HIGH* pin state. The 74HC4051 multiplexer enables the three potentiometer analog values to be read "simultaneously" by the ESP8266 microcontroller.

Listing 4-3. 74HC4051 multiplexer and ESP8266 development board

```
int Spin[] = {D0, D1, D2};              // multiplexer S0, S1 and S2
                                        // switch pins
void setup()
{
  Serial.begin(115200);                 // Serial Monitor baud rate
  for (int i=0; i<3; i++)
  {
    pinMode(Spin[i], OUTPUT);           // multiplexer pins as OUTPUT
    digitalWrite(Spin[i], LOW);         // set multiplexer pins to LOW
  }
}

void loop()
{
  for (int i=0; i<8; i++)               // 8 multiplexer pin combinations
  {                                     // set pins from bit sequence
    for (int j=0; j<3; j++) digitalWrite(Spin[j], bitRead(i, j));
    delay(10);                          // display readings
    Serial.print(analogRead(A0));Serial.print("\t");
    for (int j=0; j<3; j++) digitalWrite(Spin[j], LOW);
  }                                     // reset pins
```

```
Serial.println();
delay(1000);                            // delay between readings
}
```

For mobile control of the sound-based RGB LED strip display, values of
the *adjustVol* and *baseline* variables are determined by the output voltages
from two potentiometers. The MAX4466 electret microphone amplifier
module and potentiometers are accessible to the ESP8266 microcontroller,
by connecting the analog devices to a 74HC4051 multiplexer (see Figure 4-4).
Instead of entering the *adjustVol* and *baseline* variables on the Serial Monitor,
as in Listing 4-2, the potentiometer output voltages control the sound-based
RGB LED strip display. For example, the *adjustVol* potentiometer connected
to multiplexer pin 13, which is multiplexer input channel 0, is read with the
instructions

```
for (int j=0; j<3; j++) digitalWrite(Spin[j], bitRead(0, j))
adjustVol = analogRead(A0)/50
```

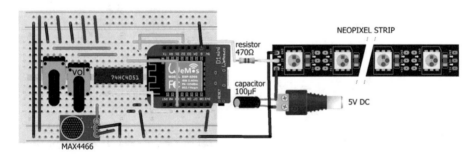

Figure 4-4. *Mobile control of RGB LED strip display with*
potentiometers and microphone

The *adjustVol* potentiometer will result in *adjustVol* values between
0 and 20. Similarly, *baseline* values are obtained from the *baseline*
potentiometer connected to multiplexer pin 14, which is input channel 1.

LED rings clock

Two 12–RGB LED rings display the hours and minutes on a clock, for example, at 16:40, with the clock turning on another LED every five minutes. When the hour changes, a Piezo transducer makes a phone ringtone of *two rings,* and a rainbow display is shown on the minute RGB LED ring. The colors of the hour and minute RGB LED rings alternate each hour. The RGB LED rings clock is powered from the ESP8266 development board 5V pin and includes a 100 µF capacitor and 470 Ω resistor as recommended (see Figure 4-5 with connections in Table 4-3).

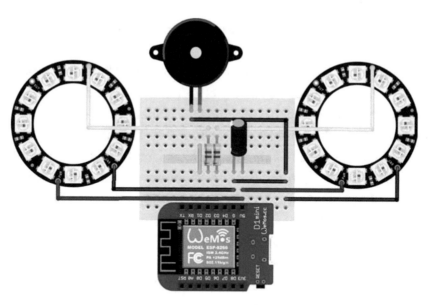

Figure 4-5. *LED rings clock*

Table 4-3. _LED rings clock_

Component	Connect to	And to
LED ring VCC	ESP8266 5V	100 µF capacitor positive
LED ring GND	ESP8266 GND	100 µF capacitor negative
LED ring IN	470 Ω resistor	ESP8266 D2, D3
Piezo transducer VCC	ESP8266 D1	
Piezo transducer GND	ESP8266 GND	

If the red, green, and blue LEDs are turned on at brightness level of 1, 40, or 100, with a scale of 1–255, then the current usage of a 12–RGB LED ring is 15, 75, or 160 mA, respectively, so two 12–RGB LED rings with maximum brightness of 100 are safely powered by the ESP8266 development board 5V pin.

The sketch in Listing 4-4 calculates the number of hour and minute LEDs to turn on based on the time that is initially set with the Unix epoch time, which is the number of seconds since January 1, 1970. The Unix epoch time is obtained from www.epochconverter.com with the GMT option, if required, and 15 s should be allowed for the sketch to compile and upload. For example, the Unix epoch time corresponding to May 31, 2020, 17:20:51 GMT was 1590945651s. The _Time_ library by Michael Margolis calculates the number of hours and minutes, based on the elapsed Unix epoch time, with the library _hour_ and _minute_ functions. The number of RGB LEDs to turn on to display hours and minutes is the remainder when the _Time_ library hours is divided by 12, as the clock is not a 24-hour clock, and the _Time_ library minutes divided by 5, as the clock turns on another LED every five minutes. An arbitrary delay of 22 s is included after the minute LEDs are updated, as the hour display takes 13 s to complete, so up to 35 s elapses before the _Time_ library hours and minutes are updated. The *display* variable prevents the hour display being repeated during the five-minute period after the hour.

The first section of Listing 4-4 sets the Unix epoch time, includes the libraries, and defines the RGB LED ring pins. Two instances of the *Adafruit NeoPixel* library are required, one for each of the two RGB LED rings. The *setup* function calls the *Time* library function *setTime* to convert the Unix epoch time to hours and minutes and the *getTime* function to convert hours and minutes to the number of RGB LEDs to turn on, with the *LEDhours* and *LEDminutes* functions. Note that instructions for the RGB LED rings are activated by the show() instruction. In the *loop* function, the *getTime* function is called; and on the hour, the *phonering* function is called with the *playTone* function generating the phone ringtone. A ringtone consists of a 400 ms pulse, a 200 ms pause, a 400 ms pulse, and a two-second pause, with a pulse generated by five cycles of a square wave, with the frequency alternating between 300 Hz for 40 ms and 350 Hz for 40 ms. The Adafruit *rainbow* function displays a variety of colors for two cycles on the minute RGB LED ring.

In the *playTone* function, the analogWriteFreq() instruction has a default PWM (pulse with modulation) frequency of 1 kHz, which is altered by defining the required frequency as the function parameter. The 50% duty cycle of the square wave, used to generate sound, is obtained by setting the variable *value* in the instruction analogWrite(pin, value) to 512, which is half of 1023 or $2^{10}-1$, as the ESP8266 microcontroller digital to analog converter has 10-bit resolution.

Listing 4-4. LED rings clock

```
#include <TimeLib.h>                      // include Time library
unsigned long pctime = 1590945651;        // set Unix epoch time
#include <Adafruit_NeoPixel.h>            // include NeoPixel library
int LEDpinM = D3;                         // ring to display minutes
int LEDpinH = D2;                         // ring to display hours
```

```
int piezoPin = D1;                      // Piezo transducer pin
int LEDnumber = 12;                     // number of LEDs on ring
unsigned long interval = 1000;          // one sec time interval
int color = 0;                  // color flag for hour LED ring
int display = 0;                // indicator hour display completed
String text;
int minutes, hours;
                // associate ringM and ringH with Neopixel library
Adafruit_NeoPixel ringM(LEDnumber, LEDpinM, NEO_GRB + NEO_KHZ800);
Adafruit_NeoPixel ringH(LEDnumber, LEDpinH, NEO_GRB + NEO_KHZ800);

void setup()
{
  setTime(pctime);              // set time to Unix epoch time
  getTime();                    // get time parameters
  ringH.begin();                // initialise hours LED ring
  ringH.setBrightness(1);       // set LED brightness (1 to 255)
  LEDhours();                   // function to display hours
  ringH.show();                 // update hours LED ring
  ringM.begin();
  ringM.setBrightness(1);
  LEDminutes();
  ringM.show();                 // update minutes LED ring
}

void loop()
{
  getTime();                    // calculate hours and minutes
  if(minutes == 0 && display ==0)       // on the hour, run the display
  {
    display = 1;                // flag to prevent repeat hour display
    phonering();               // sound of phone ringtones
    rainbow();                 // rainbow of LED colors
    ringM.clear();             // clear minutes LED ring
```

```
    ringM.show();
    color = 1 - color;        // change color flag
    ringH.clear();
    ringH.show();
    LEDhours();               // update hours LED ring
  }
  if(minutes > 0) LEDminutes();              // update minutes LEDs
  for(int i=0; i<22; i++) delay(interval);        // 22s delay
}

void getTime()              // function to calculate hours and minutes
{
  hours = hour() % 12;      // convert 24hr time to 12hr time
  minutes= int(minute()/5);               // number of 5min intervals
  if(minutes > 0 ) display = 0;        // reset hour display flag
}

void LEDminutes()           // function to turn on minute LEDs
{
  for(int i=0; i<minutes; i++)
  {                          // set LED RGB values
    ringM.setPixelColor(i, ringM.Color(255*color,
    255*(1-color), 0));
  }
  ringM.show();
}

void LEDhours()              // function to turn on hour LEDs
{
  for(int i=0; i<hours; i++)
  {
    ringH.setPixelColor(i, ringH.Color(255*(1-color),
    255*color, 0));
  }
```

```
  ringH.show();
}

void rainbow()                          // Adafruit rainbow function
{
  int cycle = 2;                        // two cycles of colors
  for(long Pixel1Hue=0; Pixel1Hue<cycle*65536; Pixel1Hue += 256)
  {
    for(int i=0; i<ringM.numPixels(); i++)
    {
      int pixelHue = Pixel1Hue + (i * 65536L / ringM.
      numPixels());
      ringM.setPixelColor(i, ringM.gamma32(ringM.
      ColorHSV(pixelHue)));
    }
    ringM.show();
    delay(10);
  }
}

void phonering()                        // function for phone ringtone
{
  for(int k=0; k<2; k++)                // two cycles
  {
    for(int j=0; j<2; j++)              // of two rings
    {
      for(int i=0; i<5; i++)           // with five repeats
      {
        playTone(300, 40);             // frequency 300Hz for 40ms
        playTone(350, 40);             // frequency 350Hz for 40ms
      }
```

```
    delay(200);                    // 200ms delay between rings
  }
  delay(2000);                     // 2s delay between cycles
 }
}

void playTone(int freq, int duration)
{
  analogWriteFreq(freq);           // frequency and duty cycle
  analogWrite(piezoPin, 512);      // to generate square wave
  delay(duration);                 // for duration (ms)
  analogWrite(piezoPin, 0);        // disable PWM on pin
}
```

Network Time Protocol

Using the internal ESP8266 or ESP32 microcontroller clock to measure time is convenient, but the internal clock is not consistently accurate, with drifting over time and the extent of the drift depending on the individual chip and the ambient temperature. The internal microcontroller clock is updated with the Network Time Protocol (NTP) service, arbitrarily at 08:30 and 20:30, with the time information obtained from a local server pool. Details of server pools are available at www.pool.ntp.org, and the IP address of the local server pool is required in the sketch. The NTP data is accessed using the *NTPtimeESP* library by Andreas Spiess that is downloaded as a *.zip* file from github.com/SensorsIot/NTPtimeESP. The LOLIN (WeMos) D1 mini board is smaller than an ESP32 development board, but an ESP32 development board is an alternative (see end of this chapter).

Listing 4-5 contains additional instructions to the first section of Listing 4-4 for connection to a Wi-Fi network and accessing the local NTP pool with the *NTPtimeESP* library. Only the additional or replacement instructions are commented, to emphasize the few changes required to the sketch. In the *setup* function, the setTime(pctime) instruction is replaced by calling the *getEpoch* function, which is also called in the *loop* function with the instruction if(hours == 8 && minutes == 30) getEpoch().

The *getEpoch* function establishes a Wi-Fi connection, accesses the NTP service for the Unix epoch time, disconnects the Wi-Fi connection, and resets the internal microcontroller clock. The Wi-Fi connection codes and their values are

```
WL_CONNECTED         3
WL_CONNECT_FAILED    4
WL_CONNECTION_LOST   5
WL_DISCONNECTED      6
```

which are accessed with the instruction WiFi.status().

Listing 4-5. LED rings clock with NTP time updating for the ESP8266 board

```
#include <Adafruit_NeoPixel.h>
int LEDpinL = D2;              // left ring to display hours
int LEDpinR = D3;              // right ring to display minutes
int piezoPin = D1;            // Piezo transducer pin
int LEDnumber = 12;
unsigned long interval = 1000;
int color = 0;
String text;
Adafruit_NeoPixel ringM(LEDnumber, LEDpinR, NEO_GRB + NEO_KHZ800);
Adafruit_NeoPixel ringH(LEDnumber, LEDpinL, NEO_GRB + NEO_KHZ800);
```

```
#include <ESP8266WiFi.h>        // library to connect to Wi-Fi network
#include <ESP8266WebServer.h>   // library for web server functionality
ESP8266WebServer server;
                    // associate server with ESP8266WebServer library
char ssid[] = "xxxx";           // replace xxxx with Wi-Fi ssid
char password[] = "xxxx";       // replace xxxx with Wi-Fi password
#include <NTPtimeESP.h>         // include NTPtime library
                                // associate NTP with NTPtime library
NTPtime NTP("uk.pool.ntp.org");    // UK server pool for NTPtime
strDateTime dateTime;
unsigned long epoch;            // Unix epoch time
#include <TimeLib.h>            // include Time library
int minutes, hours;
int display = 0;

void setup()
{
  pinMode(piezoPin, OUTPUT);    // Piezo transducer pin as output
  getEpoch();                   // get Epoch time from NTP
  getTime();
  ringH.begin();
  ringH.setBrightness(1);
  LEDhours();
  ringH.show();
  ringM.begin();
  ringM.setBrightness(1);
  LEDminutes();
  ringM.show();
}
```

```
void loop()
{
  getTime();
  if(minutes == 0 && display ==0)
  {
    display = 1;
    phonering();
    rainbow();
    ringM.clear();
    ringM.show();
    color = 1 - color;
    ringH.clear();
    ringH.show();
    LEDhours();
  }
  if(minutes > 0) LEDminutes();
  if(hours == 8 && minutes == 30) getEpoch();   // update Epoch time
  delay(interval);                 // delay between time calculations
}

void getTime()                     // as in Listing 4-4

void getEpoch()                    // function to get NTP time
{
  WiFi.begin(ssid, password);              // wait for Wi-Fi connect
  while (WiFi.status() != WL_CONNECTED) delay(500);
  epoch = 0;
  for (int i=0; i<5; i++)     // five attempts to access NTP
  {
    delay(500);                   // delay between Wi-Fi connect
    dateTime = NTP.getNTPtime(0, 1);     // and sourcing NTP data
```

```
  if(dateTime.valid)
  {
    epoch = dateTime.epochTime;        // NTP Epoch time obtained
    i = 5;                             // stop attempting connect to NTP
  }
}
WiFi.disconnect(true);        // disconnect Wi-Fi connection
WiFi.mode(WIFI_OFF);          // switch off Wi-Fi connection
setTime(epoch);              // set internal clock to Epoch time
}

void LEDminutes()             // as in Listing 4-4

void LEDhours()               // as in Listing 4-4

void rainbow()                // as in Listing 4-4

void phonering()              // as in Listing 4-4

void playTone(int freq, int duration)   // as in Listing 4-4
```

ESP32 and Internet clock

Listing 4-5 is for an Internet clock controlled by an ESP8266 microcontroller. For an ESP32 microcontroller, the Wi-Fi and web server library instructions

```
#include <ESP8266WiFi.h>           // library to connect to Wi-Fi network
#include <ESP8266WebServer.h>      // library for web server functionality
ESP8266WebServer server;           // associate server with library
```

are changed to

```
#include <WiFi.h>          // library to connect to Wi-Fi network
#include <WebServer.h>     // library for web server functionality
WebServer server (80);     // associate server with WebServer lib
```

Sound generation with a Piezo transducer differs for the ESP8266 and ESP32 microcontrollers, so the *playTone* function for the ESP8266 microcontroller is replaced with the *playToneESP32* function:

```
void playToneESP32(int freq, int duration)
{
  ledcSetup(channel, freq, 10); // 10-bit resolution
  ledcWrite(channel, 512);       // square wave with 50% duty cycle
  delay(duration);               // for duration (ms)
  ledcWrite(channel, 0);
}
```

The third parameter of the ledcSetup instruction is the resolution level, 8, 10, 12, or 15 bits, for PWM. For consistency with Listing 4-5, the *playToneESP32* function uses 10-bit resolution, with 1024 values, and a 50% duty cycle obtained with a value of 512. The Piezo transducer pin is mapped to the *channel* variable with the instruction ledcAttachPin(piezoPin, channel) in the *setup* function, with channel defined by int channel = 0. The Piezo transducer and LED ring pin numbers *D1*, *D2*, and *D3* are changed to ESP32 development board pins 25, 26, and 27, respectively.

Summary

The color of each LED on a WS2812 5050 RGB LED strip was individually defined, with a range of colors swept through the RGB LED strip. An electret microphone amplifier module measured sound levels to determine the number and color of RGB LEDs to turn on in the RGB LED strip. The limitation of one analog input pin of the ESP8266 microcontroller was resolved by incorporating a 74HC4051 multiplexer to access several analog input devices. The ESP8266 microcontroller "simultaneously" accessed voltages from two potentiometers, to control settings on the RGB LED strip and the electret microphone amplifier module. An Internet clock was built with two RGB LED rings to display the hours and minutes. On the hour, a Piezo transducer makes a phone ringtone of *two rings*, which is followed by a rainbow display on one RGB LED ring. The Wi-Fi functionality of the ESP8266 and ESP32 microcontrollers enabled access to the Network Time Protocol (NTP) service, twice every 24 hours, to update the internal microcontroller clock and maintain the RGB LED clock accuracy.

Components List

- ESP8266 microcontroller: LOLIN (WeMos) D1 mini or NodeMCU board

- ESP32 microcontroller: DEVKIT DOIT or NodeMCU board

- RGB LED ring: 2×

- RGB LED strip

- Resistor: 2× 470 Ω

- Capacitor: 100 µF

- Piezo transducer

- Electret microphone amplifier module: MAX4466

- Multiplexer: 74HC4051

CHAPTER 5

MP3 player

The DFPlayer Mini MP3 player with built-in micro-SD card module is either used as a battery-powered stand-alone module with push-button controls or connected to a microcontroller for more comprehensive control features. The MP3 player has audio output channels for earphone or amplifier input (DAC R and DAC L) and for loudspeaker input (SPK1 and SPK2), UART Serial communication (RX and TX), and four control pins (IO1, IO2, ADKEY1, and ADKEY2) that are active *LOW* (see Figure 5-1). The *BUSY* pin is *LOW* when an audio file is playing, but otherwise *HIGH*. The MP3 has a music equalizer with six settings.

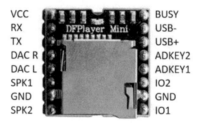

Figure 5-1. *DFPlayer Mini MP3 player*

When the MP3 player is stand-alone, a short press on tactile switches connected to the control pins, *IO1* or *IO2*, plays the previous or next track, respectively, while a long press decreases or increases the volume. Pressing the *ADKEY1* or *ADKEY2* control pin plays the first or fifth track, respectively.

© Neil Cameron 2021
N. Cameron, *Electronics Projects with the ESP8266 and ESP32*,
https://doi.org/10.1007/978-1-4842-6336-5_5

For this chapter, *mp3* audio files are stored on a micro-SD card, FAT32 formatted with up to 32 GB storage, within a folder named *mp3*. Folder names of *01–99* are permitted with the audio files, within a folder, named *001.mp3* to *255.mp3*.

Figure 5-2 illustrates tactile button control of a stand-alone MP3 player with a loudspeaker, of less than 3W, connected to the *SPK1* and *SPK2* pins through the audio and GND pins of an audio jack socket (connections given in Table 5-1). Instead of controlling the MP3 player with tactile buttons, the GND pin is directly connected to the appropriate control pin. Note that when power is applied to the MP3 player, the red indicator LED turns on after the *IO1* or *IO2* pin is connected to GND and turns off when the track has finished playing.

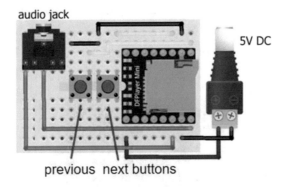

Figure 5-2. *Stand-alone MP3 player*

Table 5-1. *Stand-alone MP3 player*

Component	Connect to
MP3 player VCC	Battery 5V
MP3 player GND	Battery GND
MP3 player SPK1	Audio output
MP3 player SPK2	Audio output
MP3 player IO1 (previous track and decreases volume)	Switch right pin
MP3 player IO2 (next track and increases volume)	Switch right pin
Switch left pins	GND

Control command for the MP3 player

The MP3 player is operated by control commands transmitted using UART (Universal Asynchronous Receiver-Transmitter) Serial communication. The ten components of a control command are *start bit, version, number of bytes, command, feedback, parameter[1,2], checksum[1,2],* and *finish* bit. The *start* and *finish* bits, in HEX format, are *0x7E* and *0xEF*, the *number of bytes* is *0x06, feedback* is *0x00,* and *version* is *0xFF.* A control command has two parameters, but generally the value of *parameter[1]* is zero. The *checksum* is the negative sum of all the components, omitting the *start* and *finish* bits. The *checksum* is formatted as a high and a low byte. When a control command is transmitted to the MP3 player, the response buffer contains ten components, of which *parameter[2]* contains data.

For example, the control command to play the fourth track is *0x03* with *parameter[2]* equal to *0x04* (see Table 5-2). The checksum is $-(0xFF + 0x06 + 0x03 + 0x00 + 0x00 + 0x04) = -(255 + 6 + 3 + 0 + 0 + 4) = -268$ that maps to $2^{16} - 268 = 65268 = 0xFEF4$, with high and low bytes of *0xFE* and *0xF4*, respectively. The control command components in HEX format are start

115

bit, *0x7E*; version, *0xFF*; length, *0x06*; command, *0x03*; feedback, *0x00*; parameter[1], *0x00*; parameter[2], *0x04*; checksum[1], *0xFE*; checksum[2], *0xF4*; and finish bit, *0xEF*.

A selection of MP3 player control commands is given in Table 5-2, with a manual available at usermanual.wiki/Pdf/ DFPlayer20Mini20Manual.1647715389/pdf. The command *0x03* plays the Nth track with tracks ordered by the time that they were loaded onto the micro-SD card. The command *0x12* plays the track with file name *000N XXX*, irrespective of the time order that the audio file was loaded on the micro-SD card. The audio file name does not need to reflect the order that audio files were loaded on the micro-SD card. For example, four audio files were loaded on the micro-SD card in the order of *0014 ABC*, *0012 AAA*, *0011 XYZ*, and *0013 PQR*, which the MP3 player catalogues as tracks 1, 2, 3, and 4, respectively. The commands *(0x12, 13)* and *(0x03, 4)* will both play the audio file *0013 PQR*, which is track 4 for the MP3 player.

***Table 5-2.** MP3 player control commands*

Command	Action
0x01	Next track
0x02	Previous track
0x03	Play track number N
0x04	Increase volume by one level
0x05	Decrease volume by one level
0x06	Set volume level to N, between 0 and 30
0x07	Equalizer (Normal, Pop, Rock, Jazz, Classic, Base)
0x0D	Play current track
0x0E	Pause current track
0x12	Play track number N

(continued)

Table 5-2. (*continued*)

Command	Action
0x18	Random play order, starting at track 1
0x43	Get volume level
0x46	Get software version number
0x48	Get number of files on the SD card
0x4C	Get track number

MP3 player control with a microcontroller

Connecting the MP3 player to an ESP8266 or ESP32 microcontroller provides significantly more functionality than the stand-alone MP3 player. The MP3 player is powered by the ESP8266 or ESP32 development board 3V3 pin, as the MP3 player operates at 3.3–5 V and the transmit (*TX*) and receive (*RX*) Serial communication functions at 3.3 V. If the MP3 player is powered by 5 V, then a logic-level converter is required to reduce the 5 V voltage on the MP3 player TX pin to 3.3 V on the ESP8266 or ESP32 microcontroller RX pin. The voltage is also reduced with a voltage divider consisting of a 5 kΩ resistor and a 10 kΩ resistor, as described in Chapter 16 (Signal generation).

The ESP8266 development board *RX* and *TX* pins are required for communication with the Serial Monitor, as information is displayed on the Serial Monitor to ensure that the sketch is performing as expected. The ESP8266 microcontroller communicates with the MP3 player with software Serial, using the built-in *SoftwareSerial* library. The advantage of the compact LOLIN (WeMos) D1 mini with a powerful CPU and Wi-Fi functionality is offset, to an extent, by the constraint of available pins, as pin *D8* has a pull-down resistor and pin *D0* has no interrupt function. The ESP8266 development board pins *D4, D3, D2,* and *D8* are defined as control pins to play the next track, to increase the volume, to decrease the volume, and to change the music equalizer, respectively (see Figure 5-3 with connections in Table 5-3). Pins *D4*, *D3,* and *D2* are connected to GND for the required change, while pin *D8*, which has a built-in pull-down resistor, is connected to 3V3 to change the music equalizer.

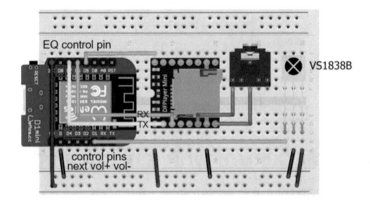

Figure 5-3. *MP3 player with LOLIN (WeMos) D1 mini*

Table 5-3. *MP3 player connections for ESP8266 and ESP32 development boards*

Component	ESP8266	ESP32
MP3 player VCC	3V3	3V3
MP3 player RX	D7	TX2 (GPIO 17)
MP3 player TX	D6	RX2 (GPIO 16)
MP3 player SPK1	Audio output	Audio output
MP3 player GND	GND	GND
MP3 player SPK2	Audio output	Audio output
MP3 player BUSY	D5	GPIO 34
IR sensor OUT	D1	GPIO 23
IR sensor GND	GND	GND
IR sensor VCC	3V3	3V3

In contrast, the ESP32 development board has an abundance of GPIO pins, with the ESP32 DEVKIT DOIT 30-pin and NodeMCU 36-pin development boards having two and three Serial communication ports, respectively (see Chapter 21 (Microcontrollers)). The MP3 player with an ESP32 DEVKIT DOIT development board is shown in Figure 5-4, with connections in Table 5-3.

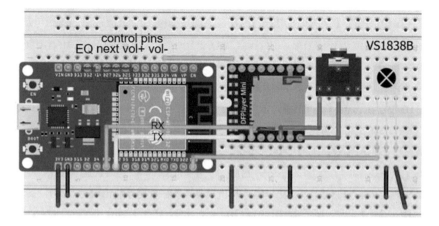

Figure 5-4. *MP3 player with the ESP32 DEVKIT DOIT development board*

The sketch in Listing 5-1 is the base for a subsequent sketch (Listing 5-3) using infrared signals to control the MP3 player. In the *setup* function of the sketch, the minimum and maximum file numbers are defined. For example, if the files titled *0009 abc.mp3* and *0013 xyz.mp3* have the lowest and highest file numbers, then the variables *fileMin* and *fileMax* are set to *9* and *13*, respectively.

The first section of the sketch defines the control pins, the music equalizer level names, the control command template, and the audio file names. The *setup* function attaches internal pull-up resistors to the control pins and defines the interrupt activated by the MP3 player *BUSY* pin changing from *LOW* to *HIGH* when a track finishes playing. The interrupt service routine (ISR) sets the variable *finish* to the value of one, which indicates that an audio file has finished playing. To determine if the micro-SD card is inserted in the MP3 player, the number of files on the micro-SD card is counted with the command *0x48;* and if no audio files are present, then a message is displayed on the Serial Monitor. The volume value is set, the first file is played, and the timer is reset to measure the audio file play time.

The *loop* function monitors the control pins for activity and calls the *cmd* (command) function. The four control pins use the commands *0x12* to play the next audio file and *0x4C* to obtain the corresponding track number, the command *0x04* or *0x05* to increase or decrease the volume level, the command *0x43* to obtain the volume value, and the command *0x07* to increment the music equalizer level.

The next audio file is played when the *nextPin* is connected to GND or the current file has finished with the instruction `if(digitalRead(nextPin) == LOW || finish == 1)`. Audio files are checked by playing each audio file for a fixed time period, for example, 5 s, by changing the first instruction of the *loop* function to `if(digitalRead(nextPin) == LOW || millis()-timed > 5000)`.

The *cmd* function builds the checksum based on the *command* and *parameter[2]*, as *parameter[1]* is zero, and splits the checksum into a high byte and a low byte for transmission to the MP3 player. The *highByte* and *lowByte* functions are functions within the Arduino IDE. The response from the MP3 player is held in the *buffer[ ]* array, and *buffer[6]* contains the data value. When the command *0x4C*, to obtain the corresponding track number, is called, both the track number and the audio file name are displayed.

Listing 5-1 is for an ESP8266 microcontroller. The ESP32 development board Serial ports enable Serial communication with more than one device, without having to utilize libraries to provide the Serial communication functionality. The instruction `Serial2.begin(baud, SERIAL_8N1, RXD2, TXD2)` establishes Serial communication on the second Serial port with the baud rate defined by the parameter *baud* on pins *RXD2* and *TXD2*. When using an ESP32 microcontroller, the following instructions for the ESP8266 microcontroller

```
#include <SoftwareSerial.h>          // include SoftwareSerial library
SoftwareSerial SoftSer(D6, D7);      // define SoftSer RX, TX pins
SoftSer.begin(9600);                 // SoftwareSerial baud rate
for (int i=0; i<10; i++) SoftSer.write(serialCom[i]);
                                     // transmit to or receive from MP3
for (int i=0; i<10; i++) buffer[i] = SoftSer.read();
```

are replaced with the instructions

```
Serial2.begin(9600, SERIAL_8N1, 16, 17);      // define RX2, TX2
for (int i=0; i<10; i++) Serial2.write(serialCom[i]);
                                     // transmit to or receive from MP3
for (int i=0; i<10; i++) buffer[i] = Serial2.read();
```

and the instruction pinMode(busyPin, INPUT) is included in the *setup* function. The *BUSY* pin, *D5*, and control pin definitions *D4, D3,* and *D2* are changed to GPIO 34 and to three suitable GPIO pins, such as GPIO 27, GPIO 26, and GPIO 25. For consistency with the sketch for an ESP8266 microcontroller, the music equalizer pin, *D8*, is changed to GPIO 12, which has a built-in pull-down resistor.

Listing 5-1. MP3 player

```
#include<SoftwareSerial.h>          // include SoftwareSerial library
SoftwareSerial SoftSer(D6, D7);     // define SoftSer RX, TX pins
int nextPin = D4;
int volUp = D3;
int volDown = D2;                   // define control pins
int EQpin = D8;
```

```
int busyPin = D5;
int EQstate = 0;                            // equaliser settings
String EQ[] = {"Normal","Pop","Rock","Jazz","Classic","Bass"};
unsigned long timed = 0;
unsigned int checksum;
byte highChk, lowChk;                       // control command template
byte serialCom[10] = {0x7E,0xFF,0x06,0x00,0x00,0x00,0x00,0x00,
0x00,0xEF};
// start version length CMD feedback para[1, 2] checksum[high, low] end
byte buffer[10];
int fileMin = 9;                // lowest and highest file number
int fileMax = 13;               // on micro SD card
int file = fileMin;
String fileName[] = {           // file names in order loaded on SD card
"0012 Nina Simone - My baby just cares for me",
"0011 Reamonn - Supergirl",
"0013 Spider Murphy Gang - Ich Grüsse Alle Und Den Rest Der Welt",
"0009 Proclaimers - I'm Gonna Be (500 Miles)",
"0010 Railroad Earth - The Good Life"
};
volatile int finish;           // variable in loop and ISR functions
int track;

void setup()
{
  Serial.begin(115200);                 // Serial Monitor baud rate
  SoftSer.begin(9600);                  // software Serial baud rate
  pinMode(nextPin, INPUT_PULLUP);       // control pins use internal
  pinMode(volUp, INPUT_PULLUP);         // pull-up resistors
  pinMode(volDown, INPUT_PULLUP);
                                // interrupt finished, BUSY pin HIGH
```

```
attachInterrupt(digitalPinToInterrupt(busyPin), finished,
RISING);
cmd(0x48, 0);                   // get number of files on SD card
cmd(0x06, 10);                  // set volume to 10 (range 0 - 30)
cmd(0x43, 0);                   // get volume value
cmd(0x12, file);                // play first audio file
finish = 0;                     // set finish variable
cmd(0x4C, 0);                   // get track number
timed = millis();               // start timer
}

void loop()
{                               // next file selected or current file ended
  if(digitalRead(nextPin) == LOW || finish == 1)
  {
    file = file+1;              // increment file name
    if(file > fileMax) file = fileMin;
                                // constrain file name <= fileMax
    cmd(0x12, file);            // play next audio file
    finish = 0;                 // set finish variable
    cmd(0x4C, 0);              // get track number
  }
  else if(digitalRead(volUp) == LOW)        // increase volume is selected
  {
    cmd(0x04, 0);                           // increase volume
    cmd(0x43, 0);                           // get volume value
  }
  else if(digitalRead(volDown) == LOW)
  {                             // decrease volume is selected
    cmd(0x05, 0);               // decrease volume
    cmd(0x43, 0);
  }
```

```
  else if(digitalRead(EQpin) == HIGH)    // change equaliser is selected
  {                                       // when pin state is HIGH
    EQstate = EQstate+1;                  // increment equaliser
    if(EQstate > 5) EQstate = 0;          // constrain equaliser value
    Serial.println(EQ[EQstate]);
    cmd(0x07, EQstate);                   // change equaliser setting
  }
}

void cmd(byte CMD, byte param2)           // command function
{
  delay(100);                             // delay to debounce button
  checksum = -(0xFF + 0x06 + CMD + 0x00 + 0x00 + param2);
                                          // build checksum
  highChk = highByte(checksum);           // split checksum into
  lowChk = lowByte(checksum);             // high byte and low bytes
  serialCom[3] = CMD;
  serialCom[6] = param2;                  // command components
  serialCom[7] = highChk;
  serialCom[8] = lowChk;                  // transmit command to MP3
  for (int i=0; i<10; i++) SoftSer.write(serialCom[i]);
  delay(100);                             // receive command from MP3
  for (int i=0; i<10; i++) buffer[i] = SoftSer.read();
  delay(100);
  if(CMD == 0x12)                         // play next audio file
  {
    Serial.print("finished track ");Serial.print(track);
    Serial.print("\ttime");
    Serial.print((millis() - timed)/1000);
    Serial.println("s");                  // display audio play time
    timed= millis();                      // reset timer
  }
```

```
  else if(CMD == 0x43)                  // get volume
  {
    Serial.print("volume ");            // display volume value
    Serial.println(buffer[6]);
  }
   else if(CMD == 0x48)                 // get number of files on SD card
  {
    if(buffer[6]<2)                     // no audio files present
    {
      Serial.println("SD card not inserted ");
      Serial.println("insert SD card and reset microcontroller");
      for(;;) delay(1000);              // do nothing
    }
  }
  else if(CMD == 0x4C)                  // get track number
  {
    track = buffer[6];                  // display track number of file
    Serial.print("playing track ");Serial.print(track);
    Serial.print("\t\t");Serial.println(fileName[track-1]);
  }                                     // array starts at [0], but track starts at [1]
}

IRAM_ATTR void finished()      // ISR
{
  finish = 1;                  // set finish variable
}
```

Infrared remote control of an MP3 player

The MP3 player is controlled by an infrared remote control and the VS1838B infrared sensor, instead of connecting control pins to GND, as in Listing 5-1. Connections for the VS1838B infrared sensor are given in Table 5-3 and shown in Figures 5-3 and 5-4. The *IRremoteESP8266* library by David Conran, Sebastien Warin, Mark Szabo, and Ken Shirriff is recommended and is available within the Arduino IDE. For an ESP32 microcontroller, the *IRremote* library by Ken Shirriff is recommended. A *.zip* file containing the *IRremote* library is downloaded from github. com/z3t0/Arduino-IRremote. The *IRremote* library that is available in the Arduino IDE is not always the latest version. When a remote button is pressed, the infrared sensor receives the signal, which is decoded and mapped to the corresponding control pin. For example, the decoded 32-bit infrared signal, *0xFF18E7*, for button 2 of an infrared remote control is shown in Figure 5-5.

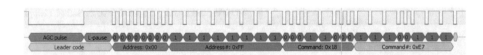

Figure 5-5. *IR remote control signal*

Listings 5-2 and 5-3 decode infrared signals and display the received signals in HEX format for an ESP8266 and ESP32 microcontroller, respectively. Listing 5-3 only includes the NEC and Sony decode types, but the library file *IRremote.h* includes a comprehensive list of decode types, for inclusion in a sketch. Listing 5-4 uses the HEX codes corresponding to pressing the next audio file, increasing volume, decreasing volume, and the stop button on a Sony infrared remote control of *0x8D1, 0x491, 0xC91,* and *0x1D1*, respectively. Similarly, the HEX codes for the remote control buttons 1–5 were *0x011, 0x811, 0x411, 0xC11,* and *0x211*, which are used for the command to play tracks 1–5.

Listing 5-2. Decoding infrared signals with an ESP8266 development board

```
#include <IRutils.h>              // include IRutils library
int IRpin = D1;                   // IR receiver pin
int BufferSize = 1024;            // longer signal length
int Timeout = 50;                 // block repeat signals
IRrecv irrecv(IRpin, BufferSize, Timeout, true);
decode_results reading;           // IRremote reading

void setup()
{
  Serial.begin(115200);           // Serial Monitor baud rate
  irrecv.enableIRIn();            // initialise the IR receiver
}

void loop()
{
  if (irrecv.decode(&reading))    // read pulsed signal
     Serial.print(resultToHumanReadableBasic(&reading));
}                                 // display signal information
```

Listing 5-3. Decoding infrared signals with an ESP32 development board

```
#include <IRremote.h>             // include IRremote library
int IRpin = 23;                   // IR receiver pin
IRrecv irrecv(IRpin);
decode_results reading;
```

```
void setup()
{
  Serial.begin(115200);
  irrecv.enableIRIn();
}

void loop()
{
  if (irrecv.decode(&reading))
  {
        if(reading.decode_type == NEC)  Serial.print("NEC: ");
    else if(reading.decode_type == SONY) Serial.print("Sony: ");
    else Serial.print("Other: ");
    Serial.print(reading.value, HEX);
    Serial.print("\tBits: ");          // display signal HEX code
    Serial.println(reading.bits);      // and bit number
    delay(200);                        // delay before next IR signal
    irrecv.resume();                   // receive the next value
  }
}
```

The infrared signals are mapped to control pin functions using the instructions associated with a control pin in Listing 5-1. For example, the instruction for increasing volume if(digitalRead(volUp) == LOW) is replaced with the instruction if(reading.value == 0x491). Mapping a remote control button to playing a specific track uses switch case instructions rather than if else instructions, with each case instruction mapping an infrared signal to a track number. Instructions to replace the control pin commands in Listing 5-1 by remote control signals are given in Listing 5-4.

In the first section of the sketch, replace

Listing 5-4. Infrared remote control of an MP3 player

```
int nextPin = D4;
int volUp = D3;
int volDown = D2;                    // define control pins
int EQpin = D8;
```

with

```
#include <IRutils.h>                 // include IR library
int IRpin = D1;                      // IR receiver pin
int BufferSize = 1024;               // longer signal length
int Timeout = 50;                    // block repeat signals
IRrecv irrecv(IRpin, BufferSize, Timeout, true);
decode_results reading;              // IRremote reading
```

for an ESP8266 microcontroller, and for an ESP32 microcontroller, the new instructions are

```
#include <IRremote.h>
int IRpin = 23;
IRrecv irrecv(IRpin);
decode_results reading;
```

For both microcontrollers, replace the instruction int track with int track, oldTrack.

In the *setup* function, replace

```
pinMode(nextPin, INPUT_PULLUP);      // control pins use internal
pinMode(volUp, INPUT_PULLUP);        // pull-up resistors
pinMode(volDown, INPUT_PULLUP);
```

with

```
irrecv.enableIRIn();                    // initialise the IR receiver
```

The complete *loop* function is replaced with the following instructions, noting that the instruction `irrecv.resume()` is required only for the ESP32 microcontroller:

```
void loop()
{
  if(finish == 1)                       // current audio file ended
  {
    cmd(0x01, 0);                       // play next track
    finish = 0;                         // set finish variable
    cmd(0x4C, 0);                       // get track number
  }
  if(irrecv.decode(&reading))           // read pulsed signal
  {
    if(reading.value == 0x8D1)          // next audio file is selected
    {
      file = file+1;                    // increment file name
      if(file > fileMax) file = fileMin;
                                        // constrain file name < fileMax
      cmd(0x12, file);                  // play next audio file
      finish = 0;                       // set finish variable
      cmd(0x4C, 0);                     // get track number
    }
    else if(reading.value == 0x491)     // increase volume is selected
    {
      cmd(0x04, 0);                     // increase volume
      cmd(0x43, 0);                     // get volume value
    }
```

```
  else if(reading.value == 0xC91)      // decrease volume is selected
  {
    cmd(0x05, 0);                      // decrease volume
    cmd(0x43, 0);                      // get volume value
  }
  else if(reading.value == 0x1D1)      // change equaliser is selected
  {
    EQstate = EQstate+1;               // increment equaliser
    if(EQstate > 5) EQstate = 0;       // constrain equaliser value
    Serial.println(EQ[EQstate]);
    cmd(0x07, EQstate);                // change equaliser setting
  }
  else
  {
    switch(reading.value)            // switch case for selected track
    {                                // map remote signal to play track
      case 0x011: track = 1; break;
      case 0x811: track = 2; break;
      case 0x411: track = 3; break;
      case 0xC11: track = 4; break;
      case 0x211: track = 5; break;
    }
    cmd(0x03, track);                  // play track
    finish = 0;                        // set finish variable
    cmd(0x4C, 0);                      // get track number
  }
//    irrecv.resume();                 // for ESP32, receive next value
  }
  delay(100);
}
```

In the *cmd* function, the instruction if(CMD == 0x12) to play the next audio file is replaced with the instruction if(CMD == 0x01 ||CMD == 0x03 || CMD == 0x12) to play the next track or the selected track or the selected audio file. Two instructions further on, the instruction Serial.print(track) is replaced with Serial.print(oldTrack). In the instruction group to get the track number, the instruction oldTrack = track is added after the instruction track = buffer[6].

Creating sound tracks and two alarm systems

The website www.fromtexttospeech.com creates MP3 files for speech corresponding to text entered into the online textbox, with different voices in several languages available. The audio files are named with a number and text combination, for example, *"0001 alarm on"*, so that audio files are accessed independently of the order that the audio files were loaded on the micro-SD card. An application of user-defined sound tracks is an alarm system with an HC-SR04 ultrasonic distance sensor or a passive infrared (PIR) sensor to detect movement, with specific announcements from the MP3 player when the sensor is triggered (see Figures 5-6 and 5-7).

Figure 5-6. *MP3 player with alarm and LOLIN (WeMos) D1 mini*

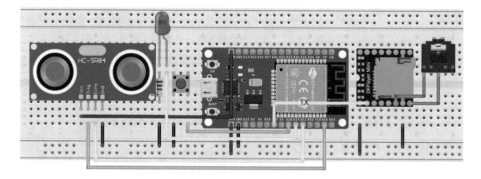

Figure 5-7. *MP3 player with alarm and the ESP32 DEVKIT DOIT development board*

The sketch in Listing 5-5 includes an HC-SR04 ultrasonic distance sensor to detect a distance change, such as when a door is opened, and if the alarm is on, then the MP3 player makes an announcement. The distance, in centimeters, between the sensor and an object is half the echo time, measured in microseconds, multiplied by 0.0343, assuming the speed of sound of 343 m/s. The first section of the sketch defines the HC-SR04 ultrasonic distance sensor and switch pins with the switch activating the interrupt *alarmISR*, which turns on or off the alarm and the indicator LED, with the MP3 player playing the corresponding audio file. In the *loop* function, the HC-SR04 ultrasonic distance sensor measures the distance every 2 s. When the measured distance is less than a threshold, the *play* function is activated with an MP3 player announcement, and the alarm is turned off. There is a time interval between playing the audio files, rather than sequential tracks being played immediately, when triggered by the MP3 player *BUSY* pin state changing to *HIGH*.

Connections for the MP3 player with alarm are given in Table 5-4. There is no MP3 player *TX* nor *BUSY* connection to the ESP8266 or ESP32 microcontroller as the MP3 player does not transmit a signal. Listing 5-5 is for an ESP8266 microcontroller, and the *NewPing8266* library is downloaded from github.com/jshaw/NewPingESP8266. For an ESP32 microcontroller, the *NewPing* library by Tim Eckel is available in the

Arduino IDE. The focus of the layouts in Figures 5-6 and 5-7 is to minimize overlapping connections, as in practice access is required to the MP3 player micro-SD card holder and to the ESP8266 and ESP32 development boards to provide power.

Table 5-4. *MP3 player with alarm and ESP8266 and ESP32 development boards*

Component	ESP8266	ESP32
MP3 player VCC	3V3	3V3
MP3 player RX	D7	TX2 (GPIO 17)
MP3 player SPK1	Audio output	Audio output
MP3 player GND	GND	GND
MP3 player SPK2	Audio output	Audio output
HC-SR04 VCC	5V	VIN
HC-SR04 Trig	D1	GPIO 22
HC-SR04 Echo	D2	GPIO 21
HC-SR04 GND	GND	GND
LED long leg	D3	GPIO 19
LED short leg	220 Ω resistor and to GND	
Switch right	D4	GPIO 18
Switch left	GND	GND

Listing 5-5 is for an ESP8266 microcontroller. When using an ESP32 microcontroller, the ESP8266 microcontroller instructions

```
#include<SoftwareSerial.h>        // include SoftwareSerial library
SoftwareSerial SoftSer(D6, D7);   // define SoftSer TX pin
#include <NewPingESP8266.h>       // include NewPingESP8266 lib
```

```
NewPingESP8266 sonar (trigPin, echoPin, maxdist);
SoftSer.begin(9600);              // software Serial baud rate
for (int i=0; i<10; i++) SoftSer.write(serialCom[i]);
```

are replaced with

```
#include <NewPing.h>             // include NewPing library
NewPing sonar (trigPin, echoPin, maxdist);
Serial2.begin(9600, SERIAL_8N1, 16, 17);   // Serial2 TX2 on GPIO 17
for (int i=0; i<10; i++) Serial2.write(serialCom[i]);
```

and pin definitions for the *trigPin, echoPin, LEDpin,* and *alarmPin* are changed to GPIO 22, GPIO 21, GPIO 19, and GPIO 18, respectively.

Listing 5-5. MP3 player alarm

```
#include<SoftwareSerial.h>          // include SoftwareSerial library
SoftwareSerial SoftSer(D6, D7); // define SoftSer TX pin
#include <NewPingESP8266.h>         // include NewPingESP8266 lib
int trigPin = D1;                   // HC-SR04 trigger pin
int echoPin = D2;                   // HC-SR04 echo pin
int maxdist = 200;                  // set max scan distance (cm)
int echoTime;
float distance;                     // scanned distance (cm)
                                    // associate sonar with NewPing
NewPingESP8266 sonar (trigPin, echoPin, maxdist);
int LEDpin = D3;                    // define LED pin
int alarmPin = D4;                  // define alarm switch pin
unsigned int checksum;
byte highChk, lowChk;               // control command template
byte serialCom[10] = {0x7E,0xFF,0x06,0x00,0x00,
0x00,0x00,0x00,0x00,0xEF};
byte buffer[10];
volatile int alarmSet = 0;          // set alarm state
```

```
String fileName[] = {              // file names in numerical order
"0001 alarm off",
"0002 alarm on",
"0003 someone entered the room",
"0004 close the door please",
"0005 press switch to reset the alarm"
};

void setup()
{
  Serial.begin(115200);        // Serial Monitor baud rate
  SoftSer.begin(9600);         // software Serial baud rate
  pinMode(trigPin, OUTPUT);    // define trigger pin as output
  pinMode(LEDpin, OUTPUT);     // define LEDpin as output
  pinMode(alarmPin, INPUT_PULLUP);
                               // alarm pin uses pull-up resistor
  attachInterrupt(digitalPinToInterrupt(alarmPin), alarmISR,
  FALLING);
}

void loop()
{
  echoTime = sonar.ping();          // echo time (µs)
  distance = (echoTime/2.0)*0.0343; // distance to target
  Serial.println(distance);         // play audio files if
                                    // distance < 100 and alarm set
  if(distance < 100 && alarmSet == 1) play();
  delay(2000);                      // delay between readings
}
```

```
void play()
{
  cmd(0x06, 10);                  // volume to 10 (range 0 to 30)
  cmd(0x12, 3);                   // play audio file named 0003
  delay(2000);                    // interval between audio files
  cmd(0x12, 4);                   // play audio file named 0004
  delay(2000);
  cmd(0x12, 5);                   // play audio file named 0005
  delay(2500);
  alarmISR();                     // turn alarm off
}

void cmd(byte CMD, byte param2)
{                                 // build checksum
  checksum = -(0xFF + 0x06 + CMD + 0x00 + 0x00 + param2);
  highChk = highByte(checksum);   // split checksum into
  lowChk = lowByte(checksum);     // high byte and low bytes
  serialCom[3] = CMD;
  serialCom[6] = param2;          // components of command
  serialCom[7] = highChk;
  serialCom[8] = lowChk;          // transmit command to MP3
  for (int i=0; i<10; i++) SoftSer.write(serialCom[i]);
}

IRAM_ATTR void alarmISR()
{
  alarmSet = 1 - alarmSet;        // turn off (0) or on (1) alarm
  digitalWrite(LEDpin, alarmSet); // turn off or on LED
  cmd(0x12, alarmSet+1);          // play audio file 0001 or 0002
}
```

Movement detection alarm

A movement detection alarm consists of a passive infrared (PIR) sensor detecting movement, which triggers the MP3 player to play a warning and to turn on an LED for ten seconds (see Figures 5-8 and 5-9). The sketch in Listing 5-6 consists of just 20 lines of code, with the ultrasonic distance sensor replaced by a PIR sensor, but using the connections in Table 5-5. Only the third track is played by the MP3 player, which requires the command *(0x12, 0x03)*. The command checksum is the negative value of the HEX representation of the signal components (*0xFF* + *0x06* + *0x12* + *0x00* + *0x00* + *0x03*), which is –(255 + 6 + 18 + 3) or –282 in decimal. The HEX representation of –282 is 2^{16} – 282 = 65256 or *0xFEE6*, which has high and low bytes of *0xFE* and *0xE6*, respectively.

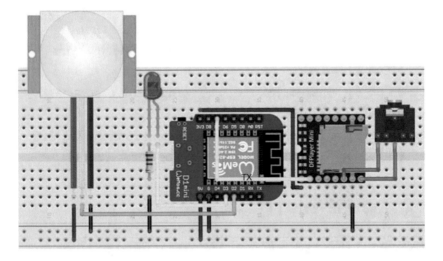

Figure 5-8. *MP3 player alarm with LOLIN (WeMos) D1 mini – short version*

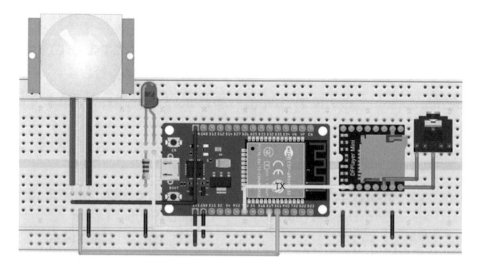

Figure 5-9. *MP3 player alarm with the ESP32 DEVKIT DOIT development board – short version*

Table 5-5. *MP3 player alarm with ESP8266 and ESP32 development boards – short version*

Component	ESP8266	ESP32
PIR sensor VCC	5V	VIN
PIR sensor OUT	D2	GPIO 21
PIR sensor GND	GND	GND

Listing 5-6 is for an ESP8266 microcontroller. When using an ESP32 microcontroller, the ESP8266 microcontroller instructions

```
#include<SoftwareSerial.h>        // include SoftwareSerial library
SoftwareSerial SoftSer(D6, D7);   // define SoftSer TX pin
SoftSer.begin(9600);              // software Serial baud rate
for (int i=0; i<10; i++) SoftSer.write(serialCom[i]);
```

are replaced with the instructions

```
Serial2.begin(9600, SERIAL_8N1, 16, 17);   // Serial2 TX2 on GPIO 17
for (int i=0; i<10; i++) Serial2.write(serialCom[i]);
```

and pin definitions for the *PIRpin* and *LEDpin* are changed to GPIO 21 and GPIO 19, respectively.

Listing 5-6. MP3 player alarm – short version

```
#include<SoftwareSerial.h>              // include SoftwareSerial library
SoftwareSerial SoftSer(D6, D7);         // define SoftSer TX pin
int PIRpin = D2;                        // PIR sensor and LED pins
int LEDpin = D3;
byte serialCom[10] = {0x7E,0xFF,0x06,0x12,0x00,
0x00,0x03,0xFE,0xE6,0xEF};              // one control command
void setup()
{
  SoftSer.begin(9600);                  // software Serial baud rate
  pinMode(LEDpin, OUTPUT);              // LED pin as OUTPUT
}

void loop()
{
  if(digitalRead(PIRpin) == HIGH)   // PIR sensor triggered
  {
    digitalWrite(LEDpin, HIGH);     // turn on LED and play sound
    for(int i=0; i<10; i++) SoftSer.write(serialCom[i]);
    delay(10000);
    digitalWrite(LEDpin, LOW);      // turn off LED after 10s
  }
}
```

Speaking clock

A speaking clock is built with a real-time clock (RTC) DS3231 and the MP3 player module. The DS3231 RTC has a built-in temperature sensor, is powered with 3.3 V or 5 V, and has a CR2032 lithium button-cell battery to power the RTC when not connected to an ESP8266 or ESP32 development board. The DS3231 RTC module uses I2C (Inter-Integrated Circuit) communication with the two bidirectional lines: serial data (SDA) and serial clock (SCL). The speaking clock time and temperature announcement is activated by pressing a button switch. One scenario is for people with a visual impairment, who can locate the large button switch, but not easily read the time on a watch, to be able to hear the time and temperature. Figures 5-10 and 5-11 illustrate the speaking clock with the ESP8266 and ESP32 development boards.

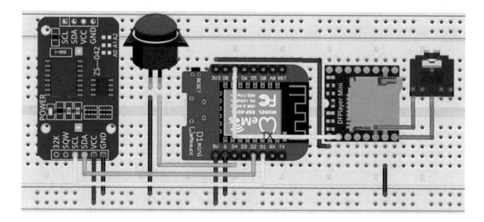

Figure 5-10. *Speaking clock with LOLIN (WeMos) D1 mini*

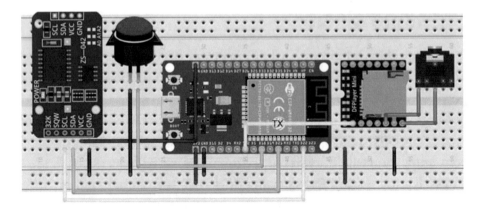

Figure 5-11. *Speaking clock with the ESP32 DEVKIT DOIT development board*

Connections for the DS3231 RTC and MP3 player modules are given in Tables 5-6 and 5-3, respectively. There is no MP3 player *TX* nor *BUSY* connection to the ESP8266 or ESP32 microcontroller as the MP3 player does not transmit a signal.

Table 5-6. *Real-time clock module with ESP8266 and ESP32 development boards*

Component	ESP8266	ESP32
DS3231 GND	GND	GND
DS3231 VCC	5V	VIN
DS3231 SDA	D2	GPIO 21
DS3231 SCL	D1	GPIO 22
Button switch right	D4	GPIO 18
Button switch left	GND	GND

The *MD_DS3231* library by Marco Colli is recommended, due to the ease of accessing time components, and the library is available in the Arduino IDE. When the sketch is first compiled and loaded, the current date and time are included in the sketch; and then the sketch is immediately compiled and loaded again, but with the date and time setting instructions commented out, as in Listing 5-7. When setting the time and date, the 24-hour time format is used without leading zeros. Compiling and loading takes about 30 seconds, so set the time forward by 30 seconds.

A total of 28 sound files are required for the numbers and temperature, with the files referenced as *0001 one, 0002 two ... 0020 twenty, 0030 thirty, 0040 forty, 0050 fifty, 0060 zero, 0070 the time is, 0080 degrees Celsius, 0090 and,* and *0100 o'clock.* Sound files 21–24 correspond to the numbers *30, 40, 50,* and *0;* files 25–28 are for *the time is, degrees Celsius, and,* and *o'clock.* The website www.fromtexttospeech.com creates mp3 files for speech corresponding to text entered into the online textbox, with different voices in several languages available.

The DS3231 RTC provides the time information, and then the track *the time is* is played by the MP3 player, and the *speak20* function is called to play the track(s) for the hour (see Listing 5-7). If the minutes are less than ten, then the *zero* track and the *one* to *nine* tracks are played; and if the minutes are less than 21, then the corresponding minutes track is played. Otherwise, the *thirty, forty,* or *fifty* track is played, which is track number 21, 22, or 23, equal to 18 plus the minutes divided by ten, followed by the track for the units digit. If the minutes are zero, then track number 28 for *o'clock* is played. The *getTemp* function for the DS3231 RTC reads the temperature, then the *and* track is played followed by the *speak20* function being called to play the track(s) for the temperature, and lastly, the track for *degrees Celsius* is played. The tracks are short, so there is no need for an interrupt to detect when a track has finished playing and the *BUSY* pin is not read.

Listing 5-7 is for an ESP8266 microcontroller. When using an ESP32 microcontroller, the ESP8266 microcontroller instructions

```
#include<SoftwareSerial.h>          // include SoftwareSerial library
SoftwareSerial SoftSer(D6, D7);     // define SoftSer TX pin
SoftSer.begin(9600);                // software Serial baud rate
for (int i=0; i<10; i++) SoftSer.write(serialCom[i]);
```

are replaced with the instructions

```
Serial2.begin(9600, SERIAL_8N1, 16, 17);        // TX2 on GPIO 17
for (int i=0; i<10; i++) Serial2.write(serialCom[i]);
```

and the *switchPin* definition is changed to GPIO 18.

Listing 5-7. Speaking clock

```
#include<SoftwareSerial.h>              // include SoftwareSerial library
SoftwareSerial SoftSer(D6, D7);         // define SoftSer TX pin
#include <MD_DS3231.h>                  // include MD_DS3231 library
unsigned int checksum;
byte highChk, lowChk;
byte serialCom[10] ={0x7E,0xFF,0x06,0x00,0x00,
0x00,0x00,0x00,0x00,0xEF};
byte buffer[10];
int switchPin = D4;                     // define switch pin
int val, deg;

void setup()
{
  SoftSer.begin(9600);                  // software Serial baud rate
  pinMode(switchPin, INPUT_PULLUP);     // switch pin uses pull-up resistor
  cmd(0x06, 10);                        // set volume to 10 (range 0 - 30)
```

```
  RTC.control(DS3231_12H, DS3231_OFF);    // 24 hour clock
            // RTC date of Wednesday 7 September 2020 at 20:37:50
/*          // instructions to set time commented out
  RTC.yyyy = 2020;                // year
  RTC.mm = 9;                     // month
  RTC.dd = 7;                     // day
  RTC.h = 20;                     // hour in 24 hour format
  RTC.m = 37;                     // minutes
  RTC.s = 50;                     // seconds, allow 30s to compile
  RTC.dow = 4;                    // day of week, Sunday = 1
  RTC.writeTime();
*/
}

void loop()
{
  if(digitalRead(switchPin) == LOW)        // switch is pressed
  {
    speak(25);                    // MP3 play "the time is"
    RTC.readTime();               // components of date and time
    speak20(RTC.h);               // MP3 play the hour
    if(RTC.m == 0) speak(28);     // MP3 play "o'clock"
    else if(RTC.m <10)
    {
      speak(24);                  // MP3 play "zero"
      speak(RTC.m);               // MP3 play minute < 10
    }
    else if(RTC.m <21) speak(RTC.m);       // MP3 play minute <21
    else
    {
      speak(RTC.m/10 + 18);       // MP3 play "30 40 or 50 mins"
      speak(RTC.m % 10);          // MP3 play minute < 10
    }                             // temperature measurement
```

```
    deg = round(RTC.readTempRegister());
    speak(27);                      // MP3 play "and"
    speak20(deg);                   // MP3 play the temperature
    speak(26);                      // MP3 play "degrees Celsius"
  }
}

void speak(int file)                // function to play MP3 file
{
  if(file == 27) delay(200);  // delay before playing "and"
  cmd(0x03, file);
  delay(300);                       // time for short track to play
  if(file == 25 || file == 27) delay(300);
}                                   // delay for "the time is" or "and"

void speak20(int val)               // function to play combination
{                                   // of "20" and units
  if(val < 21) speak(val);      // MP3 play number < 21
  else
  {
    speak(20);                      // MP3 play "20"
    speak(val % 20);                // MP3 play track numbered
  }                                 // remainder after dividing by 20
}

void cmd(byte CMD, byte param2)
{
  delay(500);                       // stop repeated button push
  checksum = -(0xFF + 0x06 + CMD + 0x00 + 0x00 + param2);
                                    // build checksum
  highChk = highByte(checksum);     // split checksum into
  lowChk = lowByte(checksum);       // high byte and low bytes
  serialCom[3] = CMD;
```

```
serialCom[6] = param2;              // components of command
serialCom[7] = highChk;
serialCom[8] = lowChk;              // transmit command to MP3
for (int i = 0; i<10; i++) SoftSer.write(serialCom[i]);
delay(20);                          // time to load command
}
```

Voice recorder

The ISD1820 record and playback module stores recorded sounds, up to 10 s duration, on the internal flash memory, which retains the information when the module is not powered. Recording is activated after a *HIGH* signal to the *REC* pin or after the *REC* button is pressed. The module LED is turned on for the 10 s recording period. The *P-E* playback option plays the entire recorded sound following a *HIGH* signal to the *P-E* pin or when the *PLAYE* button is pressed. The *P-L* playback option is also initiated on a *HIGH* signal, with recorded sound played back while the *P-L* pin is *HIGH* or the *PLAYL* button is pressed. The ISD1820 module is powered at 3.3 V and uses an 8 Ω 0.5 W speaker (see Figure 5-12 with connections in Table 5-7).

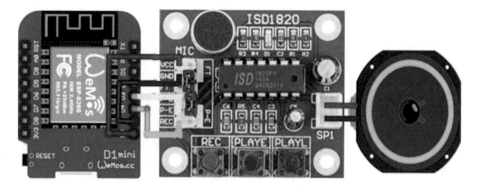

Figure 5-12. *ISD1820 record and playback module*

In Listing 5-8, the character *r* or *p* is entered on the Serial Monitor to start recording for 10 s or to start playback, respectively. When the instruction pinMode(playPin, OUTPUT) is called, the *PLAYE* pin is automatically set *LOW;* and to ensure the pin is initially set *LOW,* the instruction digitalWrite(playPin, LOW) precedes the pinMode(playPin, OUTPUT) instruction. An infrared signal to an infrared sensor connected to the ESP8266 or ESP32 development board or a door opening being detected by a PIR sensor triggers a *HIGH* signal to playback the recorded message, rather than entering a character on the Serial Monitor.

Table 5-7. *ISD1820 record and playback module*

Component	Connect to
ISD1820 VCC	ESP8266 3V3
ISD1820 GND	ESP8266 GND
ISD1820 P-E	ESP8266 D3
ISD1820 REC	ESP8266 D4

Listing 5-8. ISD1820 record and playback module

```
int playPin = D3;                  // define playback pin
int recPin = D4;                   // define record pin
char data;

void setup()
{
  Serial.begin(115200);            // Serial Monitor baud rate
  Serial.print("Enter r to record (10 seconds) or");
  Serial.println(" p to playback");
  digitalWrite(playPin, LOW);      // avoid playPin going HIGH
```

```
  pinMode(playPin, OUTPUT);            // define playPin and recPin
  pinMode(recPin, OUTPUT);             // as OUTPUT
}

void loop()
{
  while(Serial.available() > 0)        // if data available in Serial buffer
  {
    data = Serial.read();              // read Serial buffer
    if(data == 'r')
    {
      Serial.println("recording while light is on");
      digitalWrite(recPin, HIGH);   // HIGH to activate recording
      delay(10000);                 // recording time of 10s
      digitalWrite(recPin, LOW);    // reset to LOW signal
    }
    else if(data == 'p')
    {
      Serial.println("playback");
      digitalWrite(playPin, HIGH);  // HIGH to activate playback
      delay(10);                    // short delay of 10ms
      digitalWrite(playPin, LOW);   // reset to LOW signal
    }
  }
}
```

Summary

The DFPlayer Mini MP3 player operated both as a stand-alone MP3 player and when controlled by an ESP8266 or ESP32 microcontroller to play the next track, increase or decrease the volume, and change the music equalizer. The MP3 player was controlled with signals from an infrared remote control, after mapping the infrared remote control buttons to the MP3 player functions. An alarm was built with an ultrasonic distance sensor triggering announcements made by the MP3 player. A movement detection alarm, requiring only 20 lines of code, used a PIR sensor to trigger an announcement by the MP3 player and turn on an indicator LED. A button switch triggered announcements by the MP3 player of the current time and temperature, with the time and temperature information provided by the DS3231 real-time clock module. Controlling the ISD1820 record and playback module was also described.

Components List

- ESP8266 microcontroller: LOLIN (WeMos) D1 mini or NodeMCU board

- ESP32 microcontroller: DEVKIT DOIT or NodeMCU board

- DFPlayer Mini MP3 player

- Tactile switches: 2×

- Loudspeaker: Less than 3 W

- Audio jack socket and mini-loudspeaker

- Infrared sensor: VS1838B

- Resistor: 220 Ω

- LED

- Ultrasonic distance sensor: HC-SR04

- Passive infrared (PIR) sensor: HR-SC501 or HR-SC505

- Real-time clock module: DS3231

- Record and playback module: ISD1820

CHAPTER 6

Bluetooth speaker

A Bluetooth speaker complements the Internet radio in Chapter 1, the MP3 player in Chapter 5, and the WS2812 5050 RGB LED strip that responds to sound in Chapter 4. The Bluetooth stereo audio receiver module with the PAM8403 class-D audio amplifier does not require an ESP8266 or ESP32 microcontroller, but the project merits incorporation in the book because it's fun and a straightforward build. After the Bluetooth stereo audio receiver module is switched on with the announcement *"Bluetooth mode: the Bluetooth device is ready to pair,"* the Android tablet or mobile phone with Bluetooth communication is connected to the Bluetooth stereo audio receiver module, followed by another announcement *"The Bluetooth device is connected successfully."*

The Bluetooth stereo audio receiver module with the PAM8403 class-D audio amplifier powers 3 W speakers and operates at 5 V. A 18650 lithium-ion (Li-Ion) rechargeable battery powers the Bluetooth stereo audio receiver module and the speakers. An MT3608 DC to DC step-up boost converter power supply module boosts the 18650 lithium-ion battery's 3.7 V to the required 5 V. The MT3608 boost converter operates at 2–24 V and provides up to 28 V output at 2 A. The output voltage is controlled by adjusting the MT3608 potentiometer, indicated by the arrow in Figure 6-1

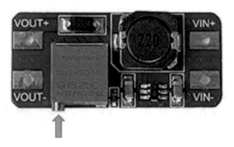

Figure 6-1. *MT3608 DC to DC step-up boost converter*

Lithium-ion batteries should neither be overcharged nor over-discharged; otherwise, the 18650 lithium-ion battery can produce substantial heat. The TP4056 battery protection module is a constant-current and constant-voltage linear charger for single-cell lithium-ion batteries. The TP4056 module monitors the voltage level of the lithium-ion battery during charging and disconnects the circuit if the lithium-ion battery voltage exceeds 4.2 V. The TP4056 module indicates when the lithium-ion battery is charging or has fully charged with a red or a blue LED. Figure 6-2 displays two TP4056 modules, with the supply voltage of 5 V provided on the left side through the mini-USB socket or by connecting the +/- points or *IN+/IN-* points to the supply voltage of 4.5–8 V. The TP4056 battery protection module on the right side of Figure 6-2 is only used for charging a lithium-ion battery and must not be connected to a load.

red LED   blue LED
charging   charge complete

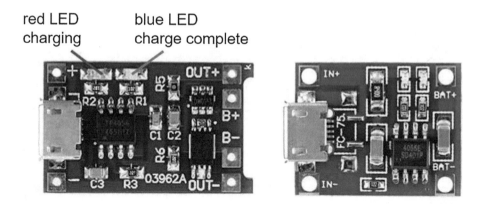

Figure 6-2. *TP4056 battery charging modules*

The TP4056 battery protection module on the left side of Figure 6-2 includes a DW01A battery protection IC, which controls an 8205A dual MOSFET (Metal Oxide Semiconductor Field Effect Transistor). When the charging lithium-ion battery voltage reaches 4.2 V, the TP4056 battery protection module switches from constant current of 1 A to a constant voltage of 4.2 V, and the current gradually reduces to zero. When the discharging lithium-ion battery voltage drops to 2.4 V, the MOSFET is switched off, which disconnects the lithium-ion battery from the load.

On the TP4056 battery protection module, the *B+* and *OUT+* points are connected together, but the *B-* and *OUT-* points are connected through the MOSFET. Figure 6-3 shows connections of the TP4056 battery protection module to the 18650 lithium-ion rechargeable battery and to the Bluetooth stereo audio receiver module (see Table 6-1). The TP4056 battery protection module in Figure 6-2 has a mini-USB socket for connecting a charging cable to a USB 5 V socket for charging the 18650 lithium-ion rechargeable battery.

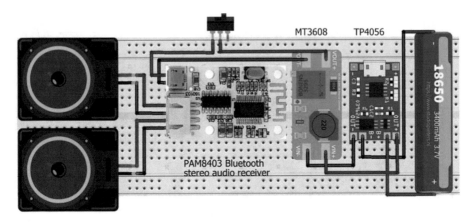

Figure 6-3. *Bluetooth stereo audio receiver module with speakers*

Table 6-1. *TP4056 protection module connections*

Component	Connect to
TP4056 B+	18650 battery positive
TP4056 B-	18650 battery negative
TP4056 OUT+	MT3608 VIN+
TP4056 OUT-	MT3608 VIN-
MT3608 VOUT+	Switch in
Switch out	Bluetooth and PAM8403 module 5V
MT3608 VOUT-	Bluetooth and PAM8403 module GND

Figure 6-3 shows the completed circuit of the 18650 lithium-ion rechargeable battery connected to the TP4056 battery charging module, which is connected to the MT3608 boost converter and, through a switch, to the Bluetooth stereo audio receiver module with the PAM8403 class-D audio amplifier and finally to the speakers.

An alternative to incorporating a TP4056 battery protection module with a MT3608 DC to DC step-up boost converter power supply module is to use a USB lithium-ion battery charge and boost converter module, such as the module included in a 18650 lithium-ion battery power bank (see Figure 6-4).

Figure 6-4. *T6845 USB lithium-ion battery charge and boost converter module*

For example, the T6845 USB lithium-ion battery charge and boost converter module boosts the battery 3.7 V voltage to the required 5 V at 1 A maximum current and incorporates battery protection, with the battery charged and battery discharged cut-off voltages of 4.2 V and 2.9 V, respectively. A USB charging cable is connected to the mini-USB socket of the T6845 USB lithium-ion battery charge and boost converter module for charging the 18650 lithium-ion rechargeable battery. A switch is fitted on the positive wire of a second USB charging cable that connects the USB power socket of the T6845 module to the mini-USB socket of the Bluetooth stereo audio receiver module (see Figure 6-5 with connections in Table 6-2).

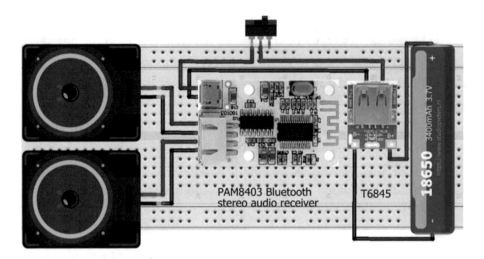

Figure 6-5. *Bluetooth stereo audio receiver and T6845 USB lithium-ion battery charge and boost converter module*

Table 6-2. *T6845 USB lithium-ion battery charge and boost converter module connections*

Component	Connect to
T6845 B+	18650 battery positive
T6845 B-	18650 battery negative
T6845 USB power socket +	Switch in
Switch out	Bluetooth and PAM8403 module 5V
T6845 USB power socket -	Bluetooth and PAM8403 module GND

The 18650 lithium-ion battery and T6845 USB lithium-ion battery charge and boost converter module, the Bluetooth stereo audio receiver module with the PAM8403 class-D audio amplifier, and the speakers are easily incorporated in a cylindrical container, such as a 40 g Pringles box! While not an ESP8266 or ESP32 microcontroller project and not requiring any programming, the project does require some soldering.

Summary

A Bluetooth speaker was built with a Bluetooth stereo audio receiver module with the PAM8403 class-D audio amplifier, powered by a lithium-ion 18650 battery coupled with a MT3608 step-up DC-DC boost converter, with battery charging and discharging controlled by a TP4056 battery protection module. Alternatively, a T6845 USB lithium-ion battery charge and boost converter module replaced the combination of a TP4056 battery protection module with a MT3608 step-up DC-DC boost converter.

Components List

- Bluetooth stereo audio receiver module with the PAM8403 amplifier

- Step-up DC-DC boost converter: MT3608

- Battery protection module: TP4056 with DW01A IC

- USB lithium-ion battery charge and boost converter module: T6845

- Lithium-ion battery: 18650

- Speaker: 2× 3 W

CHAPTER 7

Wireless local area network

A wireless local area network (WLAN) is established with an ESP8266 or ESP32 microcontroller, with networked devices requesting information from the microcontroller (see Figure 7-1). The WLAN does not have Internet access. The microcontroller is the access point (AP) for the WLAN, consisting of the microcontroller and up to four devices, and is termed a software-enabled access point or SoftAP. If the microcontroller is connected to an existing Wi-Fi network, then the microcontroller is in station (STA) mode. The WLAN client is the browser on a laptop, an Android tablet, or a mobile phone. The client connects to the WLAN by selecting the WLAN name and the access password with the browser opened at the URL (Uniform Resource Locator) of the WLAN-predefined IP (Internet Protocol) address.

Figure 7-1. *Wireless local area network with the ESP8266 or ESP32 microcontroller*

© Neil Cameron 2021
N. Cameron, *Electronics Projects with the ESP8266 and ESP32,*
https://doi.org/10.1007/978-1-4842-6336-5_7

To demonstrate establishing a WLAN with an ESP8266 or ESP32 microcontroller, the WLAN web page controls two LEDs, which are connected to the ESP8266 or ESP32 development board, and displays the LED states and a counter that is incremented when an LED state changes (see Figure 7-2). The example demonstrates using a client to remotely control devices connected to an ESP8266 or ESP32 development board, which acts as a server, and the client receipt of information, in the form of HTML (HyperText Markup Language) code that is displayed on the WLAN web page.

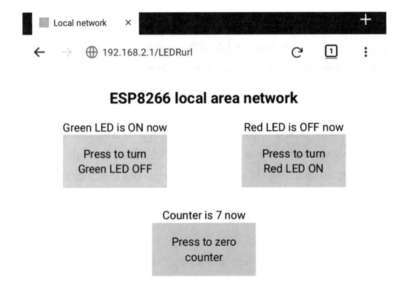

Figure 7-2. *Wireless local area network web page*

Clicking a button on the WLAN web page turns on or off the corresponding LED or resets the counter to zero. Schematics for the ESP8266 and ESP32 microcontrollers functioning as the WLAN server and connected to two LEDs are shown in Figure 7-3, with connections given in Table 7-1.

160

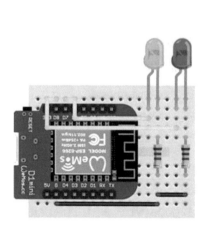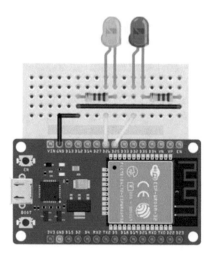

Figure 7-3. *LOLIN (WeMos) D1 mini and ESP32 DEVKIT DOIT boards and LEDs*

Table 7-1. *ESP8266 and ESP32 development boards and LEDs*

Component	ESP8266 Connections		ESP32 Connections	
LED long leg	ESP8266 D7 and D8		ESP32 GPIO 25 and GPIO 26	
LED short leg	220 Ω resistor	ESP8266 GND	220 Ω resistor	ESP32 GND

The WLAN IP address is defined in the sketch, rather than using a generated IP address, along with the IP gateway and the IP subnet mask. The WLAN IP address and gateway are identical. The IP subnet mask of (255,255,255,0) for a class-C IP address, such as 192.168.2.1, indicates that the first three elements of the IP address, *192.168.2*, define the WLAN ID and the last element defines the host ID. The WLAN password should contain at least eight alphanumeric characters. For example, instructions to set the WLAN SSID (Service Set Identifier), which is the network name, password, and IP address to *ESP8266, 12345678,* and *192.168.2.1* are

```
char ssidAP[] = "ESP8266";              // WLAN SSID
char passwordAP[] = "12345678";         // and password
IPAddress local_ip(192,168,2,1);        // pre-defined IP address,
IPAddress gateway(192,168,2,1);         // gateway
IPAddress subnet(255,255,255,0);        // and subnet mask
```

In the *setup* function of a sketch, the WLAN is initialized in access point (AP) mode with the instruction WiFi.mode(WIFI_AP). The default is joint access point and station mode, with the instruction WiFi.mode(WIFI_AP_STA), and station (STA) mode is defined by the instruction WiFi.mode(WIFI_STA). The network IP address is defined with the instructions

```
WiFi.mode(WIFI_AP);                     // WLAN in AP mode
WiFi.softAP(ssidAP, passwordAP);        // WLAN SSID, password
WiFi.softAPConfig(local_ip, gateway, subnet);   // initialise WLAN
```

The WLAN or host IP address is displayed with the instructions

```
IPAddress IP = WiFi.softAPIP();
Serial.println(IP);
```

HTTP request

A client makes an HTTP request for information by sending a URL address to the server. The server calls a function mapped to the URL and responds to the client with HTML code for the information provided by the function. For example, a URL is mapped to a function that changes the state of an LED, with the LED state displayed on the WLAN web page. In Figure 7-4, clicking a button on the WLAN web page sends an HTTP request containing the URL, associated with the button, to the server, which is the ESP8266 or ESP32 microcontroller. The server calls the function that is mapped to the URL, to change the LED state and update the HTML code for the URL. The server HTTP response is to send the updated HTML code to the client, which updates the WLAN web page.

Figure 7-4. *Client HTTP request and server HTTP response*

The sketch in Listing 7-1 displays, on the WLAN web page, the states of a green LED and a red LED and the value of a counter that can be reset to zero. The LED states are controlled by the two functions *LEDGfunct* and *LEDRfunct,* with the function *zeroFunct* resetting the counter. The corresponding three URLs, */LEDGurl, /LEDRurl,* and */zeroUrl,* are mapped to the functions, by the `server.on(URL, function)` instruction.

The server HTTP response is made with the instruction `server.send(status code, content type, content)`. Status code of *200* or *404* indicates a successful HTTP request or that the requested URL could not be found, respectively. The content type options are plain text, HTML code, or JSON text (described in Chapter 3 (*International weather station)* and Chapter 8 (*Updating a web page))* as indicated by `text/plain`, `text/html`, and `text/json`. When the content type is `text/html`, the HTML code is referenced by a string or a function. In Listing 7-1, the HTML code is referenced by the *webcode* function, which has three parameters for the states of the green LED, the red LED, and the counter value. The *webcode* function returns a string, *page,* which contains the HTML code for the WLAN web page. The server sends the HTML code to the client with the instruction `server.send(200, "text/html", webcode(LEDG, LEDR, counter))`.

In Listing 7-1, the WLAN SSID and password are defined with the WLAN IP, and URLs are mapped to the functions that control the LEDs and the counter and the HTML code for the WLAN web page is defined (see Listing 7-3). The *ESP8266WebServer* library references the *ESP8266WiFi* library, so the *ESP8266WiFi* library is not explicitly included in the sketch. Similarly, for the ESP32 microcontroller, the *WiFi* library is referenced by the *WebServer* library. The HTML code is contained in the *buildpage.h* tab to separate the HTML code from the main sketch. The additional tab is created in the Arduino IDE by selecting the triangle below the *Serial Monitor* button, on the right side of the IDE, and choosing *New Tab* from the drop-down menu. The *New Tab* is titled *buildpage.h*. Note that the *loop* function only includes the instruction server.handleClient().

Listing 7-1. WLAN and LED functions

```
#include <ESP8266WebServer.h>          // include ESP8266WebServer lib
ESP8266WebServer server;               // associate server with library
char ssidAP[] = "ESP8266";             // WLAN SSID and password
char passwordAP[] = "12345678";
IPAddress local_ip(192,168,2,1);       // pre-defined IP address values
IPAddress gateway(192,168,2,1);
IPAddress subnet(255,255,255,0);
#include "buildpage.h"                 // webpage HTML code
int LEDGpin = D7;                      // define LED pins
int LEDRpin = D8;
int LEDR = LOW;                        // default LED states
int LEDG = LOW;
int counter = 0;

void setup()
{
  WiFi.mode(WIFI_AP);                  // Wi-Fi AP mode
  delay(1000);                         // setup AP mode
```

```
  WiFi.softAP(ssidAP, passwordAP);    // initialise Wi-Fi with
  WiFi.softAPConfig(local_ip, gateway, subnet);
                                      // predefined IP address
  server.begin();                     // initialise server
  server.on("/", base);               // load default webpage
  server.on("/LEDGurl", LEDGfunct);   // map URLs to functions:
  server.on("/LEDRurl", LEDRfunct);   // LEDGfunct, LEDRfunct
  server.on("/zeroUrl", zeroFunct);   // and zeroFunct
  pinMode(LEDGpin, OUTPUT);           // define LED pins as output
  pinMode(LEDRpin, OUTPUT);
}

void base()                           // function to load default webpage
{                                     // and send HTML code to client
  server.send(200, "text.html", webcode(LEDG, LEDR, counter));
}

void LEDGfunct()                      // function to change green LED state,
{                                     // increment counter and
  LEDG = !LEDG;                       // send HTML code to client
  digitalWrite(LEDGpin, LEDG);
  counter++;
  server.send(200, "text/html", webcode(LEDG, LEDR, counter));
}

void LEDRfunct()                      // function to change red LED state,
{                                     // increment counter and
  LEDR = !LEDR;                       // send HTML code to client
  digitalWrite(LEDRpin, LEDR);
  counter++;
  server.send(200, "text/html", webcode(LEDG, LEDR, counter));
}
```

```
void zeroFunct()              // function to zero counter
{                             // and send HTML code to client
  counter = 0;
  server.send(200, "text/html", webcode(LEDG, LEDR, counter));
}

void loop()
{
  server.handleClient();      // manage HTTP requests
}
```

When the client initially loads the WLAN web page, the instruction `server.on("/", base)` calls the *base* function, which loads the default WLAN web page with values of *LEDG, LEDR,* and the counter set to *LOW, LOW,* and zero, respectively. The *base* function defines the default setting for the WLAN web page.

The server response to the client HTTP request is to update the relevant LED state, the counter value, and the HTML code for the WLAN web page. For example, if the button to turn on the red LED is clicked, then the client HTTP request contains the URL */LEDRurl*, which is displayed at the top of the WLAN web page (see Figure 7-2). The server calls the associated *LEDRfunct* function, and the state of the red LED is changed from *LOW* or zero to *HIGH* or one, and the counter is incremented. The *webcode* function then updates the HTML code to include the lines

```
<td>Red LED is ON now<a href='/LEDRurl' class='btn on'>
Press to turn Red LED OFF</a></td>
```

When the server responds to the client by sending the updated HTML code, the WLAN web page displays the text *Red LED is ON now,* and the button text is updated to *Press to turn Red LED OFF.* On the web browser, the web page loading indicator, located beside the web page title, moves across the web page as the web page loads and the URL *192.168.2.1/ LEDRurl* is displayed.

Clicking the *zero* button sends the URL */zeroUrl* to the server, and the counter value is reset to zero by the mapped function, *zeroFunct*. The *webcode* function updates the HTML code `<p>Counter is "+String(counter)+" now<a href='/zeroUrl'` with the counter value of zero, and the WLAN web page displays the text *Counter is 0 now*.

With an ESP8266 microcontroller as the WLAN access point, the web server library instructions are

```
#include <ESP8266WebServer.h>
ESP8266WebServer server
```

and the corresponding instructions for an ESP32 microcontroller are

```
#include <WebServer.h>
WebServer server(80);                    // requires a port number
```

Alternatively, at the start of a sketch, instructions in Listing 7-2 are included to accommodate both an ESP8266 and ESP32 microcontroller with the LED pin definitions.

Listing 7-2. Pin definitions for ESP8266 and ESP32 development boards

```
#ifdef ESP8266
  #include <ESP8266WebServer.h>          // include ESP8266 library
  ESP8266WebServer server;
  int LEDGpin = D7;                      // define LED pins
  int LEDRpin = D8;
#elif ESP32
  #include <WebServer.h>                 // include ESP32 library
  WebServer server (80);
  int LEDGpin = 26;                      // define LED pins
  int LEDRpin = 25;
```

```
#else                                    // Arduino IDE error message
  #error "ESP8266 or ESP32 microcontroller only"
#endif
```

HTML code

A detailed description of HTML (HyperText Markup Language) is outside the scope of the book, but www.w3schools.com is recommended for information on HTML and CSS (Cascading Style Sheets), for building and defining the style of web pages.

Briefly, an HTML page consists of a <head> section, where the web page title and styles are defined, and a <body> section, which contains the web page content. The sections are bracketed with <head>...</head> and <body>...</body>. Style defines font types and sizes, headers, and spacing that is bracketed by <style>...</style>. A specific item on a web page is separately formatted and bracketed by ....

For example (see Listing 7-3), in the <head> section, the *body* style sets the top margin at 50 pixels (96 pixels per inch) and center-aligns text of size 20 pixels in Arial font. The *button* style, btn, defines a button width of 220 pixels, 30-pixel distance between buttons, and black button text of size 30 pixels. The parameters display:block enable wrap-around of the button text, margin:auto centers the button in the web page, and text-decoration:none prevents underlining of an HTML link. The *on, off,* and *zero* styles are combined with the *button* style to define button background color. Color details are available from www.w3schools.com/colors/colors_hex.asp.

The web page includes a table with the content of a table row and a table cell bracketed by <tr>...</tr> and <td>...</td>, respectively. A table is used to align web page objects, such as the red and green LED buttons. The counter button is included in a paragraph, bracketed by <p>...</p>.

168

Listing 7-3. HTML code for WLAN web page

```
String webcode(int LEDG, int LEDR, int counter)
{
  String page = "<!DOCTYPE html><html><head>";
  page +="<title>Local network</title>";
  page +="<style>";
  page +="body {margin-top:50px; font-family:Arial;";
  page +="font-size:20px; text-align:center}";
  page +=".btn {display:block; width:220px;";
  page += "margin:auto; padding:30px}";
  page +=".btn {font-size:30px; color:black;";
  page += "text-decoration:none}";
  page +=".on {background-color:SkyBlue}";
  page +=".off {background-color:LightSteelBlue}";
  page +=".zero {background-color:Thistle}";
  page +="td {font-size:30px; margin-top:50px;";
  page += "margin-bottom:5px}";
  page +="p {font-size:30px; margin-top:50px;";
  page += "margin-bottom:5px}";
  page +="</style></head>";
  page +="<body>";
  page +="<h1>ESP8266 local area network</h1>";
  page +="<table style='width:100%'><tr>";
  if(LEDG>0)
  {
    page +="<td>Green LED is ON now";
    page +="<a href='/LEDGurl' class='btn on'>";
    page +="Press to turn Green LED OFF</a></td>";
  }
```

169

```
else
{
  page +="<td>Green LED is OFF now";
  page +="<a href='/LEDGurl' class='btn off'>";
  page +="Press to turn Green LED ON</a></td>";
}
if(LEDR>0)
{
  page +="<td>Red LED is ON now";
  page +="<a href='/LEDRurl' class='btn on' >";
  page +="Press to turn Red LED OFF</a></td>";
}
else
{
  page +="<td>Red LED is OFF now";
  page +="<a href='/LEDRurl' class='btn off'>";
  page +="Press to turn Red LED ON</a></td>";
}
page +="</tr></table>";
page +="<p>Counter is "+String(counter);
page +=" now<a href='/zeroUrl'";
page +="class='btn zero'>Press to zero counter</a></p>";
page +="</body></html>";
return page;
}
```

HTML code for a web page can be included in the main sketch, but it is included as an additional tab, for example, *buildpage.h*, to separate the main sketch from the HTML code and make the sketch easier to interpret. The additional tab is created in the Arduino IDE by selecting the triangle below the *Serial Monitor* button, on the right side of the IDE, and choosing *New Tab* from the drop-down menu. The *New Tab* is titled *buildpage.h*.

The *webcode* function (see Listing 7-3) is contained in the *buildpage.h* tab, defined by the instruction #include "buildpage.h", in the first section of Listing 7-1. The *buildpage.h* tab is referenced with quotation marks, " ", and not with angular brackets, < >, which is for a library. The *webcode* function returns a string, *page*, containing the HTML code of the WLAN web page. The HTML code is built up line-by-line as a string and includes conditional statements to change the HTML code, depending on values of the *LEDG, LEDR,* and *counter* variables.

The whole web page is reloaded even if only one data value has changed. AJAX enables updating a web page with only the updated value, rather than reloading the whole web page.

When running the sketch in Listings 7-1 and 7-3, the browser, such as *Google Chrome* or *Mozilla Firefox*, on your laptop, Android tablet, or mobile must be connected to the server listed as *ESP8266*. The URL to access the web page is 192.168.2.1, as defined in Listing 7-1.

XML HTTP requests, JavaScript, and AJAX

An XML (eXtensible Markup Language) HTTP request updates a specific variable on a web page, rather than having to reload the whole web page. The combination of an XML HTTP request with JavaScript commands, to manage the XML HTTP request, is AJAX (Asynchronous JavaScript and XML). An example AJAX code for an XML HTTP request is given in Listing 7-4. When the response to the XML HTTP request is ready, indicated by a *readyState* value of 4, and if the XML HTTP request is successful, with a *status* value of 200 (see [1] in Listing 7-4), then the XML HTTP request object sends a request to the server to update information on the variable (see [2] in Listing 7-4) for the URL (see [3] in Listing 7-4). On the web browser, the *web page loading* indicator, located beside the web page title, is now absent. Further information on XML HTTP requests, JavaScript, and AJAX is available at www.w3schools.com.

171

Listing 7-4. AJAX code for XML HTTP request

```
<script>                                // start of JavaScript
var xhr = new XMLHttpRequest();         // XMLHttpRequest object
xhr.onreadystatechange = function()
{                                       // [1] if request successful
   if(this.readyState == 4 && this.status == 200)
   document.getElementById(variable).innerHTML =
   this.responseText;                   // [2] update variable
};
xhr.open('GET', URL, true);             // [3] at URL
xhr.send();
</script>                               // end of JavaScript
```

The XML HTML code is included as a *string literal*, as there are no variables in the code, which avoids the line-by-line build-up of a string for the HTML code, as used in Listing 7-3. The JavaScript and XML HTTP request instructions, stored as a *string literal* in PROGMEM, are bracketed by R"(and)", which can be extended to R"str(and)str", where str is a string of characters that does not appear in the AJAX code. An example string is === with R"(=== and ===)" bracketing the *string literal*. In JavaScript, both a single quote, ', or double quotes, ", are used to bracket a string, with single quotes preferred in the book.

Inclusion of XML HTTP requests requires changes to the main sketch and the HTML code. For the *LEDGfunct, LEDRfunct,* and *zeroFunct* functions of the main sketch in Listing 7-1, the instruction server.send(200, "text/html", webcode(LEDG, LEDR, counter)) is replaced with server.send(200, "text/plain", str). Only the updated variable, contained in the string *str*, is sent by the server to the client for updating the web page, rather than the server sending HTML code for the whole web page. For example, changes to the function *LEDRfunct* are indicated in bold, with the function *LEDGfunct* updated similarly:

```
void LEDRfunct()                        // function to change red LED state
{
  LEDR = !LEDR;                         // change LED state
  digitalWrite(LEDRpin, LEDR);
  counter++;                            // increment counter
  String str = "ON";
  if(LEDR == LOW) str = "OFF";          // map string str to LED state
  server.send(200, "text/plain", str);  // send response to client
}
```

The function *zeroFunct* is also changed to only send the updated counter value:

```
void zeroFunct()                        // function to zero counter
{
  counter = 0;                          // reset counter
  String str = String(counter);         // convert counter to a string
  server.send(200, "text/plain", str);  // send response to client
}
```

The *base* function sends the default web page HTML code to the client with the parameter *page*, rather than calling the *webcode* function.

The HTML and AJAX code is shown in Listing 7-6. The <style> section is identical, in content, to the <style> section in Listing 7-3. The <body> section now includes HTML code for the web page layout and AJAX code for the XML HTTP requests to update the web page. JavaScript scripts, bracketed by <script> and </script>, are positioned prior to the HTML </body> code to improve web page display speed.

Differences between the HTML code in Listing 7-2 and the AJAX code in Listing 7-6 are illustrated with respect to the button controlling the green LED. In Listing 7-2, the HTML code for the table cell containing the button for the green LED, when the green LED is on, is

```
<td>Green LED is ON now<a href='/LEDGurl' class='btn on'>
    Press to turn Green LED OFF</a></td>
```

and the HTML code for when the green LED is off is

```
<td>Green LED is OFF now<a href='/LEDGurl' class='btn off'>
    Press to turn Green LED ON</a></td>
```

For each state of the green LED, the HTML code specifies the text above the button, the URL associated with the button, a `href='/LEDGurl'`, the button class, and the text on the button.

In Listing 7-6, the HTML code to update the web page button to control the green LED is

```
<td>Green LED is <span id='LEDG'>OFF</span> now</td>
<td><button class = 'btn off' id='Green LED'
    onclick = 'sendData(id)'>Press to turn Green LED ON
    </button></td>
```

The HTML code specifies the text above the button with the green LED state held by the variable with identity `'LEDG'`, which has a default value of *OFF*, the button class, and the text on the button. Clicking the button, with identity defined by id=`'Green LED'`, calls the function *sendData* with the button identity parameter.

The AJAX code for the *sendData* function relevant to controlling the green LED button is given in Listing 7-5. The *sendData* function updates the button state to *btn on* or *btn off* and the button text to *Press to turn Green LED ON* or *Press to turn Green LED OFF*. The *sendData* function sets the values of *variable* for the XML HTTP request instructions and *URL*

```
document.getElementById(variable).innerHTML = this.responseText
xhr.open('GET', URL, true)
```

and, finally, sends the XML HTTP response.

Listing 7-5. AJAX code for updating a variable

```
function sendData(butn)
{
  if(butn == 'Red LED' || butn == 'Green LED')
  {
    var state = document.getElementById(butn).className;
    state = (state == 'btn on' ? 'btn off' : 'btn on');
    text =  (state == 'btn on' ? butn + ' OFF' : butn + ' ON');
    document.getElementById(butn).className = state;
    document.getElementById(butn).innerHTML = 'Press to turn '
    + text;
  }
  var URL, variab, text;

  else if(butn == 'Green LED')
  {
    URL = 'LEDGurl';
    variab = 'LEDG';
  }
  var xhr = new XMLHttpRequest();
  xhr.onreadystatechange = function(butn)
  {
    if (this.readyState == 4 && this.status == 200)
    document.getElementById(variab).innerHTML = this.
    responseText;
  };
```

```
xhr.open('GET', URL, true);
xhr.send();
}
```

The complete AJAX code to manage XML HTTP requests and update the web page, when a button to control the red or green LED or to zero the counter is clicked, is given in Listing 7-6.

Listing 7-6. AJAX code for WLAN web page

```
char page[] PROGMEM = R"(
<!DOCTYPE html><html><head>
<title>Local network</title>
<style>
body {margin-top:50px; font-family:Arial}
body {font-size:20px; text-align:center}
.btn {display:block; width:280px; margin:auto; padding:30px}
.btn {font-size:30px; color:black; text-decoration:none}
.on {background-color:SkyBlue}
.off {background-color:LightSteelBlue}
.zero {background-color:Thistle}
td {font-size:30px; margin-top:50px; margin-bottom:5px}
p {font-size:30px; margin-top:50px; margin-bottom:5px}
</style></head>
<body>
<h1>ESP8266 local area network</h1>
<table style='width:100%'><tr>
<td>Green LED is <span id='LEDG'>OFF</span> now</td>
<td>Red LED is <span id='LEDR'>OFF</span> now</td>
</tr></table>
<table style='width:100%'><tr>
<td><button class = 'btn off' id='Green LED'
    onclick = 'sendData(id)'>Press to turn Green LED ON
    </button></td>
```

```
<td><button class = 'btn off' id='Red LED'
     onclick = 'sendData(id)'>Press to turn Red LED ON
     </button></td>
</tr></table>
<p>Counter is <span id='counter'>0</span> now</p>
<button class = 'btn zero' id = 'zero'
     onclick = 'sendData(id)'>Press to zero counter</button>

<script>
function sendData(butn)
{
  var URL, variab, text;
  if(butn == 'Red LED')              // set URL and variab values
  {                                  // for Red LED button
    URL = 'LEDRurl';
    variab = 'LEDR';
  }
  else if(butn == 'Green LED')       // or for Green LED button
  {
    URL = 'LEDGurl';
    variab = 'LEDG';
  }
  else if(butn == 'zero')            // or for the zero button
  {
    URL = 'zeroUrl';
    variab = 'counter';
  }
  if(butn == 'Red LED' || butn == 'Green LED')
  {                                  // change button class and text
    var state = document.getElementById(butn).className;
    state = (state == 'btn on' ? 'btn off' : 'btn on');
```

```
      text = (state == 'btn on' ? butn + ' OFF' : butn + ' ON');
      document.getElementById(butn).className = state;
      document.getElementById(butn).innerHTML = 'Press to turn '
      + text;
    }
    var xhr = new XMLHttpRequest();
    xhr.onreadystatechange = function(butn)
    {
      if (this.readyState == 4 && this.status == 200)
      document.getElementById(variab).innerHTML = this.
      responseText;
    };
    xhr.open('GET', URL, true);
    xhr.send();
  }
</script>
</body></html>
)";
```

When the buttons that control the red and green LEDs are clicked, an XML HTTP request is made by the client to update values of the LED states, but the counter is not automatically updated. The interval between repeated XML HTTP requests is defined with the instruction setInterval(reload, 1000), with the *reload* function making an XML HTTP request every 1000 ms, as shown in Listing 7-7. In the main sketch, the */countURL* URL is mapped to the *countFunct* function with the instruction server.on("/countUrl", countFunct) included in the *setup* function. Instructions for the *countFunct* function are

```
void countFunct()                           // function to update counter
{
  String str = String(counter);             // convert counter to a string
  server.send(200, "text/plain", str);  // send response to client
}
```

The AJAX code to periodically update the counter in Listing 7-7 is incorporated between the <script> and </script> instructions in Listing 7-6.

Listing 7-7. AJAX code to periodically update the counter

```
setInterval(reload, 1000);
function reload()
{
  var xhr = new XMLHttpRequest();
  xhr.onreadystatechange = function()
  {
    if(this.readyState == 4 && this.status == 200)
    document.getElementById('counter').innerHTML = this.
    responseText;
  };
  xhr.open('GET', 'countUrl', true);
  xhr.send();
}
```

The two approaches, with HTML code and with AJAX code, result in the same information being displayed on the web page, but with HTML code, the whole web page is reloaded with every client request. In contrast, with AJAX code, only a specific variable is updated on the web page. The AJAX code is double the length of the HTML code and may be more difficult to interpret. Updating only the specific item on a web page, rather than reloading the whole web page, is advantageous for web pages containing substantial information.

Summary

A wireless local area network was established with an ESP8266 or ESP32 microcontroller, as the WLAN server. The browser of an Android tablet or mobile phone, which is the client, accessed the WLAN using an IP address and password defined by the sketch. The WLAN web page displayed the states of two LEDs, connected to the ESP8266 or ESP32 development board, and a counter value. The LED states were remotely controlled by clicking the client web page buttons. The web page HTML code was built line-by-line as a string, and the whole web page had to be reloaded when updated information was displayed. AJAX code consisting of XML HTTP requests and JavaScript instructions, incorporated as a *string literal*, enabled updating of only specific variables on the web page, rather than reloading the whole web page.

Components List

- ESP8266 microcontroller: LOLIN (WeMos) D1 mini or NodeMCU board

- ESP32 microcontroller: ESP32 DEVKIT DOIT or NodeMCU board

- LED: 2×

- Resistor: 2× 220 Ω

CHAPTER 8

Updating a web page

Devices connect to a wireless local area network (WLAN) with Wi-Fi communication (see Chapter 7 (Wireless local area network)). A router connected to an Internet Service Provider (ISP), through a telephone line using DSL (Digital Subscriber Line) technology, provides access to the Internet (see Figure 8-1). The Internet is formed by interconnected computer networks using the Internet Protocol suite, consisting of the Transmission Control Protocol and the Internet Protocol (TCP/IP), to globally link devices. The World Wide Web (WWW) identifies information resources by URLs (Uniform Resource Locators). The client or web browser, such as *Google Chrome* or *Mozilla Firefox*, sends an HTTP (HyperText Transfer Protocol) request to the server device hosting the resource to retrieve information at the web address defined by the URL. The server responds to the client HTTP request, and the client displays the requested web page information on the Android tablet or mobile phone. The client must request web page information from the server, as the server cannot impose updates on the client. The exception is WebSocket, as discussed in Chapter 9.

© Neil Cameron 2021
N. Cameron, *Electronics Projects with the ESP8266 and ESP32*,
https://doi.org/10.1007/978-1-4842-6336-5_8

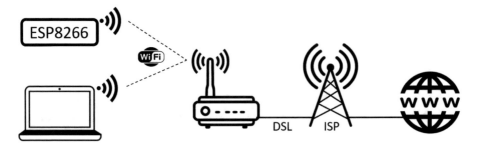

Figure 8-1. *Client, Internet Service Provider, and WWW*

In this chapter, an ESP8266 or an ESP32 microcontroller is the server. The web server library instructions for the ESP8266 development board are

```
#include <ESP8266WebServer.h>
ESP8266WebServer server
```

and for the ESP32 development board are

```
#include <WebServer.h>
WebServer server(80);            // requires a port number
```

To demonstrate the process of a client requesting information from a server, the sketch in Listing 8-1 displays the BMP280 temperature reading, a counter, and the state of an LED (see Figure 8-2). The web page is automatically refreshed, and the reloading time is determined by the web page HTML code `<meta http-equiv='refresh' content='N'>`, with a refresh every N seconds. A function, *BMP*, updates the BMP280 temperature reading, increments the counter, and changes the LED state; and the server then sends the updated web page HTML code to the client. The timing of the *BMP* function is controlled by the *Ticker* library, with the instruction `timer.attach(T, BMP)`, and the *BMP* function is called every T seconds. If the web page refresh interval, N, is substantially less than the *BMP* function call interval, T, then the client will wait $(T - N)$ seconds before the server sends the updated HTML code. In Listing 8-1, the *BMP* function call interval equals $N + 1$ seconds, but not N seconds as the server and client are not synchronized.

Figure 8-2. *BMP280 and LED counter web page*

Figure 8-3 shows the BMP280 temperature sensor and LED with an ESP8266 and ESP32 development board. Connections are given in Table 8-1. The *Adafruit_BMP280* library is available within the Arduino IDE.

Figure 8-3. *BMP280 and LED with LOLIN (WeMos) D1 mini and ESP32 DEVKIT DOIT*

183

Table 8-1. *BMP280 and LED with ESP8266 and ESP32 development boards*

Component	ESP8266 Connections		ESP32 Connections	
BMP280 VCC	3V3		3V3	
BMP280 GND	GND		GND	
BMP280 SDA	D2		GPIO 21	
BMP280 SCK	D1		GPIO 22	
BMP280 SDO	GND		GND	
LED long leg	D3		GPIO 23	
LED short leg	220 Ω resistor	GND	220 Ω resistor	GND

In the *setup* function of Listing 8-1, the Wi-Fi connection is established, the server IP address is displayed on the Serial Monitor, the WLAN web page is mapped to the *webcode* function, and the timing of the *BMP* function is defined. The *ESP8266WiFi* library is referenced by the *ESP8266WebServer* library, so does not need to be explicitly included in the sketch, similarly for the ESP32 microcontroller with *WebServer* and *WiFi* libraries. The *webcode* function returns a string, *page*, containing the web page HTML code with updated values of the temperature, counter, and LED state. There are no conditional statements in the HTML code, as in Chapter 7 (Wireless local area network), so the web page URL is mapped to the *webcode* function directly. A line-by-line build-up of the HTML code incorporates the variables *temp, counter,* and *LED*, which are not constant, so HTML code cannot be included as a *string literal*. Variable values in HTML code are enclosed in single quotes, as in the instruction "<meta http-equiv='refresh' content='9'>" with the HTML code enclosed in double quotes to indicate a string.

Listing 8-1. HTTP request with BMP280 and LED

```
#include <ESP8266WebServer.h>    // include ESP8266WebServer lib
ESP8266WebServer server;         // associate server with library
char ssid[] = "xxxx";            // change xxxx to Wi-Fi SSID
char password[] = "xxxx";        // change xxxx to Wi-Fi password
#include <Adafruit_Sensor.h>     // include Unified Sensor
#include <Adafruit_BMP280.h>     // and BMP280 libraries
Adafruit_BMP280 bmp;             // associate bmp with BMP280
int BMPaddress = 0x76;           // I2C address of BMP280
#include <Ticker.h>              // include Ticker library
Ticker timer;                    // associate timer with Ticker lib
int lag = 10;                    // set timer interval at 10s
int LEDpin = D3;                 // LED pin on D3
String LED = "off";              // initial LED state
int count = 0;
String temp, counter;

void setup()
{
  Serial.begin(115200);                      // Serial Monitor baud rate
  WiFi.begin(ssid, password);                // initialise Wi-Fi
  while (WiFi.status() != WL_CONNECTED) delay(500);
                                             // wait for Wi-Fi connect
  Serial.print("IP address: ");
  Serial.println(WiFi.localIP());            // display server IP address
  server.begin();
  server.on("/", webcode);                   // map URL to function
  bmp.begin(BMPaddress);                     // initialise BMP280
  timer.attach(lag, BMP);                    // BMP called every lag seconds
  pinMode(LEDpin, OUTPUT);
  digitalWrite(LEDpin, LOW);                 // turn off LED
}
```

```
void BMP()                                    // function to get readings
{
  temp = String(bmp.readTemperature());   // update BMP280 reading
  counter = String(count++);                // increment counter
  digitalWrite(LEDpin, !digitalRead(LEDpin));
                                            // turn on or off the LED
  if(LED == "on") LED = "off";              // update LED state
  else LED = "on";
  server.send (200, "text/html", webcode());
}                                           // send response to client
String webcode()                            // return HTML code
{
  String page;
  page = "<!DOCTYPE html><html><head>";     // refresh every 9s
  page += "<meta http-equiv='refresh' content='9'>";
  page += "<title>ESP8266</title></head>";
  page += "<body>";
  page += "<h2>BMP280</h2>";                // display temp
  page += "<p>Temperature: " + temp + " " + "&degC</p>";
  page += "<p>Counter: " + counter + "</p>";  // counter
  page += "<p>LED is " + LED + "<p>";         // LED state
  page += "</body></html>";
  return page;
}

void loop()
{
  server.handleClient();          // manage HTTP requests
}
```

The client HTTP request results in the server sending the HTML code for the whole web page with the whole web page then reloaded. The web page in Listing 8-1 is for example purposes only, but if the web page contained more information and images, then the time to reload the whole web page would be important.

Listing 8-1 is for an ESP8266 microcontroller. The only changes to the sketch for an ESP32 microcontroller are including the *WebServer* library, rather than the *ESP8266WebServer* library, and defining the LED pin. An alternative to microcontroller-specific sketch instructions is to use the compiler directive equivalent of an *if..then..else* group for conditional compilation of the sketch. Instructions for both the ESP8266 and ESP32 microcontrollers are included in the sketch. If the microcontroller is not an ESP8266 or ESP32, then an error message is displayed in the Arduino IDE. Further details are included in Chapter 21 (Microcontrollers). For example, Listing 8-2 contains the instructions to include at the start of Listing 8-1.

Listing 8-2. Pin definitions for ESP8266 and ESP32 development boards

```
#ifdef ESP32
  #include <WebServer.h>                // include ESP32 library
  WebServer server (80);                // and define LED pin
  int LEDpin = 23;
#elif ESP8266
  #include <ESP8266WebServer.h>         // include ESP8266 library
  ESP8266WebServer server;              // and define LED pin
  int LEDpin = D3;
#else                                   // Arduino IDE error message
  #error "ESP8266 or ESP32 microcontroller only"
#endif
```

XML HTTP requests, JavaScript, and AJAX

Chapter 7 (Wireless local area network) describes updating a specific variable on a web page with an XML HTTP request, rather than having to reload the whole web page. Converting the sketch in Listing 8-1 from HTML code to AJAX code does not require the *Ticker* library, so the following instructions are deleted

```
#include <Ticker.h>
Ticker timer
int lag = 10
timer.attach(lag, BMP)
```

as timing of web page updates is managed by AJAX code. The *BMP* function in Listing 8-1 is no longer required and is split into three functions, *tempFunct, countFunct,* and *LEDfunct,* to update the BMP280 temperature reading, increment the counter, and change the LED state. Each function sends updated information for one variable to the client. The *base* function replaces the *webcode* function, in Listing 8-1, and sends the default web page HTML code to the client when the web page is initially loaded. URLs are mapped to the four functions with the instructions

```
server.on("/", base);
server.on("/tempUrl", tempFunct);
server.on("/countUrl", countFunct);
server.on("/LEDurl", LEDfunct);
```

The sketch in Listing 8-3 lists the functions to source data and instruct the server to send the information to the client. Note that the parameters *"text/html"* and *page* are included in the *base* function for the server to return HTML code to the client, while the *tempFunct, countFunct,* and *LEDfunct* functions include *"text/plain"* and the variable name.

Listing 8-3. XML HTTP requests for the BMP280 temperature, counter, and LED state

```
void base()                        // function to load default webpage
{                                  // and send HTML code to client
  server.send (200, "text/html", page);
}

void tempFunct()                   // function to get temperature reading
{                                  // and send value to client
  temp = String(bmp.readTemperature());
  server.send (200, "text/plain", temp);
}                                  // send plain text not HTML code

void countFunct()                  // function to increment counter
{                                  // and send value to client
  counter = String(count++);
  server.send (200, "text/plain", counter);
}

void LEDfunct()                    // function to update LED
{                                  // and send LED state to client
  digitalWrite(LEDpin, !digitalRead(LEDpin));
  if(LED == "on") LED = "off";
  else LED = "on";
  server.send (200, "text/plain", LED);
}
```

Listing 8-4 contains the AJAX code for the web page and XML HTTP requests, defined as a *string literal*. The AJAX code is contained in the *buildpage.h* tab to separate the AJAX code from the main sketch with the instruction #include "buildpage.h". The additional tab is created in the Arduino IDE by selecting the triangle below the *Serial Monitor* button, on the right side of the IDE, and choosing *New Tab* from the drop-down menu. The *New Tab* is titled *buildpage.h*. Note that the *loop* function only includes the instruction server.handleClient().

The <body> section contains the web page HTML code; and the variables *tempId*, *countId*, and *LEDid* correspond to the XML HTTP requests. The JavaScript instruction setInterval(function, time) controls the time interval, in milliseconds, between the XML HTTP requests, which is five seconds for the *reload* function to obtain the temperature reading and one second for the counter and LED state. JavaScript scripts, bracketed by <script>...</script>, are positioned prior to the HTML </body> code to improve web page display speed.

The whole web page is no longer reloaded when the temperature or LED state is updated, as only specific variables are renewed. On the web browser, the *web page loading* indicator, located beside the web page title, is now absent.

Listing 8-4. AJAX request with BMP280 and LED

```
char page[] PROGMEM = R"(
<!DOCTYPE html><html>
<head><title>ESP8266</title></head>
<body>
<h2>BMP280</h2>
<p>Temperature: <span id = 'tempId'>0</span>&degC</p>
<p>Counter: <span id = 'countId'>0</span></p>
<p>LED is <span id = 'LEDid'> </span><p>

<script>
setInterval(reload, 5000);          // time in milliseconds
function reload()                    // reload function called every 5s
{                                    // to get tempId from tempUrl
   var xhr = new XMLHttpRequest();
```

```
  xhr.onreadystatechange = function()
  {
    if(this.readyState == 4 && this.status == 200)
    document.getElementById('tempId').innerHTML =
    this.responseText;
  };
  xhr.open('GET', 'tempUrl', true);
  xhr.send();
}

setInterval(LEDreload, 1000);
function LEDreload()              // LEDreload function called every 1s
{                                // to get countId from countUrl
  var xhr = new XMLHttpRequest();        // and LEDid from LEDurl
  xhr.onreadystatechange = function()
  {
    if(this.readyState == 4 && this.status == 200)
    document.getElementById('countId').innerHTML =
    this.responseText;
  };
  xhr.open('GET', 'countUrl', true);
  xhr.send();

  var xhr = new XMLHttpRequest();
  xhr.onreadystatechange = function()
  {
    if(this.readyState == 4 && this.status == 200)
    document.getElementById('LEDid').innerHTML =
    this.responseText;
  };
  xhr.open('GET', 'LEDurl', true);
  xhr.send();
}
```

```
</script>
</body></html>
)";
```

Each variable displayed on the web page is associated with an XML HTTP request, the URL associated with the variable, and a function to obtain the variable value. For consistency and to make the sketch more readily interpretable, a variable named *X* is referenced as *Xid* in the web page HTML code and XML HTTP request, and the URL is referenced as *Xurl* in both the *setup* function of the main sketch and the XML HTTP request, with the function sourcing the variable value referenced as *Xfunct* in the main sketch.

JSON

In Listing 8-3, each variable was associated with a specific function attached to a specific URL; and in Listing 8-4, each variable was updated by a separate XML HTTP request. For data collected simultaneously, it is more efficient to have one XML HTTP request for all variables and one function, attached to one URL, to source the information. JSON (JavaScript Object Notation) combines several variable values as text, which are sent by the server to the client. The client parses the JSON text to the component variables when updating the web page. JSON text consists of variable name and value pairs, each in double quotes and separated by a colon, with variable name and value pairs separated by a comma and the JSON text contained in curly brackets, {}. An example JSON text with three variable name and value pairs is {"device": "LED", "state": "off", "pin": "15"}.

In Listing 8-4, the counter and LED state are updated simultaneously, so two XML HTTP requests, two URLs, and two functions are combined. The combined URL, "*/countLEDurl*", and combined function, *countLEDfunct*, are defined by the instruction server.on("/countLEDurl", countLEDfunct) in the *setup* function of the main sketch. The *countLEDfunct* function in the main sketch consists of the instructions

```
void countLEDfunct()
{
  count++;                                  // increment count
  digitalWrite(LEDpin, !digitalRead(LEDpin));
                                            // turn on or off the LED
  if(LED == "on") LED = "off";             // update LED state
  else LED = "on";
  JsonConvert(count, LED);                 // convert to JSON text
  server.send (200, "text/json", json);   // send JSON text to client
}
```

The string *json* is defined in the main sketch, with the instruction String json. Note the server.send() instruction indicates that JSON text is being sent. The *JsonConvert* function, to combine the integer *count* and string *LED* into JSON text, consists of the instructions

```
String JsonConvert(int val1, String val2)
{
  json  = "{\"var1\": \"" + String(val1) + "\",";
  json += " \"var2\": \"" + val2          + "\"}";
  return json;
}
```

which produce the JSON text of {"var1": "123", "var2": "off"} when the counter, *val1*, is equal to *123* and the LED state, *val2*, is *off*. The character pair, \", which is underlined to emphasize that the characters are paired, is interpreted as a double quote character and not an end of a string indicator. The \ character is termed the *backslash escape character*.

The HTML code to display the counter and LED state is changed to

```
<p>Counter: <span id = 'var1'>0</span></p>
<p>LED is <span id = 'var2'> </span><p>
```

which references the JSON names of *var1* and *var2*. The JavaScript code to process the text sent by the server

```
document.getElementById('Xid').innerHTML = this.responseText
```

is changed to

```
var obj = JSON.parse(this.responseText);
document.getElementById('var1').innerHTML = obj.var1
document.getElementById('var2').innerHTML = obj.var2
```

which parses the JSON text into the two name and value pairs for the counter, *var1*, and LED state, *var2*.

Listing 8-5 contains the updated AJAX code for the web page by combining the two XML HTTP requests and two URLs for the counter and LED state in Listing 8-4 and parsing JSON text, with the updates highlighted in bold.

Listing 8-5. AJAX code with JSON parsing

```
char page[] PROGMEM = R"(
<!DOCTYPE html><html>
<head><title>ESP8266</title></head>
<body>
<h2>BMP280</h2>
<p>Temperature: <span id = tempId>0</span>&degC</p>
<p>Counter: <span id = 'var1'>0</span></p>
<p>LED is <span id = 'var2'> </span><p>

<script>
setInterval(reload, 5000);        // time in milliseconds
function reload()                  // update the temperature every 5s
{
```

```
  var xhr = new XMLHttpRequest();
  xhr.onreadystatechange = function()
  {
    if(this.readyState == 4 && this.status == 200)
    {document.getElementById('tempId').innerHTML = this.
    responseText;}
  };
  xhr.open('GET', '/tempUrl', true);
  xhr.send();
}

setInterval(countLEDreload, 1000);
function countLEDreload()          // update the counter and
{                                  // LED state every second
  var xhr = new XMLHttpRequest();
  xhr.onreadystatechange = function()
  {
    if(this.readyState == 4 && this.status == 200)
    {                              // parse JSON text
      var obj = JSON.parse(this.responseText);
      document.getElementById('var1').innerHTML = obj.var1;
      document.getElementById('var2').innerHTML = obj.var2;
    }
  };
  xhr.open('GET', '/countLEDurl', true);
  xhr.send();
}
</script>
</body></html>
)";
```

Accessing WWW data

Displaying, on a web page, data supplied by an ESP8266 or ESP32 microcontroller does not require access to the Internet, as a WLAN to connect the client with the server can be established by the microcontroller, acting as the server, as discussed in Chapter 7 (Wireless local area network). To demonstrate displaying data accessed from the World Wide Web, date and time information is accessed from the websites www.calendardate.com/todays.htm and 24timezones.com/Edinburgh/time, with temperature and humidity for Edinburgh, Scotland, accessed from the website www.metoffice.gov.uk.

Information is obtained with an API (Application Programming Interface) key, to retrieve data using HTTP requests, which is issued by *ThingSpeak* (www.thingspeak.com). Under the *ThingSpeak Apps* menu, the *ThingHTTP* option generates an API key to access a specific item on a given web page. For example, an API key to source the current time from the 24timezones.com/Edinburgh/time website is generated by right-clicking the displayed time and selecting *Inspect Element (Q)*. On the displayed *Web Console*, click the three dots and select *Dock to Right*. The HTML code corresponding to the selected time is highlighted in blue, and moving the cursor over the HTML code generates a box surrounding the selected item on the web page. Right-click the highlighted HTML code and select *Copy* and *XPath*. On the web page thingspeak.com/apps/thinghttp, select *New ThingHTTP*, and enter a name for the API and the URL of the web page containing the data, for example, 24timezones.com/Edinburgh/time, and in the *Parse String* box, paste the copied *XPath* and click *Save ThingHTTP*. An API key is generated by *ThingSpeak* to access the required information, which is tested by loading a web page with URL api.thingspeak.com/apps/thinghttp/send_request?api_key=API *key*.

If the *ThingSpeak* API key returns the message *"Error parsing document, try a different parse string,"* then an alternative data source on the web page or a linked web page is required.

Information obtained with a *ThingSpeak* API key will require parsing. For example, date and time information is generated as *<p>Today's Date is Monday June 15, 2020</p>* and *6:05:34 PM, Monday 15, June 2020*, respectively, while temperature and humidity are provided in HTML code as *<div data-value="14.66">15°</div>* and *<span class="humidity" data-type="percentage" data-value="90">90%</span>*, respectively. The *date* substring is generated as the text following the text *is*. The *time* substring is text prior to the comma. Both the *temperature* and *humidity* substrings are bracketed by the = and > characters. The *toInt* and *toFloat* functions extract an integer and a real number, respectively, from a string, provided the first character of the string is a digit.

The sketch in Listing 8-6 accesses the current date, time, temperature, and humidity with *ThingSpeak* API keys and parses the information into a JSON string for inclusion in the server response to the client HTTP request. Note that the web page updates at 30 second intervals, so the initial values are all zero.

Listing 8-6. Parsing data accessed with ThingSpeak API keys

```
#include <ESP8266WebServer.h> // include web server library
ESP8266WebServer server;        // associate server with library
WiFiClient client;              // associate client with Wi-Fi library
#include "buildpage.h"          // webpage AJAX code
char ssid[] = "xxxx";           // change xxxx to  your Wi-Fi SSID
char password[] = "xxxx";       // change xxxx to your Wi-Fi password
char APItime[] = "xxxx";
char APIdate[] = "xxxx";         // change xxxx to ThingSpeak API key
char APItemp[] = "xxxx";
char APIhumid[] = "xxxx";
char url[] = "/apps/thinghttp/send_request?api_key=";
char host[] = "api.thingspeak.com";
int indexS, indexF, chk, humid;
float temp;
String data, ndata, text, json, mdy, tim;
```

```
void setup()
{
  Serial.begin(115200);                 // Serial Monitor baud rate
  WiFi.begin(ssid, password);           // connect and initialise Wi-Fi
  while (WiFi.status() != WL_CONNECTED) delay(500);
  Serial.print("IP address: ");
  Serial.println(WiFi.localIP());       // display server IP address
  server.begin();                       // initialise server
  server.on("/", base);                 // load default webpage
  server.on("/API", APIfunct);
}

void APIfunct()
{
  getData(APIdate, "date");             // call function to access date
  getData(APItime, "time");             // time
  getData(APItemp, "temp");             // temperature
  getData(APIhumid, "humid");           // humidity
  JsonConvert(mdy, tim, temp, humid);   // convert to JSON text
  server.send (200, "text/json", json);
}

String JsonConvert(String val1, String val2, float val3, int val4)
{
  json  = "{\"var1\": \"" + val1          + "\","; // start with {
  json += " \"var2\": \"" + val2          + "\",";
                                          // end with comma
  json += " \"var3\": \"" + String(val3) + "\",";
  json += " \"var4\": \"" + String(val4) + "\"}"; // end with }
  return json;
}
```

```
void getData(String APIkey, String text)   // function to access data
{
  for (int i=0; i<5; i++)          // with up to five attempts
  {
    getVal(APIkey, text);          // call function to get information
    if(chk > 0) i = 5;             // data accessed successfully
  }
}

void getVal(String APIkey, String text)
{                                  // function to access information
  chk = 0;
  Serial.print("sourcing ");Serial.println(text);
  client.connect(host, 80);
  client.println(String("GET ") + url + APIkey);
  client.println(String("Host: ") + host);
  client.println("User-Agent: ESP8266/0.1");
  client.println("Connection: close");
  client.println();
  client.flush();
  delay(100);
  while(client.connected())        // while connected to ThingSpeak
  {
    if(client.available())         // if data is available
    {                              // read data till end of line
      data = client.readStringUntil('\n');
      Serial.println(data);
      if(text == "humid")          // parse humidity data
      {
        indexS = data.lastIndexOf("="); // position of last "=" in string
        indexF = data.indexOf("%");
        ndata = data.substring(indexS+2, indexF-2);
```

```
      humid = ndata.toInt();
      chk = data.length();
    }
    else if(text == "temp")            // parse temperature data
    {
      indexS = data.indexOf("=");    // position of first "=" in string
      ndata = data.substring(indexS+2);
      temp = ndata.toFloat();
      chk = data.length();
    }
    else if(text == "date")            // date: day month dd, yyyy
    {
      indexS = data.indexOf("is");
      mdy = data.substring(indexS+2);
      chk = data.length();
    }
    else if(text == "time")            // time: hh:mm:ss AM or PM
    {
      indexF = data.indexOf(",");
      tim = data.substring(0, indexF);
      chk = data.length();
    }
    client.stop();                // close connection after data collected
    delay(100);
  }
 }
}
void base()                        // function to return HTML code
{
  server.send (200, "text/html", page);
}
```

```
void loop()
{
  server.handleClient();        // handle HTTP requests
}
```

The parsed information is displayed on a web page at 30-second intervals (see Listing 8-7), for example purposes only as weather doesn't generally change that fast. Different time intervals can be selected for the date, time, and weather parameters by defining separate *reload* functions with appropriate time intervals.

Listing 8-7. AJAX code with JSON parsing

```
char page[] PROGMEM = R"(
<!DOCTYPE html><html>
<head><title>ESP8266</title></head>
<body>
<h2>BMP280</h2>
<p>Date: <span id = 'var1'>00 000 0000</span></p>
<p>Time1: <span id = 'var2'>00:00:00</span></p>
<p>Temp is <span id = 'var3'>0</span>&degC<p>
<p>Humidity is <span id = 'var4'>0</span>%<p>

<script>
setInterval(APIreload, 30000);            // time in milliseconds
function APIreload()
{
  var xhr = new XMLHttpRequest();
  xhr.onreadystatechange = function()
  {
    if(this.readyState == 4 && this.status == 200)
    {
      var obj = JSON.parse(this.responseText);
      document.getElementById('var1').innerHTML = obj.var1;
```

```
        document.getElementById('var2').innerHTML = obj.var2;
        document.getElementById('var3').innerHTML = obj.var3;
        document.getElementById('var4').innerHTML = obj.var4;
      }
    };
    xhr.open('GET', 'API', true);
    xhr.send();
}
</script>
</body></html>
)";
```

MQTT broker and IFTTT

Communication between devices on different Wi-Fi networks requires a different solution than communication between devices within a Wi-Fi network. The MQTT (Message Queuing Telemetry Transport) protocol enables communication between devices and an MQTT broker to pass information between it and one device and between it and a second device, with the two devices on different Wi-Fi networks. The MQTT broker enables data transfer between devices without breaching firewall safeguards. When a device on one Wi-Fi network requests information from a second device on another network, the information is allowed through the network firewall, as the request came from the Wi-Fi network. Provision of information to the MQTT broker is termed *publish,* and *subscribe* is the term to access information from the MQTT broker. There are several MQTT brokers, and the Cayenne MQTT broker is used in this chapter.

Cayenne (see mydevices.com/cayenne/features) provides a dashboard to display information from devices connected to an ESP8266 or ESP32 microcontroller (see Figure 8-4). The Cayenne dashboard is visible locally or remotely on `cayenne.mydevices.com/cayenne/dashboard/start`. Information from devices is displayed numerically, as a dial, or graphically, with binary variables displayed as *ON/OFF*. A device is turned on or off from the Cayenne dashboard, which provides both local and remote access to a device.

Figure 8-4. *Cayenne dashboard*

An *IFTTT* (If This, Then That) function enables event triggering based on sensors connected to an ESP8266 or ESP32 development board and visible on the Cayenne dashboard. For example, if the incident light on a light-dependent resistor (LDR) increases above a threshold due to a door opening or time of day, then an *IFTTT* instruction is sent to the Cayenne MQTT broker to forward an email or text message to the email address or mobile phone number stored on the Cayenne dashboard.

Details about Cayenne are accessed at `mydevices.com/cayenne/docs/intro`, and the *CayenneMQTT* library is available in the Arduino IDE. Communication between the ESP8266 or ESP32 microcontroller and Cayenne MQTT is through virtual channels, which are arbitrarily numbered V0, V1, V2, and so on. The instruction to send data to the

Cayenne dashboard is `Cayenne.virtualWrite(virtual channel, variable, type code, unit code)` where the *type* and *unit* codes define attributes of the variable. Several *type* and *unit* codes are given in Table 8-2, with a complete list in the library file *CayenneMQTT>src>Caye nneUtils>CayenneTypes.h*. For example, if the variable *light* is a measure of luminosity in lux, then the instruction to send the value of *light* to the Cayenne dashboard on virtual channel *V3* is `Cayenne.virtualWrite(V3, light, "lum", "lux")`.

Table 8-2. *Variable type names and codes*

Description	Type Name	Type Code
Barometric pressure	TYPE_BAROMETRIC_PRESSURE	"bp"
Proximity	TYPE_PROXIMITY	"prox"
Luminosity	TYPE_LUMINOSITY	"lum"
Relative humidity	TYPE_RELATIVE_HUMIDITY	"rel_hum"
Temperature	TYPE_TEMPERATURE	"temp"
Description	**Unit Name**	**Unit Code**
Hectopascal	UNIT_HECTOPASCAL	"hpa"
Meter	UNIT_METER	"m"
Lux	UNIT_LUX	"lux"
Fahrenheit	UNIT_FAHRENHEIT	"f"
Celsius	UNIT_CELSIUS	"c"

Including *type* and *unit* codes in the `Cayenne.virtualWrite()` instruction automatically configures the Cayenne dashboard with the variable description, relevant icon, and unit of measurement. Note that `Cayenne.virtualWrite()` instructions are limited to 60 per minute, so Listing 8-8 has a ten-second interval between the MQTT messages.

The instruction to read an integer variable on virtual channel 3 in the Cayenne dashboard is

```
CAYENNE_IN(3)                          // define virtual channel number 3
{
  int variable = getValue.asInt();  // read value of integer variable
}
```

The functions `getValue.asDouble()` and `getValue.asString()` read a real number and a string, respectively, with the channel number not preceded by *V*, as in the `Cayenne.virtualWrite()` instruction.

Information on declaring devices or variables, such as LED state or an LDR reading, on the Cayenne dashboard is available at `mydevices.com/cayenne/docs/features/#features-dashboard`.

An ESP8266 or ESP32 microcontroller is added as a Cayenne dashboard device by

1. Selecting *Add new* at the top left side of the dashboard

2. Selecting *Device/Widget* and selecting *Microcontrollers* ➤ *Generic ESP8266* or selecting *Bring Your Own Thing* for an ESP8266 or ESP32 microcontroller, respectively

The corresponding MQTT username and password, Client ID, MQTT server, and port details are generated by the Cayenne MQTT broker. Copy the MQTT username and password and the Client ID to the sketch; then compile and upload the sketch. The ESP8266 or ESP32 microcontroller will then connect to the Cayenne MQTT broker. Adding a device name in Cayenne differentiates between ESP8266 and ESP32 microcontrollers.

Cayenne dashboard widgets are defined by

1. Selecting *Add new* at the top left side of the dashboard

2. Selecting *Device/Widget*, selecting *Custom Widgets*, and selecting *Button (Controller widget)*

3. Entering the chosen widget name, such as LED

4. Entering the device name, such as *ESP32-A* or *ESP8266-project1*

5. Selecting *Data ➤ Digital Actuator* and selecting *Unit ➤ Digital (0/1)*

6. Selecting the virtual channel number to correspond with the sketch

7. Choosing an icon and selecting *Add Widget*

Figure 8-5 shows examples of defining a controller widget, *LED*, linked to virtual channel 0 and formatting the count variable on virtual channel 6 to be displayed as a gauge on the Cayenne dashboard.

Figure 8-5. *Cayenne variables and devices*

Listing 8-8 displays on a Cayenne dashboard or app (see Figure 8-4) temperature and pressure measurements from a BMP280 sensor, ambient light using a light-dependent resistor, and a counter. In the series of Cayenne.virtualWrite instructions, the virtual channel *V2* is not used to avoid confusion with GPIO 2 for the *flashPin* variable. Variable headings are defined with the variable settings option in the Cayenne dashboard, and graphical displays are also selected for each variable. A controller widget on virtual channel 0 is created in the Cayenne dashboard, with the binary widget value from the *CAYENNE_IN(0)* function used to turn on or off the LED attached to the ESP8266 development board.

Listing 8-8. Cayenne and ESP8266 with LED, LDR, and BMP820 sensor

```
#include <CayenneMQTTESP8266.h>      // Cayenne MQTT library
char ssid[] = "xxxx";                 // change xxxx to your Wi-Fi ssid
char password[] = "xxxx";   // change xxxx to Wi-Fi password
char username[] = "xxxx";   // change xxxx to Cayenne username
char mqttpass[] = "xxxx";   // change xxxx to Cayenne password
char clientID[] = "xxxx";   // change xxxx to Cayenne client identity
#include <Adafruit_Sensor.h>      // include Adafruit_Sensor library
#include <Adafruit_BMP280.h>      // include Adafruit_BMP280 library
Adafruit_BMP280 bmp;              // bmp with BMP280 library
int LEDpin = D3;                  // LED pin
int LDRpin = A0;                  // light dependent resistor pin
int flashPin = D4;                // flashing LED pin
unsigned long count = 0;
int interval = 10000;         // 10s interval between MQTT messages
unsigned long lastTime = 0;
float temp, pressure, BasePressure, altitude;
int light;

void setup()
{
  bmp.begin(0x76);                       // initiate bmp with I2C address
                                         // initiate Cayenne MQTT
  Cayenne.begin(username, mqttpass, clientID, ssid, password);
  pinMode(LEDpin, OUTPUT);               // define LED pins as output
  digitalWrite(LEDpin, LOW);
  pinMode(flashPin, OUTPUT);
}

void loop()
```

```
{
  Cayenne.loop();                          // Cayenne loop function
  if(millis()-lastTime > interval)
  {
    temp = bmp.readTemperature();          // BMP280 temperature
    pressure = bmp.readPressure()/100.0;   // and pressure
    BasePressure = pressure + 10.0;        // assumed sea level pressure
    altitude = bmp.readAltitude(BasePressure);
                                           // predicted altitude (m)
    light = analogRead(LDRpin);            // ambient light intensity
    light = constrain(light, 0, 1023);     // constrain light reading
    count++;                               // increment counter
    if(count>99) count = 0;
    digitalWrite(flashPin, LOW);           // turn on then off flashing LED
    delay(10);
    digitalWrite(flashPin, HIGH);
                         // send readings to Cayenne on virtual channels
    Cayenne.virtualWrite(V1, temp, "temp", "c");
                                           // temperature reading
    Cayenne.virtualWrite(V3, pressure, "bp", "pa");   // pressure
    Cayenne.virtualWrite(V4, altitude, "prox", "m");  // altitude
    Cayenne.virtualWrite(V5, light, "lum", "lux");    // luminosity
    Cayenne.virtualWrite(V6, count,"prox","");        // counter
    lastTime=millis();                     // update time
  }
}

CAYENNE_IN(0)                              // Cayenne virtual channel 0
{
  digitalWrite(LEDpin, getValue.asInt());  // turn on or off LED
}
```

Listing 8-9 uses the Cayenne MQTT functionality to mimic an alarm system, which is triggered by the light intensity reading on a light-dependent resistor, such as when a door is opened. If the light intensity increases above a threshold of 500 and the alarm on the Cayenne dashboard is set to *ON*, an email and/or text is sent to notify that the event has occurred. If the alarm setting is set to *OFF*, then there is no response to changes in light intensity. The ESP8266 or ESP32 development board LED is flashed every two seconds to indicate that the microcontroller is powered on.

If the alarm setting is set to *ON*, then the light intensity reading is sent to the Cayenne MQTT broker on virtual channel 1, but with a value of zero if the alarm is set to *OFF*. Alarm and LED controller widgets on virtual channels 3 and 0 are created on the Cayenne dashboard to turn on or off the alarm and to provide an indicator that the alarm has been triggered. Attached to the ESP8266 or ESP32 development board are a blue (*alarmPin*) and a red (*LEDpin*) LED to correspondingly indicate the alarm state and that the alarm has been triggered. The two LEDs are turned on or off with the *CAYENNE_IN(3)* and *CAYENNE_IN(0)* functions. Triggers for the LED widget and for email and text notification, based on the alarm widget, are defined in the Cayenne dashboard *IFTTT* function. Figure 8-6 shows the Cayenne dashboard with the alarm set to *ON* and a light intensity reading of 268, which is below the threshold to trigger the alarm and turn on the indicator LED widget. Figure 8-7 shows the schematic with connections in Table 8-3.

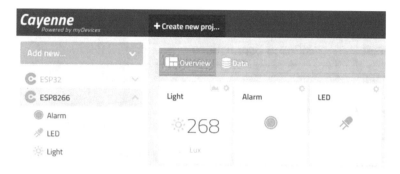

Figure 8-6. *Alarm, LED, and light intensity*

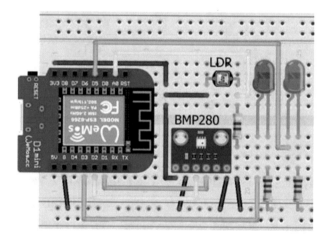

Figure 8-7. *Alarm, LED, and light intensity with LOLIN (WeMos) D1 mini*

Table 8-3. *Alarm, LED, and light intensity*

Component	ESP8266 Connections		ESP32 Connections	
BMP280 VCC	3V3		3V3	
BMP280 GND	GND		GND	
BMP280 SDA	D2		GPIO 21	
BMP280 SCK	D1		GPIO 22	
BMP280 SDO	GND		GND	
LDR left	3V3		3V3	
LDR right	4.7 kΩ resistor	GND	4.7 kΩ resistor	GND
LDR right	A0		GPIO 36	
LED long legs	D3, D5		GPIO 23	
LED short legs	220 Ω resistor	GND	220 Ω resistor	GND

Listing 8-9. Alarm, LED, and light intensity

```
#include <CayenneMQTTESP8266.h>  // Cayenne MQTT library
char ssid[] = "xxxx";            // change xxxx to your Wi-Fi ssid
char password[] = "xxxx";        // change xxxx to your Wi-Fi password
char username[] = "xxxx";        // change xxxx to Cayenne username
char mqttpass[] = "xxxx";        // change xxxx to Cayenne password
char clientID[] = "xxxx";        // change xxxx to Cayenne client identity
int LEDpin = D3;
int alarmPin = D5;               // define LED, alarm and LDR pins
int LDRpin = A0;
int flashPin = D4;               // flashing LED
int reading, alarm, alert;
int interval = 2000;             // 2s interval between LDR readings
unsigned long LDRtime = 0;
```

```
void setup()
{
  Cayenne.begin(username, mqttpass, clientID, ssid, password);
  pinMode(LEDpin, OUTPUT);              // define LED pins as output
  pinMode(alarmPin, OUTPUT);
  pinMode(flashPin, OUTPUT);
  alarm = 0;                            // set alarm to OFF
}

void loop()
{
  Cayenne.loop();                       // Cayenne loop function
  if(millis() - LDRtime > interval)
  {
    LDRtime = millis();
    reading = analogRead(LDRpin);
    if (alarm == 1) Cayenne.virtualWrite(V1, reading, "lum", "lux");
    else Cayenne.virtualWrite(V1, 0, "lum", "lux");
    digitalWrite(flashPin, LOW);
    delay(10);                          // flash LED to indicate power on
    digitalWrite(flashPin, HIGH);
  }
}

CAYENNE_IN(0)                           // Cayenne virtual channel 0
{
  alert = getValue.asInt();             // get alarm triggered status
  digitalWrite(LEDpin, alert);          // update alarm triggered LED
}
```

```
CAYENNE_IN(3)                          // Cayenne virtual channel 3
{
  alarm = getValue.asInt();            // get alarm set state
  digitalWrite(alarmPin, alarm);       // update alarm set indicator LED
}
```

The *IFTTT* (If This, Then That) function to trigger an event on the Cayenne dashboard is defined on the Cayenne dashboard and not in the sketch. Information on the *IFTTT* features of the Cayenne dashboard is available at mydevices.com/cayenne/docs/features/#features-triggers. Three *IFTTT* triggers are required by the alarm system. When the light intensity increases above a threshold of 500, with the alarm widget set to *ON*, the email and text notification of the event is triggered, and a second trigger turns on the LED widget, on virtual channel 0, to indicate that the alarm has been triggered. The third *IFTTT* trigger turns off the alarm widget, on virtual channel 3, which indicates that the alarm is now set to *OFF*. The LEDs attached to the ESP8266 or ESP32 development board are turned on or off depending on the values of the alarm and LED widgets on the Cayenne dashboard.

Cayenne *IFTTT* triggers are accessed by

1. Selecting *User Menu* ➤ *Triggers and Alerts* at the top right side of the dashboard

2. Selecting *Trigger* and naming the trigger, such as *LEDon*

3. Dragging the device, *ESP8266*, into the *if* box

4. Selecting the trigger, such as *light*, and selecting the *threshold* and *Sensor above* or *Sensor below*

5. Dragging the device, *ESP8266*, into the *then* box

6. Selecting the action, such as *LED* in Figure 8-8, and selecting either *On(1)* or *Off (0)*

7. *Selecting Save*

When sending a notification as a text message, include the mobile phone number plus the +country code in the *Add custom recipient* box.

Figure 8-8. *Cayenne IFTTT trigger*

Figures 8-8 illustrates the *IFTTT* trigger to turn on the LED widget, on virtual channel 0, when the light intensity, on virtual channel 1, exceeds the threshold of 500. The second and third *IFTTT* triggers send the email/text notification and turn off the alarm widget, on virtual channel 3, when the LED widget is turned on. Figure 8-9 illustrates the corresponding email notification triggered by *IFTTT*.

Hi Neil Cameron,
Your mqtt sensors need your attention.

Device Notification

Channel 1

has reached the threshold value of

500

This is connected to ESP8266.

Cayenne Dashboard

Figure 8-9. *Cayenne IFTTT notification*

Listings 8-8 and 8-9 include the library for an ESP8266 microcontroller. The library for an ESP32 microcontroller is accessed with the instruction #include <CayenneMQTTESP32.h>, which is included in the *CayenneMQTT* library. No changes, other than pin numbers for attached sensors, are required for the sketches with an ESP32 microcontroller.

Parsing text

Parsing text is often required, such as data from the Serial buffer or data uploaded following an HTTP request. The instruction Serial.read() reads the next available character in the Serial buffer, while the instruction Serial.readStringUntil('\n') reads all the data in the Serial buffer until end-of-line character. The content of the Serial buffer is stored as a string, str, with the instruction str = Serial.readString() and parsed into an integer or a real number with the instruction `Serial.parseInt()` or `Serial.parseFloat()`. For example, if the Serial buffer contains the text *abc25* or *abc3.14*, then parsing returns the integer 25 or the real number 3.14, respectively. Parsing ignores the initial non-digit characters, other than a decimal point or a minus sign, and stops when a non-digit character is read after the last digit character. Parsing instructions are repeated to extract more than one number from the Serial buffer. For example, if the Serial buffer contains *abc-25de3.14*, then the integer -25 and the real number 3.14 are returned with the instructions

```
if(Serial.available()>0)
{
  x = Serial.parseInt();
  y = Serial.parseFloat();
}
```

The *parseInt* and *parseFloat* functions are blocking functions, which prevent the microcontroller from processing other instructions until parsing is completed.

Strings are parsed to integers or real numbers with the instructions `toInt()` or `toFloat()`, respectively, provided the first character of the string is a digit, a decimal point, or a minus sign. For example, if a string *str* equals *-25abc* or *3.14abc*, then the instructions `str.toInt()` or `str.toFloat()` return the integer -25 or the real number 3.14, respectively. Parsing stops when a non-digit character is read after a digit character or a decimal point. Note that a real number is stored with a total number of six or seven digits, so converting the string *2.7182818284* to a real number results in a value of *2.718282*.

A string that does not start with a digit character is parsed by extracting a substring that does start with a digit character, a decimal point, or a minus sign. For a string `str`, the instruction `str.substring(x, y)` creates the substring between positions *x* (inclusive) and *y* (exclusive). For example, comma positions of the string `str = "abc,def,gh"` are 4 and 8, so the instruction `str.substring(4+1, 8)` creates the substring *def* with characters 5, 6, and 7 of the string. If the end parameter is omitted, as in the instruction `str.substring(x)`, then the substring extends to the end of the string. For example, the instruction `str.substring(5)` creates the substring *def,gh*.

The instructions `str.indexOf("x")` and `str.indexOf("x", y)` locate the position of the substring *x* within the string, by searching from the first to the last character or from position *y* to the last character. Similarly, the instructions `str.lastIndexOf("x")` and `str.lastIndexOf("x", y)` locate the position of the substring *x* within the string by searching from the last to the first character or from position *y* to the first character. The *indexOf* and *lastIndexOf* functions are combined with the *substring* function to create a specific substring of a string, when there are several substring delimiters in a string.

For example, the decimal humidity value contained in the string str = *<span class="humidity" data-value="68.1">68%</span>* is bracketed by an = character and a > character, but there are two of each character in the string. The *toFloat* function cannot extract the humidity value, as the first character of the string is not a digit, so a substring is created to extract the decimal value, but not the integer value. The instructions indexS = `str.lastIndexOf("=")` and indexF = `str.indexOf("%")` locate positions of the last = character and the % character, with the substring defined by the instruction `str.substring(indexS+2, indexF-2)` containing the characters *68.1">*, from which the decimal value is extracted with the *toFloat* function.

The instruction `str.length()` determines the length of the string, which does not include the null terminating character, \n, and the string length is used to ensure that a substring position does not exceed the length of the string. To check if a string, *str*, starts or ends with a substring, *abc*, the instructions `str.startsWith("abc")` and `str.endsWith("abc")` return a value one if true or value zero if false.

Console log

When debugging a sketch or checking the progress of a sketch, information on a variable is displayed on the Serial Monitor with the `Serial.print("text")` instruction. The equivalent to displaying information on the Serial Monitor for a web browser is the console log, when using JavaScript code, to display the value of a variable or text, such as "*button pressed.*" The console log is accessed in the browser by pressing the *F12* keyboard key and selecting *Console* and *Logs* (see Figure 8-10). To define the character set for the console log, the instruction `<meta charset='UTF-8'>` must be included in the `<head>` section of the web page HTML code. The instruction `console.log(variable)` displays information on the console log, where *variable* can equal a variable, some text, or the server response to the client. For example, in Listing 8-5, the instruction `console.log(this.responseText)` is included after `document.getElementById('tempId').innerHTML = this.responseText` and the instructions

```
console.log("LED updated");
console.log(this.responseText);
console.log(obj.var1);
var value = document.getElementById('var2').innerHTML;
console.log(value);
```

are included after the instruction `document.getElementById('var2').innerHTML = obj.var2`. To generate repeated temperature readings, the *reload* function interval was reduced to one second, and the *countLEDreload* function interval for the counter and LED was increased to five seconds. The console log produced the output in Figure 8-10, showing the five temperature readings, the text "*LED updated,*" the JSON text received by the client, the counter, and the LED state defined as a new variable, *value.*

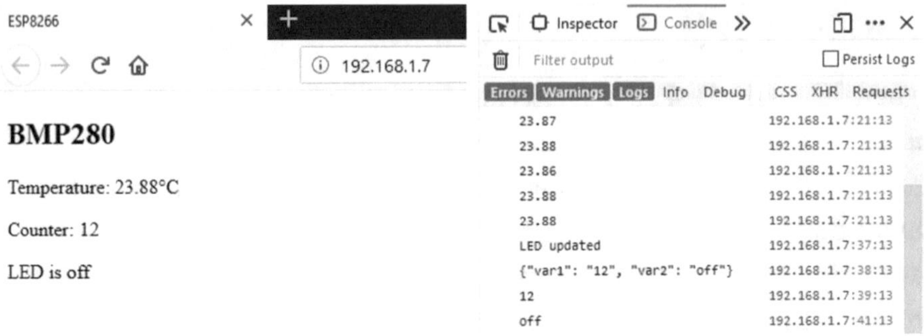

Figure 8-10. *Console log*

Wi-Fi connection

The ESP8266 and ESP32 libraries are automatically installed when the *esp8266* by *ESP8266 Community* and *esp32* by *Espressif Systems* are installed in the Arduino IDE Boards Manager. Library versions 2.7.4 and 1.0.4 were used in this chapter. If the error message "*Downloading* `http://downloads.arduino.cc/packages/packages_index.json`" is displayed in the Arduino IDE Boards Manager, then delete all *.tmp* files in *user* ➤ *AppData* ➤ *Local* ➤ *Arduino15* folder and restart the Arduino IDE.

The Wi-Fi connection between the ESP8266 or ESP32 microcontroller and the WLAN router is tested using the *ping* command given the ESP8266 or ESP32 IP address. Either right-click the *Windows logo* at the bottom-left side of the screen and select *Run* or press the *Windows* key and *R* key, simultaneously, to open the Command window. Type *cmd* and click *OK*. In the *C:\\WINDOWS\system32\cmd.exe* window, the *Command prompt* window, type *ping* followed by the ESP8266 or ESP32 IP address, as shown in Figure 8-11. The *ping* command sends small data packets to the ESP8266 or ESP32 IP address that are transmitted back to the sender. In the example, four data packets were sent and received, which indicated that the Data Link, the Wi-Fi connection, and the Internet Protocol were functioning correctly.

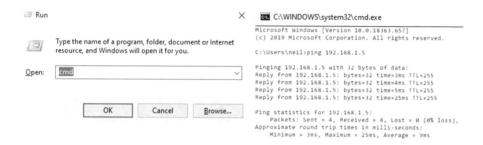

Figure 8-11. *Wi-Fi connection test*

Access information file

Access to a Wi-Fi network, ThingSpeak data (see Listing 8-6), or a MQTT broker (see Listing 8-8) requires a password, an SSID, an API key, or MQTT broker keys. Instead of storing the access information in the sketch with instructions like char mqttpass[] = "abcdef", the information is stored in a library that is referenced by the sketch. A text file with the extension .*h* is created to hold the access information, with the file placed in the Arduino IDE libraries folder. To determine the location of the Arduino IDE libraries folder, select *File* ➤ *Preferences* in the Arduino IDE; and the libraries folder is shown in the sketchbook location, for example, *C:\Users\user\Documents\ Arduino*. The access information file is referenced by the sketch with the instruction #include <access_info.h>. An example access information file, in Listing 8-10, includes the access keys for Wi-Fi, ThingSpeak, and Cayenne.

Listing 8-10. Access information

```
char ssid[] = "PhoneNetwork12";        // Wi-Fi access
char password[] = "diff1cu1t";
char APItime[] = "efth1234";
char APIdate[] = "mhtd5678";           // ThingSpeak API keys
char APItemp[] = "plmf4567";
char APIhumid[] = "thkl6789";
```

221

```
char username[] = "ABC-234";          // Cayenne access
char mqttpass[] = "XYZ-567";
char clientID[] = "GHJ-876";
```

Summary

A web page displayed the temperature reading from a BMP280 module, a counter, and the state of an LED, with the ESP8266 or ESP32 microcontroller functioning as the server. The web page HTML code was built line-by-line as a string, and the whole web page was reloaded to display the updated information. AJAX code, consisting of XML HTTP requests and JavaScript instructions, incorporated as a *string literal*, enabled updating the web page with only specific variables, rather than reloading the whole web page. Data on several variables was combined as JSON text in the server response to the client HTTP request, and options for parsing text were described. Information from the World Wide Web was accessed with API keys and displayed on a web page using both AJAX and JSON code. Access to an MQTT broker allowed uploading of sensor data to a web page, with a sensor value above a threshold triggering an email or text message notification of the event. The console log verified data sent by the server and received by the client.

Components List

- ESP8266 microcontroller: LOLIN (WeMos) D1 mini or NodeMCU board

- ESP32 microcontroller: ESP32 DEVKIT DOIT or NodeMCU board

- BMP280 module

- LED: 2×

- Resistor: 2× 220 Ω

CHAPTER 9

WebSocket

The WebSocket protocol (`www.websocket.org`) allows a two-way real-time conversation between the web server and client, through a standardized connection to allow both the server and the client to send data at any time. The client sends a request to the server to switch from an HTTP protocol to a WebSocket protocol; and if the server can host the WebSocket protocol, the HTTP connection is replaced with a WebSocket connection, but using the same port as HTTP.

An example of the WebSocket protocol is transmitting and receiving text in a conversation between the web server and the client (see Figure 9-1). To transmit to the server, text is entered in the web page *transmit text* box, and the *send text* button is clicked. The transmitted text is then displayed on the Serial Monitor connected to the server. Conversely, when text is entered on the Serial Monitor, followed by the computer or laptop keyboard *<Enter>* key, the text received by the client is displayed in the web page *receive text* box. Clicking the web page *receive text* box clears the text received from the server. Both the *transmit text* and *receive text* boxes are increased in size by dragging the bottom-right corner of a box.

© Neil Cameron 2021
N. Cameron, *Electronics Projects with the ESP8266 and ESP32*,
https://doi.org/10.1007/978-1-4842-6336-5_9

Websocket

transmit text	receive text (click to clear)
Sent message by client	received message from server

send text

Figure 9-1. *WebSocket web page*

The *WebSocketsServer* library, listed under *WebSockets*, by Markus Sattler is available in the Arduino IDE. The WebSocket is connected on port 81, as the default HTTP COM port is 80, and the *wsEvent* function displays the received message from the client. Listing 9-1 contains the sketch for the transmit and receive text example. The `Serial.write()` instruction converts ASCII code for an alphanumeric character to display the alphanumeric character, while `Serial.print()` displays the ASCII (American Standard Code for Information Interchange) code. The *loop* function in Listing 9-1 still includes the `server.handleClient()` instruction to manage HTTP requests, but when text is transmitted by the server to the client, the instruction `websocket.broadcastTXT` `(str.c_str(), str.length())` sends the content of the Serial buffer to the client. The text string is converted to a C-style, null-terminated string with the instruction `string.c_str()`. The *base* function sends the default web page AJAX code to the client, when the web page is initially loaded.

In this chapter, an ESP8266 or an ESP32 microcontroller is the server. The web server library instructions for the ESP8266 microcontroller are

```
#include <ESP8266WebServer.h>
ESP8266WebServer server
```

and for the ESP32 microcontroller are

```
#include <WebServer.h>
WebServer server(80);          // requires a port number
```

The web server library references the Wi-Fi library, so the #include <ESP8266WiFi.h> or #include <WiFi.h> instructions are not required.

Listing 9-1. WebSocket main sketch

```
#include <ESP8266WebServer.h>          // include web server library
ESP8266WebServer server;               // associate server with library
#include <WebSocketsServer.h>          // include WebSocket library
WebSocketsServer websocket = WebSocketsServer(81);
                                       // set WebSocket port 81
#include "buildpage.h"                 // webpage AJAX code
char ssid[] = "xxxx";                  // change xxxx to Wi-Fi SSID
char password[] = "xxxx";              // change xxxx to Wi-Fi password
String str;

void setup()
{
  Serial.begin(115200);               // Serial Monitor baud rate
  WiFi.begin(ssid, password);         // connect and initialise Wi-Fi
  while (WiFi.status() != WL_CONNECTED) delay(500);
  Serial.print("IP address: ");
  Serial.println(WiFi.localIP());     // display web server IP address
  server.begin();
  server.on("/", base);               // load default webpage
  websocket.begin();                  // initialise WebSocket
  websocket.onEvent(wsEvent);         // call wsEvent function
}                                     // on WebSocket event

void wsEvent(uint8_t num, WStype_t type, uint8_t * message,
size_t length)
{
```

```
  if(type == WStype_TEXT)              // when text received from client
  {                                    // display text on Serial Monitor
    for(int i=0; i<length; i++) Serial.write(message[i]);
    Serial.println();
  }
}

void loop()
{
  server.handleClient();               // manage HTTP requests
  websocket.loop();                    // handle WebSocket data
  if(Serial.available() > 0)
  {                                    // read text in Serial buffer
    str = Serial.readString();         // and send to client
    websocket.broadcastTXT(str.c_str(), str.length());
  }
}

void base()                            // function to return HTML code
{
  server.send (200, "text/html", page);
}
```

Implementation of the WebSocket protocol is contained in the JavaScript section of Listing 9-2, which includes the web page AJAX code. When the web page is loaded, a table with headers is created to display the received and transmitted text, and the *init* function is called to open the WebSocket connection at *ws://web server IP address:81/*. When the client transmits a message to the server, the instruction send(document.getElementById('txText').value) in the *sendText* function sends the content of the variable *txText*, which is then cleared. When the client receives a message from the server, the message content is stored in the variable *rxText*, which is displayed on the web page.

The transmitted message, *txText*, is contained in an HTML *textarea*, within an HTML *form*, with the form *action* property associated with the JavaScript *sendText* function. The transmitted message is not included in an HTML *input field*, as an *input field* does not permit text wrap-around. If an HTML *input field* is required, then the *sendText* function is called by a carriage return at the end of the sent message with the instruction onkeydown='if(event.keyCode == 13) sendText()', as the ASCII code 13 corresponds to a carriage return. The received message, *rxText*, is included in an HTML *textarea*, which allows text wrap-around.

Listing 9-2. WebSocket web page AJAX code

```
char page[] PROGMEM = R"(
<!DOCTYPE html><html>
<head><title>ESP8266</title>
<style>
body {font-family:Arial}
td {vertical-align: top;}
textarea {font-family:Arial; width:300px; height:50px;}
input[type=submit] {background-color:yellow;}
</style></head>
<body id='initialise'>
<h2>WebSocket</h2>
<table><tr>
<td>transmit text</td>
<td>receive text (click to clear)</td>
</tr><tr>
<td><form action='javascript:sendText()'>
<textarea id='txText'></textarea><br>
<input type='submit' value="send text">
</form></td>
```

```
<td><textarea id='rxText'
onfocus='this.value=""'></textarea><br></td>
</tr></table>

<script>
var wskt;
document.getElementById('initialise').onload = function()
{init()};

function init()                          // open WebSocket
{
  wskt = new WebSocket('ws://' + window.location.hostname +
  ':81/');
  wskt.onmessage = function(rx)
  {                                      // client receive message
    var obj = rx.data;
    document.getElementById('rxText').value = obj;
  };
}
function sendText()·                      // client transmit message
{
  wskt.send(document.getElementById('txText').value);
  document.getElementById('txText').value = "";
}
</script>
</body></html>
)";
```

Remote control and WebSocket communication

A laser, mounted on a tilt bracket with a servo motor attached to an ESP8266 or ESP32 development board, is remotely controlled by moving a slider on the client web page with the slider position information transmitted to the server, which is the ESP8266 or ESP32 microcontroller. The client receives information on the servo position and the laser state from the server (see Figure 9-2). The microcontroller moves the servo motor and turns on or off the laser according to the control information received from the client. Information on the web page is continuously updated, as the WebSocket protocol enables the server to transmit information to the client, without the client requesting the information.

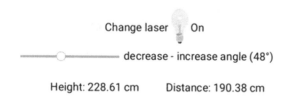

Figure 9-2. *Web page with laser position and state*

An application for a remotely controlled laser mounted on a tilt bracket is measurement of vertical and horizontal distance to a point identified by the laser. The vertical distance to the point is determined from the angle of tilt, and the horizontal distance from the object is measured with an ultrasonic distance sensor attached to the front of the tilt bracket. In Figure 9-3, the hinge of the tilt bracket is 5 cm above the base, with an

229

8 cm distance between the hinge and the front of the HC-SR04 ultrasonic distance sensor and a 2 cm height difference between the hinge and the laser. The vertical distance (cm), above the base, to a point marked by the laser is $5 + (8 + d)tan(x) + 2/cos(x)$, where $x°$ is the angle of the tilt bracket.

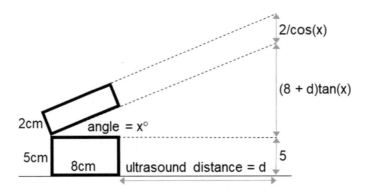

Figure 9-3. *Derivation of height and distance measurement*

Connections for an ESP8266 or ESP32 development board, with the ultrasonic distance sensor, laser module, and servo motor are given in Table 9-1 and shown in Figure 9-4. The HC-SR04 ultrasonic distance sensor requires a regulated 5 V supply, which is not provided by a 5 V USB power bank. The servo motor requires an external power supply, such as a 5V battery or a 9V battery with the L4940V5 voltage regulator, as the motor can use hundreds of milliamps during a few milliseconds that the rotor is turning, which is more than the output of the ESP8266 or ESP32 development board 5V or VIN pins. A 9V battery with an L4940V5 voltage regulator, with 100nF and 22μF capacitors (see Figure 9-3), powers the ultrasonic distance sensor and the servo motor. The KY-008 laser operates at 650 nm, with the red light wavelength in the 635–700 nm range.

Table 9-1. *Height and distance measurement with ESP8266 and ESP32 microcontrollers*

Component	Connect to	And to
Ultrasonic distance sensor VCC	VCC rail	
Ultrasonic distance sensor TRIG	ESP8266 D8 or ESP32 GPIO 13	
Ultrasonic distance sensor ECHO	ESP8266 D7 or ESP32 GPIO 27	
Ultrasonic distance sensor GND	GND rail	
Laser module S	ESP8266 D6 or ESP32 GPIO 26	
Laser module -	GND rail	
Servo motor signal (orange or white)	ESP8266 D5 or ESP32 GPIO 25	
Servo motor (red)	VCC rail	
Servo motor (brown or black)	GND rail	
ESP8266 or ESP32 GND	GND rail	
L4940V5 supply	9 V battery positive	100 nF capacitor positive
L4940V5 GND	GND rail	
L4940V5 demand	VCC rail	22 µF capacitor positive
9 V battery negative	GND rail	
100 nF capacitor negative	GND rail	
22 µF capacitor negative	GND rail	

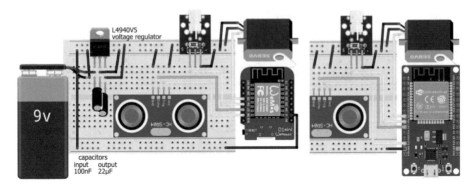

Figure 9-4. *Height and distance measurement with the LOLIN (WeMos) D1 mini or ESP32 DEVKIT DOIT development board*

Listing 9-3 is for an ESP8266 microcontroller, and the *NewPing8266* library is downloaded from `github.com/jshaw/NewPingESP8266`. For an ESP32 microcontroller, the *WebServer* and *NewPing* libraries replace the *ESP8266WebServer* and *NewPing8266* libraries, with the *NewPing* library available in the Arduino IDE. The instruction `ESP8266WebServer server` is replaced with `WebServer server (80)`. The ESP32 microcontroller also requires an ESP32-specific *Servo* library, rather than the Arduino IDE built-in *Servo* library. The *ESP32Servo* library by Kevin Harrington and John K. Bennett is recommended, and the library is available in the Arduino IDE. The ESP8266 microcontroller instructions with the *Servo* library

```
#include <Servo.h>              // include Servo library
servoFB.attach(FBpin)          // initialise servo motor to FBpin
```

are replaced with the *ESP32Servo* library instructions for the ESP32 microcontroller

```
#include <ESP32Servo.h>
servoFB.setPeriodHertz(F)           // define servo frequency (F)
servoFB.attach(FBpin, min, max)     // initialise servo motor to FBpin
```

The square wave frequency, *F*, is included in the instruction `servoFB.setPeriodHertz(F)`, which is generally 50 Hz. In the `servoFB.attach(FBpin, min, max)` instruction, the *min* and *max* parameters refer to the pulse width, in microseconds, of a square wave to move the servo motor to 0° and 180°, respectively. Default values for the *min* and *max* parameters are 1000 μs and 2000 μs, with values of 500 μs and 2500 μs for the Tower Pro SG90 servo.

There is no change to the following instructions:

```
Servo servoFB                       // associate servoFB with Servo lib
servoFB.writeMicroseconds(T)        // move to position mapped to Tμs
servoFb.write(N)                    // move to angle N°
```

In the sketch in Listing 9-3, the majority of instructions relate to including libraries, defining variables associated with the servo motor and the ultrasonic distance sensor, establishing the Wi-Fi connection, and loading the default web page by calling the *base* function to access the AJAX code, contained in the string literal *page* located in the *buildpage* tab. Instructions related to WebSocket are included in the *wsEvent* function. When the server receives, from the client, a message containing the servo angle and laser state, the *wsEvent* function is called, which loads the received message into a string that is parsed into the servo angle and laser state by locating the position of the comma separating the two values. The servo angle is mapped to the number of microseconds for a square wave pulse length to move the servo motor to the required angle. The laser state is also updated. The horizontal distance is measured by the ultrasonic distance sensor, and the vertical distance is calculated from the servo angle and horizontal distance. The two distances are converted to name and value pairs in JSON format with the *JsonConvert* function, which transmits the information to the client. The distance, in centimeters, between the ultrasonic distance sensor and an object is half the echo time, measured in microseconds, multiplied by 0.0343, assuming the speed of sound of 343 m/s.

Listing 9-3. Height and distance measurement

```
#include <ESP8266WebServer.h>       // include Webserver library
ESP8266WebServer server;            // associate server with library
char ssid[] = "xxxx";               // change xxxx to Wi-Fi SSID
char password[] = "xxxx";           // change xxxx to Wi-Fi password
#include <WebSocketsServer.h>       // include Websocket library
WebSocketsServer websocket = WebSocketsServer(81);
                                    // set WebSocket port 81
#include "buildpage.h"              // webpage AJAX code
#include <Servo.h>
Servo servoFB;                      // associate servoFB with Servo lib
int FBpin = D7;                     // forward-backward servo pin
int laserPin = D8;
int minMicrosec = 450;              // minimum and maximum time
int maxMicrosec = 1150;             // for servo motor pulse length
#include <NewPingESP8266.h>         // include NewPing library
int trigPin = D5;                   // ultrasonic trigger and echo pins
int echoPin = D6;
float maxdist = 300;                // ultrasound maximum distance
NewPingESP8266 sonar(trigPin, echoPin, maxdist);
float distance, height, temp, angle;
int microsec, laser, comma;
String text[2];                     // strings in JSON text
String str, json;
unsigned long timer = 0;

void setup()
{
  Serial.begin(115200);             // Serial Monitor baud rate
  WiFi.begin(ssid, password);       // connect and initialise Wi-Fi
  while (WiFi.status() != WL_CONNECTED) delay(500);
```

```
  Serial.print("IP address: ");
  Serial.println(WiFi.localIP());   // display web server IP address
  server.begin();
  server.on("/", base);             // load default webpage
  websocket.begin();                // initialise WebSocket
  websocket.onEvent(wsEvent);       // wsEvent on WebSocket event
  servoFB.attach(FBpin);            // initialise servo motor
  servoFB.writeMicroseconds(minMicrosec);
                                    // and move to initial position
  pinMode(laserPin, OUTPUT);        // define laser pin as output
}
                        // function called when message received from client
void wsEvent(uint8_t n, WStype_t type, uint8_t * message,
size_t length)
{
  if(type == WStype_TEXT)
  {
    str = "";                       // convert message to string
    for (int i=0; i<length; i++) str = str + char(message[i]);
    comma = str.indexOf(",");       // location of comma
    text[0] = str.substring(0, comma);   // extract substrings
    text[1] = str.substring(comma+1);
    angle = text[0].toFloat();      // parse servo angle
    microsec = map(angle,20,90,minMicrosec,maxMicrosec);
                                    // map angle to µs
    servoFB.writeMicroseconds(microsec);  // move servo to angle
    delay(10);                      // time to move servo
    laser = text[1].toInt();        // parse laser state
    digitalWrite(laserPin, laser);  // turn on or off laser
    distance = (sonar.ping_median(10)/2.0)*0.0343;
                                    // get horizontal distance
```

```
  angle = angle*PI/180.0;                  // convert angle to radians
  height = 5.0+(distance+8.0)*tan(angle)+2.0/cos(angle);
                                           // vertical distance
  JsonConvert(height, distance);           // convert to JSON format
  websocket.broadcastTXT(json.c_str(), json.length());
 }                                         // send JSON text
}
                  // function converts variables to JSON name/value pairs
String JsonConvert(float val1, float val2)
{                                          // start with open bracket
  json  = "{\"var1\": \"" + String(val1) + "\",";
                                           // partition with comma
  json += " \"var2\": \"" + String(val2) + "\"}";
                                           // end with close bracket
  return json;
}

void base()                               // function to return HTML code
{
  server.send(200, "text/html", page);
}

void loop()
{
  server.handleClient();                  // manage HTTP requests
  websocket.loop();                       // handle WebSocket data
}
```

WebSocket and AJAX

On the web page (see Figure 9-5), clicking the *Change laser* button turns on or off the laser, and the relevant image is displayed on the web page. Moving the slider changes the angle of the tilt bracket, with the angle displayed on the web page. The client transmits the servo angle and laser state to the server, and the server responds by sending the client the measured horizontal distance and calculated height that the client displays on the web page.

Servo control

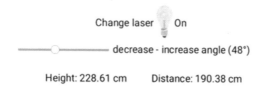

Change laser   On

decrease - increase angle (48°)

Height: 228.61 cm   Distance: 190.38 cm

Figure 9-5. *Height and distance measurement*

AJAX code for the web page (see Listing 9-4) is included in the string literal *page*, bracketed by the characters R"(and)", with variables identified by single apostrophes, '. In the HTML code, the <head> section includes two <meta> instructions that are required to format text in the console log, which displays data received and transmitted by the client, for example, console.log(FBVal). The <style> section centers text on the web page and defines the slider, the size of an image, and the height of a table row. The content of the web page is formatted in a table, with the first row, which spans two columns, containing the *Change laser* button, a bulb image, and text, *laserId*, describing the laser state of *On* or *Off*. The

second table row contains a slider to select the tilt angle, ranging from 20°
to 90°, followed by text and the angle value. The slider is defined with the
instruction

```
<input autocomplete='on' type='range' min='20' max='90' value='20'
  class='slider' id='FBSlider' oninput='sendFB()'>
```

which sets *autocomplete* to *on* with the slider initial position set at *value*,
as setting *autocomplete* to *off* positions the slider in the default middle
position. The instruction associates the slider with the *sendFB* function,
which is called when the slider is moved. The third table row displays the
calculated height and measured distance.

When the web page is loaded, the *init* function is called to open the
WebSocket connection at *ws://web server IP address:81/*. When the client
receives a message, the message content is stored in the variable *rx.
data*, which is parsed to the variables *vertical* and *horizontal* for display
on the web page. A message is transmitted by the client with the *sendFB*
function, which combines the angle selected by the slider with the laser
state. When the *Change laser* button is clicked, the *changeLaser* function
is called, which changes the value of the laser state, *laserVal,* updates the
laser state in the web page code, and alternates the *bulb* image, which
is downloaded from the `www.w3schools.com` website. The location of an
image to download from a website is obtained by right-clicking the image
and selecting *View Image Info* or *Copy Image Location* and including the
image location in the AJAX code.

When either the slider position is changed or the *Change laser*
button is clicked, the angle selected by the slider and the laser state
are transmitted by the client to the server with the instruction
`wskt.send(FBVal +','+ laserVal)`. For sketch testing purposes, the
instructions `console.log(obj.var1)` and `console.log(FBVal)` display, in
the console log, values of the received vertical distance and the transmitted
angle by the client, respectively.

Listing 9-4. AJAX code for height and distance measurement

```
char page[] PROGMEM = R"(
<!DOCTYPE html><html>
<head>
<meta name='viewport' content='width=device-width,
initial-scale=1.0'>
<meta charset='UTF-8'>
<title>ESP8266</title>
<style>
html {text-align: center}
.slider {-webkit-appearance: none; height: 2px;
background: DarkGrey}
img {width:25px; height:50px}
td {height:50px}
</style>
<title>WebSocket</title>
</head>
<!-- initiate WebSocket when webpage loaded-->
<body id='initialise'>
<h2>Servo control</h2>
<table align='center'><tr>
<td colspan='2'><input type='radio' id='r1'
onclick='changeLaser()'>  Change laser
<img id='bulb' src='https://www.w3schools.com/jsref/
pic_bulboff.gif'>
<span id='laserId'>Off</span></td>
</tr>
<tr>
<!--autocomplete='off': returns slider to default mid-point
position-->
```

```
<td><input autocomplete='on' type='range' min='20' max='90'
value='20' class='slider' id='FBSlider' oninput='sendFB()'></td>
<td><label id='FBId'>decrease - increase angle (20&deg)
</label></td>
</tr>
<tr>
<td style='width:200px'>Height: <span id='vertical'>0</span>
cm</td>
<td>Distance: <span id='horizontal'>0</span> cm</td>
</tr></table>

<script>
var FBVal = 20;
var laserVal = 0;
document.getElementById('initialise').onload = function()
{init()};

function init()
{
  wskt = new WebSocket('ws://' + window.location.hostname +
':81/');
  wskt.onmessage = function(rx)
  {
    var obj = JSON.parse(rx.data);
    console.log(obj.var1);
    console.log(obj.var2);
    document.getElementById('vertical').innerHTML = obj.var1;
    document.getElementById('horizontal').innerHTML = obj.var2;
  };
}
```

```
function sendFB()
{
  FBVal = document.getElementById('FBSlider').value;
  document.getElementById('FBId').innerHTML = 'decrease -
  increase angle ('+FBVal.toString() + '&deg)';
  wskt.send(FBVal +','+ laserVal);
  console.log(FBVal);
  console.log(laserVal);
}

function changeLaser()
{
  laserVal = 1 - laserVal;
  if(laserVal == 1) {laserTag = 'On';}
  else {laserTag = 'Off';}
  document.getElementById('laserId').innerHTML = laserTag;
  document.getElementById('r1').checked=false;
  wskt.send(FBVal +',' + laserVal);
  var image = document.getElementById('bulb');
  if (image.src.match('bulboff')) {image.src =
              'https://www.w3schools.com/js/pic_bulbon.gif';}
  else {image.src = 'https://www.w3schools.com/js/
  pic_bulboff.gif';}
}
</script>
</body></html>
)";
```

The *Servo* library instruction servo.write(N) moves the servo motor to an angle of N°. An alternative instruction is servo.writeMicroseconds(microsec), with the number of microseconds defining the pulse length of the square wave. A *standard* servo motor moves to angle 0° or 180° when the square wave pulse length is 500 µs or 2500 µs, while the pulse length for other *standard* servo motors is 1000 µs or 2000 µs. For the two *standard* cases, the formula for the number of required microseconds to move to a given angle is *500 + angle × 200/18* and *1000 + angle × 100/18*. The servo motor used in this chapter was calibrated with the sketch in Listing 9-5, by entering different microsecond values on the Serial Monitor and measuring servo motor angle. For example, 700 µs and 1150 µs were required to position the servo motor at 45° and 90°, giving the equation *microseconds = 250 + angle × 10* or *250 + angle × 180/18.*

Listing 9-5. Servo motor calibration

```
#include <Servo.h>              // include Servo library
Servo servoFB;                  // associate servoFB with Servo library
int FBpin = D7;                 // servo pin
int microsec;

void setup()
{
  Serial.begin(115200);         // Serial Monitor baud rate
  servoFB.attach(FBpin);        // initialise servo motor
}

void loop()
{
  if(Serial.available() > 0)    // text entered in Serial Monitor
  {                             // parse Serial buffer to integer
    microsec = Serial.parseInt();
    servoFB.writeMicroseconds(microsec);
  }                             // move servo motor
}
```

Access images, time, and sensor data over the Internet

Another example of the WebSocket protocol is the graphic display of data on a web page with the graph properties: Y-axis minimum and maximum values and the X-axis time interval, changed by the user in real time. Changing the graph Y-axis only impacts the client making the change, so the Y-axis of the graph is client specific. In contrast, when the X-axis time interval is transmitted to the server, the graphic display is updated at the same time for all clients connected to the server. Figure 9-6 illustrates a web page displaying sensor data in real time with the option to change the minimum and maximum values of the Y-axis and the time interval for data updates. The browser current date and time are also displayed as well as an image downloaded from the Internet.

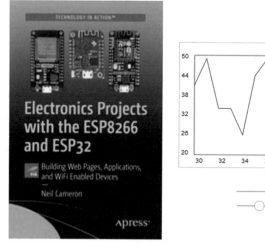
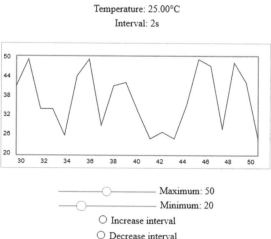

Figure 9-6. *Real-time sensor graphics*

The BMP280 sensor measures temperature and pressure, communicates with I2C or SPI, and operates at 3.3 V. For I2C communication, the I2C address of the BMP280 sensor is *0x76*, with the BMP280 module SD0 pin connected to GND. Connections between a BMP280 sensor and an ESP8266 or ESP32 development board are shown in Figure 9-7 and given in Table 9-2.

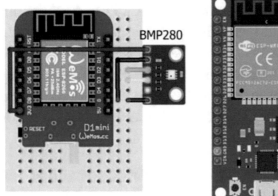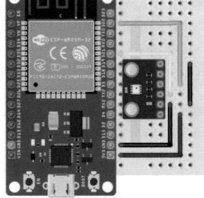

Figure 9-7. *BMP280 with LOLIN (WeMos) D1 mini and ESP32 DEVKIT DOIT boards*

Table 9-2. *BMP280 with ESP8266 and ESP32 microcontrollers*

Component	ESP8266 Connections	ESP32 Connections
BMP280 VCC	3V3	3V3
BMP280 GND	GND	GND
BMP280 SDI	D2	GPIO 21
BMP280 SCK	D1	GPIO 22
BMP280 SD0	GND	GND

The first section and the *setup* function of the sketch in Listing 9-6 are essentially the same as in Listing 9-3. The *Adafruit_Sensor* library, listed under *Adafruit_Unified_Sensor* in the Arduino IDE, and the *Adafruit_BMP280* library are installed for the BMP280 sensor, which is initialized with its I2C address in the *setup* function. The *tempUrl* URL is mapped to the *tempFunct* function, which is attached to the *Ticker* library for timing web page updates.

When the server receives, from the client, a message containing the timing interval, the WebSocket *wsEvent* function is called, which loads the received message for parsing. In Listing 9-6, the message only contains the timing interval variable, *interval*, and the message string is converted to an integer with the *atoi()* C++ function. The *tempFunct* function updates the *interval* variable, for the *Ticker* library to control the timing of calls to the *tempFunct* function, and obtains the temperature reading from the BMP280 sensor. Both the temperature and timing interval are converted to name and value pairs in JSON format, with the *JsonConvert* function, and transmitted to the client. If several clients are connected to the server and one client changes the timing interval, then the timing interval displayed by each client is also updated. The *base* and *loop* functions of Listing 9-6 are identical to those in Listing 9-3. When testing the sketch, the instruction `JsonConvert(bmp.readTemperature(), interval)` is replaced with `JsonConvert(random(20, 50)*1.0, interval)` to generate variation between values.

Listings 9-1, 9-3, and 9-6 illustrate three examples of handling the client WebSocket message. The message is displayed on the Serial Monitor with the instruction `Serial.write(message[i])`, converted to a string as `str = str + char(message[i])` or converted to an integer by `interval = atoi((char *) &message[0])`. The C++ equivalent of the *atoi* function for a real number is the *atof* function.

Listing 9-6. Real-time sensor graphics

```
#include <ESP8266WebServer.h>        // include WebServer library
ESP8266WebServer server;             // associate server with library
char ssid[] = "xxxx";                // change xxxx to Wi-Fi SSID
char password[] = "xxxx";            // change xxxx to Wi-Fi password
#include <WebSocketsServer.h>        // include Websocket library
WebSocketsServer websocket = WebSocketsServer(81);
                                     // set WebSocket port 81
#include "buildpage.h"               // webpage AJAX code
String json;
#include <Ticker.h>                  // include Ticker library
Ticker timer;                        // associate timer with Ticker lib
int interval = 1;
int oldInterval = 1;
#include <Adafruit_Sensor.h>         // include Adafruit Sensor
#include <Adafruit_BMP280.h>         // and BMP280 libraries
Adafruit_BMP280 bmp;                 // associate bmp with BMP280
int BMPaddress = 0x76;               // BMP280 I2C address

void setup()
{
  Serial.begin(115200);             // Serial Monitor baud rate
  WiFi.begin(ssid, password);       // connect and initialise Wi-Fi
  while(WiFi.status()!= WL_CONNECTED ) delay(500);
  Serial.print("IP address: ");
  Serial.println(WiFi.localIP());   // display web server IP address
  server.begin();
  server.on("/",base);              // load default webpage
  server.on("/tempUrl", tempFunct);
                                     // map URL to tempFunct
```

```
  websocket.begin();                  // initialise WebSocket
  websocket.onEvent(wsEvent);         // wsEvent on WebSocket event
  bmp.begin(BMPaddress);              // initialise BMP280 sensor
  timer.attach(interval, tempFunct);
}                   // attach timer to tempFunct
                    // function called when message received from client
void wsEvent(uint8_t n, WStype_t type, uint8_t * message,
size_t length)
{                   // convert message to integer
  if(type == WStype_TEXT) interval = atoi((char *)
&message[0]);
}

void tempFunct()
                    // function to transmit temperature and update interval
{                   // convert to JSON format
  JsonConvert(bmp.readTemperature(), interval);
  websocket.broadcastTXT(json.c_str(), json.length());
                                // send JSON text
  if(interval != oldInterval)
  {
    timer.detach();
    timer.attach(interval, tempFunct);
    oldInterval = interval;       // update timer interval
  }
}
                    // function converts variables to JSON name/value pairs
String JsonConvert(float val1, int val2)
{                   // start with open bracket
  json  = "{\"var1\": \"" + String(val1) + "\",";
                                // partition with comma
```

```
    json += " \"var2\": \"" + String(val2) + "\"}";
                                            // end with close bracket
    return json;
}
void base()                                 // function to return HTML code
{
    server.send(200, "text/html", page);
}

void loop()
{
    server.handleClient();                  // manage HTTP requests
    websocket.loop();                       // handle WebSocket data
}
```

AJAX code for the web page is given in Listing 9-7. The content of
the web page is formatted as a table with a header row containing the
browser current date and time, with two columns consisting of seven
rows. The first column, which spans all seven rows, with the instruction
<td rowspan='7'>, contains the image that is downloaded when the web
page is initialized. The first three rows in the second column contain the
updated temperature and time interval, both transmitted by the server,
and a <canvas> for the graph. The four sliders to control the graph Y-axis
maximum and minimum values and the buttons to increase or decrease
the time interval call the functions *setMaxy, setMiny, sendadd,* and
sendsub, respectively.

The *graph* function uses the canvas.getContext() instruction to
access functions for drawing on a canvas, with details available at
www.w3schools.com/tags/ref_canvas.asp. The clearRect and
strokeRect instructions clear a rectangular space (445 × 200 pixels) in
which the graph rectangle (400 × 160 pixels) is outlined, starting at pixel

position (25, 20) within the rectangular space with position (0, 0) being the top-left corner. Six Y-axis labels are positioned with the instruction

```
ctx.fillText(Math.round(maxy-i*(maxy-miny)/5), 3, 25+31*i)
```

that calculates the label values from the maximum and minimum Y-axis values. The Y-axis labels are positioned in rows that are 31 pixels apart, starting at pixel position (3, 25). The 11 X-axis labels are continuously updated, based on the total number of data values, *Ndata*, with the instruction

```
ctx.fillText(String(Ndata+i-20), 27+19*i, 193)
```

The X-axis labels are positioned in columns that are 19 pixels apart, starting at pixel position (27, 193). Instructions to draw a line connecting the data points together are beginPath with the initial data point moveTo(x,y) and subsequent data points lineTo(x,y) followed by stroke. The graph is plotted in batches of 21 points, which are constantly updated with the 21st point being the most recent value with the instructions

```
Ndata++;                        // increment the number of data points
if(Ndata>maxVal) datay.shift();
                                // remove the first element of datay[ ]
datay.push(obj.var1);           // add new data point to end of datay[ ]
```

JavaScript array command details are available at www.w3schools.com/jsref/jsref_obj_array.asp.

The graph Y-axis maximum and minimum values are the corresponding slider values, and the functions *setMaxy* and *setMiny* convert a slider value to a string for displaying on the web page to the right of the slider. The functions *sendadd* and *sendsub* increase and decrease the time interval between updates of the web page by one second, with the updated value sent to the server.

When the first web page is loaded, the *init* function opens the WebSocket connection at *ws://web server IP address:81/*. When the client receives a message, the message content, stored in the variable *rx.data*, is parsed to the variables *temp* and *interval* for displaying, on the web page, the temperature and time interval between readings. The browser current time is obtained and formatted with the instructions

```
var dt = new Date();
var tm = dt.toLocaleTimeString
   ('en-GB', {weekday: 'long', day: '2-digit', month: 'long'});
document.getElementById('timeNow').innerHTML = tm;
```

The resulting time format is *Tuesday, 16 June, 10:11:47*, but if innerHTML = dt, then the display format is *Tue Jun 16 2020 10:11:47 GMT+0100 (British Summer Time)*. If the time in *hh:mm:ss* format is required, then the variable *tm* is defined as var tm = dt.toLocaleTimeString ('en-GB'). Details on date formatting are available at www.w3schools.com/Jsref/jsref_obj_date.asp.

Listing 9-7. AJAX code for real-time sensor graphics

```
char page[] PROGMEM = R"(
<!DOCTYPE html><html>
<head>
<meta name='viewport' content='width=device-width,
initial-scale=1.0'>
<meta charset='UTF-8'>
<!-- padding top right bottom left-->
<style>
html {text-align: center}
.slider {-webkit-appearance: none; height: 2px;
background: DarkGrey}
td {padding: 0px 0px 0px 25px}
```

```
img {width:253px; height:384px}
</style>
<title>ESP8266</title>
</head>
<body onload='javascript:init()'>
<table>
<tr><th></th><th><h2>BMP280 at <span id = 'timeNow'></span>
</h2></th></tr>
<tr>
<td rowspan='7'>
<img src=
'https://images.springer.com/sgw/books/medium/9781484263358.jpg'
    alt='book'></td>
<td>Temperature: <span id = 'temp'>0</span>&degC</td>
</tr>
<tr><td>Interval: <span id='interval'>1</span>s</td></tr>
<tr><td>
<canvas id = 'myCanvas' width = '445' height = '200'
    style = 'border:1px solid DarkGrey'>
    Your browser does not support the canvas element.
</canvas>
</td></tr>
<tr><td>
<input autocomplete='off' type='range' min='1' max='100'
value='25' class='slider' id='maxySlider' oninput='setMaxy()' >
<label id='maxyId'>Maximum: 25</label>
</td></tr>
<tr><td>
<input autocomplete='off' type='range' min='0' max='100'
value='15' class='slider' id='minySlider' oninput='setMiny()' >
<label id='minyId'>Minimum: 15</label>
</td></tr>
```

```
<tr><td>
<input type='radio' id='r1' oninput='sendadd()'> Increase
interval
</td></tr>
<tr><td>
<input type='radio' id='r2' oninput='sendsub()'> Decrease
interval
</td></tr>
</table>
<script>
var canvas = document.getElementById('myCanvas');
var ctx = canvas.getContext('2d');
ctx.strokeStyle = 'red';
ctx.strokeRect(25, 20, 400, 160);
ctx.lineWidth = 1;
var y = 0;
var miny = 15;
var maxy = 25;
var timeval = 1;
var datay = [0];
var Ndata = 0;
var maxVal = 20;
var dt = 0;
var tm = 0;
function init()
{
  webSocket = new WebSocket('ws://' + window.location.hostname
  + ':81/');
  webSocket.onmessage = function(rx)
  {
    var obj = JSON.parse(rx.data);
    document.getElementById('temp').innerHTML = obj.var1;
```

```
    document.getElementById('interval').innerHTML = obj.var2;
    Ndata++;
    if(Ndata>maxVal) datay.shift();
    datay.push(obj.var1);
    dt = new Date();
    tm = dt.toLocaleTimeString
      ('en-GB', {weekday: 'long', day: '2-digit', month:
      'long'});
    document.getElementById('timeNow').innerHTML = tm;
    graph()
  };
}
function graph()
{
  ctx.clearRect(0, 0, 445, 200);
  ctx.strokeStyle = 'red';
  ctx.strokeRect(25, 20, 400, 160);
  for (i=0; i<6; i++)
    ctx.fillText(Math.round(maxy-i*(maxy-miny)/5), 3, 25+31*i);
  if(Ndata<21) {for (i=0; i<21; i=i+2)
    ctx.fillText(String(i), 27+19*i, 193);}
  if(Ndata>20) {for (i=0; i<21; i=i+2)
    ctx.fillText(String(Ndata+i-20), 27+19*i, 193);}
  ctx.beginPath();
  y = 20+160*(maxy-datay[0])/(maxy-miny);
  if(y<20) y=20;
  if(y>180) y=180;
  ctx.moveTo(25, y);
  for(i=1; i<21; i++)
  {
    y = 20+160*(maxy-datay[i])/(maxy-miny);
    if(y<20) y=20;
```

```
    if(y>180) y=180;
    ctx.strokeStyle = 'blue';
    ctx.lineTo(25+20*i, y);
  }
  ctx.stroke();
}
function setMaxy()
{
  maxy = document.getElementById('maxySlider').value;
  document.getElementById('maxyId').innerHTML =
    'Maximum: ' + maxy.toString();
}
function setMiny()
{
  miny = document.getElementById('minySlider').value;
  document.getElementById('minyId').innerHTML =
    'Minimum: ' + miny.toString();
}
function sendadd()
{
  timeval = parseInt(document.getElementById('interval').
  innerHTML) + 1;
  document.getElementById('interval').innerHTML = timeval;
  document.getElementById('r1').checked=false;
  webSocket.send(timeval);
}
function sendsub()
{
  timeval = parseInt(document.getElementById('interval').
  innerHTML) - 1;
  if(timeval<1) timeval = 1;
  document.getElementById('interval').innerHTML = timeval;
```

```
    document.getElementById('r2').checked=false;
    webSocket.send(timeval);
}
</script>
</body></html>
)";
```

Summary

Three examples illustrate the advantage of using the WebSocket protocol for a two-way real-time conversation between the client and the web server. In the first example, a web page enabled the client to send text to and receive text from the server in real time. In the second example, the client used a web page slider and button to remotely control the position and state of a laser attached to a servo motor on a tilt bracket. The server responded with the height and distance to an object identified by the laser, with the horizontal distance measured by an ultrasonic sensor. The third example demonstrated the real-time graphic display, on a web page, of temperature sensor data transmitted by the server, with the graph properties and the interval between temperature measurements controlled remotely by the client using a web page slider and buttons.

Components List

- ESP8266 microcontroller: LOLIN (WeMos) D1 mini or NodeMCU board

- ESP32 microcontroller: DEVKIT DOIT or NodeMCU board

- Temperature sensor: BMP280 module

- Ultrasonic distance sensor: HC-SR04

- Laser module: KY-008

- Servo motor: SG90

- Servo pan and tilt bracket

- Capacitor: 100 nF, 22 µF

- Voltage regulator: L4940V5

- Battery: 9 V

CHAPTER 10

Build an app

A mobile app, short for application, is a computer program for mobile devices, such as an Android tablet or mobile phone. Apps are available for mobile games, providing information, location and route finding, playing music, and controlling external devices. The *MIT App Inventor* provides the opportunity to design your own app, rather than using an app downloaded from *Google Play Store*. After completing the app design stage, the app is immediately available to download to an Android tablet or mobile phone.

The *MIT App Inventor* app design website, `ai2.appinventor.mit.edu`, is accessed by clicking the *Create Apps* button at `appinventor.mit.edu`. When building an app, the option to simultaneously display the developing app on an Android tablet or mobile phone is provided by the *MIT App Inventor Companion* app (*MIT AI2 Companion*), which is downloaded from *Google Play Store*. For example, the effect of changing the screen position of a button or an image in *MIT App Inventor* is instantly realized in the *Companion* app. Both the computer, on which the app is being developed, and the Android tablet or mobile phone hosting the *MIT App Inventor Companion* app must be on the same Wi-Fi local area network. Full details are available at `appinventor.mit.edu/explore/ai2/setup-device-wifi.html`.

After logging on to the *MIT App Invento*r website and selecting *Start new project*, the app Designer window is displayed (see Figure 10-1). On the left side of the Designer window, the *User Interface* palette adds buttons, images, labels, and sliders to the app screen with *drag and drop*. On the right side of the Designer window in the *Properties* section, properties of selected items, such as the app name, screen background color, orientation, and title, are modified. The app screen is subdivided into different sections by inserting *HorizontalArrangements* from the *Layout* palette on the left side of the Designer window. The choice of a meaningful name for each item is recommended for app programming, which uses a block-based visual language that resembles *Scratch,* with information at scratch.mit.edu/about. For example, a button to control an LED is named *LEDbutton*, with the font size, button height and width, and text all defined in the *Properties* section on the right side of the Designer window. Images are uploaded in the *Media* palette at the bottom right side of the Designer window. *MIT App Inventor* tutorials are available at appinventor.mit.edu/explore/ai2/tutorials.html.

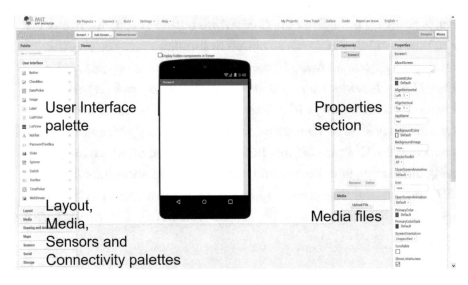

Figure 10-1. *MIT App Inventor initial window*

Control and feedback app

An example app controls the brightness of an LED, attached to an ESP8266 or ESP32 microcontroller, with feedback provided by a light-dependent resistor (LDR) (see Figure 10-2). The app includes a button to turn on or off the LED and displays an image indicating the LED state. When the slider on the app is moved with the LED turned on, the app transmits a signal to the microcontroller to change the LED brightness. Every two seconds, the microcontroller transmits the LDR reading to the app. The brighter the LED, the higher the LDR reading. Controlling the brightness of an LED is only an example application. In a practical application, the state and speed of a remotely located motor would be controlled through the app, which would indicate if the motor was running and at what speed, without the user being able to observe the motor.

Figure 10-2. *Bluetooth and LED control app*

The app uses Bluetooth to communicate with the ESP8266 or ESP32 microcontroller. ESP32 development boards have Bluetooth functionality, but ESP8266 development boards must be connected to an HC-05 Bluetooth module. The HC-05 Bluetooth module is powered from 3.6 V to 6 V and is connected to the ESP8266 development board 5V pin. The HC-05 Bluetooth module transmit (*TXD*) and receive (*RXD*) serial data function at 3.3 V, which is the operating voltage of the

ESP8266 microcontroller, and are directly connected to the ESP8266
development board *RX* and *TX* pins. The ESP8266 microcontroller uses
Serial communication to upload a compiled sketch. During uploading,
the ESP8266 development board *RX* pin is disconnected, or uploading will
fail. Connections for both the ESP8266 and ESP32 development boards are
shown in Figure 10-3 and given in Table 10-1.

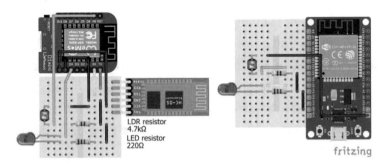

Figure 10-3. *Bluetooth and LED control with ESP8266 and ESP32
development boards*

Table 10-1. *Bluetooth and LED control with ESP8266 and ESP32
development boards*

Component	Connect to	ESP8266	ESP32
Bluetooth HC-05 VCC		5V	
Bluetooth HC-05 GND		GND	
Bluetooth HC-05 TX1		RX	
Bluetooth HC-05 RX0		TX	
LED long leg		D4	GPIO 27
LED short leg	220 Ω resistor	GND	GND
LDR bottom leg		A0	GPIO 33
LDR bottom leg	4.7 kΩ resistor	GND	GND
LDR top leg		5V	3V3

The sketch on the left side of Table 10-2 is for an ESP8266 microcontroller. When the ESP8266 microcontroller receives a message, from the app, consisting of the string "C", then the ESP8266 microcontroller changes the LED state and transmits the string "H" for *HIGH* or "L" for *LOW* to the app, to indicate the updated LED state. If the received message read by the microcontroller is not "C", then the LED brightness is set to the message value, by parsing the message, read as a string, to an integer with the instruction toInt(string), but only if the LED is turned on. Every two seconds, the microcontroller transmits the LDR reading to the app. The delay of 20 ms after the microcontroller transmits the LED state signal blocks the transmission of a simultaneous signal with the LDR reading.

The app transmits to the microcontroller the one-letter string "C", when the *Change LED* button is clicked, or the value of the brightness slider, when the slider is moved. When the app receives the one-letter string "H" or "L", the app displays the *bulbon* or the *bulboff* image, and the brightness slider is moved to position 255 or 0, respectively. The app continuously displays the updated LDR values.

The corresponding sketch for an ESP32 microcontroller, on the right side of Table 10-2, differs from the sketch for the ESP8266 microcontroller by the inclusion of the *BluetoothSerial* library, the PWM instructions, and the ESP32 microcontroller building the message string. Differences between the sketches, other than in pin numbers, are highlighted in bold. The ESP32 microcontroller accumulates characters in the Serial buffer into a string, while the ESP8266 instruction Serial.readString() reads the whole Serial buffer as a string. If the app slider is moved rapidly, the instruction Serial.readString() combines several slider values into a string. The high CPU frequency of the ESP32 microcontroller enables differentiation between slider values, when the slider is moved quickly. The ESP32 PWM instruction ledcWrite(channel, value) is the ESP8266 equivalent of the digitalWrite and analogWrite instructions. The ESP32 instruction ledcSetup(channel, 1000, 8) sets the square wave frequency for the LED to 1000 Hz with 8-bit resolution, resulting in a maximum value of 255, for consistency with the ESP8266 sketch. Chapter 21 (Microcontrollers) includes details of PWM with an ESP32 microcontroller.

Table 10-2. *Bluetooth and LED control sketches for ESP8266 and ESP32 microcontrollers*

ESP8266 Microcontroller	ESP32 Microcontroller
	`#include <BluetoothSerial.h>`
	`BluetoothSerial SerialBT;`
`int LEDpin = D4;`	`int LEDpin = 27;`
`int LDRpin = A0;`	`int LDRpin = 33;`
`int bright, LDR;`	`int bright, LDR;`
`int LEDstate = 0;`	`int LEDstate = 0;`
	`int channel = 0;`
	`char c;`
`String str;`	`String str;`
`unsigned int lastTime = 0;`	`unsigned int lastTime = 0;`
`void setup()`	`void setup()`
`{`	`{`
`  Serial.begin(9600);`	`  SerialBT.begin("ESP32 Bluetooth");`
`  pinMode(LEDpin, OUTPUT);`	`  pinMode(LEDpin, OUTPUT);`
	`  ledcAttachPin(LEDpin, channel);`
	`  ledcSetup(channel, 1000, 8);`
`  digitalWrite(LEDpin, LEDstate);`	`  ledcWrite(channel, LEDstate);`
`}`	`}`

(*continued*)

Table 10-2. (*continued*)

ESP8266 Microcontroller	ESP32 Microcontroller

```
void loop()                    void loop()
{                              {
 if(Serial.available()>0)       if(SerialBT.available()>0)
 {                              {
                                  str = "";
                                  while(SerialBT.available()>0)
                                  {
  str = Serial.                    c = SerialBT.read();
  readString();

                                   str = str + String(c);
                                  }
  if(str == "C")                if(str == "C" )
  {                             {
   LEDstate = 1- LEDstate;        LEDstate = 1 - LEDstate;
   if(LEDstate == 1)             if(LEDstate == 1)
     Serial.print("H");            SerialBT.print("H");
   else Serial.print("L");       else SerialBT.print("L");
   digitalWrite(LEDpin,          ledcWrite(channel,
         LEDstate);                         LEDstate*255);
   delay(20);                    delay(20);
  }                             }
  else if(LEDstate == 1)        else if(LEDstate == 1)
```

(*continued*)

Table 10-2. (*continued*)

ESP8266 Microcontroller	ESP32 Microcontroller
| ```
  {
    bright = str.toInt();
    analogWrite(LEDpin,
    bright);
  }
}
if(millis()-lastTime >
2000)
{
  lastTime = millis();
  LDR = analogRead(LDRpin);
  Serial.println(LDR);
}
}
``` | ```
  {
    bright = str.toInt();
    ledcWrite(channel, bright);
  }
}
if(millis()-lastTime > 2000)
{
  lastTime = millis();
  LDR = analogRead(LDRpin);
  SerialBT.println(LDR);
}
}
``` |

The app layout consists of several *HorizontalArrangements* containing the app title, the *ChangeLED* button and the *LEDimage* image, *BrightLabel* and *BrightValue* labels with a *BrightSlider* slider, *LDRlabel* and *LDRvalue* labels, the *SelectBluetooth ListPicker* button, and the *DisconnectBluetooth* button with the *Bluetoothimage* image and *StatusLabel* label (see Figure 10-4). All items are listed in the *User Interface* palette on the left side of the Designer window. The choice of a meaningful name for each item is recommended for app programming. The *Bluetoothimage* image is mapped to the *bluetooth.png* file that is uploaded in the *Media* palette at the bottom right of the Designer window, by clicking the *Bluetoothimage* in the *Components* section and selecting the image file name in the *Picture* box of the *Properties* section, with the image height and width set to 40 and 50 pixels. When a *ListPicker* button is clicked, the list corresponding to the button is displayed, which will be the list of available Bluetooth connections. The *Clock* and *BluetoothClient* components, located in the *Sensors* and *Connectivity* palettes on the left side of the Designer window, are displayed below the app layout. Text for buttons is added in the *Properties* section of each button. *VerticalArrangements* are used to insert spaces between objects in a *HorizontalArrangement*.

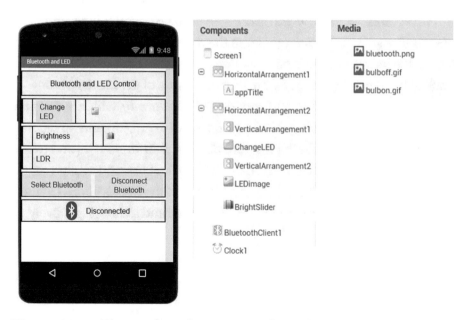

Figure 10-4. *Bluetooth and LED control app layout*

Once the layout is finalized, the app programming is started by clicking *Blocks* at the top-right side of the Designer window. The app program defines variables and procedures, establishes a Bluetooth communication, controls the LED, and processes the received signal from the microcontroller (see Figures 10-5, 10-6, 10-7, and 10-8). Blocks are color coded, and the importance of meaningful names for each item on the app screen is apparent.

Variables and procedures are defined at the start of the block program, just as when creating a sketch in the Arduino IDE. On the left side of the Blocks window, clicking *Variables* produces a series of options including *initialize global name to*, which is dragged to the Blocks window, and *name* is changed to *Receive*, to refer to the received signal by the app. From *Text* on the left side of the Blocks window, select and drag the blank " " block to the Blocks window. Again, on the left side of the Blocks window, clicking *Procedures* produces the option *to Procedure do*, which is dragged to the Blocks window, and *procedure* is changed to *LED*, to refer to LED control. A procedure is similar to a function in the Arduino IDE, and two inputs to the procedure are defined by clicking the blue-and-white gear symbol and twice dragging the *input x* block into the *inputs* block. On the *LED* procedure block, change *x* and *x2* to *picture* and *slider*, respectively (see Figure 10-5).

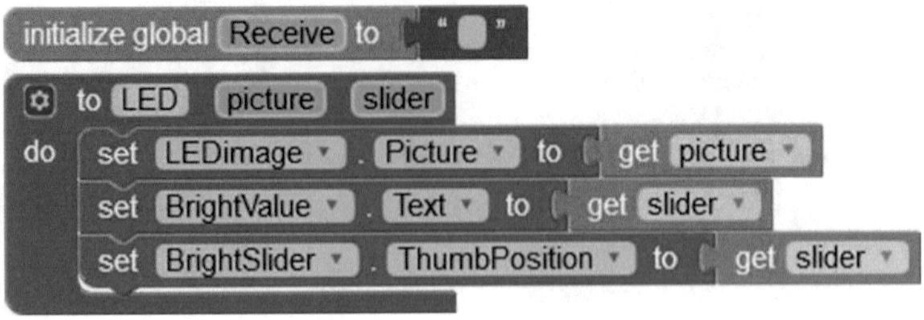

Figure 10-5. Variable and procedure definition

The *LED* procedure sets the *LEDimage* to the appropriate image when the LED is changed and sets the variables *BrightValue* and *BrightSlider* to the slider position, when the slider is moved. The three *LED* procedure actions are defined by

1. Clicking *LEDimage* on the left side of the Blocks window, selecting the option *set LEDimage.Picture to,* and dragging it to the Blocks window

2. Clicking *BrightValue* on the left side of the Blocks window, selecting the option *set BrightValue.Text to,* and dragging it to the Blocks window

3. Clicking *BrightSlider*, selecting the option *set BrightSlider.ThumbPosition to,* and dragging it to the Blocks window

From *Variables* on the left side of the Blocks window, select the option *get* three times. The nine blocks are connected together as shown in Figure 10-5. In the first *get* block, select *picture;* and in the other two *get* blocks, select *slider.*

For Bluetooth communication, there are three functions: display available Bluetooth connections and connect or disconnect the Bluetooth connection. The available Bluetooth connections are displayed as a list, using the *SelectBluetooth ListPicker* button. On the left side of the Blocks window, clicking the *SelectBluetooth ListPicker* button produces options including *when SelectBluetooth.BeforePicking* and *set SelectBluetooth.Elements to* which are dragged onto the Blocks window. Clicking *BluetoothClient1* produces options including *BluetoothClient1. AddressesAndNames*, which is also dragged onto the Blocks window. The three blocks are connected together as shown in Figure 10-6.

When the *SelectBluetooth ListPicker* button is clicked, the selected Bluetooth connection is made, the text *Connected* is displayed in black text, and the *LED* procedure is called. Blocks are added by clicking the

SelectBluetooth ListPicker button, *BluetoothClient1,* and the *StatusLabel* label. The *if then* block is selected after clicking *Control* and the blank " " block by clicking *Text* and then changing the blank " " block to *Connected* or to *bulbon.gif* and by clicking *Procedures* and then selecting the *LED* procedure created earlier (see Figure 10-5). The block for the value zero is selected after clicking *Math*.

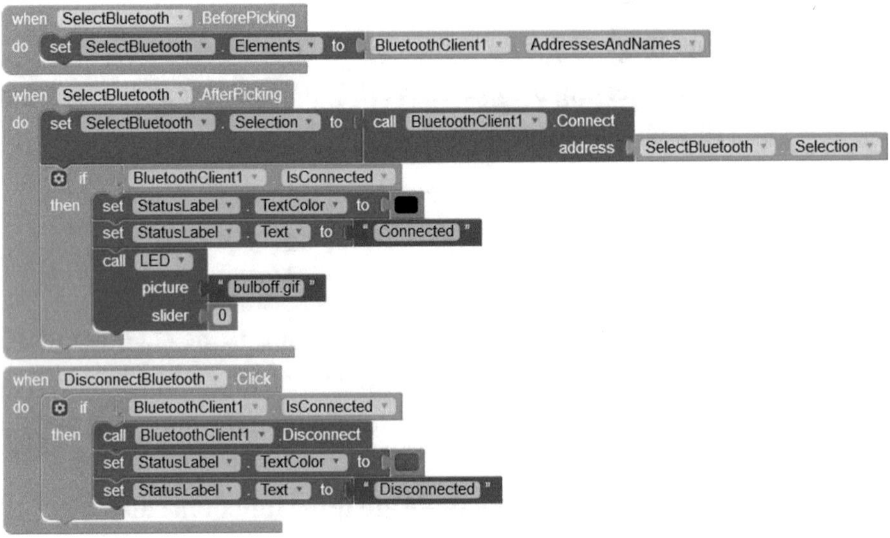

Figure 10-6. *Bluetooth communication*

Blocks to disconnect the Bluetooth connection are added by clicking the *BluetoothDisconnect* button and including *when DisconnectBluetooth. Click*. The text color of the *StatusLabel* label is set by selecting a color block from the color list in *Colors*. The visibility of a label is defined in the *Properties* section, on the right side of the Designer window, or in the Blocks window by clicking the label and selecting the *set Label.visible to* block and adding a *true* or *false* block.

Clicking a block in the Block section and then right-clicking *Duplicate* is an alternative to clicking and selecting blocks from the left side of the Blocks window.

Clicking the *ChangeLED* button on the app sends a message with the string *"C"*, and the block is constructed as shown in Figure 10-7. When the slider is moved, the app sends a message with the slider value, which is a real number. The *round* block, located in the *Math* palette, rounds up or down a real number to an integer. On the left side of the Blocks window, clicking the *BrightSlider* slider produces the option *when BrightSlider. PositionChanged*. To the *call Bluetooth1.SendText text* block, add the *get ThumbPosition* block, which is obtained by hovering the mouse over *ThumbPosition* in the *when BrightSlider.PositionChanged* block and dragging the *get ThumbPosition* block into position (see Figure 10-7).

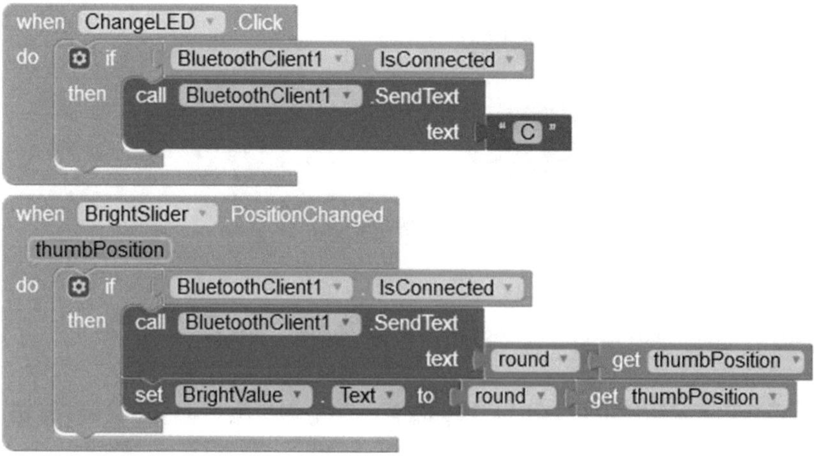

Figure 10-7. *Control the LED*

When the app receives a message, containing the string *"H"* or *"L"*, the *LED* procedure displays the *bulbon.gif* or *bulboff.gif* image and moves the slider to position 225 or 0, respectively. Otherwise, the *LDRvalue* label is updated.

On the left side of the Blocks window, clicking *Clock1* produces the option *when Clock1.Timer do*, clicking *Text* produces the option *contains text piece,* and clicking *Variables* produces the *get* option and *global*

Receive is selected. The *length* block is obtained by clicking *Text*. The *greater than* condition block is obtained by clicking *Math* and selecting the *equals* condition block, which is changed to a *greater than* condition block. The *if then, else if then, else* block is created from an *if then* block, clicking the blue-and-white gear symbol and dragging an *else if* and an *else* block into the *if* block. Component blocks are added as shown in Figure 10-8.

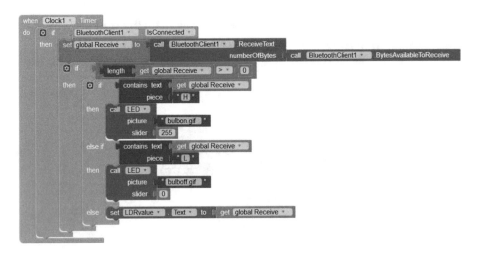

Figure 10-8. *Process the received Bluetooth signal*

The block *is number?*, obtained by clicking *Math*, is applied to a text variable to provide a conditional action on the received text. For example, the *else* block before the *set LDRvalue.Text* block at the bottom of Figure 10-8 is replaced by the *else if then* block and the *is number?* block as shown in Figure 10-9.

Figure 10-9. *Condition on numerical value*

270

Install the app

After designing the app layout and programming the app with the block-based visual language, the app is built by selecting *App (save .apk to my computer)* from the *Build* menu at the top of the Designer window. The *.apk* (Android Package Kit) file is then downloaded to the Android tablet or mobile phone with the app installed using an installer. Alternatively, a QR (Quick Response) code to download the app *.apk* file is created by selecting *App (provide QR code for .apk)*, with the QR code scanned to initiate downloading the *.apk* file and the app installed using an installer.

To install the app, the Android tablet or mobile phone *Security* setting *Unknown sources* must be set to *Allow installation of app from unknown sources*. After installing the app, reset the *Security* setting.

The default app icon of the *MIT App Inventor* (see Figure 10-10) is replaced with a user-defined image. In the *Properties* section of the app Designer window for *Screen1*, the *Icon* property of *None* is the default. The app icon is replaced by uploading the required JPG or PNG image, which should be no larger than 50 × 50 pixels.

Figure 10-10. *MIT App Inventor logo*

Servo-robot control app

In Chapter 9 (WebSocket), a servo motor, attached to a microcontroller, was controlled by moving a slider on the client web page with the slider position transmitted to the server, which was the microcontroller, to move the servo motor to the required angle. In this chapter, two servo motors are moved to required positions, with the app controlling the servo motors connected to the ESP8266 or ESP32 development board. The servo motor positions are saved and then played back to imitate an automated robotic movement sequence. The app controls one servo motor for left-right (LR) movement and the other servo motor for forward-backward (FB) movement of the pan-tilt bracket (see Figure 10-11). Clicking the appropriate app button moves a servo motor continuously until the *Stop* button is clicked. The servo motor positions are saved by clicking the *Save position* button with the app displaying the number of saved positions. The saved sequence of movements is replayed by clicking the *Playback* button. The *Reset* button cancels the saved servo motor positions.

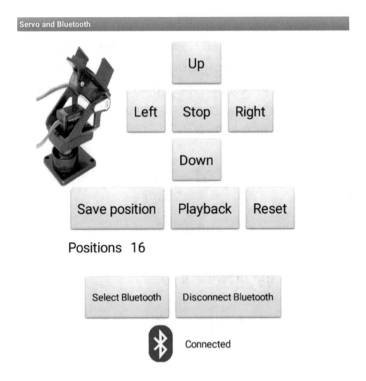

Figure 10-11. *Servo motor control*

The app on the Android tablet or mobile phone communicates with the ESP8266 or ESP32 microcontroller, connected to two servo motors, by Bluetooth (see Figure 10-12) with connections in Table 10-3. Clicking a button on the app transmits a command letter, which moves the corresponding servo motor in the required direction. The servo motors are externally powered with 5 V, as the motors can use hundreds of milliamps during a few microseconds that the rotor is turning, which is more than the 12 mA maximum output of an ESP8266 or ESP32 development board.

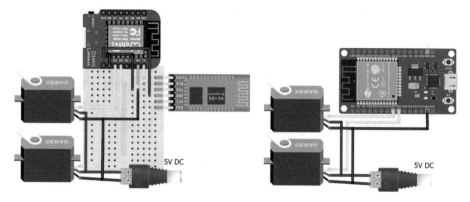

Figure 10-12. *Servo motors and Bluetooth with ESP8266 and ESP32 development boards*

The ESP32 microcontroller requires the ESP32-specific *Servo* library, rather than the Arduino IDE built-in *Servo* library. The *ESP32Servo* library by Kevin Harrington and John K. Bennett is recommended, and the library is available in the Arduino IDE. The built-in *Servo* library instructions for the ESP8266 microcontroller

```
#include <Servo.h>           // include Servo library
servoFB.attach(FBpin)        // initialise servo motor to FBpin
```

are replaced with the *ESP32Servo* library instructions for the ESP32 microcontroller

273

```
#include <ESP32Servo.h>
servoFB.setPeriodHertz(F)          // define servo frequency (F)
servoFB.attach(FBpin, min, max)    // initialise servo motor to FBpin
```

The square wave frequency, *F*, is included in the instruction servoFB.setPeriodHertz(F), which is generally 50 Hz. In the servoFB. attach(FBpin, min, max) instruction, the *min* and *max* parameters refer to the pulse width, in microseconds, of a square wave to move the servo motor to 0° and 180°, respectively. Default values for the *min* and *max* parameters are 1000 μs and 2000 μs, with values of 500 μs and 2500 μs for the Tower Pro SG90 servo.

There is no change to the following instructions:

```
Servo servoFB                      // associate servoFB with servo lib
servoFB.writeMicroseconds(T)       // move to position mapped to Tμs
servoFb.write(N)                   // move to angle N°
```

The ESP8266 microcontroller uses Serial communication to upload a compiled sketch. During uploading, the ESP8266 microcontroller RX pin must be disconnected, or uploading will fail.

Table 10-3. *Servo motors and Bluetooth communication with ESP8266 and ESP32 development boards*

Component	Connect to	ESP8266	ESP32
Servo VCC (red)	Battery 5 V		
Servo GND (brown or black)	Battery GND	GND	GND
Servo signals (orange or white)		D3, D4	GPIO 25, GPIO 26
Bluetooth HC-05 VCC		5V	
Bluetooth HC-05 GND		GND	
Bluetooth HC-05 TX1		RX	
Bluetooth HC-05 RX0		TX	

The sketch in Listing 10-1 is commented for the ESP8266 development board. Instructions for the ESP32 development board include the *BluetoothSerial* library with `SerialBT` replacing `Serial` instructions (see Table 10-2), as the transmitted messages only contain one character. The received command letter by the ESP8266 or ESP32 microcontroller either increments the position of a servo motor or calls a function to save, playback, or reset the servo motor positions. When moving servo motors, the movement speed is determined by the delay between movements, and a delay of 100 ms enables the servo motors to be precisely moved to the required positions. After a servo motor position is saved, the microcontroller transmits the position number for display on the app. When the servo motor position sequence is played back, the delay of 15 ms is a compromise between moving the servo motors quickly and providing sufficient time for the servo motors to move to the saved positions. The servo motors are moved to an initial or home position before playing back the saved servo motor position sequence, but not after the playback, as the end position does not have to equal the starting position.

The servo motor position sequence is saved in two arrays, one for each servo motor, but the information is not retained in memory when the ESP8266 or ESP32 development board is powered down. Saving the servo motor positions in EEPROM (Electrically Erasable Programmable Read-Only Memory) would retain the information when the ESP8266 or ESP32 development board is turned off, as described in Chapter 20 (OTA and saving data to EEPROM, SPIFFS, and Excel).

The *playServo* function controls playback of the saved servo motor position sequence. Two saved positions can differ for one servo motor only, if the position change was only a pan (left-right) or a tilt (forward-backward) movement. If the new position is different from the previous position for only one servo motor, the number and direction of 5° *steps* to move to the new position is determined, with no change to the other servo motor position.

Listing 10-1. Servo motors and Bluetooth

```
#include <Servo.h>              // include Servo library
Servo servoFB;                  // associate servos with library
Servo servoLR;
int FBpin = D3;                 // servo motor pins
int LRpin = D4;
int FBpos[20];                  // arrays for saved servo positions
int LRpos[20];
int Nservo = 0;                 // number of saved positions
int FB, LR, steps, stepsize;
char c;

void setup()
{
  Serial.begin(9600);                   // Bluetooth module baud rate
  servoFB.attach(FBpin);                // servo motor pin to Servo lib
  servoLR.attach(LRpin);
  startPosition();                      // set initial servo positions
}

void loop()
{                                       // read character in Serial buffer
  if(Serial.available()>0) c = Serial.read();
       if(c == 'U') FB = FB-5;          // move servo forward (up)
  else if(c == 'D') FB = FB+5;          // move servo backward
  else if(c == 'L') LR = LR+5;          // move servo left
  else if(c == 'R') LR = LR-5;          // move servo right
  else if(c == 'Z') delay(100);         // stop moving both servos
  else if(c == 'S') saveServo();        // save both servo positions
  else if(c == 'P') playServo(15);      // playback servo positions
  else if(c == 'E') resetServo();       // reset saved positions
  if(c != 'Z' && c !=' ') moveServo(FB, LR, 100);
}                                       // move both servos
```

```
void startPosition()              // function to set initial servo positions
{
  FB = 50;                        // arbitrary home position
  LR = 70;
  moveServo(FB, LR, 100);         // move servos to initial position
}

void moveServo(int vFB, int vLR, int lag)
{                                 // function to move servos
  vFB = constrain(vFB, 5, 100);   // constrain servo positions
  vLR = constrain(vLR, 5, 175);
  servoFB.write(vFB);             // move forward-backward servo
  delay(lag);                     // time between servo movements
  servoLR.write(vLR);             // move left-right servo
  delay(lag);
}

void saveServo()                  // function to save servo positions
{
  Nservo++;                       // increment number of positions
  Serial.println(Nservo);         // transmit position number to app
  FBpos[Nservo] = FB;             // save forward-backward position
  LRpos[Nservo] = LR;             // save left-right position
  c = ' ';                        // reset command value
}

void playServo(int lag)           // function to play back servo positions
{
  startPosition();                // move servos to initial position
  FBpos[0] = FB;
  LRpos[0] = LR;
  for (int i=1; i<Nservo+1; i++)  // cycle through saved positions
```

```
  {
    if(FBpos[i] != FBpos[i-1])        // forward-back position change
    {
      steps = abs((FBpos[i] - FBpos[i-1])/5);   // number of steps
      stepsize = 5;                     // magnitude of step size
      if(FBpos[i] < FBpos[i-1]) stepsize = -5;
                        // change in FB from FBpos[i-1],LRpos[i-1]
      for (int j = 0; j<steps; j++)
moveServo(FBpos[i-1]+j*stepsize, LRpos[i-1], lag);
    }
    if(LRpos[i] != LRpos[i-1])          // left-right position change
    {
      steps = abs((LRpos[i] - LRpos[i-1])/5);
      stepsize = 5;
      if(LRpos[i] < LRpos[i-1]) stepsize = -5;
                        // now at FBpos[i], so change in LR to LRpos[i]
      for (int j = 0; j<steps; j++)
moveServo(FBpos[i], LRpos[i-1]+j*stepsize, lag);
    }
  }
  c = ' ';                          // reset command value
}

void resetServo()                   // function to reset saved positions
{
  Nservo = 0;                       // reset position number to zero
  Serial.println(Nservo);           // transmit position number to app
  c = ' ';                          // reset command value
}
```

The app layout consists of five buttons to control servo motor movements, with the buttons positioned in a *TableArrangement*, which is located in the *Layout* palette on the left side of the Designer window, with the table consisting of three rows and columns (see Figure 10-13). The second *HorizontalArrangement* contains three buttons to save, playback, and reset the servo motor positions. The app layout for Bluetooth connection is the same as described in the app for Figure 10-4. In the *User Interface* palette, an *Image* logo is positioned in the first *HorizontalArrangement*. The image of the pan-tilt bracket with servo motors is uploaded in the *Media* palette at the bottom right of the Designer window. In the *Properties* section on the right side of the Designer window, the image is selected under *Picture*, with the image height and width set to *Fill parent* and 90 pixels, respectively.

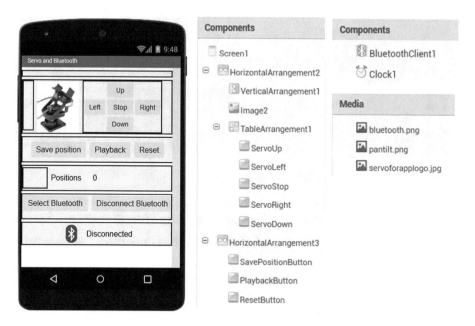

Figure 10-13. *App layout for servo motor control*

The app blocks are all based on a button click, which transmits the appropriate command letter to the ESP8266 or ESP32 microcontroller connected to the two servo motors (see Figure 10-14). The command letters are the first letter of each command, such as "L" for left, with the exception of "Z" and "E" for stop and reset.

Figure 10-14. *Servo motor commands*

The block for the app to receive the transmitted number of saved servo motor positions sets the *PositionsLabel* text to the transmitted message (see Figure 10-15).

Figure 10-15. *Number of saved servo motor positions*

The *SelectBluetooth.BeforePicking, SelectBluetooth.AfterPicking,* and *DisconnectBluetooth* blocks are identical to those in Figure 10-6.

Speech recognition app

Speech recognition is used to control an app rather than clicking app buttons. The app requests the user to speak and converts the spoken sound into text using the speech recognition function of the Android tablet or mobile phone, which may require Internet access. The app layout consists of *HorizontalArrangements* containing the app title, the *Speech* button, and the *SpokenText* textbox. An image of a person speaking, *speech. png*, is uploaded in the *Media* palette and mapped to the *Speech* button in the *Properties* section. The label *SpokenText* contains the text generated by the speech recognition function (see Figure 10-16).

Figure 10-16. *Speech recognition app layout*

The Blocks window consists of just four blocks (see Figure 10-17). When the user clicks the *Speech* button, the *SpeechRecognizer* function, located in the *Media* palette on the right side of the Designer window, clears the content of the *SpokenText* label, asks the user to speak, and converts the speech to text, which is displayed in the *SpokenText* label.

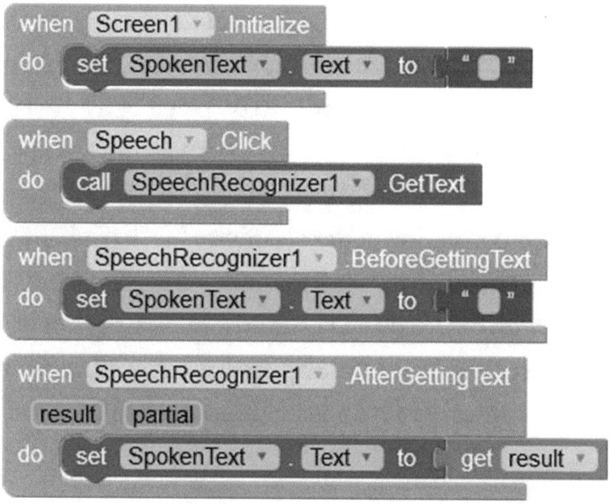

Figure 10-17. *Speech recognition*

Devices are controlled based on the content of the text, derived from the *SpeechRecognizer* function. For example, if the speech and the corresponding *SpokenText* label contain the phrase *LED on* or *LED off*, then the appropriate image, indicating the LED state, is displayed on the app (see Figure 10-18). The *bulbon.png* and *bulboff.png* images are uploaded in the *Media* palette in the Designer window, with the *bulboff. png* image mapped to the *LEDimage* in the *Properties* section.

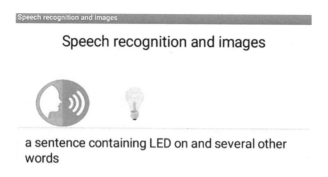

Figure 10-18. *Speech recognition with image control*

The *SpeechRecognizer.AfterGetting Text* function in Figure 10-17 now calls the app *LED* procedure with an image dependent on the app *SpokenText* label containing the phrase *LED on* or *LED off* (see Figure 10-19). The app *LED* procedure in Figure 10-5 that displays an image on the app to indicate the LED state is combined with the app *Change LED* procedure in Figure 10-7 that sends a message consisting of the character "*C*" to the ESP8266 or ESP32 microcontroller. The sketches for an ESP8266 or ESP32 microcontroller in Table 10-2 to turn on or off the LED, when a message, consisting of the character "*C*", was received from the app, are not altered, as there is no change in the microcontroller response to messages sent by the app.

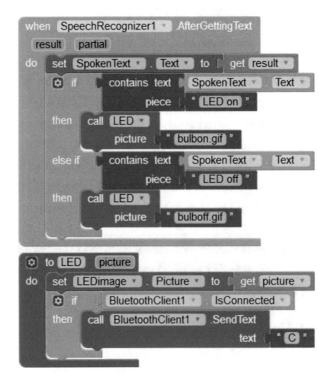

Figure 10-19. *Speech recognition with image control and Bluetooth*

Note that the *SelectBluetooth ListPicker* button, the *DisconnectBluetooth* button, and the Bluetooth image with *StatusLabel* label are included in the app layout (see Figure 10-4) along with the corresponding blocks for Bluetooth connection (see Figures 10-16 and 10-20).

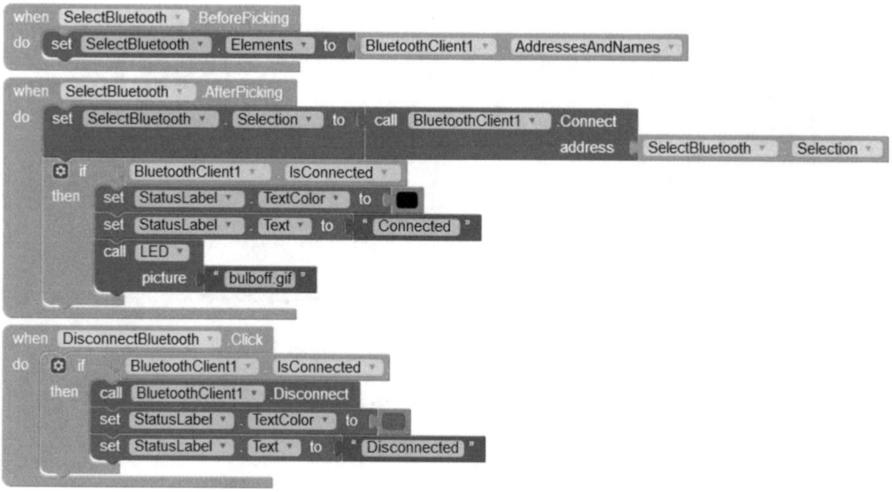

Figure 10-20. *Bluetooth connection*

Instead of the speech recognition app turning on or off an LED, a device is controlled through a relay attached to the ESP8266 or ESP32 development board. The sketches in Table 10-2 are not changed, but the *SpokenText* label of the speech recognition app (see Figure 10-19) is changed from *LED on* and *LED off* to *Relay on* and *Relay off,* as required. Chapter 15 (Radio frequency communication) includes a description of controlling a device with a relay. For example, the *IRF520 MOSFET* relay module can switch up to 100 V direct current (DC) at 10 A, to provide power for a motor, a light, or other devices (see Figure 10-21).

If the load is a DC motor, then the motor, which is partially an inductor, will generate a voltage to maintain current when power to the motor is switched off. Fitting a diode across the motor prevents a voltage spike and dissipates energy through the motor when power is switched off. A Schottky diode, which is a fast switching diode with a low forward voltage drop, is recommended.

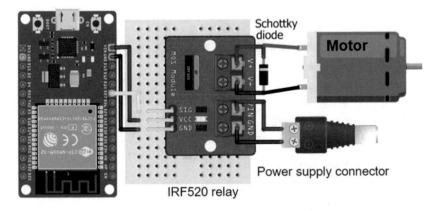

Figure 10-21. *IRF520 MOSFET relay module and the ESP32 development board*

Summary

An app to control the brightness of an LED attached to an ESP8266 or ESP32 development board with feedback from a light-dependent resistor was developed for an Android tablet or mobile phone. The app is programmed with *MIT App Inventor* with a block-based visual language. The ESP8266 or ESP32 development board and the Android tablet or mobile phone communicate using Bluetooth. The ESP32 development board has built-in Bluetooth functionality, but an HC-05 Bluetooth module is attached to the ESP8266 development board. Two servo motors were controlled with an app with servo motor positions saved for playback to imitate an automated robotic movement sequence. An app based on speech recognition controlled the state of an LED attached to an ESP8266 or ESP32 development board, with images displayed on the app on the Android tablet or mobile phone to indicate the LED state.

Components List

- ESP8266 microcontroller: LOLIN (WeMos) D1 mini or NodeMCU board

- ESP32 microcontroller: ESP32 DEVKIT DOIT or NodeMCU board

- LED

- Light-dependent resistor

- Resistors: 220 Ω, 4.7 kΩ

- Bluetooth module: HC-05

- Relay: IRF520 module

CHAPTER 11

App database and Google Maps

MIT App Inventor contains a database function for storing data within an app. *Google Maps* is accessible with *MIT App Inventor*, provided the Android tablet or mobile phone hosting the app has Internet access. This chapter outlines a method to store route data in an app database, with the app displaying route information using *Google Maps*. Building the app database and incorporation of *Google Maps* are the basis for Chapter 12 (GPS tracking app with Google Maps) to develop a GPS tracking app for the GPS module connected to an ESP8266 or ESP32 development board.

MIT App Inventor database

The database function of *MIT App Inventor* retains data when the app is switched off. Databases store data in a structured format, with data referenced to an index or an *MIT App Inventor tag*. The database enables addition, modification, and deletion of data, with searching for a specific database tag using an *MIT App Inventor ListPicker* and displaying the database contents with an *MIT App Inventor ListView*. A database item consists of two components: the database tag

© Neil Cameron 2021
N. Cameron, *Electronics Projects with the ESP8266 and ESP32*,
https://doi.org/10.1007/978-1-4842-6336-5_11

and the value associated with that tag. For example, a database item may consist of *"Longest_day, June, 21"*, with *"Longest_day"* being the database tag and *"June, 21"* being the value associated with tag *"Longest_day"*. The value associated with a tag is a string that includes several components, each separated by a comma, backslash, hash, or ampersand. The database tag is alphanumeric text, so the format for an address and birthday database item is *"Alexander, 44 Scotland Street, 1 January"*, where *"Alexander"* is the database tag that references the value consisting of two components: address of *"44 Scotland Street"* and birthday of *"1 January"*. Database information is accessed by searching on the database tag and not on the associated value.

In an example database, which demonstrates adding, deleting, altering, and displaying database contents, the app consists of two screens (see Figures 11-1 and 11-2). A database item includes the database tag, *Text1*, which is case sensitive, and the database value consisting of two text components, *Text2* and *Text3*, which are alphanumeric. In *Screen1*, a database item is entered into the corresponding three textboxes and saved in the database by clicking the *SavetoDbase* button (see Figure 11-1). A database item is searched for by entering text in the *FindDbaseText1* textbox and clicking the *FindTextButton* button to initiate a database search for the database tag that matches the entered text, and the database item is then displayed in the three textboxes: *Text1*, *Text2,* and *Text3*. A displayed database item is deleted from the database by clicking the *DeleteDbaseItem* button. *Screen1* is cleared by clicking the *ClearScreen* button.

Figure 11-1. *Database app screen 1 layout*

Database contents are displayed by clicking the *ViewDbaseContents* button, which moves to the second screen, *Screen2*, with the database items displayed in a *ListView* as *"Text1 AND Text2&Text3"* (see Figure 11-2). Clicking the *ClearDbaseDisplay* button clears the *Screen2* display of database items. Clicking the *SelectandDisplay ListPicker* button produces a list of the database tags, *Text1*. When a database tag is selected, the database item is displayed as *"Text1 Text2&Text3"* in the *DbaseTag* and *DbaseValue* labels, respectively. Clicking the *ClearDisplay* button clears the database item from *Screen2*. The effect of the *GotoScreen1* button is self-explanatory.

Figure 11-2. *Database app screen 2 layout*

The *TinyDB1* database of *MIT App Inventor* is accessed from the *Storage* palette on the left side of the Designer window, and the *TinyDB* component is dragged onto *Screen1*. *ListView* and *ListPicker* are located in the *User Interface* palette.

A database item is saved, with the TinyDB *StoreValue* function, provided both *Text1* and *Text3* are not blank, with the database value components, *Text2* and *Text3*, joined with the ampersand, &, character (see Figure 11-3).

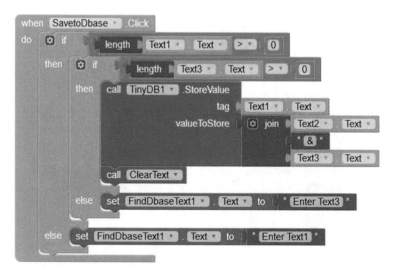

Figure 11-3. *Save a database item*

The contents of *Screen1* are cleared with the *ClearText* procedure, which replaces textboxes with blank text (see Figure 11-4). A database item is deleted from the database with the TinyDB *ClearTag* function, which clears *Text1* from the database, as *Text2* and *Text3* are subsequently overwritten. The entire database content is deleted with the TinyDB *ClearAll* function.

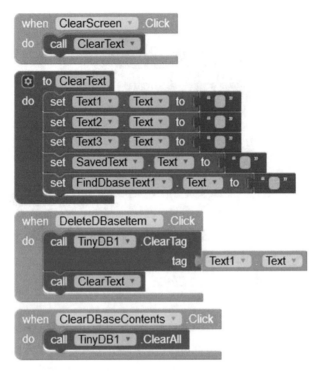

Figure 11-4. *Delete a database item or clear all database items*

A database item is accessed by the database tag, *Text1*, with the database value components indexed as list items 1, 2, *and so on.* If the database tag is found, the database value is parsed into components using the ampersand, &, partitioning character; otherwise, an error message is displayed (see Figures 11-3 and 11-5).

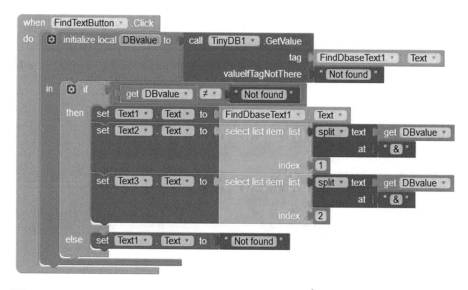

Figure 11-5. *Locate a database item*

Database contents are displayed by allocating database tags to a list, *DBlist*, with the TinyDB *GetTags* function. The corresponding database values are added to the list, with the TinyDB *GetValue* function, and the contents of the list are displayed with the *ListView* function (see Figure 11-6).

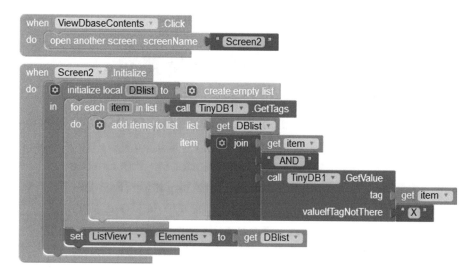

Figure 11-6. *Display database content*

A database item is selected from a list with the TinyDB *GetTags* and *GetValue* functions. The list is deleted with the TinyDB *create empty list* function. The app is moved to another screen with the *open another screen* control option (see Figure 11-7).

```
when SelectandDisplay  .BeforePicking
do  set SelectandDisplay . Elements  to ( call TinyDB1  .GetTags

when SelectandDisplay  .AfterPicking
do  set DBaseTag . Text  to  SelectandDisplay  Selection
    set DBaseValue . Text  to ( call TinyDB1  .GetValue
                                                    tag  SelectandDisplay  Selection
                                         valueIfTagNotThere  " "

when ClearDBaseDisplay  .Click
do  set ListView1 . Elements  to (  create empty list

when ClearDisplay  .Click
do  set DBaseTag . Text  to  " "
    set DBaseValue . Text  to  " "

when GotoScreen1  .Click
do  open another screen  screenName  " Screen1 "
```

Figure 11-7. *Display or clear the display of a selected database item*

MIT App Inventor and Google Maps

 *Google Maps* is accessible with *MIT App Inventor*, provided the Android tablet or mobile phone hosting the app has Internet access. The example app demonstrates accessing *Google Maps*, storing location latitude (North-South position) and longitude (East-West position) information in the app database, placing markers on the map view, zooming in and zooming out of the map view, and displaying road or aerial map views (see Figure 11-8). The map is moved by dragging the map, a double touch zooms in the map, and the

latitude and longitude of the touched position are displayed. A location is saved in the app database after entering the location name and clicking the *AddLocation* button. The *ChooseLocation* button displays a list of saved locations in the app database, with the map centered on the chosen location. The *DeleteLocation* button removes a saved location from the app database.

Figure 11-8. Location database app

The first *HorizontalArrangement* of the location database layout includes the map with a marker, which is accessed from the *Maps* palette (see Figure 11-9). The map is centered and the marker positioned on the latitude-longitude defined in the *CenterFromString* property. The map properties include the *EnableZoom* option, with a height and width of 200 pixels and *Fill parent*, respectively, and the *ShowScale* option. Latitude and longitude labels for displaying values and buttons to zoom in and zoom out of the map and to clear markers from the map are included in the second and third *HorizontalArrangements*. In *MIT App Inventor*, labels are for displaying alphanumeric text, while textboxes enable the user to enter alphanumeric text. A textbox *Hint* property positions text in the textbox to provide information to the user. The *Location* textbox *Hint* is "*enter name then click*". The *AddLocation*, *ChooseLocation,* and *DeleteLocation* buttons are clicked to update location information on the app database. Finally, the *RoadView* and *AerialView* buttons change the map view format, although high aerial-view resolution is only available for the USA.

Figure 11-9. *Location database app layout*

Blocks to display location latitude and longitude when the map is tapped or double-tapped, with the latter increasing the zoom level, are shown in Figure 11-10. The *setText* procedure updates the latitude and longitude textboxes for the map position touched by the user. A global variable *zoom* is defined as the map zoom level. The *drawMap* procedure redraws the map with the updated zoom level and centers the map on the touched location. Blocks to change the map zoom level are shown in Figure 11-11, with the *zoom* procedure updating the zoom level.

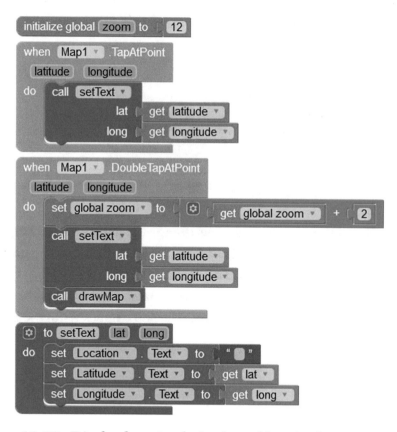

Figure 11-10. *Display location latitude and longitude on tapping map*

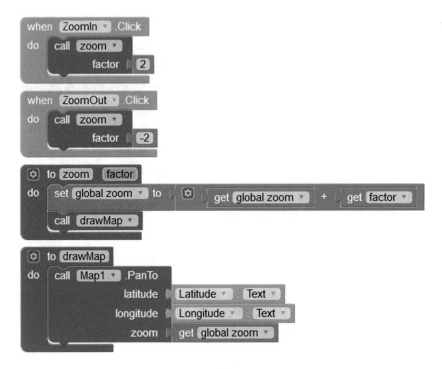

Figure 11-11. Change map zoom level

Location data is saved to the *TinyDB1* app database with the TinyDB *StoreValue* function, with the database tag equal to the location name, as entered in the *Location* textbox. The database value is the location latitude and longitude, which are joined with the ampersand character (see Figure 11-12). A location is deleted from the app database with the TinyDB *ClearTag* function.

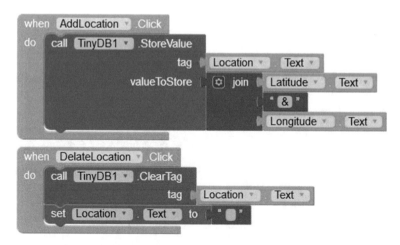

Figure 11-12. *Save location data to the app database*

When a location is selected from the list of locations saved in the app database, the database tag is set to the selected location. The corresponding database value obtained with the TinyDB *GetValue* function, consisting of the location latitude and longitude joined by the ampersand character, is split into two indexed components (see Figure 11-13). The map type is set one, corresponding to the *road view*, the map zoom level is set, and the map is redrawn centered on the location latitude and longitude with a map marker positioned on the map at the selected location. The *ClearMarkers* button sets the *Map Features* to an empty list, which removes all map markers when the map is next updated.

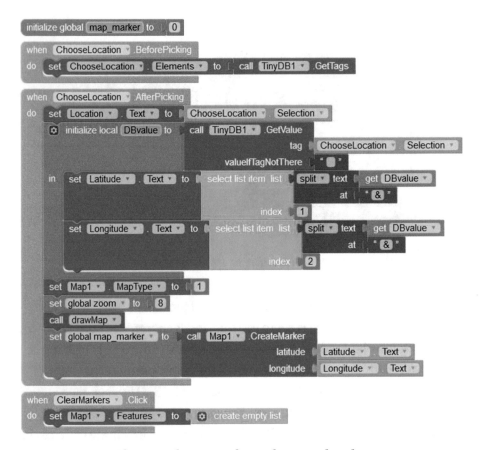

Figure 11-13. *Choose a location from the app database*

Finally, for a *road* or an *aerial* map view, the map type is set to one or two, respectively, and the road view has higher resolution than the aerial view (see Figure 11-14). The resolution of the aerial view is only high for the USA, so the map zoom level is set to eight before redrawing the map.

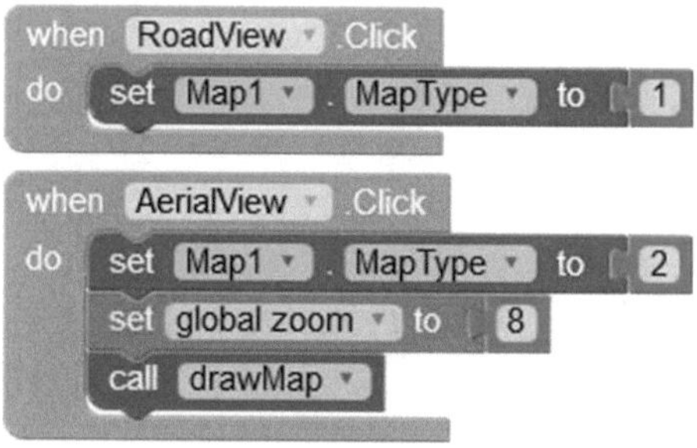

Figure 11-14. Map type definition

Summary

Demonstration apps were developed to illustrate the *MIT App Inventor* database functionality and use of *Google Maps* in a location app. An *MIT App Inventor* database contains database items, consisting of a database tag and the corresponding database value, to include several variables separated by the ampersand character. Database items are added to, altered in, or deleted from the database, with the option to display the database contents or only the database value corresponding to a selected database tag. A database app, built with *MIT App Inventor,* stored the latitude and longitude data of selected locations. Markers were positioned on the map view at the stored locations. The app had a map zoom function with the road and aerial views provided by *Google Maps.*

Components List

- Android tablet or mobile phone
- Internet access

CHAPTER 12

GPS tracking app with Google Maps

In Chapter 11 (App database and Google Maps), an app is developed to display map locations using *Google Maps* on an Android tablet or mobile phone with Internet access. In this chapter, a GPS location app displays the position of a remotely located GPS module or the route taken by the GPS module using *Google Maps*. An nRF24L01 module, connected to an ESP8266 or ESP32 development board attached to the GPS module, transmits the GPS location to a receiving nRF24L01 module, attached to an ESP32 development board. The GPS location information is transmitted to the app on the Android tablet or mobile phone by the ESP32 microcontroller using Bluetooth communication. The GPS location is displayed on the app using *Google Maps*, with the Android tablet or mobile phone accessing *Google Maps* data from the World Wide Web through the Internet Service Provider (ISP) (see Figure 12-1). The transmission range of the nRF24L01 transceiver module of at least 1 km combined with the 10 m range of Bluetooth provides a degree of flexibility in the distance between the app user, the receiving nRF24L01 module, and the remotely positioned GPS module.

© Neil Cameron 2021
N. Cameron, *Electronics Projects with the ESP8266 and ESP32*,
https://doi.org/10.1007/978-1-4842-6336-5_12

Figure 12-1. *GPS tracking app with nRF24L01 transceiver modules*

The receiving nRF24L01 module could be connected to an ESP8266 development board, but an HC-05 Bluetooth module would have to be connected to the ESP8266 development board for Bluetooth communication with the Android tablet or mobile phone.

Alternatively, LoRa (long range) communication, between the transmitting ESP8266 or ESP32 development board connected to the GPS module and the receiving ESP32 microcontroller, could replace the Radio Frequency (RF) communication of the nRF24L01 modules. LoRa communication is described in Chapter 14 (ESP-NOW and LoRa communication).

The app displays the current GPS location with a zoom map function and the option to display a completed route by connecting location tracking markers. The received GPS latitude and longitude values are filtered to avoid erroneous marker positions, caused by transmission noise, from being plotted on the map. An initial base position is entered on the app, to which received GPS positions are compared (see Figure 12-2).

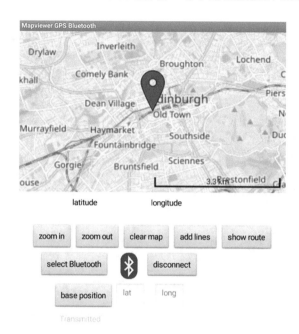

Figure 12-2. *GPS tracking app*

After the Bluetooth connection is established between the app and the
receiving ESP32 microcontroller, the GPS position is identified on the map,
with the map automatically centered at the GPS position (see Figure 12-3 (a)).
Every two seconds, the GPS position is transmitted to the receiving
nRF24L01 module, and the map is updated with the GPS position
(see Figure 12-3 (b)). Clicking the app *add lines* button connects the GPS
position markers with a joining line (see Figure 12-3 (c)). Clicking the app
clear map button clears the map of the GPS markers and the joining line.
Clicking the app *show route* button displays the route taken as the joining
line of GPS positions (see Figure 12-3 (d)).

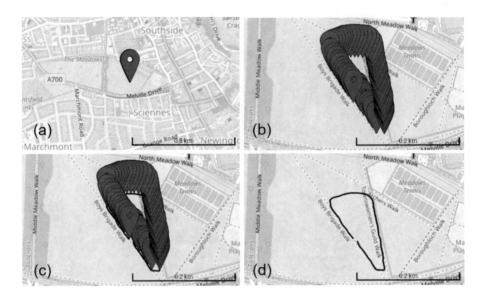

Figure 12-3. *GPS tracking app position markers and route taken*

The app layout in Figure 12-4 consists of the map with a location marker and the *LineString* function, available in the *Maps* palette on the left side of the *MIT App Inventor* Designer window. The GPS latitude and longitude are displayed in the corresponding *Latitude* and *Longitude* labels. The second *HorizontalArrangement* contains the *ZoomIn*, *ZoomOut*, *ClearMarkerLines*, *AddLines,* and *ShowRoute* buttons, which control the map zoom function, clear all markers from the map, connect location markers with a joining line, and display the completed route using the joining lines without the markers.

Figure 12-4. *GPS tracking app layout*

When the app is loaded, clicking the *SelectBluetooth ListPicker* button displays a list of available Bluetooth connections, the selected Bluetooth connection is made, and the text *connected* is displayed in gray text. The *DisconnectBluetooth* button disconnects the Bluetooth connection, and the text *disconnected* is displayed in red.

Entering the base latitude and longitude into the corresponding *BaseLatitude* and *BaseLongitude textboxes* and then clicking the *BasePosition* button displays the entered values, and the app subsequently screens the received latitude and longitude values before displaying location markers on the map with *Google Maps*. The last *HorizontalArrangement* displays the signal, *TransmittedLocation*, as received by the receiving nRF24L01 module. The app *Clock*, *TinyDB*, and *BluetoothClient* components are located in the *Sensors*, *Storage,* and *Connectivity* palettes of the Designer window.

MIT App Inventor blocks to build the app are shown in Figures 12-5 to 12-10. Blocks to connect and disconnect to and from the Bluetooth device, which is the ESP32 microcontroller, are shown in Figure 12-5. The *StatusLabel* label displays the Bluetooth connection status. Building the Bluetooth connection blocks was described in Chapter 10 (Build an app).

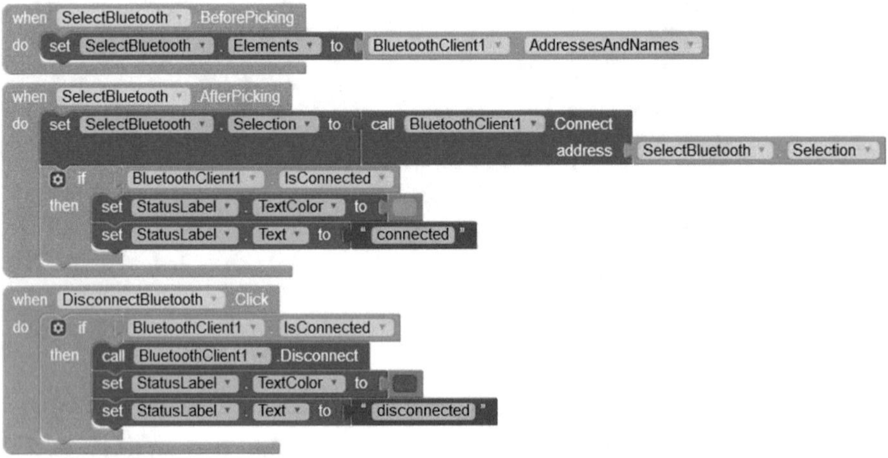

Figure 12-5. *Connect or disconnect to or from a Bluetooth device*

The *Clock1* timer monitors, at 1000 ms intervals, the Bluetooth device for a signal, which is analogous to the instruction if(Serial.available() > 0) in a sketch in the Arduino IDE. The received signal is displayed at the bottom of the app screen in the *TransmittedLocation* label. The received signal should contain three comma-separated components: a counter, the GPS latitude, and the GPS longitude. If the received signal contains a comma, then the signal text is parsed, with each signal component indexed 1, 2, or 3 and allocated to the components of a list, *datalist*. If the *datalist* contains three components, then the *check* procedure is called to validate the signal information (see Figure 12-6). If the received signal does not contain a comma or does not contain three components, then the signal is ignored.

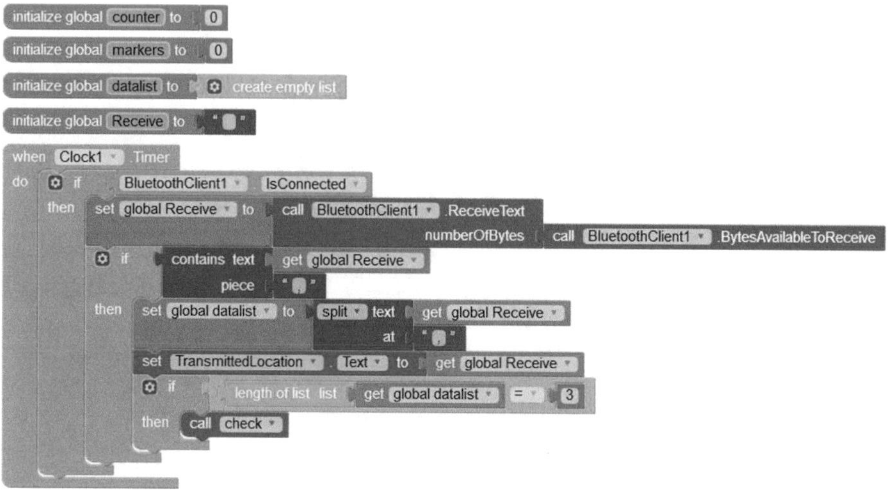

Figure 12-6. *Receive and process Bluetooth signal*

The *check* procedure validates the signal information by checking that the GPS latitude and longitude are both numbers and that the absolute deviation from the base position, which was entered on the app by the user, is less than two degrees (see Figure 12-7). One degree of latitude is 111 km, while a degree of longitude is 78 km at 45° North or South, given a spherical Earth radius of 6371 km. Comparing the GPS latitude and longitude to the base position ensures that spurious positions, due to transmission noise, are not plotted on the map. The GPS position is updated on the map by creating a map marker at the GPS latitude and longitude, with the map centered on the marker location. The GPS position is stored in the TinyDB database with the database tag equal to a marker counter, which is only incremented for verified GPS position data, rather than for all received GPS position data.

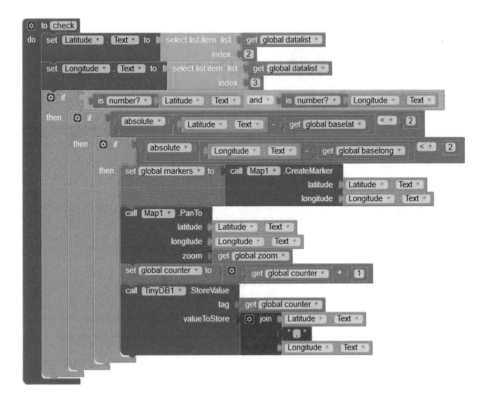

Figure 12-7. *Validate position data, plot position on the map, and store position data*

The blocks to create position marker joining lines are shown in Figure 12-8. The *linetext* text is essentially a series of (X, Y) co-ordinates. When the *AddLines* button is clicked, the *linetext* text is initialized as a blank character and incremented with each GPS position stored in the TinyDB database to form the sequence of (X, Y) co-ordinates. When all the GPS position data is incorporated in the *linetext* text, the points on a *Map LineString* are generated from the *linetext* text, and the *Map LineString* is made visible on *Google Maps*. The *Map LineString* is also made visible, but without the map markers, when the *ShowRoute* button is clicked, after clicking both the *AddLines* and then the *ClearMarkerLines* buttons.

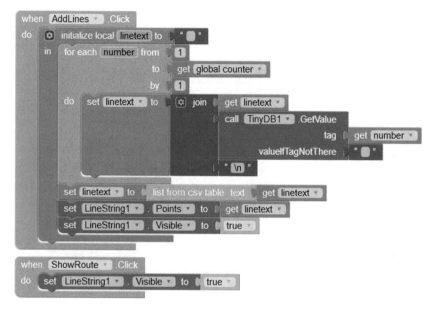

Figure 12-8. *Create marker connecting lines*

Blocks to clear the map markers and/or the map marker joining line are shown in Figure 12-9. When the *ClearMarkerLines* button is clicked, the *Map LineString* is no longer visible, the displayed latitude and longitude are cleared, and the *Map Features*, such as the map markers, are all reset, except for the first item of *Map Features*.

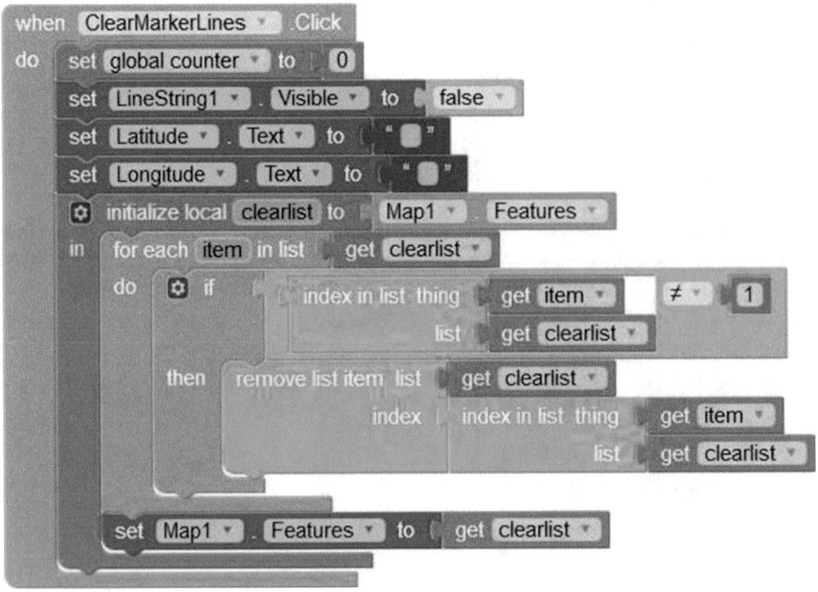

Figure 12-9. *Clear map markers and connecting lines*

The blocks for the map zoom functions and incorporation of the base position information are shown in Figure 12-10. When the *ZoomIn* or *ZoomOut* button is clicked, the map zoom factor is increased or decreased, and the map is redrawn with the updated zoom level and centered at the GPS location. When the *BasePosition* button is clicked, the values entered by the user in the *BaseLatitude* and *BaseLongitude textboxes* are stored in the global *baselat* and *baselong* variables, for screening received GPS position information, with the *BaseLabel* updated with values of the *baselat* and *baselong* variables.

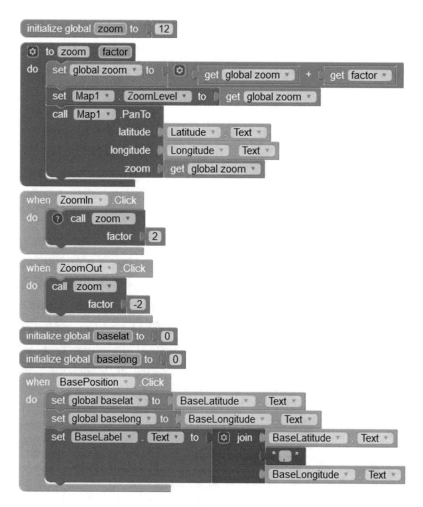

Figure 12-10. *Map zoom function and base position values*

GPS position transmit

GPS positional information is transmitted with an nRF24L01 transceiver module attached to an ESP8266 or ESP32 development board. The nRF24L01 module pins are shown in Figure 12-11, with the GND pin indicated by a square surround. The nRF24L01 module communicates with Serial Peripheral Interface (SPI), with the MOSI (Main-Out Secondary-In), MISO (Main-In Secondary-Out), and SCK (serial clock) pins connected to the microcontroller SPI pins. The CE (transmit/receive) and CSN (standby/ active mode) pins do not have a predefined microcontroller pin. The nRF24L01 module operates at 3.3 V, but the logic pins are 5 V tolerant.

GND		VCC	3.3V
CE	pin 6	CSN	pin 7
SCK	pin 13	MOSI	pin 11
MISO	pin 12	IRQ	

Figure 12-11. *nRF24L01 pin connections*

GPS position data, from a u-blox NEO-7M GPS module, is transmitted by an ESP8266 or ESP32 microcontroller, powered by a 5 V power bank.

Connections for the transmitting nRF24L01 module with the u-blox NEO-7M GPS module and an ESP8266 or ESP32 development board and for the receiving nRF24L01 module with an ESP32 development board are shown in Figure 12-12 and in Table 12-1. The 10 µF capacitor reduces signal noise. Only the u-blox NEO-7M GPS module transmit pin is connected to the microcontroller, as the module receive pin is not required.

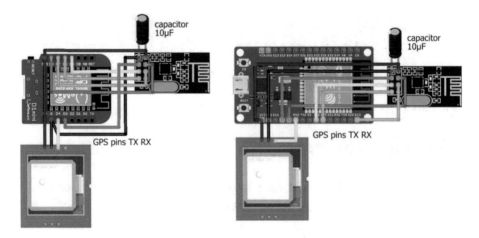

Figure 12-12. *Transmitting nRF24L01 module and u-blox NEO-7M GPS module with a LOLIN (WeMos) D1 mini board and a transmitting or receiving nRF24L01 module and ESP32 DEVKIT DOIT board*

Table 12-1. *Connections for nRF24L01 and u-blox NEO-7M GPS modules with ESP8266 and ESP32 development boards*

Component	Transmitting nRF24L01	Transmitting or Receiving nRF24L01
nRF24L01 VCC	ESP8266 3V3	ESP32 3V3
nRF24L01 CSN	ESP8266 D8	ESP32 GPIO 4
nRF24L01 MOSI	ESP8266 D7	ESP32 GPIO 23
nRF24L01 IRQ	Not connected	Not connected
nRF24L01 GND	ESP8266 GND	ESP32 GND
nRF24L01 CE	ESP8266 D3	ESP32 GPIO 2
nRF24L01 SCK	ESP8266 D5	ESP32 GPIO 18
nRF24L01 MISO	ESP8266 D6	ESP32 GPIO 19
u-blox NEO-7M VCC	ESP8266 3V3	ESP32 3V3
u-blox NEO-7M GND	ESP8266 GND	ESP32 GND
u-blox NEO-7M TXD	ESP8266 D4	ESP32 RX2 (GPIO 16)
10 µF capacitor positive leg	nRF24L01 VCC	nRF24L01 VCC
10 µF capacitor negative leg	nRF24L01 GND	nRF24L01 GND

Instructions for the transmitting nRF24L01 module connected to the u-blox NEO-7M GPS module and an ESP8266 development board are given in Listing 12-1. NMEA (National Marine Electronics Association) messages from the u-blox NEO-7M GPS module are extracted with the *NeoGPS* library, which uses the *AltSoftSerial* library software Serial connection. The *AltSoftSerial* library is not compatible with the ESP8266 microcontroller, so the *SoftwareSerial* library is used instead. The *NeoGPS* library by Slash Devin and the *RF24* library by James Coliz are available in the Arduino IDE, and the *SoftwareSerial* library is built-in. The ESP32

DEVKIT DOIT 30-pin board and the ESP32 NodeMCU 36-pin board have a second Serial port on GPIO 16 (RX2) and GPIO 17 (TX2).

Listing 12-1 is for an ESP8266 microcontroller. When using an ESP32 microcontroller, the following instructions for the ESP8266 microcontroller

```
#include <SoftwareSerial.h>        // include SoftwareSerial library
SoftwareSerial SoftSer(D4, D0); // associate SoftSer with SoftwareSerial
RF24 radio(D3, D8);                 // associate radio with RF24 library
SoftSer.begin(9600);                // SoftwareSerial baud rate
while(nmea.available(SoftSer)>0)  // GPS data available
```

are replaced with instructions for an ESP32 microcontroller

```
RF24 radio(2, 4);                          // associate radio with RF24 library
Serial2.begin(9600, SERIAL_8N1, 16, 17);   // ESP32 RX2 on GPIO 16
while(nmea.available(Serial2)>0)  // GPS data available
```

The u-blox NEO-7M GPS module transmits NMEA messages every second. The *RMC* message, which is the recommended minimum message, contains latitude and longitude. In the *NeoGPS* library folder, open the file *NMEAGPS_cfg.h* in the *src* folder and ensure that the instruction #define NMEAGPS_PARSE_RMC on line 38 is not commented out. If only the RMC message is required, then the instruction on line 48 should equal #define LAST_SENTENCE_IN_INTERVAL NMEAGPS::NMEA_RMC. Information about the structure of NMEA messages is available at github. com/SlashDevin/NeoGPS.

GPS latitude and longitude values are transformed to strings, which are converted to character arrays for inclusion in a data structure transmitted by the nRF24L01 module. A *GPSsend* counter is incremented on receipt of valid GPS location data, with a condition on the counter value defining the interval between transmissions by the nRF24L01 module. Details on *RF24* library instructions accompany Listing 12-2.

Listing 12-1. nRF24L01 transmit signal with position data for the ESP8266 board

```
#include <SoftwareSerial.h> // include SoftwareSerial library
SoftwareSerial SoftSer(D4, D0);
                            // associate SoftSer with SoftwareSerial
#include <NMEAGPS.h>        // include NeoGPS library
NMEAGPS nmea;              // associate nmea and gps
gps_fix gps;              // with NMEAGPS library
float GPSlat, GPSlong;     // real numbers for GPS location
int GPSsend = 0;          // GPS send counter
#include <SPI.h>           // include SPI library
#include <RF24.h>          // include RF24 library
RF24 radio(D3, D8);        // associate radio with RF24 library
byte addresses[ ][6] = {"12"};          // data pipe address
typedef struct            // define data structure to include
{
  char GPSlat[10];        // character arrays for
  char GPSlong[10];       // GPS latitude and longitude
} dataStruct;
dataStruct data;          // name the data structure as data
int interval = 2;          // interval (s) between GPS transmissions

void setup()
{                         // Serial connection to GPS module
  SoftSer.begin(9600);     // SoftwareSerial baud rate
  delay(500);
  radio.begin();          // start radio
  radio.setChannel(50);    // set channel number,
  radio.setDataRate(RF24_2MBPS);          // baud rate
```

319

```
  radio.setPALevel(RF24_PA_HIGH);         // and power amplifier
  radio.setAutoAck(true);                 // set auto-acknowledge (default)
  radio.openWritingPipe(addresses[0]);    // initiate data transmit pipe
  radio.stopListening();                  // nRF24L01 as transmitter
}

void loop()
{
  while(nmea.available(SoftSer)>0)        // GPS data available
  {
    gps = nmea.read();                    // latest satellite message
    if(gps.valid.location)                // validated GPS location
    {
      GPSlat = gps.latitude();
      GPSlong = gps.longitude();
      GPSsend++;                // increment GPS send counter
    }
    if(GPSsend > interval)    // transmit every (interval+1)s
    {                  // convert number to string and then to character array
      String(GPSlat,6).toCharArray(data.GPSlat,10);
      String(GPSlong,6).toCharArray(data.GPSlong,10);
      radio.write(&data, sizeof(data));
                                          // transmit signal as data structure
      GPSsend = 0;                // reset GPS send counter
    }
  }
}
```

GPS position receive

Instructions for the receiving nRF24L01 module connected to an ESP32 development board are given in Listing 12-2. The *RF24* library by James Coliz is available in the Arduino IDE. Communication between nRF24L01 transceiver modules is through data pipes that require an address of a five-letter string, such as "*node1*" or "*12*" for each data pipe, a transmission channel number, a data rate, and a power amplifier level. The nRF24L01 module operates at frequencies of 2.4 GHz with 126 channels of bandwidth of less than 1 MHz, resulting in a range of frequencies between 2.4 GHz (2400 MHz) and 2525 MHz, corresponding to channel numbers 0–125. Channel number, *N*, is set with the instruction setChannel(N). Data rates, of 250 kbps, 1 Mbps, and 2 Mbps, measured in bits per second, are available in the RF24 library using the instruction setDataRate() with values *RF24_250KBPS, RF24_1MBPS, and RF24_2MBPS*. The power amplifier levels of *RF24_PA_MIN, LOW, HIGH,* and *MAX* correspond to -18, -12, -6, and 0 dB that equate to power outputs of approximately 1/64, 1/16, 1/4, and 1 mW, respectively, as power = $10^{(dB/10)}$mW. Power amplifier levels are set with the instruction setPALevel().

A data structure combines several data types, but has a limit of 32 bytes with an integer, a real number, or a character requiring 2, 4, or 1 byte, respectively. The received nRF24L01 signal, containing GPS location data, is combined with a counter value and transmitted as a text string to the GPS location app.

Listing 12-2. nRF24L01 receive signal transmitted with Bluetooth

```
#include <BluetoothSerial.h>        // include Bluetooth library
BluetoothSerial SerialBT;           // associate SerialBT with library
#include <SPI.h>                    // include SPI library
#include <RF24.h>                   // include RF24 library
RF24 radio(2, 4);                   // associate radio with RF24 lib
byte addresses[ ][6] = {"12"};      // data pipe address
typedef struct                      // define data structure to include
{
  char GPSlat[10];                  // character arrays for
  char GPSlong[10];                 // GPS latitude and longitude
} dataStruct;
dataStruct data;                    // name the data structure as data
int count = 0;                      // received message counter
int textLen;
String text;
char c;

void setup()
{
  radio.begin();                    // start radio
  radio.setChannel(50);             // set channel number
  radio.setDataRate(RF24_2MBPS);    // baud rate
  radio.setPALevel(RF24_PA_HIGH);   // and power amplifier
  radio.setAutoAck(true);           // set auto-acknowledge (default)
  radio.openReadingPipe(0, addresses[0]);
                                    // initiate data receive pipe
  radio.startListening();           // nRF24L01 module as receiver
  SerialBT.begin("ESP32 Bluetooth");        // identify Bluetooth
}
```

```
void loop()
{
  if(radio.available())              // if signal received
  {                                  // received signal to data structure
    radio.read(&data, sizeof(data));
    count++;                         // increment counter
    text = String(count) + "," + String(data.GPSlat) + "," +
    String(data.GPSlong) + ",";    // build string of position data
    textLen = text.length();
    for (int i=0; i<textLen; i++)
    {
      c = text[i];                   // for each message character
      SerialBT.write(c);             // transmit to Bluetooth device
    }
  }
}
```

The receiving nRF24L01 module is monitored by displaying the received data on the Serial Monitor using the Serial connection with the instructions

```
Serial.begin(115200);              // Serial Monitor baud rate
Serial.println(text);              // display GPS position data
```

Validate transmission of GPS position

The Wi-Fi functionality of ESP8266 and ESP32 microcontrollers enables data display on a web page, in addition to the Serial Monitor. When checking the development of a tracking app, the received GPS location data is displayed on a web page using an Android tablet or mobile phone connected to a wireless local area network (WLAN). Transmission of GPS location data is tested by changing the GPS location within the WLAN connection radius of several meters.

Building and updating a web page is described in Chapter 8 (Updating a web page). Instructions to update a web page with GPS location data are combined with Listing 12-2, as shown in Listing 12-3. The sketch demonstrates different time intervals for updating, displaying, and transmission of GPS location data. The u-blox Neo-7M GPS location data is automatically updated every second, which is displayed on the Serial Monitor. The web page updates a counter every second, but the web page GPS location data is updated every five seconds. The nRF24L01 transceiver module transmits GPS location data every three seconds. In Listing 12-2, GPS latitude and longitude were transformed to strings, converted to character arrays, and sent as a text string to the GPS location app, with the instruction `String(GPSlat,6).toCharArray(data.GPSlat,10)`. In Listing 12-3, GPS latitude and longitude are declared in a data structure, *data*, and transmitted directly with the instruction `radio.write(&data, sizeof(data))`. The `flashLED` function creates a double flash of the LED when GPS location data is transmitted, as an indicator that the combination of the ESP8266 or ESP32 microcontroller and u-blox NEO-7M GPS module is functioning.

Listing 12-3 is for an ESP8266 microcontroller. If the transmitting nRF24L01 module is connected to an ESP32 development board, then the *WiFi*, *WebServer* and *SoftwareSerial* libraries, nRF24L01 CE and CSN pins, and the LED pin definition instructions for the ESP8266 microcontroller

```
#include <ESP8266WiFi.h>          // include ESP8266 Wi-Fi and
#include <ESP8266WebServer.h>     // web server libraries
ESP8266WebServer server;          // associate server with library
#include <SoftwareSerial.h>       // include SoftwareSerial library
SoftwareSerial SoftSer(D4, D0);
                                  // associate SoftSer with SoftwareSerial
SoftSer.begin(9600);              // serial connection to GPS module
```

```
while(nmea.available(SoftSer)>0)  // GPS data available
RF24 radio(D3, D8);               // associate radio with RF24 library
int LEDpin = D1;                  // define LED
```

are replaced with instructions for the ESP32 microcontroller

```
#include <WiFi.h>                 // include ESP8266 Wi-Fi and
#include <WebServer.h>            // web server libraries
WebServer server (80);            // requires a port number
Serial2.begin(9600, SERIAL_8N1, 16, 17);
                                  // ESP32 RX2, TX2 on GPIO 16 and 17
while(nmea.available(Serial2)>0)  // GPS data available
RF24 radio(2, 4);                 // associate radio with RF24 library

int LEDpin = D1;                  // define LED pin
```

Listing 12-3. nRF24L01 transmit signal with position data and display on web page

```
#include <ESP8266WiFi.h>          // include ESP8266 Wi-Fi and
#include <ESP8266WebServer.h>     // web server libraries
ESP8266WebServer server;          // associate server with library
char ssid[] = "xxxx";             // change xxxx to your Wi-Fi SSID
char password[] = "xxxx";         // change xxxx to your Wi-Fi password
#include "buildpage.h"            // webpage HTML code
#include <SoftwareSerial.h>       // include SoftwareSerial library
SoftwareSerial SoftSer(D4, D0);   // associate SoftSer with SoftwareSerial
#include <NMEAGPS.h>              // include NeoGPS library
NMEAGPS nmea;                     // associate nmea with NMEAGPS lib
gps_fix gps;                      // associate gps with NMEAGPS library
float GPSlat, GPSlong, GPSalt, GPSspd;
                                  // real numbers for GPS location
```

```
int GPSsend = 0;                    // GPS send counter
String json;
int count = 0;
String counter;                     // counter increment every second
#include <SPI.h>                     // include SPI library
#include <RF24.h>                    // include RF24 library
RF24 radio(D3, D8);                  // associate radio with RF24 library
byte addresses[ ][6] = {"12"};       // data pipe address
typedef struct                       // define data structure to include
{
  float GPSlat;                      // GPS latitude
  float GPSlong;                     // GPS longitude
  float GPSalt;                      // GPS altitude (m)
  float GPSspd;                      // GPS ground speed (kmph)
  int sigCount;                      // signal counter
} dataStruct;
dataStruct data;                     // name the data structure as data
int LEDpin = D1;                     // define LED pin
int LED = 0;                         // LED turned off
int interval = 1;                    // (interval+1)s between transmissions

void setup()
{
  Serial.begin(115200);              // define Serial output baud rate
  SoftSer.begin(9600);               // serial connection to GPS module
  WiFi.begin(ssid, password);        // initialise and connect Wi-Fi
  while (WiFi.status() != WL_CONNECTED) delay(500);
  Serial.print("IP address: ");
  Serial.println(WiFi.localIP());    // display web server IP address
  server.begin();                    // initialise server
```

```
  server.on("/", base);          // call base function as webpage loaded
  server.on("/GPSurl", GPSfunct);
                                  // call GPSfunct with GPSurl loaded
  server.on("/countUrl", countFunct);
  delay(500);
  radio.begin();                 // start radio
  radio.setChannel(50);          // set channel number,
  radio.setDataRate(RF24_2MBPS);    // baud rate and
  radio.setPALevel(RF24_PA_HIGH);   // power amplifier level
  radio.setAutoAck(true);        // set auto-acknowledge (default is true)
  radio.openWritingPipe(addresses[0]);   // initiate data transmit pipe
  radio.stopListening();         // set nRF24L01 module as transmitter
  pinMode(LEDpin, OUTPUT);       // define LEDpin as OUTPUT
}

void GPSfunct()                  // function to transmit GPS position data
{
  while(nmea.available(SoftSer)>0)   // GPS data available
  {
    gps = nmea.read();           // latest satellite message
    if(gps.valid.location)       // validated GPS location
    {
      GPSlat = gps.latitude();
      GPSlong = gps.longitude();
      GPSsend++;                 // increment GPS send counter
    }
    if(gps.valid.altitude) GPSalt = gps.altitude(); // altitude
    if(gps.valid.speed) GPSspd = gps.speed_kph();
                                 // ground speed
    JsonConvert(GPSlat, GPSlong, GPSalt, GPSspd);
                                 // convert to JSON text
```

```
    server.send(200, "text/json", json);  // send JSON text to client
    Serial.println(json);
    if(GPSsend > interval)       // transmit every (interval+1)s
    {
      data.GPSlat = GPSlat;      // convert GPS readings to data structure
      data.GPSlong = GPSlong;
      data.GPSalt = GPSalt;
      data.GPSspd = GPSspd;
      data.sigCount++;           // increment signal counter
      radio.write(&data, sizeof(data));
                                 // transmit signal as data structure
      GPSsend = 0;               // reset GPS send counter
      flashLED();
    }
  }
}
                                 // function to convert data to JSON text
String JsonConvert(float val1, float val2, float val3, float val4)
{                                // start with open bracket
  json  = "{\"var1\": \"" + String(val1,4) + "\",";
  json += " \"var2\": \"" + String(val2,4) + "\",";
                                 // end with comma
  json += " \"var3\": \"" + String(val3)   + "\",";
  json += " \"var4\": \"" + String(val4)   + "\"}";
                                 // end with close bracket
  return json;
}

void countFunct()                // function to increment counter
{                                // and send value to client
  count++;
  counter = String(count);
```

```
  server.send (200, "text/plain", counter);
}

void flashLED()                    // function to flash LED
{
  for (int i=0; i<4; i++)
  {
    LED = 1 - LED;                 // alternate LED state four times
    digitalWrite(LEDpin, LED); // ON – OFF – ON - OFF
    delay(50);
  }
}

void base()                        // function to return HTML code
{
  server.send (200, "text/html", page);
}

void loop()
{
  GPSfunct();                      // function to transmit GPS location data
  server.handleClient();       // manage HTTP requests
}
```

Listing 12-4 contains the AJAX code for the web page and XML HTTP requests, which is defined as the string literal *page*. The first part of the <body> section is the web page HTML code with the variables referenced as the variable names in the XML HTTP request. The JavaScript instruction setInterval() controls the time interval between XML HTTP requests, which is five seconds for the *reload* function to obtain the GPS location data. JavaScript scripts, bracketed by <script>...</script>, are positioned prior to the HTML </body> code to improve web page display speed.

Listing 12-4. AJAX request with GPS position data

```
char page[] PROGMEM = R"(
<!DOCTYPE html><html>
<head><title>ESP8266</title>
<meta charset="UTF-8">
</head>
<body>
<h2>GPS</h2>
<p>Latitude: <span id = 'latId'>0</span></p>
<p>Longitude: <span id = 'longId'>0</span></p>
<p>Altitude: <span id = 'altId'>0</span> m</p>
<p>Speed: <span id = 'speedId'>0</span> kph<p>
<p>Counter: <span id = 'countId'>0</span></p>

<script>
setInterval(reload, 5000);              // reload function called every 5s
function reload()
{
  var xhr = new XMLHttpRequest();
  xhr.onreadystatechange = function()
  {
    if(this.readyState == 4 && this.status == 200)
    {
      var obj = JSON.parse(this.responseText);
      document.getElementById('latId').innerHTML = obj.var1;
      document.getElementById('longId').innerHTML = obj.var2;
      document.getElementById('altId').innerHTML = obj.var3;
      document.getElementById('speedId').innerHTML = obj.var4;
      console.log(obj.var3);
    }
  };
```

```
  xhr.open('GET', '/GPSurl', true);
  xhr.send();
}

setInterval(reload2, 1000);
function reload2()                      // reload2 function called every 1s
{                                       // to obtain countId from /countUrl
  var xhr = new XMLHttpRequest();
  xhr.onreadystatechange = function()
  {
    if(this.readyState == 4 && this.status == 200)
    {document.getElementById('countId').innerHTML = this.
    responseText;
    console.log(this.responseText);}
  };
  xhr.open('GET', '/countUrl', true);
  xhr.send();
}
</script>
</body></html>
)";
```

To complement testing the updating of transmitted GPS location data by changing the GPS position, testing the updating of the received GPS location data by changing the position of the receiving nRF24L01 module requires a mobile display, such as an OLED screen. The sketch in Listing 12-5 displays GPS location data on a 128 × 64–pixel OLED screen (see Figure 12-13). Connections for ESP8266 development boards with transmitting and receiving nRF24L01 modules are given in Table 12-2. The *Adafruit_SSD1306* library for the OLED screen is available in the Arduino IDE.

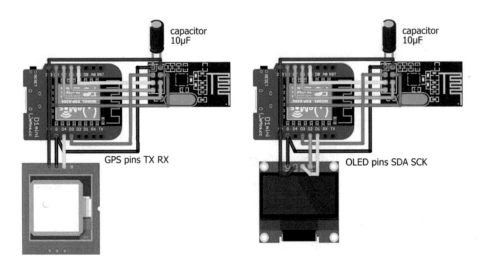

Figure 12-13. *Transmitting and receiving GPS signals with nRF24L01 modules*

Table 12-2. *ESP8266 development board connections to transmitting and receiving nRF24L01 modules with the u-blox NEO-7M GPS module and 128 × 64–pixel OLED screen*

Component	ESP8266	Connect to
nRF24L01 VCC	3V3	10 µF capacitor positive leg
nRF24L01 CSN	D8	
nRF24L01 MOSI	D7	
nRF24L01 IRQ	Not connected	
nRF24L01 GND	GND	10 µF capacitor negative leg
nRF24L01 CE	D3	

(*continued*)

Table 12-2. (*continued*)

Component	ESP8266	Connect to
nRF24L01 SCK	D5	
nRF24L01 MISO	D6	
u-blox NEO-7M VCC	3V3	
u-blox NEO-7M GND	GND	
u-blox NEO-7M TXD	D4	
128 × 64–pixel OLED GND	3V3	
128 × 64–pixel OLED VDD	GND	
128 × 64–pixel OLED SCK	D1	
128×64 pixel OLED SDA	D2	

In Listing 12-5, the transmitted GPS position data from Listing 12-3, which is displayed on a web page, is also displayed on an OLED screen to provide a mobile test of signal transmission and reception.

Listing 12-5. nRF24L01 receive signal with position data and display on OLED

```
#include <SPI.h>                        // include SPI library
#include <RF24.h>                       // include RF24 library
RF24 radio(D3, D8);                     // associate radio with RF24 lib
byte addresses[ ][6] = {"12"};          // data pipe address
typedef struct                          // define data structure to include
{
   float GPSlat;                        // character arrays for
```

```
    float GPSlong;                          // GPS latitude and longitude
    float GPSalt;                           // GPS altitude (m)
    float GPSspd;                           // GPS ground speed (kmph)
    int sigCount;                           // signal counter
} dataStruct;
dataStruct data;                            // name the data structure as data
float lagTime = 0;
#include <Adafruit_SSD1306.h>               // library 128×64 OLED screen
int width = 128;                            // OLED screen dimensions
int height = 64;
Adafruit_SSD1306 oled(width, height, &Wire, -1);
unsigned long lastTime, nowTime = 0;

void setup()
{
  radio.begin();                           // start radio
  radio.setChannel(50);                    // set channel number
  radio.setDataRate(RF24_2MBPS);           // baud rate
  radio.setPALevel(RF24_PA_HIGH);          // and power amplifier
  radio.setAutoAck(true);                  // set auto-acknowledge (default)
  radio.openReadingPipe(0, addresses[0]);
                                           // initiate data receive pipe
  radio.startListening();                  // nRF24L01 as receiver
  oled.begin(SSD1306_SWITCHCAPVCC, 0x3C);
  oled.clearDisplay();                     // initialise OLED screen
  oled.setTextColor(WHITE);
  oled.setTextSize(1);                     // text size of 6×8 pixels
  oled.display();
}
```

```
void loop()
{
  if(radio.available())            // if signal received
  {
    radio.read(&data, sizeof(data));    // set signal to data structure
    nowTime = millis();
    lagTime = (nowTime-lastTime)/1000.0;
                                   // time since last signal received
    lastTime = nowTime;
    screen();                      // call OLED screen function
  }
}

void screen()
{
  oled.clearDisplay();             // clear display
  oled.setCursor(0,0);             // position cursor
  oled.print(data.GPSlat,4);       // display GPS latitude
  oled.setCursor(65,0);            // and GPS longitude
  oled.print(data.GPSlong,4);
  oled.setCursor(0,10);
  oled.print("alt ");oled.print(data.GPSalt,1);
                                   // display GPS altitude
  oled.setCursor(65,10);           // and GPS speed
  oled.print("spd ");oled.print(data.GPSspd);
  oled.setCursor(0, 20);
  oled.print("lag ");oled.print(lagTime,2); // time since last signal
  oled.setCursor(65, 20);
```

```
oled.print("chk ");oled.print(data.sigCount);        // signals sent
oled.display();
}
```

Improve GPS position signal

Signal transmission and reception with nRF24L01 transceivers is improved by choosing a transmission channel with low activity, the data rate, and the power amplifier level. In Listing 12-6, an ESP8266 microcontroller uses the *RF24* library to display, on the Serial Monitor, the carrier activity on each of the 126 channels. If an ESP32 development board is used for channel scanning with an nRF24L01 transceiver module, then the instruction RF24 radio(D3, D8) is replaced with RF24 radio(2, 4), for consistency with earlier listings in the chapter.

Listing 12-6. Channel scanning

```
#include <SPI.h>                    // include SPI library
#include <RF24.h>                   // include RF24 library
RF24 radio(D3, D8);                 // associate radio with library
const int nChan = 126;              // 126 channels available
int chan[nChan];                    // store counts per channel
int nScan = 100;                    // number of scans per channel
int scan;

void setup()
{
  Serial.begin(115200);             // define Serial output baud rate
  radio.begin();                    // start radio
}
```

```
void loop()
{
  for (int i=0;i<nChan;i++)              // for each channel
  {
    chan[i] = 0;                         // reset counter
    for (scan=0; scan<nScan; scan++)     // repeat scanning
    {
      radio.setChannel(i);               // define channel
      radio.startListening();
      delayMicroseconds(128);            // listen for 128µs
      radio.stopListening();
      if(radio.testCarrier()>0) chan[i]=chan[i]+1;
                                         // a carrier on the channel
    }
    delay(1);                            // avoid watchdog reset
  }
  for (int i=0; i<nChan; i++)            // for each channel
  {
    if(i%10 == 0) Serial.print("|");
    Serial.print(chan[i], HEX);          // display carrier activity
  }                                      // format in HEX for values <16
  Serial.println();                      // new line
}
```

Signal transmission and reception by two nRF24L01 transceiver modules is assessed by determining the number of signals successfully received in a second, given repeated transmission of a signal. In the sketch in Listing 12-7, a message containing the time (minutes and seconds) and a counter value is repeatedly transmitted, with the counter equal to the number of transmissions in the previous second. With the default setting for signal auto-acknowledge of *true*, the number of received signals would equal the number of transmitted signals, as a signal is repeatedly transmitted until acknowledged. In the sketch, auto-acknowledge is set to *false*.

Listing 12-7. Signal transmission to monitor nRF24L01 transceiver modules

```
#include <SPI.h>                     // include SPI library
#include <RF24.h>                    // include RF24 library
RF24 radio(D3, D8);                  // associate radio with library
byte addresses[ ][6] = {"12"};       // data pipe address
typedef struct                       // define data structure to include
{
  unsigned long counted;             // counter
  unsigned long mins;                // time (minute and second)
  unsigned long secs;
} dataStruct;
dataStruct data;
unsigned long lastTime, nowTime = 0;
int count = 0;
int mins = 0, secs = 0;

void setup()
{
  radio.begin();                             // start radio
  radio.setChannel(50);                      // set channel number,
  radio.setDataRate(RF24_2MBPS);             // data rate and
  radio.setPALevel(RF24_PA_HIGH);            // power amplifier
  radio.setAutoAck(false);                   // set auto-acknowledge
  radio.openWritingPipe(addresses[0]);  // initiate data transmit pipe
  radio.stopListening();                     // set nRF24L01 as transmitter
```

```
  mins = 0;
  secs = 0;
}

void loop()
{
  nowTime = millis();
  if(nowTime - lastTime > 1000)          // determine minutes
  {                                      // and seconds
    secs++;
    if(secs > 59)                        // after 60 seconds
    {
      secs = 0;                          // reset second variable
      mins++;                            // increment minute variable
    }
    data.counted = count;                // convert values to data structure
    data.mins = mins;
    data.secs = secs;
    count = 0;                           // reset counter
    lastTime = nowTime;                  // update time of "second"
  }
  radio.write(&data, sizeof(data));      // transmit signal
  count++;                               // increment signal counter
}
```

The complementary sketch for an nRF24L01 transceiver module to receive the signal is given in Listing 12-8. Signal information for the receiving nRF24L01 module is displayed on a 128 × 64–pixel OLED screen to determine the impact of different positions of the receiving nRF24L01, relative to the position of the transmitting nRF24L01 module (see Figure 12-14). The *Adafruit SSD1306* library references the *Adafruit GFX* and *Wire* libraries, so the #include <Adafruit_GFX.h> and #include

<Wire.h> instructions are not required. The number of signals transmitted and received every second is stored in an array, acting as a circular buffer, for calculation of a moving average number of signals transmitted and received.

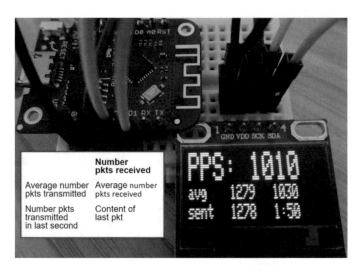

Figure 12-14. *nRF24L01 packets (received/transmitted) per second*

Listing 12-8. Signal reception to monitor nRF24L01 transceiver modules

```
#include <SPI.h>                      // include SPI library
#include <RF24.h>                     // include RF24 library
RF24 radio(D3, D8);                   // associate radio with library
byte addresses[ ][6] = {"12"};        // data pipe address
typedef struct                        // define data structure to include
{
  unsigned long sent;                 // sent signals
  unsigned long mins;                 // time (minute and second)
  unsigned long secs;
```

```
} dataStruct;
dataStruct data;
#include <Adafruit_SSD1306.h>        // library 128×64 OLED screen
int width = 128;                     // OLED screen dimensions
int height = 64;
Adafruit_SSD1306 oled(width, height, &Wire, -1);
const int Nval = 20;                 // size of circular buffer
int pkts[Nval], sents[Nval];         // arrays for circular buffer
int N = 0, pkt = 0;
unsigned long sumPkt = 0, sumSent = 0;
float avgPkt, avgSent;
unsigned long lastTime, nowTime = 0;  // variables to store time values

void setup()
{
  radio.begin();                      // start radio
  radio.setChannel(50);               // set channel number
  radio.setDataRate(RF24_2MBPS);      // data rate
  radio.setPALevel(RF24_PA_HIGH);     // and power amplifier
  radio.setAutoAck(false);            // set auto-acknowledge
  radio.openReadingPipe(0, addresses[0]);
                                      // initiate data receive pipe
  radio.startListening();             // set nRF24L01 as transmitter
  oled.begin(SSD1306_SWITCHCAPVCC, 0x3C);
  oled.clearDisplay();                // initialise OLED screen
  oled.setTextColor(WHITE);
  oled.display();
  data.sent = 0;
  for (int i=0; i<10; i++)            // set circular buffer arrays to zero
  {
    pkts[i] = 0;
```

341

```
    sents[i] = 0;
  }
}

void loop()
{
  if(radio.available())                // signal available
  {
    radio.read(&data, sizeof(data));     // read signal and
    pkt++;                               // increment signal counter
  }
  nowTime = millis();
  if(nowTime - lastTime > 1000)    // update values every second
  {
    sumPkt = sumPkt - pkts[N];       // subtract oldest value from sum
    sumPkt = sumPkt + pkt;           // add current value to sum
    pkts[N] = pkt;                   // update circular buffer
    sumSent = sumSent - sents[N];
    sumSent = sumSent + data.sent;
    sents[N] = data.sent;
    N++;
    if(N > Nval-1) N = 0;            // back to "start" of circular buffer
    avgPkt = 1.0*sumPkt / Nval;      // calculate moving averages
    avgSent = 1.0*sumSent / Nval;
    screen();                       // call OLED screen function
    pkt = 0;
    data.sent = 0;
    lastTime = nowTime;             // update time of last "second"
  }
}
```

```
void screen()
{
  oled.clearDisplay();                  // clear display
  oled.setCursor(0,0);                  // position cursor
  oled.setTextSize(2);                  // text size of 12×16 pixels
  oled.print("PPS: ");oled.print(pkt);  // signal (packets) per second
  oled.setCursor(0,16);
  oled.setTextSize(1);                  // text size of 6×8 pixels
  oled.setCursor(0,16);
  oled.print("avg");
  oled.setCursor(40,16);
  oled.print(avgSent,0);                // average of transmitted signals
  oled.setCursor(80,16);
  oled.print(avgPkt,0);                 // average of received signals
  oled.setCursor(0,25);
  oled.print("sent");
  oled.setCursor(40,25);
  oled.print(data.sent);                // last number of sent signals
  oled.setCursor(80,25);
  oled.print(data.mins);oled.print(":");  // signal content
  oled.print(data.secs);
  oled.display();
}
```

The impact of different transmission channels, data rates, and power amplifier levels is quantified using the sketches in Listings 12-7 and 12-8 to identify optimal settings for a specific environment. Note that data rates for the two nRF24L01 transceiver modules must be equal. For a pair of nRF24L01 transceivers and ESP8266 microcontrollers, a transmission rate of 2 Mbps and a *RF24_PA_HIGH* power amplifier level resulted in the highest number of packets received. Although, the number of packets sent for a 2 Mbps transmission rate was lower, relative to the transmission rate, than for the 250 kbps and 1 Mbps rates. For a 1 Mbps transmission rate, the number of packets received declined with higher amplification levels (see Table 12-3). Packets received rate will depend on the nRF24L01 transceivers, the transmission distance, and ambient electrical noise.

Table 12-3. *nRF24L01 packets received/transmitted per second*

Amplifier Level	Transmission Rate (bps)		
	250 k	**1 M**	**2 M**
MIN	150/250	420/1040	880/1280
LOW	10/250	300/1040	900/1280
HIGH	-	100/1040	1030/1280
MAX	-	-	400/1280

Summary

A GPS location app, built with *MIT App Inventor*, displayed with *Google Maps* the position of a remotely located u-blox NEO-7M GPS module or the route taken by the GPS module. An nRF24L01 module, connected to an ESP8266 or ESP32 development board attached to the GPS module, transmitted the GPS location to a receiving nRF24L01 module, attached to an ESP32 development board. The GPS location information was transmitted to the app by the ESP32 microcontroller using Bluetooth communication. The GPS location app displayed the GPS position information on the Android tablet or mobile phone, by accessing *Google Maps* data from the World Wide Web through the Internet Service Provider. The tracking app included a map zoom function and the option to connect location tracking markers and display the completed route. A web page to display transmitted GPS data was built for testing GPS signal transmission and reception. The impact of different transmission channels, data rates, and power amplifier levels was quantified by the number of signals successfully received in a second, given repeated transmission of a signal.

Components List

- ESP8266 microcontroller: LOLIN (WeMos) D1 mini or NodeMCU board

- ESP32 microcontroller: ESP32 DEVKIT DOIT or NodeMCU board

- u-blox NEO-7M GPS module

- nRF24L01 transceiver module: 2×

- OLED display: 128 × 64 pixels

CHAPTER 13

USB OTG communication

In Chapter 12 (GPS tracking app with Google Maps), data is transmitted to an app on an Android tablet or mobile phone by an ESP32 microcontroller with Bluetooth communication. In Chapter 10 (Build an app), an HC-05 Bluetooth module is connected to an ESP8266 development board to communicate with an app. If the device to transfer data to an app does not have Bluetooth functionality, then USB OTG (On-the-Go) communication connects the device with the app. In this chapter, the device without Bluetooth functionality is an Arduino Uno. An HC-05 Bluetooth module could be connected to the Arduino Uno for Bluetooth communication with the Android tablet or mobile phone, but this chapter focuses on USB OTG communication.

USB OTG communication enables an Android tablet or mobile phone to transmit and receive signals to and from a USB peripheral device. The Android tablet or mobile phone is the OTG-A device acting as a host for that app and providing power to the USB peripheral or OTG-B device, which is the Arduino Uno. A USB OTG cable connects the host to the USB peripheral device. The *Easy OTG Checker* app by Kjarvel on *Google Play Store* determines if an Android tablet or mobile phone supports OTG, by attaching the USB peripheral device with a USB OTG cable (see Figure 13-1).

N. Cameron, *Electronics Projects with the ESP8266 and ESP32*, https://doi.org/10.1007/978-1-4842-6336-5_13

Figure 13-1. *Easy OTG Checker app connected to Arduino Uno*

MIT App Inventor provides a *Serial* component for USB OTG communication that is located in the *Connectivity* palette on the left side of the Designer window. The *Serial* component communicates with the ATmega16U2 USB to serial converter of the Arduino Uno, but not with the CH340 chip on the Arduino Nano or ESP8266 development boards. If the *MIT App Inventor Serial* component is extended to the CH340 chip, then the framework for building USB OTG communication apps, as described in this chapter, will be applicable to the ESP8266 microcontroller.

App receive

To demonstrate the Android tablet or mobile phone, the OTG-A device, receiving data from the Arduino Uno, the OTG-B device, a pair of numbers is transmitted by the Arduino Uno. An app, hosted by the OTG-A device, parses the number pair into components and displays both the number pair and its components (see Figure 13-2). The number pair could be latitude and longitude from a GPS module, temperature and humidity from a BMP280 sensor, or voltage and current from an INA219 sensor attached to the Arduino Uno. The app provides the framework for more complex signal transmit and receive projects.

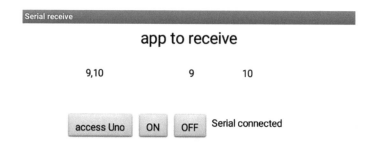

Figure 13-2. *App to receive message from the OTG-B device*

The *accessUno, OnButton,* and *OffButton* buttons enable the OTG-B device to be connected and disconnected to and from the OTG-A device with the connection status displayed in the *StatusLabel* label. When the *accessUno* button is clicked, after the Arduino Uno is attached to the Android tablet or mobile phone, a USB device access request is made (see Figure 13-3). The access request *OK* is selected, and the app *OnButton* button is clicked to connect the OTG-B device to the OTG-A device.

Figure 13-3. *USB device access request*

The sketch in Listing 13-1 writes to the Serial Monitor the number pairs at one-second intervals. When the Arduino Uno is connected to an Android tablet or mobile phone with a USB OTG cable, the Arduino Uno and Android tablet or mobile phone communicate by USB OTG communication, once the Serial port is opened by the app.

Listing 13-1. Transmit number pairs

```
String text;
int count = 0;
unsigned long timer;

void setup()
{
  Serial.begin(9600);                  // define serial baud rate
}

void loop()
{
  if(millis() - timer > 1000)          // after 1sec has elapsed
  {
    count++;                           // increment count
    if(count > 254) count = 0;         // arbitrary limit on counter
    text = String(count)+ "," +String(count+1);
                                       // combine numbers into text
    Serial.println(text);              // transmit text
    timer = millis();                  // reset timer
  }
}
```

The app layout consists of the app title and two *HorizontalArrangements* containing the *sentText, Part1Text,* and *Part2Text* labels to display text and the buttons (see Figure 13-4). The *accessUno, OnButton,* and *OffButton* buttons to connect or disconnect the OTG-B device to or from the OTG-A device and a *StatusLabel* label are contained in the second *HorizontalArrangement.* The *Serial* and *Clock* components are displayed below the app layout.

Figure 13-4. *OTG-B to OTG-A app layout*

Blocks to manage the Serial connection of the OTG-B device to the
OTG-A device, read the message transmitted by the OTG-B device, and
display the message on the OTG-A device screen are shown in
Figures 13-5, 13-6, and 13-7. The OTG-B device or *Serial1* is initialized and
the baud rate defined, just as with the instruction `Serial.begin(9600)`
when setting the Serial Monitor baud rate in the Arduino IDE. The
StatusLabel label displays the connection status of the OTG-B device with
the OTG-A device (see Figure 13-5).

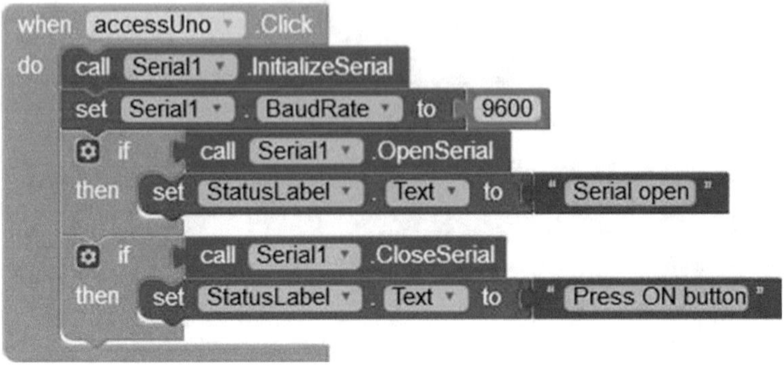

Figure 13-5. *Connect the OTG-B device*

The app includes the facility to connect and disconnect the OTG-B device (see Figure 13-6). Clicking the *OnButton* or *OffButton* button connects or disconnects the OTG-B device using the *connect* or *close* procedure. The connection status is displayed by the *StatusLabel* label, as the *connect* procedure returns the value one when the Serial port is connected and similarly for the *close* procedure.

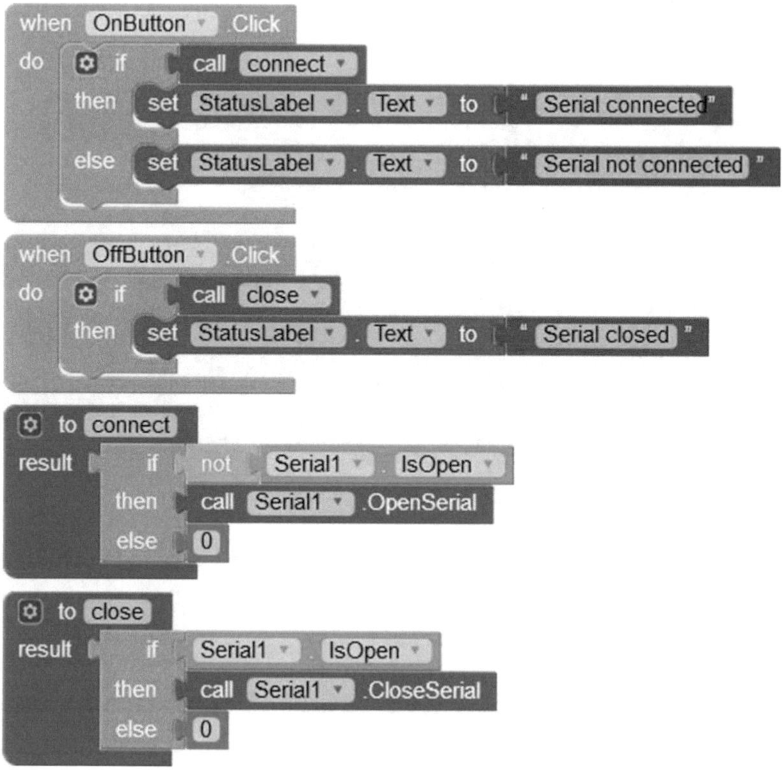

Figure 13-6. *Connect and disconnect the OTG-B device*

The message receipt section of the app runs the *Clock1* timer at 1000 ms intervals to monitor the OTG-B device for a message. The *Clock1* timer interval is set in the *Properties* section on the right side of the Designer window. If the OTG-B device is connected and the received message contains a comma, then the message is parsed to the components of a list, indexed *1* and *2*, which are displayed on the OTG-A device screen as the text variables *Part1text* and *Part2text* (see Figures 13-2 and 13-7).

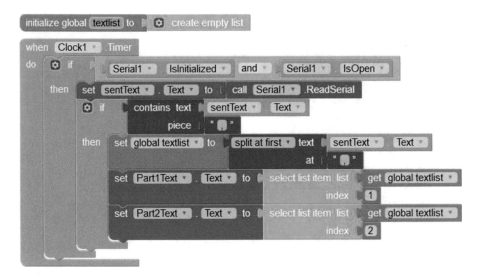

Figure 13-7. *Receive and display message from the OTG-B device*

App transmit

The converse of the OTG-B device, which is the Arduino Uno, transmitting to the OTG-A host device, which is the Android tablet or mobile phone, is the OTG-A device transmitting to the USB peripheral or OTG-B device. When the *RedButton*, *GreenButton*, or *BlueButton* button is clicked, the OTG-A device transmits to the OTG-B device the number 1, 2, or 3 corresponding to the red, green, or blue LED and the associated slider value, with the color of the updated LED indicated on the OTG-A device (see Figure 13-8 after the *RedButton* was clicked).

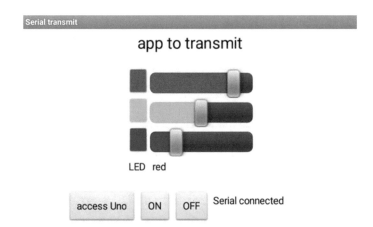

Figure 13-8. *App to control LEDs attached to the OTG-B device*

Connections to the Arduino Uno are shown in Figure 13-9 and given in Table 13-1. The app provides the framework for more complex signal transmit and receive projects.

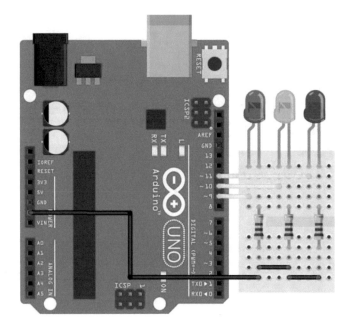

Figure 13-9. *OTG-A to OTG-B*

Table 13-1. *OTG-A to OTG-B*

Component	Connect to	And to
LED long leg	Arduino Uno PWM pins 9, 10, 11	
LED short leg	220 Ω resistor	Arduino Uno GND

The sketch in Listing 13-2 parses the Serial buffer into the number of the LED to be updated and the PWM value. The brightness of the LED is then updated. If the LED value is zero, then all LEDs are turned off. Note that the LEDs are connected to Arduino Uno PWM pins.

Listing 13-2. OTG-A to OTG-B

```
int redLED = 9;
int greenLED = 10;                       // define LED PWM pins
int blueLED = 11;
int LED;
int bright[] = {0,0,0,0};                // initial PWM values

void setup()
{
  Serial.begin(9600);                    // set Serial baud rate
  pinMode(redLED, OUTPUT);
  pinMode(greenLED, OUTPUT);             // set LED pins as output
  pinMode(blueLED, OUTPUT);
}

void loop()
{
  if(Serial.available() > 0)            // wait for app message
  {
```

```
    LED = Serial.parseInt();                    // parse message to LED
    bright[LED] = Serial.parseInt();            // and PWM value
    if(LED < 1) for (int i=1; i<4; i++) bright[i] = 0;
                                                // all LEDs off
    analogWrite(redLED, bright[1]);
    analogWrite(greenLED, bright[2]);           // update LED brightness
    analogWrite(blueLED, bright[3]);
  }
}
```

The app layout contains the app title and two *HorizontalArrangements*. A *TableArrangement,* located in the *Layout* palette on the left side of the Designer window, consists of two columns of four rows, containing the *RedButton, GreenButton*, and *BlueButton* buttons with associated sliders to control PWM values, with the *LEDlabel* and *LEDcolor* labels to indicate which LED was last updated (see Figure 13-10). The second *HorizontalArrangement* includes the *accessUno, OnButton,* and *OffButton* buttons to connect or disconnect the OTG-B device to or from the OTG-A device and a *StatusLabel* label. The *Serial* component is displayed below the app layout. Minimum and maximum slider values, 0 and 255, respectively, are set in the *Properties* section, with the left and right colors, *ColorLeft* and *ColorRight*, for the slider and the initial slider position of *127.*

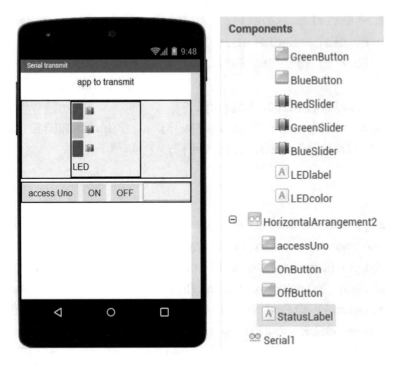

Figure 13-10. *OTG-A to OTG-B app layout*

Managing connection of the OTG-A device to the OTG-B device is
the same as in the OTG-B to OTG-A example (see Figures 13-5 and 13-6).
However, when the OTG-A device disconnects the OTG-B device, the *LED*
procedure transmits a zero LED value to the OTG-B device, which then
turns off all LEDs (see Figure 13-11).

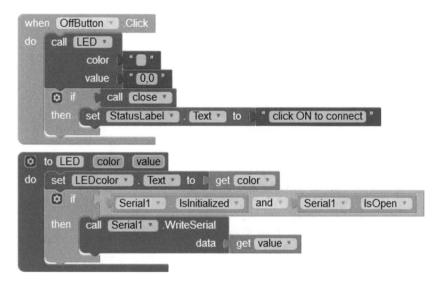

Figure 13-11. *Disconnect the OTG-A to OTG-B connection*

Clicking the *RedButton* button on the OTG-A device calls the *LED* procedure (see Figure 13-12) to transmit, to the OTG-B device, the value "*1*" and the comma-separated red LED slider position. The *round* block rounds up or down the slider position, which is a real number, to an integer. A global variable, *RedValue*, is initially set at the mid-slider position of *127* and stores the current slider position. Similar blocks are used for the green and blue LEDs, but with LED values of "*2*" and "*3*", respectively.

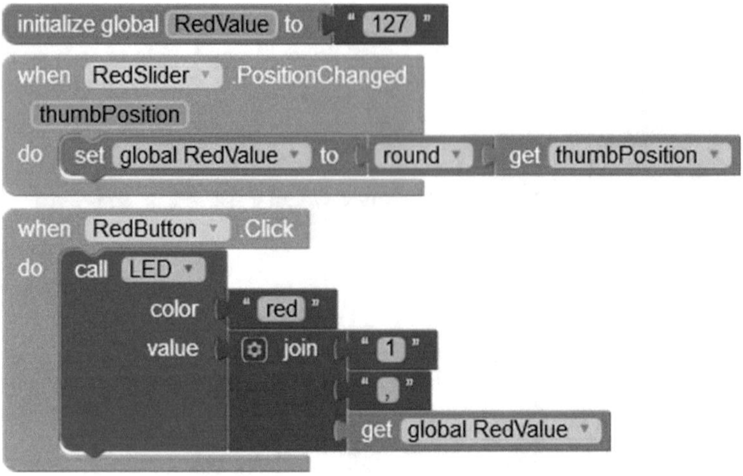

Figure 13-12.   *Control the LEDs*

App receive and transmit

An app to both receive and transmit data from and to the OTG-B device combines the previous app receive and app transmit examples. Figure 13-13 is a screenshot of the receive and transmit app after the OTG-B device transmitted the message containing the number pair *9, 10*, which was processed by the OTG-A device. The screenshot is also after the *RedButton* was clicked on the OTG-A device for transmission of a message to the OTG-B device to update the brightness of the red LED. The receive and transmit app combines the screenshots of Figures 13-2 and 13-8.

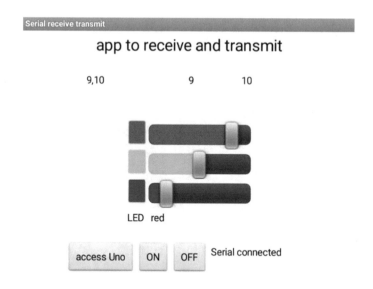

Figure 13-13. *App to receive and transmit data*

The receive and transmit app design layout in Figure 13-14 is a direct combination of the app layouts of the receive app (see Figure 13-4) and the transmit app (see Figure 13-10).

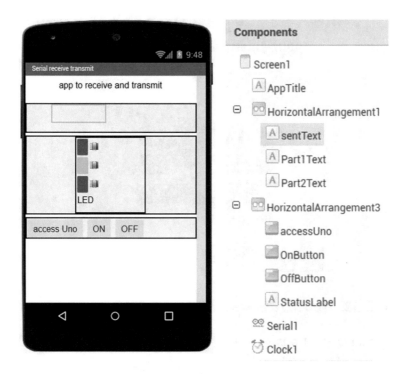

Figure 13-14. *App layout to receive and transmit data*

The sketch for the app to both receive and transmit data consists of the OTG-A to OTG-B transmit app sketch in Listing 13-2 and the contents of the loop function from the OTG-B to OTG-A receive app sketch in Listing 13-1, plus the variable definition instructions

```
String text
int count = 0
unsigned long timer
```

When a button is clicked on the receive and transmit app, the OTG-A device transmits a message to the OTG-B device to control the LEDs while processing the received messages from the OTG-B device. The two conditional instructions if(millis() - timer > 1000) and if(Serial. available() > 0), used in Listings 13-1 and 13-2, respectively, enable the OTG-B device, the Arduino Uno, to "simultaneously" receive a signal from and transmit a signal to the OTG-A host device, the Android tablet or mobile phone.

Summary

USB OTG communication connected the OTG-B device, an Arduino Uno, with an app hosted by the OTG-A device, the Android tablet or mobile phone, and the two devices were connected by a USB OTG cable. A receive app processed signals transmitted by the OTG-B device to the OTG-A host device. Similarly, a transmit app sent signals to the OTG-B device to control the brightness of several LEDs by PWM. The two apps were combined into a receive and transmit app, with the OTG-A device both receiving a signal from and transmitting a signal to the OTG-B device. The *MIT App Inventor Serial* component communicates with the ATmega16U2 USB to serial converter of the Arduino Uno, but not with the CH340 chip on the Arduino Nano or ESP8266 development boards.

Components List

- Arduino Uno

- USB OTG cable: Female USB A to male micro-USB B

- RGB LED or LED: 3×

- Resistor: 3× 220 Ω

CHAPTER 14

ESP-NOW and LoRa communication

Communication with nRF24L01 transceivers and with Bluetooth for transmission of GPS location data is described in Chapter 12 (GPS tracking app with Google Maps), On-The-Go communication in Chapter 13 (USB OTG Communication) and Wi-Fi communication for updating webpage information in Chapter 9 (WebSocket) or for an internet radio in Chapter 1. Two other communication protocols, ESP-NOW and LoRa, are described in this Chapter.

ESP-NOW

 Espressif Systems developed ESP-NOW to enable ESP8266 and ESP32 microcontrollers to communicate without requiring a Wi-Fi connection. ESP-NOW operates at 2.4 GHz, the same frequency as Wi-Fi and Bluetooth, with microcontrollers paired prior to communication. A microcontroller transmits and receives messages to and from several microcontrollers, with a network consisting of 20 microcontrollers without message encryption, but 10 microcontrollers with encryption. If power to a microcontroller is lost and then restored, the microcontroller

N. Cameron, *Electronics Projects with the ESP8266 and ESP32*,
https://doi.org/10.1007/978-1-4842-6336-5_14

automatically reconnects to the paired microcontroller. In practice, a transmission range of 250 m over open ground was achieved with two ESP32 microcontrollers.

The *ESP-NOW* library is automatically included in the Arduino IDE, when the ESP8266 or ESP32 Boards Manager is installed. In a sketch, the *ESP-NOW* library is included with <espnow.h> or <esp_now.h> for the ESP8266 or ESP32 microcontroller, respectively.

Pairing a microcontroller requires the MAC (Media Access Control) address of the microcontroller, which is the address for communication within a network. Listing 14-1 obtains the MAC address of an ESP8266 microcontroller. For an ESP32 microcontroller, the instruction #include <ESP8266WiFi.h> is replaced with #include <WiFi.h>. The MAC address contains six numbers in HEX format, such as *3C:71:BF:F1:CC:9C*. The MAC address is also displayed by the Arduino IDE when a sketch is compiled and loaded (see Figure 14-1).

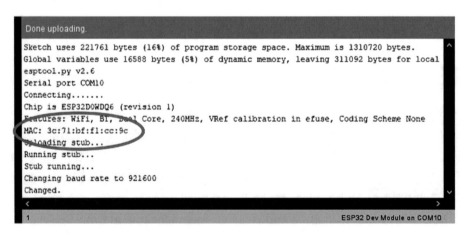

Figure 14-1. *MAC address from Arduino IDE*

Listing 14-1. MAC address

```
#include <ESP8266WiFi.h>            // include Wi-Fi library

void setup()
{
  Serial.begin(115200);            // Serial Monitor baud rate
  Serial.println(WiFi.macAddress()); // get MAC address
}

void loop()                        // nothing in loop function
{}
```

Information transmitted with ESP-NOW includes an integer, a real number, and text or a data structure containing a combination of the three data types. To provide some generality, the sketches in this chapter include a data structure. For ESP-NOW, the maximum size of a data structure is 250 bytes, with an integer, real number, or character requiring 2, 4, or 1 byte, respectively. In Listing 14-2, an example data structure consists of two integers, a real number, and a character array. Note that the length of the character array is the maximum number of characters plus one, to allow for the end-of-line, */n*, character.

Listing 14-2. Example data structure

```
typedef struct                     // define structure to include
{
  int count = 5;                   // two integers,
  int total;
  float value = 3.14;              // a real number
  char text[12] = "text";          // and a character array
} dataStruct;
dataStruct payload;                // name the structure as payload
```

The structure is transmitted or received with the structure name, *payload*, with each component of the structure individually accessible, such as *payload.value*.

The following section includes instructions for an ESP8266 microcontroller. Instruction differences between the ESP8266 and ESP32 microcontrollers are listed in Table 14-1. An ESP8266 microcontroller is allocated the role of transmitter *(CONTROLLER)*, receiver *(SLAVE)*, or both transmitter and receiver *(COMBO)*, with the instruction esp_now_set_self_role(role). The terminology is, unfortunately, the current convention for ESP-NOW with an ESP8266 microcontroller. A receiving ESP8266 microcontroller is identified to the transmitting ESP8266 microcontroller by the MAC address, role, and communication channel with the instruction esp_now_add_peer(receiveMAC, ESP_NOW_ROLE_SLAVE, channel, NULL, 0), where *receiveMAC* is the MAC address of the receiving ESP8266 microcontroller. The data structure, *payload*, is transmitted to the receiving ESP8266 microcontroller with the instruction esp_now_send(receiveMAC, (uint8_t *) & payload, sizeof(payload)). If the receiver MAC address is replaced with *{0xFF, 0xFF, 0xFF, 0xFF, 0xFF, 0xFF}*, then the transmission will be to all the receiving ESP8266 microcontrollers. The ampersand, &, and asterisk, *, characters relate to the memory address of the structure, *payload*. The address of a variable in memory is accessed by preceding the variable with the ampersand, such as &payload, and a pointer stores the memory address of another variable by preceding the pointer with an asterisk, such as *pointer. The pointer is defined with the same data type as the variable, such as float * pointer. The value of a variable is accessed with a pointer, as illustrated in Listing 14-3.

Listing 14-3. Variable, pointer, and memory address

```
int sum = 25;              // allocate value to variable
int * pointer;             // define pointer
int number;
```

```
void setup()
{
  Serial.begin(115200);
  pointer = &sum;                        // set pointer to address of sum
  number = *pointer;                     // set number to pointer content
  Serial.print("\nnumber ");Serial.println(number);
}

void loop()                              // nothing in loop function
{}
```

The transmitting ESP8266 microcontroller registers for a callback that the transmitted data was received by the receiving ESP8266 microcontroller with the instruction esp_now_register_send_cb(sendData). The *sendData* function returns the MAC address of the receiving ESP8266 microcontroller and the callback value. Listing 14-4 also displays the MAC address of the receiving ESP8266 microcontroller, using the *printf* function that converts the content of the *mac* array to HEX format with the 0 character padding for up to two digits, with the parameter *%02*. Upper- or lowercase HEX format is printed with the parameter *%X* or *%x*.

Listing 14-4. Transmitter callback

```
void sendData(uint8_t * mac, uint8_t chk)
{
  for (int i=0; i<6; i++)                // receiver MAC address
  {
    Serial.printf("%02x", mac[i]);       // convert to HEX format
    if(i < 5) Serial.print(":");         // include colons
  }
  Serial.print("\tcallback ");
  if(chk == 0) Serial.println("OK ");    // transmission received
  else Serial.println("fail");           // or not
}
```

The receiving ESP8266 microcontroller also registers for a callback with the instruction esp_now_register_recv_cb(receiveData). The *receiveData* function returns the MAC address of the transmitting ESP8266 microcontroller, *mac*; copies the received data, *data*, to the memory address of the payload structure, *&payload*; and displays the byte number of the received data, *len*, and the *text* character array on the Serial Monitor.

Listing 14-5. Receiver callback

```
void receiveData(uint8_t * mac, uint8_t * data, uint8_t len)
{                              // copy received data to payload
  memcpy(&payload, data, sizeof(payload));
  Serial.print("bytes ");Serial.print(len);Serial.print("\t");
  Serial.print("text ");Serial.println(payload.text);
}
```

The complete sketch for the transmitting ESP8266 microcontroller to send an integer, a real number, and text with ESP-NOW is given in Listing 14-6. Note that the MAC address in Listing 14-6 must be replaced with the MAC address of your receiving ESP8266 microcontroller or use the generic value of *{0xFF, 0xFF, 0xFF, 0xFF, 0xFF, 0xFF}*.

Listing 14-6. ESP-NOW for a transmitting ESP8266 microcontroller

```
#include <espnow.h>                     // include ESP-NOW library
uint8_t receiveMAC[] = {0x84,0xF3,0xEB,0x0D,0xB5,0xB3};
typedef struct                          // receiver MAC address
{
  int count = 0;                        // data structure with
  float value = 3.14;                   // integer, real number
  char text[10] = "abcdef";             // and character array
} dataStruct;
dataStruct payload;
```

```
int channel = 1;                            // set transmission channel
int chk;

void setup()
{
  Serial.begin(115200);                     // Serial Monitor baud rate
  if(esp_now_init() != 0)                   // initialise ESP-NOW
  {
    Serial.println("error initialising ESP-NOW");
    return;
  }                                         // transmitter device
  esp_now_set_self_role(ESP_NOW_ROLE_CONTROLLER);
  chk = esp_now_add_peer(receiveMAC, ESP_NOW_ROLE_SLAVE,
  channel, NULL, 0);                        // add receiver device
  if(chk == 0) Serial.println("receiver added");
  else
  {
    Serial.println("error adding receiver");
    return;
  }
  esp_now_register_send_cb(sendData);   // link to sendData function
}

void loop()
{
  payload.count++;                          // increment counter
  payload.value = payload.value + 1.0; // and real number
  if(strcmp(payload.text,"abcdef") == 0)   // alternate text
strncpy(payload.text, "xyz", sizeof(payload.text));
  else strcpy(payload.text, "abcdef");
  Serial.print(payload.count);
  Serial.print(payload.value);              // display transmitted data
```

```
Serial.print(payload.text);
chk = esp_now_send(receiveMAC, (uint8_t *) & payload,
sizeof(payload));
Serial.print("\tsent ");
if(chk == 0) Serial.print("OK  ");     // transmission sent or not
else Serial.println("fail");
delay(2000);
}

void sendData(uint8_t * mac, uint8_t chk)      // callback function
{
  for (int i = 0; i < 6; i++)         // display receiving MAC address
  {
    Serial.printf("%02x", mac[i]);
    if (i < 5)Serial.print(":");
  }
  Serial.print("\tcallback ");        // transmission received or not
  if(chk == 0) Serial.println("OK  ");
  else Serial.println("fail");
}
```

The complementary sketch for the receiving ESP8266 microcontroller is given in Listing 14-7, with the received message displayed on the Serial Monitor.

Listing 14-7. ESP-NOW for a receiving ESP8266 microcontroller

```
#include <espnow.h>                  // include ESP-NOW library
typedef struct
{
  int count;                         // data structure with
  float value;                       // integer, real number
  char text[10];                     // and character array
} dataStruct;
```

```
dataStruct payload;
int rcv = 0;                            // counter of received signals

void setup()
{
  Serial.begin(115200);
  if(esp_now_init() != 0)               // initialise ESP-NOW
  {
    Serial.println("error initialising ESP-NOW");
    return;
  }
  esp_now_set_self_role(ESP_NOW_ROLE_SLAVE);  // receiver device
  esp_now_register_recv_cb(receiveData);
}                                       // link to receiveData function

void receiveData(uint8_t * mac, uint8_t * data, uint8_t len)
{
  rcv++;                                // increment signal counter
  memcpy(&payload, data, sizeof(payload));
                                        // copy received data to payload
  for (int i = 0; i < 6; i++)
  {                                     // display transmitting MAC address
    Serial.printf("%02x", mac[i]);
    if (i < 5)Serial.print(":");
  }                                     // display contents of payload
  Serial.print("\t");
  Serial.print("received ");Serial.print(rcv);Serial.print("\t");
  Serial.print("bytes ");Serial.print(len);Serial.print("\t");
  Serial.print("count ");Serial.print(payload.count);
  Serial.print("\t");
```

```
  Serial.print("value ");Serial.print(payload.value);
  Serial.print("\t");
  Serial.print("text ");Serial.println(payload.text);
}

void loop()                                    // nothing in loop function
{}
```

The WebSocket protocol enables a server to transmit information to the client, with the information displayed on a web page, as described in Chapter 9 (WebSocket). Listing 14-8 automatically updates a web page with the message and the time of receipt (see Figure 14-2). An application is the display of sensor information.

Figure 14-2. *Receiving ESP8266 microcontroller with ESP-NOW and WebSocket*

Listing 14-8. Receiving ESP8266 microcontroller with ESP-NOW and WebSocket

```
#include <ESP8266WebServer.h>      // include web server library
ESP8266WebServer server;
#include <WebSocketsServer.h>      // include WebSocket library
WebSocketsServer websocket = WebSocketsServer(81);
                                   // set WebSocket port 81
#include "buildpage.h"             // webpage AJAX code
char ssid[] = "xxxx";              // change xxxx to Wi-Fi SSID
char password[] = "xxxx";          // change xxxx to Wi-Fi password
#include <espnow.h>                // include ESP-NOW library
typedef struct
{
  int count;                       // data structure with
  float value;                     // integer, real number
  char text[10];                   // and character array
} dataStruct;
dataStruct payload;
String strMAC, message, json;

void setup()
{
  Serial.begin(115200);            // Serial.Monitor baud rate
  WiFi.begin(ssid, password);      // initialise Wi-Fi
  while (WiFi.status() != WL_CONNECTED) delay(500);
  Serial.print("IP address: ");
  Serial.println(WiFi.localIP());  // display web server IP address
  Serial.print("MAC address: ");   // and MAC address
  Serial.println(WiFi.macAddress());
  server.begin();
  server.on("/", base);            // default webpage
```

```
  websocket.begin();
  if(esp_now_init() != 0)                 // initialise ESP-NOW
  {
     Serial.println("error initialising ESP-NOW");
     return;
  }                                        // receiver device
  esp_now_set_self_role(ESP_NOW_ROLE_SLAVE);
  esp_now_register_recv_cb(receiveData);
}                                          // link to receiveData function

void receiveData(uint8_t * mac, uint8_t * data, uint8_t len)
{                                          // copy received data to payload
  memcpy(&payload, data, sizeof(payload));
  strMAC = "";
  for (int i = 0; i < 6; i++)           // transmitting MAC address
  {                                       // convert to HEX format
     strMAC = strMAC + String(mac[i], HEX);
     if (i < 5)strMAC = strMAC + ":";
  }
  strMAC.toUpperCase();                   // convert to upper case
  JsonConvert(strMAC, payload.count, payload.value,
  payload.text);
  websocket.broadcastTXT(json.c_str(), json.length());
}

String JsonConvert(String val1, int val2, float val3, String val4)
{                                              // start with open bracket
  json  = "{\"var1\": \"" + val1          + "\",";
                                            // partition with comma
  json += " \"var2\": \"" + String(val2) + "\",";
  json += " \"var3\": \"" + String(val3) + "\",";
```

```
  json += " \"var4\": \"" + String(val4) + "\"}";
                                    // end with close bracket
  return json;
}

void base()                              // function to return HTML code
{
  server.send (200, "text/html", page);
}

void loop()
{
  server.handleClient();                 // handle server requests
  websocket.loop();                      // handle WebSocket data
}
```

Implementation of the WebSocket protocol is contained in the JavaScript section of Listing 14-9, which includes the web page AJAX code that is included as the *string literal* page[ ] in the *buildpage.h* tab.

Listing 14-9. WebSocket web page AJAX code

```
char page[] PROGMEM = R"(
<!DOCTYPE html><html>
<head>
<meta name='viewport' content='width=device-width,
initial-scale=1.0'>
<meta charset='UTF-8'>
<title>ESP-NOW</title>
<style>
body {font-family:Arial}
</style></head>
<body id='initialise'>
```

```
<h2>ESP-NOW with ESP8266</h2>
<p>last message at <span id='timeNow'</span></p>
<p>received from <span id='MAC'> </span></p>
<p>counter <span id='count'>0</span></p>
<p>number <span id='value'>0</span></p>
<p>message <span id='text'> </span></p>
<script>
var wskt;
document.getElementById('initialise').onload=function(){init()};
function init()
{
 wskt = new WebSocket('ws://' + window.location.hostname + ':81/');
  wskt.onmessage = function(rx)
  {
    var obj = JSON.parse(rx.data);
    document.getElementById('MAC').innerHTML = obj.var1;
    document.getElementById('count').innerHTML = obj.var2;
    document.getElementById('value').innerHTML = obj.var3;
    document.getElementById('text').innerHTML = obj.var4;
    var dt = new Date();
    var tm = dt.toLocaleTimeString ('en-GB');
    document.getElementById('timeNow').innerHTML = tm;
  };
}
</script>
</body></html>
)";
```

Data from several microcontrollers is received by one microcontroller by allocating a specific channel value to each transmitting microcontroller, with the instruction

```
chk = esp_now_add_peer(receiveMAC, ESP_NOW_ROLE_SLAVE, channel,
NULL, 0)
```

In a sketch, the MAC address of a transmitting microcontroller or an index value included in the message is used to allocate a received message to a specific transmitting microcontroller. For example, two ESP8266 microcontrollers, running a sketch based on Listing 14-6, transmitted messages every two and nine seconds that were received by an ESP8266 microcontroller running the sketch in Listing 14-7. Inclusion of the instruction `if((mac[5]-0x9B)==0) Serial.print("\t\t\t\t\t\t")` offset displaying the message, from the microcontroller with MAC address ending in 0x9B, on the Serial Monitor (see Figure 14-3).

```
COM14                                                    —    □    ×

|                                                              [ Send ]

count 14        value 17.14      text pqrst                          ^
count 15        value 18.14      text ijk
                                            count 4 value 6.18      text xyz
count 16        value 19.14      text pqrst
count 17        value 20.14      text ijk
```

Figure 14-3. *Messages from two transmitting ESP8266 microcontrollers*

Listings 14-4 to 14-8 are for an ESP8266 microcontroller. There are several differences in ESP-NOW instructions between libraries for the ESP8266 and ESP32 microcontrollers that are listed in Table 14-1 with the detail highlighted in bold. The transmitting and receiving ESP32 microcontrollers both require the *WiFi* library and are defined as Wi-Fi station mode, `WIFI_STA`, immediately after the `Serial.begin(115200)` instruction. The function *esp_now_set_self_role* is not required, and the function *esp_now_peer_info_t* to define the receiving ESP32 microcontroller replaces the *esp_now_add_peer* function. In the *sendData* function, the send status variable is specifically defined; and in the *receiveData* function, parameter types are defined as const uint8_t or int instead of uint8_t.

Table 14-1. *ESP-NOW instructions for ESP8266 and ESP32 microcontrollers*

ESP8266	ESP32
	#include <WiFi.h>
#include <espnow.h>	#include <esp_now.h>
	WiFi.mode(WIFI_STA)
esp_now_set_self_role(ESP_NOW _ROLE_XX) *where XX is CONTROLER or SLAVE*	Not required
chk = esp_now_add_ peer(receiveMAC, ESP_NOW_ROLE_SLAVE, channel, NULL, 0)	esp_now_peer_info_t receiver; memcpy(receiver.peer_addr, receiveMAC, 6); receiver.channel = channel; receiver.encrypt = false; chk = esp_now_add_peer(&receiver);
void sendData(uint8_t * mac, uint8_t chk)	void sendData(**const** uint8_t * mac, **esp_ now_send_status_t** chk)
void receiveData(uint8_t *mac, uint8_t *data, uint8_t len)	void receiveData(**const** uint8_t * mac, **const** uint8_t * data, **int** len)

If the received message is displayed on a web page, then an ESP-NOW channel between the transmitting and receiving ESP32 microcontrollers and a Wi-Fi channel between the receiving ESP32 microcontroller and the WLAN are required.

The transmitting ESP32 microcontroller is defined as a software-enabled Wi-Fi access point, SoftAP, on default channel one with a default IP address of 192.168.4.1, which is displayed with the instruction Serial. println(WiFi.softAPIP()). The SoftAP password should contain at least eight alphanumeric characters. Instructions to define the SoftAP with SSID, password, and channel number for the transmitting ESP32 microcontroller are given in Table 14-2.

Table 14-2. *Web page instructions for transmitting and receiving ESP32 microcontrollers*

ESP32 Transmitter	ESP32 Receiver
	#include <WebServer.h>
	WebServer server(80)
char ssidAP[ ] = "abcdefg"	char ssid[ ] = "xxxx"
char passwordAP[ ] = "12345678"	char password[ ] = "xxxx"
int channelAP = 3	
WiFi.mode(WIFI_AP)	WiFi.mode(WIFI_AP_STA)
WiFi.softAP(ssidAP, passwordAP, channelAP)	
Serial.print("Soft-AP IP address ")	
Serial.println(WiFi.softAPIP())	
WiFi.begin(ssidAP, passwordAP)	WiFi.begin(ssid, password);
receiver.channel = channelAP	

The receiving ESP32 microcontroller has joint access point and station mode, with the instruction WiFi.mode(WIFI_AP_STA), to connect to the SoftAP and to the Wi-Fi network (see Table 14-2). The Wi-Fi network SSID and password are defined, with the *xxxx* in Table 14-2 replaced by the SSID and password of your Wi-Fi router. Note that the `WiFi.begin()` instruction for the transmitting ESP32 microcontroller references the generated SoftAP SSID and password, while the receiving ESP32 microcontroller references the Wi-Fi router SSID and password.

Further information on ESP-NOW is available at `www.espressif.com/sites/default/files/documentation/2c-esp8266_non_os_sdk_api_reference_en.pdf`, in Section 3.8, for the ESP8266 microcontroller, with details for the ESP32 microcontroller at `docs.espressif.com/projects/esp-idf/en/latest/esp32/api-reference/network/esp_now.html`.

LoRa communication

 Several communication systems are available, each operating at different frequencies, over different distances, and with different data rates. RFID (Radio Frequency IDentification), Bluetooth, and Bluetooth Low Energy (BLE) technologies have lower data rates than Wi-Fi communication, which has lower range than the mobile telecommunication technology standards 2G–5G (see Figure 14-4). LoRa (long range) is a low-power wide area network (LPWAN) technology developed by Semtech. LoRa communication operates with a form of frequency modulation (FM), rather than amplitude modulation (AM), uses lower frequencies than the 2.4 GHz of Wi-Fi and Bluetooth communication, and has low power consumption. LoRaWAN (Long Range Wide Area Network) is the protocol for creating LoRa-based networks. This chapter describes point-to-point communication with LoRa.

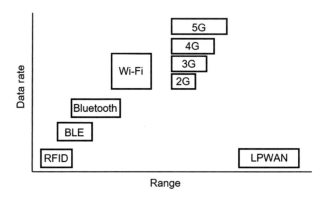

Figure 14-4. *Communication technologies*

The Semtech SX1276 and SX1278 LoRa modules are powered by 1.8–3.6 V, but differ in frequency range, 137–1020 MHz and 137–525 MHz, respectively, with the SX1278 module applicable in Europe (433 MHz), while the SX1276 module is suitable for Europe (868 MHz), Australia and North America (915 MHz), and Asia (923 MHz). Both the SX1276 and SX1278 modules have LoRa spreading factors of 6–12 and a bandwidth of 8–500 kHz, giving effective bit rates of up to 37.5 kbps.

This chapter uses the SX1278 LoRa module at 433 MHz and the *LoRa* library by Sandeep Mistry that is available in the Arduino IDE (with details available at github.com/sandeepmistry/arduino-LoRa/blob/master/API.md). The LoRa module communicates with an ESP8266 or ESP32 microcontroller using SPI (Serial Peripheral Interface), with connections between a LoRa module and an ESP8266 or ESP32 development board shown in Figure 14-5 and listed in Table 14-3. The LoRa module antenna (ANT) length is $\lambda/4$, where λ is the wavelength equal to c/f, with c equal to the speed of light (299,792,458 m/s or approximately 300 Mm/s) and f the LoRa transmission frequency. A LoRa transmission frequency of 433, 868, or 915 MHz requires an antenna 173, 86, or 82 mm long. The LoRa module digital input-output pins are marked DIO.

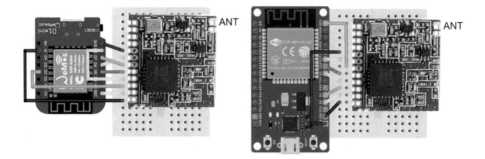

Figure 14-5. *SX1278 LoRa module with LOLIN (WeMos) D1 mini and ESP32 DEVKIT DOIT development boards*

The image of the SX1278 LoRa module in Figure 14-5 was increased in size to match the mini-breadboard holes and illustrate the connections. In reality, the 12 connection pins of the SX1278 LoRa module span 14 mm rather than 30 mm on a breadboard. One solution is to bend the eight pins of a long-pin header block to align with the SX1278 LoRa module connections (see Figure 14-6).

Figure 14-6. *Pin header block with long and normal pins*

Table 14-3. *SX1278 LoRa module with ESP8266 and ESP32 microcontrollers*

Component	ESP8266	ESP32
SX1278 GND (pin 1)		
SX1278 DIO1		
SX1278 DIO2		
SX1278 DIO3		
SX1278 VCC	3V3	3V3
SX1278 MISO	D6	GPIO 19
SX1278 MOSI	D7	GPIO 23
SX1278 SLCK	D5	GPIO 18
SX1278 NSS (CSS)	D8	GPIO 5
SX1278 DIO0	D2	GPIO 4
SX1278 REST	RST	GPIO 2
SX1278 GND (pin 12)	GND	GND
OLED GND	GND	GND
OLED VCC	3V3	3V3
OLED SCK	D1	GPIO 22
OLED SDA	D2	GPIO 21

A sketch for LoRa communication with an ESP8266 microcontroller is given in Listing 14-10. The LoRa transmission frequency of 433, 868, or 915 MHz is defined with the instruction LoRa.begin(NE6), with N equal to 433, 868, or 915. The LoRa module connection pins for the chip select (CSS) and reset (RST) and an interrupt (DIO0) pin are defined in the sketch, as the *LoRa* library default values are GPIO 10, GPIO 9, and GPIO 2.

When the LoRa module reset pin is connected to the ESP8266 or ESP32 microcontroller reset pin, the LoRa module reset pin is defined as *-1.* The default SPI pins are defined implicitly. The LoRa spreading factor (SF6–SF12) spreads a transmission across the available bandwidth, with a higher SF increasing the transmission range, but decreasing the transmission bit rate. The *LoRa* library has bandwidth values from 7.8 kHz to 250 kHz, with lower bandwidth corresponding to longer transmission range. The default signal bandwidth of 125 kHz is changed with the instruction LoRa.setSignalBandwidth(N), for bandwidth *N*, with possible values listed on the *LoRa* library website. For example, set *N* equal to *31.25E3* for a bandwidth of 31.25 kHz. The maximum LoRa transmission size with the *LoRa* library is 255 bytes.

In the sketch, a message is transmitted at five-second intervals, which is displayed on the OLED screen along with a received message from the receiving microcontroller (see Figure 14-7). The value in the received message is equal to the packet transmitted, assuming no messages were lost. The feedback message confirms receipt of the transmitted message by the receiving microcontroller. The receiving microcontroller displays the number of seconds between received messages, the signal RSSI (received signal strength indicator) and SNR (signal-to-noise ratio), and then the received message.

Figure 14-7. *Characterizing LoRa message reception with feedback*

Listing 14-10. Transmitting LoRa module with feedback

```
#include <SPI.h>                          // include SPI and
#include <LoRa.h>                         // LoRa libraries
int CSS = D8;                             // define SX1278 pins
int RST = -1;                             // RESET pin
int DIO0 = D2;                            // interrupt pin
#include <Wire.h>                         // include libraries for OLED
#include <Adafruit_SSD1306.h>
int width = 128;                          // OLED dimensions
int height = 32;                          // associate oled with library
Adafruit_SSD1306 oled(width, height, &Wire, -1);
int counter = 0;
unsigned long lastTime;
String packet, recv;
int packetSize;                           // size of received message

void setup()
{
  digitalPinToInterrupt(DIO0);            // set pin as interrupt
  LoRa.setPins(CSS, RST, DIO0);           // define LoRa module pins
  LoRa.setSpreadingFactor(9);             // define spreading factor
  LoRa.setSignalBandwidth(62.5E3);        // set bandwidth to 62.5kHz
  while (!LoRa.begin(433E6)) delay(500);  // 433MHz transmission
  oled.begin(SSD1306_SWITCHCAPVCC, 0x3C);
                                          // OLED display I2C address
  oled.setTextColor(WHITE);               // set font color
  oled.setTextSize(2);                    // text size 12×16 pixels
  oled.display();
}
```

```
void loop()
{
  if(millis() - lastTime > 5000)        // 5s transmission interval
  {
    screen();                           // OLED display function
    packet = String(counter);           // create packet
    LoRa.beginPacket();                 // start LoRa transmission
    LoRa.print(packet);                 // send packet
    LoRa.endPacket();                   // close LoRa transmission
    counter++;                          // increment counter
    lastTime = millis();                // update transmission time
  }
  packetSize = LoRa.parsePacket();      // detect received packet
  if (packetSize > 0)
  {
    recv = "";                          // read packet
    while(LoRa.available()) recv = recv + ((char)(LoRa.read()));
    screen();                           // OLED display function
  }
}

void screen()                           // function for OLED display
{
  oled.clearDisplay();
  oled.setCursor(0,0);
  oled.print("sent ");oled.println(packet);    // transmitted value
  oled.print(recv);                            // received message
  oled.display();
}
```

During packet reception, the LoRa module measures, in decibels (dB), the received signal strength indicator (RSSI) and the signal-to-noise ratio (SNR). The received signal power is $10^{(dB/10)}$mW. The RSSI ranges from 0 dBm to -120 dBm, with a value greater than -50 dBm indicating a strong signal, while a weak signal has a RSSI of less than -90 dBm. The SNR is the difference between the signal and the background noise RSSI values, with a positive SNR indicating that the received signal operates above the noise baseline. LoRa can operate below the noise baseline, which is the normal limit of signal sensitivity.

The sketch for characterizing LoRa message reception is given in Listing 14-11, which displays the interval between message reception, RSSI, SNR, and the message on an OLED display. A received message is read as a byte, which is converted to a character with the instruction (char)(LoRa.read()). On receiving a message, the sketch also returns the received message to the transmitting microcontroller, as feedback. The *Adafruit SSD1306* library references the *Adafruit GFX* library, so the #include <Adafruit_GFX.h> instruction is not required.

Listing 14-11. Characterizing LoRa message reception

```
#include <SPI.h>                          // include SPI and
#include <LoRa.h>                         // LoRa libraries
int CSS = D8;                             // define SX1278 pins
int RST = -1;                             // RESET pin
int DIO0 = D2;                            // interrupt pin
int width = 128;                          // OLED dimensions
int height = 64;
#include <Wire.h>                         // include libraries for OLED
#include <Adafruit_SSD1306.h>
Adafruit_SSD1306 oled(width, height, &Wire, -1);
                                          // Reset pin not required
```

```
String packet;
int RSSI, packetSize, interval;
float SNR;
unsigned long lastTime = 0;

void setup()
{
  digitalPinToInterrupt(DIO0);           // set pin as interrupt
  LoRa.setPins(CSS, RST, DIO0);          // define LoRa module pins
  while (!LoRa.begin(433E6)) delay(500);   // 433MHz transmission
  oled.begin(SSD1306_SWITCHCAPVCC, 0x3C);
                                         // OLED display I2C address
  oled.setTextColor(WHITE);              // set font color
  oled.setTextSize(2);                   // text size 12×16 pixels
  oled.display();
}

void loop()
{
  packetSize = LoRa.parsePacket();       // detect received packet
  if (packetSize > 0)
  {
    interval = round((millis() - lastTime)/1000);    // interval (s)
    lastTime = millis();                 // update message time
    packet = "";                         // read packet
    while(LoRa.available()) packet = packet +
    ((char)(LoRa.read()));
    RSSI = LoRa.packetRssi();
    SNR = LoRa.packetSnr();              // signal : noise
    screen();                            //  OLED display function
```

```
    LoRa.beginPacket();                    // start LoRa transmission
    LoRa.print("recv " + packet);          // send packet
    LoRa.endPacket();                      // close LoRa transmission
  }
}

void screen()                              // function for OLED display
{
    oled.clearDisplay();
    oled.setCursor(0,0);
    oled.print("lag  ");oled.println(interval);
                                // display time since last message
    oled.print("RSSI ");oled.println(RSSI);
                                // display interval, RSSI and SNR
    oled.print("SNR  ");oled.println(SNR);
    oled.print("msg  ");oled.print(packet);
                                   // display received message
    oled.display();
}
```

The WebSocket protocol enables a server to transmit information to the client, with the information displayed on a web page. Listing 14-12 automatically updates a web page with the message and the time of receipt (see Figure 14-8). An application is the display of sensor information.

Figure 14-8. *LoRa reception with WebSocket*

Listing 14-12 is for an ESP8266 development board as the server. The web server library instructions for the ESP8266 microcontroller of

```
#include <ESP8266WebServer.h>
ESP8266WebServer server
```

are replaced when using an ESP32 microcontroller with

```
#include <WebServer.h>
WebServer server(80);                      // requires a port number
```

The web server library references the Wi-Fi library, so the #include <ESP8266WiFi.h> or #include <WiFi.h> instructions are not required. The *CSS, RST,* and *DIO0* pin numbers are changed to 5, 2, and 4 for an ESP32 microcontroller.

Listing 14-12. Receiving LoRa module and WebSocket

```
#include <ESP8266WebServer.h>        // include Webserver library
ESP8266WebServer server;             // associate server with library
#include <WebSocketsServer.h>        // include WebSocket library
WebSocketsServer websocket = WebSocketsServer(81);
                                     // set WebSocket port 81
```

```
#include "buildpage.h"                // webpage AJAX code
char ssid[] = "xxxx";                 // change xxxx to Wi-Fi SSID
char password[] = "xxxx";             // change xxxx to Wi-Fi password
String message, json;
int RSSI;
float SNR;
#include <SPI.h>                      // include SPI library
#include <LoRa.h>                     // and LoRa library
int CSS = D8;                         // define SX1278 pins
int RST = -1;                         // RESET pin
int DIO0 = D2;                        // interrupt pin
int packetSize;

void setup()
{
  Serial.begin(115200);              // Serial Monitor baud rate
  WiFi.begin(ssid, password);        // initialise and connect Wi-Fi
  while (WiFi.status() != WL_CONNECTED) delay(500);
  Serial.print("IP address: ");
  Serial.println(WiFi.localIP());    // display web server IP address
  server.begin();
  server.on("/", base);              // load default webpage
  websocket.begin();                 // initialise WebSocket
  digitalPinToInterrupt(DIO0);       // set pin as interrupt
  LoRa.setPins(CSS, RST, DIO0);      // define LoRa module pins
  while (!LoRa.begin(433E6)) delay(500);   // 433MHz transmission
  Serial.println("LoRa connected");
}

void loop()
{
  server.handleClient();             // handle HTTP requests
  websocket.loop();                  // handle WebSocket data
```

```
packetSize = LoRa.parsePacket();        // detect received packet
if (packetSize > 0)
{
  message = "";                         // read packet
  while(LoRa.available()) message = message +
  ((char)(LoRa.read())));
  RSSI = LoRa.packetRssi();
  SNR = LoRa.packetSnr();               // signal : noise
  JsonConvert(message, RSSI, SNR);      // convert to JSON format
  websocket.broadcastTXT(json.c_str(), json.length());
  }
}

String JsonConvert(String val1, int val2, float val3)
{                                       // start with open bracket
  json  = "{\"var1\": \"" + String(val1) + "\",";
                                        // partition with comma
  json += " \"var2\": \"" + String(val2) + "\",";
  json += " \"var3\": \"" + String(val3) + "\"}";
                                        // end with close bracket

  return json;
}

void base()                             // function to return HTML code
{
  server.send (200, "text/html", page);
}
```

The corresponding AJAX code for the web page is given in Listing 14-13. When the web page is loaded, the *init* function opens the WebSocket connection at *ws://web server IP address:81/*. When the SX1278 LoRa module receives a message, the WebSocket protocol forwards the message to the client as the variable *rx.data*, which is parsed to the *rxText, RSSI,* and

SNR variables for display on the web page. The time of message receipt is obtained from the JavaScript date reference, as described in Chapter 9 (WebSocket), with details available at www.w3schools.com/Jsref/jsref_obj_date.asp.

Listing 14-13. WebSocket and AJAX code for the web page

```
char page[] PROGMEM = R"(
<!DOCTYPE html><html>
<head>
<meta name='viewport' content='width=device-width,
initial-scale=1.0'>
<meta charset='UTF-8'>
<title>ESP8266</title>
<style>
body {font-family:Arial}
</style></head>
<body id='initialise'>
<h2>LoRa and WebSocket</h2>
<p>last message at <span id='timeNow'</span></p>
<p>received <span id='rxText'> </span></p>
<p>RSSI <span id='RSSI'>0</span> dBm</p>
<p>SNR <span id='SNR'>0</span> dB</p>
<script>
var wskt;
document.getElementById('initialise').onload = function()
{init()};
function init()                              // open WebSocket
{
  wskt = new WebSocket('ws://' + window.location.hostname +
  ':81/');
  wskt.onmessage = function(rx)
```

```
  {
    var obj = JSON.parse(rx.data);
    document.getElementById('rxText').innerHTML = obj.var1;
    document.getElementById('RSSI').innerHTML = obj.var2;
    document.getElementById('SNR').innerHTML = obj.var3;
    var dt = new Date();
    var tm = dt.toLocaleTimeString ('en-GB');
    document.getElementById('timeNow').innerHTML = tm;
  };
}
</script>
</body></html>
)";
```

Summary

ESP-NOW and LoRa technologies were described for communication between ESP8266 and ESP32 microcontrollers. ESP-NOW requires no additional components than the ESP8266 or ESP32 development board, while LoRa requires the SX1278 module. ESP-NOW operates at 2.4 GHz, which is higher than the 7.8–250 kHz operating frequencies of LoRa, with the protocols having limits of 250 and 255 bytes per message, respectively. LoRa has a greater transmission range than ESP-NOW. With ESP-NOW, the transmitting microcontroller receives a callback that the message was received with information displayed on the Serial Monitor or on a web page updated with the WebSocket procedure. With LoRa communication, the received message was either displayed on an OLED screen attached to the ESP8266 or ESP32 development board or on a web page, also using the WebSocket procedure.

Components

- ESP8266 microcontroller: LOLIN (WeMos) D1 mini or NodeMCU board

- ESP32 microcontroller: DEVKIT DOIT or NodeMCU board: 2×

- LoRa transceiver: SX1278 module 2×

- OLED display: 128 × 32 pixels, 128 × 64 pixels

CHAPTER 15

Radio frequency communication

In telecommunications and signal processing, information is transferred on a radio carrier wave by either modulating the amplitude or the frequency of a radio carrier wave. Radio waves have frequencies between 20 kHz and 300 GHz, corresponding to wavelengths of 15 km to 1 mm, and travel at the speed of light. Radio waves with frequencies above 300 MHz are termed microwaves. For Radio Frequency (RF) communication with amplitude modulation (AM), the transmission amplitude is proportional to the signal amplitude, and the transmission frequency is constant (see Figure 15-1). Conversely, for frequency modulation (FM), the amplitude of the transmitted signal is constant, and the transmission frequency is proportional to the signal amplitude. AM is used for communication between two-way radios, citizens band radios, and VHF (very-high-frequency) aircraft radios. FM is used in telemetry and radio broadcasting of music, as FM has a higher signal-to-noise ratio than AM at the same transmission power.

© Neil Cameron 2021
N. Cameron, *Electronics Projects with the ESP8266 and ESP32*,
https://doi.org/10.1007/978-1-4842-6336-5_15

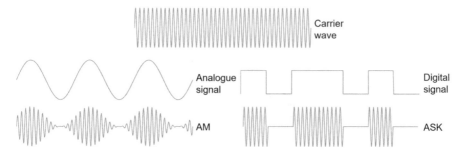

Figure 15-1. *Amplitude modulation (AM) and Amplitude Shift Keying (ASK)*

Amplitude Shift Keying (ASK) is a form of amplitude modulation for representing a digital signal, such as *1234*, which would require four distinct signal amplitudes. The simplest form of ASK, called On-Off Keying (OOK), consists of a binary signal represented by either transmitting the carrier signal or no signal. In Figure 15-1, the signal 1011010 is illustrated both as a digital signal and as an ASK signal.

The 433 MHz transmitter and receiver pairs (see Figure 15-2) are short-range devices designed for signal transmission, usually on a license-exempt basis, at a low power level and excluding voice. The transmitter is the smaller of the transmitter and receiver pair in Figure 15-2. The standard transmitter and receiver pair are often coded MX-FS-03V and MX-05V and marked as FS1000A and MX-RM-5V, respectively. The superheterodyne transmitter and receiver pair are often coded WL102-341 and WL101-341. A superheterodyne transmitter uses frequency mixing to convert the transmitted signal into a signal with intermediate frequency that is more efficiently processed than a signal at the original carrier frequency. Superheterodyne is a compound of supersonic (frequencies above human hearing), hetero (different), and dyne (unit of power).

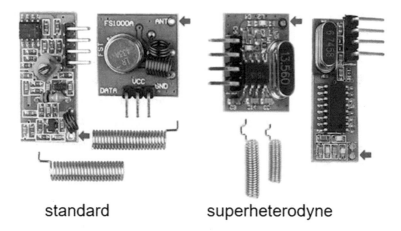

standard   superheterodyne

Figure 15-2. *433 MHz standard and superheterodyne transmitter and receiver pairs*

The transmitter and receiver pairs in Figure 15-2 are shown with coiled antennas, but transmission and reception is improved with uncoiled antennas of length $\lambda/2$ or $\lambda/4$, where λ is the wavelength equal to c/f, with c equal to the speed of light (299,792,458 m/s or approximately 300 Mm/s) and f the carrier wave frequency. For a carrier wave frequency of 433.29 MHz, an antenna of length a quarter wavelength is 173 mm long. In Figure 15-2, antenna connection points are indicated with red arrows.

Connections for the transmitter and receiver with ESP8266 and ESP32 development boards are shown in Figures 15-3 and 15-4, respectively, for both the superheterodyne and standard devices. On the superheterodyne transmitter PCB, the + and *EN* pins are pre-connected, as are the *DO* (data out) and unmarked pins of the superheterodyne receiver PCB and the two unmarked pins on the standard receiver PCB. The *RH_ASK* library by Mike McCauley, which is downloaded from `www.airspayce.com/mikem/arduino/RadioHead`, and the *rc-switch* library by Suat Özgür, which is available in the Arduino IDE, are both recommended.

For both libraries, the RF transmit and receive data pins are connected to the ESP8266 development board D1 and D2 pins or pins 26 and 27 for the ESP32 development board (see Table 15-1) with the receive data pin defined as an interrupt pin for the *rc-switch* library. In Listings 15-1 and 15-2, the instruction to define the ESP8266 development board pins, RH_ASK rf (2000, D2, D1, 0), is replaced with the instruction RH_ASK rf (2000, 27, 26, 0) for an ESP32 microcontroller. The choice of transmit and receive pins is arbitrary.

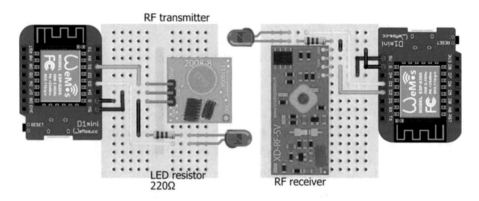

Figure 15-3. *433 MHz RF transmitter and receiver with LOLIN (WeMos) D1 mini*

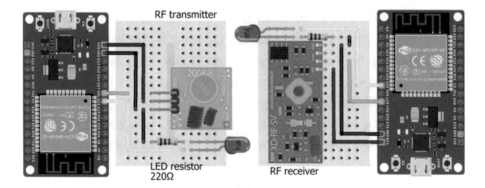

Figure 15-4. *433 MHz RF transmitter and receiver with the ESP32 DEVKIT DOIT board*

Table 15-1. *Transmitter and receiver connections for ESP8266 and ESP32 microcontrollers*

	Transmitter				**Receiver**		
Superheterodyne	_	+	DAT	EN	GND	DO	VCC
Standard	GND	VCC	Data		GND	Unmarked pins	VCC
Connect to							
ESP8266	GND	5V	D1		GND	D2	5V
ESP32	GND	VIN	GPIO 26		GND	GPIO 27	VIN

Transmitting and receiving text

The *RH_ASK* library is used to transmit messages containing character strings. The *RH_ASK* driver uses a timer-driven interrupt to generate eight interrupts per bit period, with *Timer1* being the default timer. Several libraries use *Timer1*, such as the *Servo* library, but the *RH_ASK* driver can use *Timer2* instead of *Timer1* by uncommenting the line #define RH_ASK_ARDUINO_USE_TIMER2 on line 32 of the file *RH_ASK.cpp* that is located in the *user/Arduino/libraries/RadioHead* folder. The instruction RH_ASK rf (2000, receive pin, transmit pin, 0) defines the transmission speed in bits per second (bps) with the receive data and transmit data pins, respectively.

For the *RH-ASK* library, signals are formatted with a 36-bit training preamble consisting of 18 0-1 bit pairs, a 12-bit start symbol (*0xB38*), a 1-byte number for the payload length, a 4-byte header, *N* bytes containing the *N* characters of the message with a maximum of 60 characters per message, and 2 bytes for frame check sequences (FCS). The payload length is the number of characters in the message plus seven (payload length, 1; header, 4; FCS, 2). Apart from the preamble and start symbol, each byte is split into high and low 4-bit sequences, which are mapped to 6-bit sequences and transmitted least significant bit (LSB) first. Table 15-2 provides the mapping of the 4-bit sequences (*0x0* to *0xF*) to 6-bit sequences (*0xD* to *0x34*), formatted as HEX. The signal length is 36 + 12 + (N + 7) × 12 bits for a message of N characters. A message of 60 characters takes 426 ms to transmit with a transmission speed of 2 kbps.

Table 15-2. *Mapping of 4-bit to 6-bit sequences in the RH_ASK library*

4-bit	0x0	0x1	0x2	0x3	0x4	0x5	0x6	0x7
6-bit	0xD	0xE	0x13	0x15	0x16	0x19	0x1A	0x1C
4-bit	0x8	0x9	0xA	0xB	0xC	0xD	0xE	0xF
6-bit	0x23	0x25	0x26	0x29	0x2A	0x2C	0x32	0x34

For example, the character A has ASCII code 65 and HEX code *0x41* with high and low HEX codes (and 4-bit sequences) of *0x4* (0100) and *0x1* (0001) that are mapped to HEX codes (and 6-bit sequences) of *0x16* (010110) and *0xE* (001110), respectively. The 6-bit sequences are transposed from most significant bit (MSB) first to least significant bit (LSB) first. The transposed high sequence and then low sequence is (011010)(011100), which is equivalent to (0110)(1001)(1100), when expressed as three 4-bit sequences, corresponding to HEX codes of *0x6*, *0x9*, and *0xC*. The message character A is converted to a signal corresponding to *69c*, as shown in Figure 15-5.

The purpose of recoding is to ensure that a 12-bit sequence contains 6 bits with value one and 6 bits with value zero, which is termed *DC-balanced*. In the example of transmitting the character *A*, the two 4-bit sequences corresponding to the HEX code of *0x41* are (0100)(0001), which are not DC-balanced, but after recoding, the three 4-bit sequences of (0110)(1001)(1100) are DC-balanced.

Analysis of the complete signal for the message *ABC*, as captured by a logic analyzer with the *sigrok PulseView* program, using OOK decoder type *NRZ* and filter length 4 with OOK visualization display *Nibble-Hex* and Sync offset of -1 is illustrated in Figure 15-5. The *sigrok PulseView* program and manual are available to download at `sigrok.org`. After the 36-bit training preamble and the start symbol, *0xB38*, the payload length of 10, equal to the message length of three characters plus seven, is displayed as *b19*, which is derived exactly as for the preceding example with the character *A*. The number 10 has a HEX code of *0x0A* with high and low HEX codes (*0x0* and *0xA*) mapping to *0xD* and *0x26*, which have transposed binary representation of (1011)(0001)(1001) corresponding to HEX code *b19*. Following the signal header sequence, the HEX sequence *0x6, 0x9, 0xC* for the message character *A* is displayed as *69c*, and similarly the message characters *B* and *C* with HEX sequences *0x6, 0xB, 0x2* and *0x6, 0xA, 0xA* are displayed as *6b2* and *6aa*, respectively.

Figure 15-5. *Logic analyzer signal analysis with RH_ASK format*

Listings 15-1 and 15-2 illustrate using the *RH_ASK* library to transmit and receive a message of variable length consisting of text, a real number, and an integer, with a maximum message length of 60 characters. In Listing 15-1, an example message is generated with the transmission number, *val*, determined from the sketch elapsed time divided by the time interval between transmissions, *timelag*. A different text string for each message is generated by the instruction text[val%3] that calculates the remainder when the variable *val* is divided by three, given three strings in the *text* array. The message contains text; a real number, *1.2*val*; and an integer, *val*, separated by commas. For example, the fifth message transmitted is *ijkl,6.0,5,*. The interval between transmissions is set at 2 s, and an LED is turned on or off after each transmitted or received message. It may be necessary to repeat the instruction rf.send((uint8_t *)msg, strlen(msg)) for a long message.

The instruction msg = message.c_str() uses a *C++* command to create an array, *msg*, equal to the *message* string with a terminating null character, *\0*, and returns a pointer, *msg*, to the array. If a string is defined with the instruction String text = "abc", then the null character, *\0*, is automatically included at the end of the string. When an array string is defined as String text[4] = {'a', 'b', 'c', '\0'}, the null character is included as the last array element, with array elements defined as characters using a single apostrophe rather than the double apostrophe for a string.

Listing 15-1. Transmit message with the RH_ASK library

```
#include <RH_ASK.h>                    // include the RH_ASK library
#include <SPI.h>                       // SPI library required to compile
RH_ASK rf (2000, D2, D1, 0);          // associate rf with RH_ASK lib
int LEDpin = D3;                       // define LED pin
String text[] = {"abcdef", "ijkl", "rst"};
                                       // strings of different lengths
const char * msg;                      // pointer to array with message
String message;
int timelag = 2000;                    // interval between transmissions
int LED = 0;                           // initial LED state
int val, len, spd;
```

```
void setup()
{
  Serial.begin(115200);                 // Serial Monitor baud rate
  rf.init();                            // initialise radio transmission
  pinMode(LEDpin, OUTPUT);              // define LED pin as output
  len = rf.maxMessageLength();          // get maximum message length
  spd = rf.speed();                     // get transmission speed
  Serial.print("max message length: ");   // display message length
  Serial.println(len);
  Serial.print("transmission speed: ");   // and transmission speed
  Serial.println(spd);
}

void loop()
{
  val = millis()/timelag;               // transmission number
  message = text[val%3] + "," + String(1.2*val) + "," +
 String(val) + ",";
  Serial.println(message);              // display transmitted string
  msg = message.c_str();                // convert string
  rf.send((uint8_t *)msg, strlen(msg));  // transmit signal
  rf.waitPacketSent();                  // wait for transmission to finish
  LED = 1 - LED;
  digitalWrite(LEDpin, LED);            // turn on or off LED
  delay(timelag);
}
```

In Listing 15-2, the number of comma-separated items within the message is defined in the sketch. The instruction const int nItem = 3 enables the size of two arrays, text[nItem] and comma[nItem+1], to be implicitly defined. When a new message is received, a blank string is

407

incremented with each character of the message, and the comma positions are determined with the instruction message.indexOf("x", y), which locates the position of the substring *x* within the *message* string starting from position *y*. The *message* substrings are generated with the instruction message.substring(x, y), which is the substring of the *message* string between positions *x* (inclusive) and *y* (exclusive). The instructions string.toFloat() and string.toInt() convert a string to a real number and an integer, respectively. Further details on parsing text to substrings are given in Chapter 8 (Updating a web page). The variables *valFlt* and *valInt* in Listing 15-2 are generated to demonstrate the use of converted text in calculations.

Listing 15-2. Receive message with the RH_ASK library

```
#include <RH_ASK.h>                    // include the RH_ASK library
#include <SPI.h>                       // SPI library required to compile
RH_ASK rf (2000, D2, D1, 0);          // associate rf with RH_ASK lib
int LEDpin = D3;                       // define LED pin
uint8_t msg[RH_ASK_MAX_MESSAGE_LEN];   // maximum message length
const int nItem = 3;                   // number of items in message
String text[nItem];                    // define text array
int comma[nItem+1];                    // comma positions in message
int LED = 0;                           // initial LED state
String message;
float valFlt;
int valInt;

void setup()
{
  Serial.begin(115200);               // Serial Monitor baud rate
  rf.init();                          // initialise radio transmission
  pinMode(LEDpin, OUTPUT);            // define LED pin as output
}
```

```
void loop()
{                              // message length based on new message
  uint8_t msglen = sizeof(msg);
  if (rf.recv(msg, &msglen))     // message of correct length available
  {
    message = "";               // increment message with each character
    for (int i=0; i<msglen; i++) message = message +
    char(msg[i]);
    comma[0] = -1;
    for (int i=0; i<nItem; i++)   // comma positions in message
    {                              // get substrings between commas
      comma[i+1] = message.indexOf(",", comma[i]+1);
      text[i] = message.substring(comma[i]+1, comma[i+1]);
      Serial.print(text[i]);             // print message substring
      Serial.print(" ");
    }
    valFlt = text[1].toFloat();        // second substring to float
    valInt = text[2].toInt();          // third substring to integer
    Serial.print(text[0]);Serial.print("\t");
    Serial.print(valFlt + 0.05);Serial.print("\t");
    Serial.println(valInt * 2);
    LED = 1 - LED;
    digitalWrite(LEDpin, LED);       // turn on or off LED
  }
}
```

Decode remote control signals

The *rc-switch* library is used to decode wireless signals from wireless digital remote controls. The *rc-switch* library by Suat Özgür is available within the Arduino IDE. The transmitted signal is in *Tri-state* format, which represents (00), (11), and (01) bit pairs with a bit of value *0, 1,* or *F.* For example, the decimal number 19 has binary representation of 010011; and with the most significant bit (MSB) first, the bit pairs are (01), (00), and (11) resulting in *Tri-state* format of *F01.* Codes for wireless digital remote control buttons are obtained with the sketch in Listing 15-3.

For example, the RF codes for the *Power* and *25% PWM* buttons of an RF wireless remote control were *3163905* and *3163913*, respectively, in decimal format. Binary representation of the *3163905* code of (00)(11)(00) (00)(01)(00)(01)(11)(00)(00)(00)(01) has *Tri-state* format of 0100F0F1000F, and similarly the 3163913 code has *Tri-state* format of 0100F0F100UF, with *Tri-state* format U for the (10) bit pair. Analysis of the signals for *3163905* and *3163913*, as captured by a logic analyzer with the *sigrok PulseView* program and the RC encode decoder setting, is illustrated in Figure 15-6.

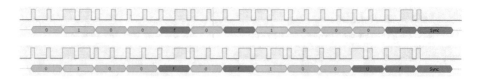

Figure 15-6. *Logic analyzer signal analysis with Tri-state coding*

Listings 15-3 and 15-4 illustrate decoding and transmitting a RF signal with the *rc-switch* library. In Listing 15-3, after receiving an RF signal, the Serial Monitor displays the signal, in decimal format, with the signal bit length and protocol number. An LED is also turned on or off to indicate that a signal was received. The variable *value* to hold the received button code is defined as an unsigned long with an upper limit of 2^{32} – 1 to accommodate RF wireless remote control codes. An unsigned int variable has an upper limit of 2^{16} – 1 or 65535. For the *rc-switch* library, the receive data pin is defined as an interrupt pin and enabled with the instructions digitalPinToInterrupt() and rc.enableReceive() with a pin value of *D2* or *27* for an ESP8266 or ESP32 microcontroller, respectively.

Listing 15-3. Receive and decode an RF code with the rc-switch library

```
#include <RCSwitch.h>              // include the rc-switch library
RCSwitch rc = RCSwitch();          // associate rc with rc-switch lib
int LEDpin = D3;                   // define LED pin and state
int LED = 0;
unsigned long value;

void setup()
{
  Serial.begin(115200);           // Serial Monitor baud rate
  digitalPinToInterrupt(D2);      // set pin as interrupt
  rc.enableReceive(D2);           // receive data on interrupt pin
  pinMode(LEDpin, OUTPUT);        // define LED pin as output
}

void loop()
{
  if (rc.available())             // if a signal is received
  {
    value = rc.getReceivedValue(); // signal in decimal format
    if (value != 0)                // non-zero signal value
    {
      Serial.print("Decimal ");Serial.print(value);
      Serial.print(" (");
      Serial.print(rc.getReceivedBitlength()); // signal bit length
```

```
    Serial.print("bit)\tProtocol ");    // print a tab between text
    Serial.println(rc.getReceivedProtocol());
                                    // signal protocol class
    LED = 1 - LED;
    digitalWrite(LEDpin, LED);    // turn on or off the LED
  }
  else Serial.println("Unknown encoding");
  rc.resetAvailable();                    // ready to receive signal
 }
}
```

With the *rc-switch* library, RF codes in either decimal, binary, or *Tri-state* format are transmitted with the instruction send(number, bitlength), send(pointer), or sendTriState(pointer), respectively, where *pointer* is the pointer to the array containing the string including the number in binary or *Tri-state* format. The converted RF code is formatted as a string with a terminating null character, \0, by the instruction pointer = code.c_str(). Irrespective of the RF code format, the *rc-switch* library converts the RF code to binary format for transmission. The signal is repeatedly transmitted, with a default of ten repeats corresponding to three received signals. The minimum number of repeat transmissions to receive a signal is four, using the instruction setRepeatTransmit(4). Transmissions repeated four to ten times result in the signal being received 1, 1, 2, 2, 3, 3, and 3 times.

Listing 15-4 transmits the RC codes *3163905–3163913*, corresponding to several buttons of an RF wireless remote control, with the codes transmitted in decimal, binary, and *Tri-state* format. An LED is turned on or off to indicate when a signal is transmitted.

In Listing 15-4, the functions *binary* and *tristate* convert a decimal number to binary format and a binary number to *Tri-state* format, respectively. A decimal number is converted to binary format by repeatedly dividing the integer part of the number by two and retaining the remainders, with the first remainder being the least significant bit (LSB) of the binary representation. For example, to convert the decimal number 19 to binary format, repeated division by two results in the remainders 1,1,0,0,1, and 0 equal to ($19 - 2 \times 9, 9 - 2 \times 4, 4 - 2 \times 2, 2 - 2 \times 1, 1 - 2 \times 0$). The first remainder is the LSB, so the binary representation of 19 is 010011, with the LSB last. The *rc-switch* library uses 24-bit format to represent a number in binary format, so converting a decimal number to binary format requires 24 divisions by two.

Conversion of a binary-formatted number into *Tri-state* format starts with the MSB pair and finishes with the LSB pair. For the decimal number 19, the bit pairs are (01), (00), and (11) that map to *Tri-state* format of *F01*. In Listing 15-4, the character at position *x* of a string *bin* is identified by the instruction bin.charAt(x). In Listing 15-4, the *Tri-state* format for the numbers 3163905, 3163907, 3163908, 3163909, and 3163911 is valid, but the transmitted values are not correct for the numbers 3163906, 3163910, 316312, and 3163913, so the term *U* is included in the *Tri-state* format for the (10) bit pair.

Listing 15-4. Transmit an RF code with the rc-switch library

```
#include <RCSwitch.h>                    // include the rc-switch library
RCSwitch rc = RCSwitch();                // associate rc with rc-switch lib
unsigned long value = 3163905;           // code to be transmitted
const char * biCode;                     // pointers to arrays with number
const char * triCode;                    // in binary or Tri-state format
int LEDpin = D3;                         // define LED pin
int LED = 0;                             // initial LED state
int delTime = 1000;                      // delay between transmissions
String bin, tri;

void setup()
{
  Serial.begin(115200);                  // Serial Monitor baud rate
  pinMode(LEDpin, OUTPUT);               // define LED pin as output
  rc.enableTransmit(D1);                 // transmit data pin
```

```
  rc.setPulseLength(351);              // optional with time in ms
  rc.setProtocol(1);                   // default is 1
  rc.setRepeatTransmit(4);             // define number of transmissions
 }

void loop()
{
  rc.send(value, 24);                  // send number in decimal format
  Serial.print(value);Serial.print("\t");    // display value
  digitalWrite(LEDpin, LED);           // turn on or off LED
  LED = 1 - LED;
  delay(delTime);                      // interval between transmissions
  binary(value);                       // convert to binary format
  rc.send(biCode);                     // send array in binary format
  Serial.print(biCode);Serial.print("\t");
                                       // display value in binary format
  delay(delTime);
  tristate(bin);                       // convert to Tri-state format
  rc.sendTriState(triCode);            // send array in Tri-state format
  Serial.println(triCode);             // display in Tri-state format
  delay(delTime);
  value++;
  if(value > 3163913) for (;;) delay(1000);
}                                      // stop after sending all codes

void binary(long number)      // function to convert to binary format
{
  bin = "";
  for (int i=0; i<24; i++)    // 24 bits starting with LSB
  {                           // next bit precedes lower significant bits
    if(number%2 == 1) bin = "1" + bin;
                              // number is an unsigned long integer
    else bin = "0" + bin;
```

```
    number = number/2;
  }
  biCode = bin.c_str();        // create pointer to array
}

void tristate(String val)    // function to convert to Tri-state format
{
  tri = "";
  for (int i=0; i<12; i++)   // start with MSB which is charAt(0)
  {                          // next bit follows higher significant bits
        if(val.charAt(2*i)=='0' && val.charAt(2*i+1)=='0')
        tri = tri + "0";
   else if(val.charAt(2*i)=='1' && val.charAt(2*i+1)=='1')
   tri = tri + "1";
   else if(val.charAt(2*i)=='0' && val.charAt(2*i+1)=='1')
   tri = tri + "F";
   else if(val.charAt(2*i)=='1' && val.charAt(2*i+1)=='0')
   tri = tri + "U";
  }
  triCode = tri.c_str();       // create pointer to array
}
```

Control pan-tilt servos with RF communication

A remotely positioned laser mounted on a pan and tilt bracket, which is rotated by two servo motors, is controlled by transmitting a message containing the joystick position and the laser state. A joystick, such as the KY-023 module, consists of two potentiometers for controlling the left-right direction (X-axis) and the forward-backward direction (Y-axis). The joystick values range from 0 to 1023, with 0 corresponding to right and forward, while 1023 maps to left and backward. Pressing down on the joystick activates a switch to turn on or off the laser. The RF transmitter and joystick are connected to an Arduino Nano or an ESP32 development board (see Figure 15-7 and Table 15-3); and the RF receiver, two servo motors with external power, and the laser module are attached to an ESP8266 development board (see Figure 15-8 and Table 15-4). The KY-008 laser operates at 650 nm, within the red light wavelength range of 635–700 nm.

Two analog pins are required to read the joystick values. The ESP8266 microcontroller has only one analog pin, so either a 74HC4051 multiplexer is connected to the ESP8266 development board to enable the ESP8266 microcontroller to access both analog input devices (see Chapter 4 (Internet clock)) or the ESP8266 development board is replaced by an Arduino Nano or an ESP32 development board.

The default transmit and receive pins for an Arduino Nano with the *RH_ASK* library are pins 12 and 11, respectively. The ESP32 microcontroller GPIO 27 is defined as the transmit pin with the instruction RH_ASK rf (2000, 26, 27, 0). The value of GPIO 26 for the receive pin is arbitrary, as, in the sketch, the ESP32 microcontroller does not receive messages. The ESP32 microcontroller ADC (analog to digital converter) has 12-bit resolution, with values from 0 to 4095, while the Arduino Nano ADC has 10-bit resolution. Either the ESP32 microcontroller ADC values are divided by four before transmission in Listing 15-5 or the mapping of received joystick value to servo angle is changed to FB = map(text[0]. toInt(),0,4095,5,100) in Listing 15-6 and similarly for the LR mapping.

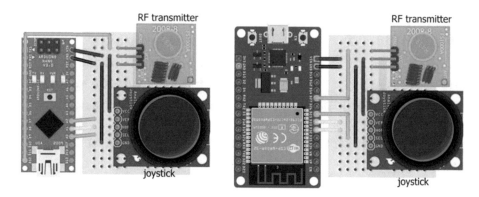

Figure 15-7. *Transmit joystick signals*

Table 15-3. *Joystick, RF transmitter, and Arduino Nano or ESP32 development board*

Component	Arduino Nano	ESP32
Joystick VCC (+)	5V	VIN
Joystick SEL (B)	A0	GPIO 25
Joystick HOR (X)	A1	GPIO 32
Joystick VER (Y)	A2	GPIO 33
Joystick GND (-)	GND	GND
RF transmitter VCC (+)	5V	VIN
RF transmitter GND (-)	GND	GND
RF transmitter DAT	Pin 12	GPIO 27

The sketch in Listing 15-5 reads the joystick position and switch state and then combines the information into a string for transmission. The joystick switch state is *HIGH* when pressed. The *RH_ASK* library is used to transmit and receive the RF signals. Joystick and RF transmitter pin definitions in Listing 15-5 are for the Arduino Nano, and for an ESP32 microcontroller, the pin definitions are

```
RH_ASK rf (2000, 26, 27, 0)          // associate rf with RH_ASK lib
int switchPin = 25                   // joystick switch pin
int LRpin = 32                       // left-right joystick pin
int FBpin = 33                       // forward-backward joystick pin
pinMode(switchPin, INPUT)            // define switchPin as input
```

Listing 15-5. Transmit joystick signal to control the servo motors and laser

```
#include <RH_ASK.h>                  // include the RH_ASK library
#include <SPI.h>                     // SPI library required to compile
RH_ASK rf;                           // associate rf with RH_ASK lib
int timelag = 50;                    // interval between transmissions
int switchPin = A0;                  // joystick switch pin
int LRpin = A1;                      // left-right joystick pin
int FBpin = A2;                      // forward-backward joystick pin
int FB, LR, SW;
const char * msg;
String message;

void setup()
{
  rf.init();                         // initialise radio transmission
}

void loop()
{        // string for joystick forward-backward, left-right and switch state
  FB = analogRead(FBpin);
  LR = analogRead(LRpin);            // get joystick position
  SW = digitalRead(switchPin);       // and switch state
  message = String(FB) +","+ String(LR) + "," + String(SW) + ",";
```

```
msg = message.c_str();                    // convert string
rf.send((uint8_t *)msg, strlen(msg));     // transmit message
rf.waitPacketSent();                      // wait for transmission to finish
delay(timelag);                           // delay between transmissions
}
```

The laser and the two servos for the pan and tilt bracket are connected to an ESP8266 development board with the RF receiver (see Figure 15-8), with connections given in Table 15-4. The servo motors are powered from an external 5 V battery, as the motor can use hundreds of milliamps during a few milliseconds that the rotor is turning, which is more than the output of the ESP8266 development board 5V pin.

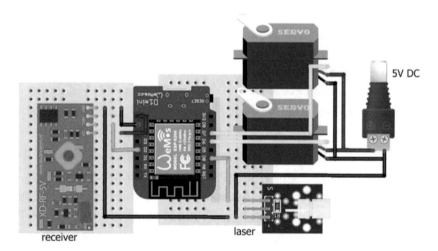

Figure 15-8. *Control the servo motors and laser with the received signal*

Table 15-4. *Servo motors, laser, RF receiver, and ESP8266 development board*

Component	Connect to	And to
Servo VCC (red)	Battery 5V	
Servo GND (brown or black)	ESP8266 GND	Battery GND
Servo signals (orange or white)	ESP8266 D6 and D7	
Laser signal (S)	ESP8266 D0	
Laser GND (-)	ESP8266 GND	
RF receiver VCC (+)	ESP8266 5V	
RF receiver GND (-)	ESP8266 GND	
RF receiver DAT	ESP8266 D2	

Listing 15-6 contains the sketch for the RF receiver, servo motors, and laser module. As noted at the start of this chapter, the *RH_ASK* driver uses *Timer1*, the default timer, which is also used by the *Servo* library. The *RH_ASK* driver uses *Timer2* by uncommenting the line #define RH_ASK_ARDUINO_USE_TIMER2 on line 32 of the file *RH_ASK.cpp*. The sketch associates both *servoFB* and *servoLR* objects with the *Servo* library, as there are two servo motors. The instruction const int nItem = 3 enables the size of two arrays, text[nItem] and comma[nItem+1], to be implicitly defined. When the RF receiver receives a message, the message substrings are converted to integers, which are mapped to the servo forward-backward and left-right angles between 5° and 100° and between 5° and 175°, respectively. A *HIGH* state on the laser pin indicates that the joystick switch was pressed.

The servo motors can shudder when there is no change in the servo motor angle. To stop the shudder, the servo motor is detached and then reattached prior to moving to the new angle. For example, the left-right

servo instruction, `servoLR.write(LR)`, to move to angle *LR*, is replaced
with the instructions

```
servoLR.attach(LRpin)
servoLR.write(LR)
servoLR.detach()
```

Listing 15-6. Receive signal with joystick positions to control the
servo motors and laser

```
#include <RH_ASK.h>                  // include the RH_ASK library
#include <SPI.h>                     // SPI library required to compile
#include <Servo.h>                   // include Servo library
RH_ASK rf (2000, D2, D1, 0);         // associate rf with RH_ASK lib
Servo servoFB;                       // associate servoFB and servoLR
Servo servoLR;                       // with Servo library
int FBpin = D6;                      // forward-backward servo pin
int LRpin = D7;                      // left-right servo pin
int laserPin = D0;                   // define laser pin
uint8_t msg[RH_ASK_MAX_MESSAGE_LEN];
const int nItem = 3;                 // number of items in message
String text[nItem];                  // array of strings
int comma[nItem+1];                  // array of comma positions
String string;
int laser, FB, LR;

void setup()
{
  rf.init();                         // initialise radio transmission
  servoFB.attach(FBpin);             // initialise servo motors
  servoLR.attach(LRpin);
  pinMode(laserPin, OUTPUT);         // define laser pin as output
}
```

```
void loop()
{                            // define message length based on new message
  uint8_t msglen = sizeof(msg);
  if (rf.recv(msg, &msglen))      // message of correct length available
  {
    string = "";         // increment string by each message character
    for (int i=0; i<msglen; i++) string = string + char(msg[i]);
    comma[0] = -1;
    for (int i=0; i<nItem; i++)   // get message comma positions
    {                             // get substrings between commas
      comma[i+1] = string.indexOf(",", comma[i]+1);
      text[i] = string.substring(comma[i]+1, comma[i+1]);
    }                             // map joystick signals to angles
    FB = map(text[0].toInt(),0,1023,5,100);
    LR = map(text[1].toInt(),0,1023,5,175);
    laser = text[2].toInt();      // update laser status
    if(laser == HIGH) digitalWrite(laserPin,
    !digitalRead(laserPin));
    servoFB.write(FB);                 // move servos to angles
    servoLR.write(LR);
  }
}
```

If the servo motors are attached to an ESP32 development board, then an ESP32-specific library for the servo motor is required, rather than the Arduino IDE built-in *Servo* library. The *ESP32Servo* library by Kevin Harrington and John K. Bennett is recommended, and the library is available in the Arduino IDE. The built-in *Servo* library instructions for the forward-backward (FB) servo motor with an ESP8266 microcontroller

```
#include <Servo.h>               // include Servo library
servoFB.attach(FBpin)            // initialise servo motor to FBpin
```

are replaced with the *ESP32Servo* library instructions for an ESP32 microcontroller

```
#include <ESP32Servo.h>
servoFB.setPeriodHertz(F)              // define servo frequency (F)
servoFB.attach(FBpin, minPW, maxPW) // initialise servo motor to FBpin
```

There is no change to the following instructions:

```
Servo servoFB                          // associate servoFB with Servo lib
servoFB.writeMicroseconds(T)           // move to position mapped to Tµs
servoFB.write(N)                       // move to angle N°
```

Similar changes are made for the left-right (LR) servo motor.

The square wave frequency, *F*, is included in the instruction servoFB. setPeriodHertz(F), which is generally 50 Hz. In the servoFB.attach(FBpin, minPW, maxPW) instruction, the *minPW* and *maxPW* parameters refer to the pulse width, in microseconds, of a square wave to move the servo motor to 0° and 180°, respectively. Default values for the *minPW* and *maxPW* parameters are 1000 µs and 2000 µs, with values of 500 µs and 2500 µs for the Tower Pro SG90 servo. The servo motor used in this chapter required 250 µs and 2050 µs to move to 0° and 180°, respectively. A sketch to calibrate a servo motor is given in Chapter 9 (WebSocket). The preceding instructions for the forward-backward servo, *servoFB*, are repeated for the left-right servo, *servoLR*.

Control relay with RF communication

Pressing a specific button on an RF wireless remote control is used to turn on or off an *IRF520* MOSFET or *KY-019* relay module, which switches the power supply to as load, such as a motor. The *IRF520* MOSFET switches 100 V direct current (DC) at 10 A, while the *KY-019* relay module switches either 240 V alternating current (AC) or 30 V DC at 10 A. The *rc-switch* library is used to transmit and receive the remote control button codes. Connections for the RF receiver, *IRF520* MOSFET or *KY-019* relay module, and a load, such as a motor, are shown in Figure 15-9 and listed in Tables 15-5 and 15-6.

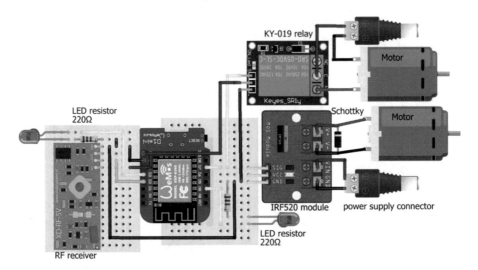

Figure 15-9. *Receiver signal to control load with the IRF520 MOSFET or KY-019 relay module*

Table 15-5. *IRF520 MOSFET and KY-019 relay modules, RF receiver, and ESP8266 development board*

Component	Connect to	And to
IRF520 SIG or KY-019 SIG	ESP8266 D7	
IRF520 VCC	Not connected	
KY-019 VCC	ESP8266 5V	
IRF520 GND or KY-019 GND	ESP8266 GND	
LED long legs	ESP8266 D3 and D0	
LED short leg	220 Ω resistor	ESP8266 GND
RF receiver VCC (+)	ESP8266 5V	
RF receiver GND (-)	ESP8266 GND	
RF receiver DAT	ESP8266 D2	

The *IRF520* MOSFET and *KY-019* relay modules are two options for controlling an external power supply for the load. The *IRF520* MOSFET module has two pairs of connections: one pair for the load and one pair for the external power supply. For the *KY-019* relay module, the positive and negative of the external power supply are connected to the *KY-019* module Common (C) and to the load negative, respectively. The *KY-019* relay module Normally Open (NO) pin is connected to the load positive. The *KY-019* Normally Open (NO) is recommended rather than the Normally Closed (NC) pin.

Table 15-6. *IRF520 MOSFET and KY-019 relay module connections to load and power*

Component	Connect to	And to
IRF520 V+	Load (motor) positive	Schottky diode cathode (stripe)
IRF520 V-	Load (motor) negative	Schottky diode anode
IRF520 VIN	External power supply	
IRF520 GND	External power GND	
KY-019 Normally Open (NO)		Load (motor) positive
KY-019 Common (C)	External power supply	
	External power GND	Load (motor) negative

In Listing 15-7, when the *LIGHT* button on the RF wireless remote is pressed, the LED attached to the ESP8266 development board pin *D3* is turned on or off. RF codes of buttons in Listing 15-7 are only specific to the RF wireless remote used in this chapter. When the *BRIGHT+* or *BRIGHT-* button on the RF wireless remote is pressed, the *IRF520* MOSFET or *KY-019* relay module supplying power to the load is turned on or off, as is the LED attached to ESP8266 development board pin *D0*. The *KY-019* relay module is active when the state of the *relayPin, D7*, is *HIGH*.

Listing 15-7. Receive signal to control load

```
#include <RCSwitch.h>                  // include the rc-switch library
RCSwitch rc = RCSwitch();              // associate rc with rc-switch lib
int LEDpin = D3;                       // LED to change state
int LEDrelayPin = D0;                  // LED associated with relay
int relayPin = D7;                     // define MOSFET/relay pin
unsigned long value;

void setup()
{
  Serial.begin(9600);                  // Serial output baud rate
  digitalPinToInterrupt(D2);           // set pin as interrupt
  rc.enableReceive(D2);                // receive data on interrupt pin
//  digitalWrite(relayPin, HIGH);      // set relayPin HIGH before
  pinMode(relayPin, OUTPUT);           // defining relayPin
  pinMode(LEDpin, OUTPUT);
  pinMode(LEDrelayPin, OUTPUT);
}

void loop()
{
  if (rc.available())                  // if a signal is received
  {
    value = rc.getReceivedValue();
    if (value != 0)                    // signal value not equal to zero
    {                                  // display signal value
      Serial.print("code ");Serial.print(value);
      if(value == 3163908)            // Light button pressed
```

```
  {
    Serial.print("\tchange LED");              // display action
    digitalWrite(LEDpin, !digitalRead(LEDpin));
  }                                  // turn on or off LED
  else if(value == 3163909)       // Bright+ button pressed
  {
    Serial.print("\trelay on");
    digitalWrite(LEDrelayPin, HIGH);       // turn on relay LED
    digitalWrite(relayPin, HIGH);          // turn on relay
  }
  else if (value == 3163910)     // Bright- button pressed
  {
    Serial.print("\trelay off");
    digitalWrite(LEDrelayPin, LOW);        // turn off relay LED
    digitalWrite(relayPin, LOW);           // turn off relay
  }
  else Serial.print("\tno action");
  Serial.print("\tLED    ");
  Serial.print(digitalRead(LEDpin));
                                   // display LED and relay states
  Serial.print("\trelay ");
  Serial.println(digitalRead(relayPin));
  }
  else Serial.println("Unknown encoding");
  rc.resetAvailable();                 // ready to receive new signal
 }
}
```

Relays

A relay is an electromagnetic switch, controlled by a small current, that is used to turn on or off a large current. When an ESP8266 or ESP32 microcontroller pin that controls the relay is *HIGH*, a small current on the base of the relay switching transistor permits a larger current from the ESP8266 or ESP32 development board 5V pin to flow through the transistor, activating the relay electromagnet, and the resultant magnetic field attracts and closes the metallic relay switch (see Figure 15-10). When the ESP8266 or ESP32 microcontroller pin is *LOW*, no current flows through the transistor, and a spring returns the metallic relay switch to the normally open position. A relay module includes a resistor to reduce the current to the switching transistor and a diode to short-circuit the relay coil when the current is turned off. The energy in the coil is absorbed through the internal resistance of the relay coil and the voltage drop of the diode. Without the diode, a large voltage spike could arc across the switch and destroy the transistor. Figures 15-10 to 15-16 illustrate an ESP8266 microcontroller controlling a relay, but the discussion also applies to an ESP32 microcontroller.

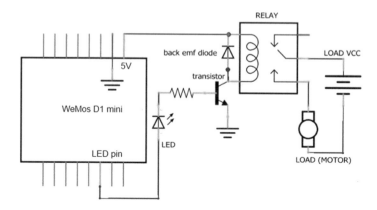

Figure 15-10. *Relay module: schematic*

To control a relay, such as the *KY-019* module in Figure 15-11, a *HIGH* signal on the ESP8266 development board pin *D4* turns on the relay transistor, activating the relay switch to provide the load, such as a motor, with external power. The ESP8266 development board GND is connected to the *KY-019* module, as the module indicator LED, relay transistor, and relay electromagnet source power from the ESP8266 development board.

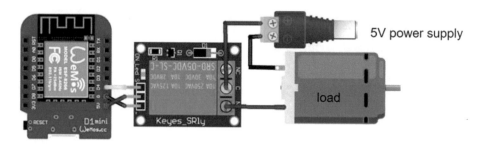

Figure 15-11. *Relay module and LOLIN (WeMos) D1 mini*

A relay module with an optocoupler extends separation of the ESP8266 microcontroller from the load with its external power supply (see Figures 15-12 and 15-13). The *FOD817C* optocoupler consists of a near-infrared LED and a phototransistor, which generates a current in response to detection of light. Both the optocoupler and the relay transistor are powered by the ESP8266 development board. A jumper between the relay module pins marked RY-VCC or JD-VCC and VCC connects the relay transistor to the ESP8266 development board 5V pin. A relay with an optocoupler sinks current to the ESP8266 microcontroller pin, in contrast to the *KY-019* relay which sources current, and the relay is active when the ESP8266 microcontroller pin is *LOW*. The dashed connecting line between the optocoupler VCC and the relay VCC in Figure 15-12 represents the jumper.

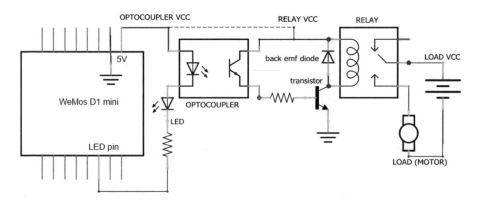

Figure 15-12. *Relay module with optocoupler schematic*

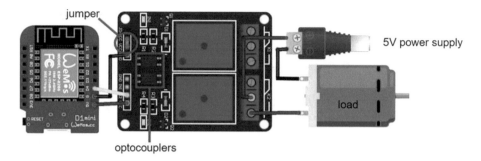

Figure 15-13. Relay module with optocoupler (1)

The ESP8266 microcontroller is completely isolated from the load and its external power supply by providing the relay with a separate power supply (see Figure 15-14 with connections given in Table 15-7). The jumper between the relay module pins marked RY-VCC or JD-VCC and VCC is removed, and power is separately supplied to the relay RY-VCC or JD-VCC and GND pins. The ESP8266 microcontroller GND is not connected to the relay module, as the optocoupler and indicator LED sink current through the ESP8266 microcontroller pin set to *LOW*.

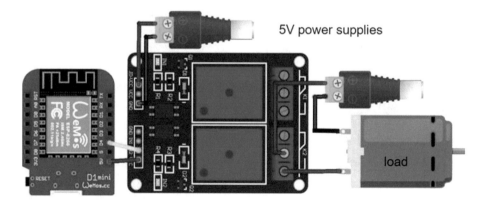

Figure 15-14. Relay module with optocoupler (2)

Table 15-7. *Relay module connections without and with an external power to relay*

Relay Module	Component	Connect to
Without external power	Relay optocoupler JD-VCC and VCC pins	Jumper
	Relay optocoupler GND	ESP8266 GND
	Relay optocoupler SIG or L1	ESP8266 D7
	Relay optocoupler VCC	ESP8266 5V
With external power	Relay optocoupler JD-VCC	External power positive
	Relay optocoupler GND	External power negative
	Relay optocoupler SIG or L1	ESP8266 D7
	Relay optocoupler VCC	ESP8266 5V

In Listing 15-7, the *KY-019* relay is activated when the ESP8266 microcontroller pin is *HIGH*, with the instructions

```
digitalWrite(relayPin, HIGH);            // turn on relay
digitalWrite(relayPin, LOW);             // turn off relay
Serial.print("\trelay ");Serial.println(digitalRead(relayPin));
```

For a relay with an optocoupler, the ESP8266 microcontroller pin state is inverted, with changes highlighted in bold:

```
digitalWrite(relayPin, LOW);             // turn on relay
digitalWrite(relayPin, HIGH);            // turn off relay
Serial.print("\trelay ");Serial.println(!digitalRead(relayPin));
```

When the instruction pinMode(relayPin, OUTPUT) is called, the relay pin is automatically set *LOW*, which will activate the relay if the relay module contains an optocoupler. To prevent a relay with an optocoupler being inadvertently turned on, the instruction digitalWrite(relayPin, HIGH) precedes the pinMode(relayPin, OUTPUT) instruction.

Solid-state relay

 The solid-state relay incorporates semiconductors for high-speed switching, without mechanical moving parts, of 240 V alternating current (AC) at 2 A. The solid-state relay phototriac coupler consists of a near-infrared LED and a photosensitive triac, which transfers a signal to a trigger circuit on the output side of the relay allowing a current to flow to the load (see Figure 15-15). The solid-state relay incorporates additional circuitry and functions on both the infrared LED input side and the output photosensitive side. Further information is available at www.ia.omron.com/support/guide/18/introduction.html.

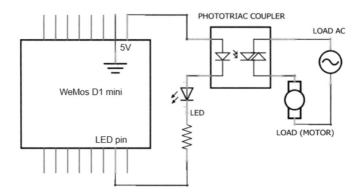

Figure 15-15. *Simplified solid-state relay schematic*

The solid-state relay is active when the ESP8266 microcontroller pin, connected to the relay phototriac coupler, is *LOW,* similar to the mechanical relay with an optocoupler. Connections for the ESP8266 development board with the solid-state relay module are shown in Figure 15-16 and given in Table 15-8.

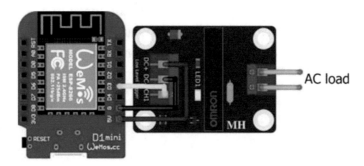

Figure 15-16. *Solid-state relay and LOLIN (WeMos) D1 mini*

Table 15-8. *Solid-state relay and*
ESP8266 development board

Component	Connect to ESP8266
Solid-state relay DC+	5V
Solid-state relay DC-	GND
Solid-state relay CH1	D3

Summary

Radio Frequency communication with Amplitude Shift Keying (ASK) and On-Off Keying (OOK) was described. A 433 MHz superheterodyne transmitter and receiver pair transmitted and received alphanumeric data by ASK radio communication over distances of 150 m. Signals from a 433 MHz wireless digital remote control were decoded with the superheterodyne receiver. Binary and *Tri-state* data formatting was discussed. The state and position of a laser attached to a pan-tilt bracket, operated with servo motors attached to an ESP8266 or ESP32 microcontroller, was controlled by a remote joystick, with joystick position and laser state information transmitted with ASK radio communication by a superheterodyne transmitter connected to an ESP32 microcontroller. Remotely powering a load, such as motors, through an electro-mechanical relay, was controlled by transmitting control codes with an RF wireless remote control. Electro-mechanical relays with and without an optocoupler, for supplying DC to a load, were described, as was the solid-state relay.

Components List

- ESP8266 microcontroller: LOLIN (WeMos) D1 mini or NodeMCU board

- ESP32 microcontroller: ESP32 DEVKIT DOIT or NodeMCU board

- Multiplexer: 74HC4051 or Arduino Nano

- 433 MHz transmitter: Standard, MX-FS-03V; superheterodyne, WL102-341

- 433 MHz receiver: Standard, MX-05V; superheterodyne, WL101-341

- Laser module: KY-008

- LED: 2×

- Resistors: 2× 220 Ω

- Joystick: KY-023

- Servo motors: 2× SG90

- Servo pan and tilt bracket

- RF wireless remote control

- Relay module without optocoupler: KY-019

- Relay module with optocoupler

- MOSFET module: IRF520

- Solid-state relay

CHAPTER 16

Signal generation

Telecommunication uses digital signals to transfer information. For example, the instruction `Serial.print("12AB")` transmits the ASCII code for each character (see Figure 16-1) in binary format with the microcontroller UART (Universal Asynchronous Receiver-Transmitter). ASCII (American Standard Code for Information Interchange) is an 8-bit character encoding standard for electronic communication, with the least significant bit (LSB) transmitted first. For example, the letter A has ASCII code of 65, which is B01000001 LSB or $(1 \times 2^6 + 1 \times 2^0)$. The transmitted $<S>$ and $<T>$ bits are the start and stop bits.

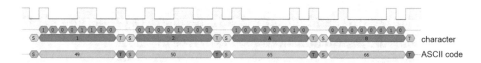

Figure 16-1. *Serial data transmission*

Note that the transmission order is important. For example, if the ASCII code for the number 2 of 50, which is B00110010 or $(1 \times 2^5 + 1 \times 2^4 + 1 \times 2^1)$, is transmitted with the most significant bit (MSB) first, then the signal could be interpreted as $(1 \times 2^6 + 1 \times 2^3 + 1 \times 2^2) = 76$, which is the ASCII code for the letter L.

Signals, consisting of a square wave at a given frequency, are also used to control industrial motor speed, audio amplification, and the brightness of an alarm clock LED. Pulse width modulation (PWM) modifies the amount of time that the square wave is *HIGH*, the pulse width, with a

© Neil Cameron 2021
N. Cameron, *Electronics Projects with the ESP8266 and ESP32*,
https://doi.org/10.1007/978-1-4842-6336-5_16

long pulse width corresponding to a fast motor speed, even though the power to the motor is being repeatedly turned on and off. Several ESP8266 and ESP32 microcontroller pins support PWM signals, and Figure 16-2 illustrates two square waves differing in frequency and duty cycle. For context, the human ear can hear sounds with frequencies of 20 Hz to 20 kHz, FM radio stations broadcast at 100 MHz, and wireless networks operate at 2.4 GHz.

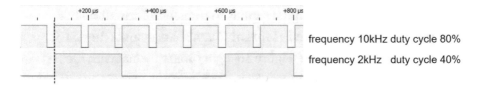

Figure 16-2. *PWM signals of different frequencies and duty cycles*

The square waves in Figure 16-2 are simultaneously generated with an ESP8266 or an ESP32 microcontroller, using the sketches in Table 16-1. The ESP8266 microcontroller default PWM frequency is 1 kHz with 10-bit resolution. The frequency of N Hz is set with the instruction analogWriteFreq(N), and the duty cycle is defined as a proportion of 1023 or $2^{10} - 1$ with the instruction analogWrite(wavePin, duty).

The ESP32 microcontroller PWM has 8, 10, 12 or 15-bit resolution with maximum frequency of $80 \text{ MHz}/2^{resolution}$. A separate channel is defined for each PWM signal, with PWM instructions for the ESP32 microcontroller of

```
ledcAttachPin(wavePin, channel)        // attach channel to pin
ledcSetup(channel, freq, resolution)   // define frequency
ledcWrite(channel, duty)               // generate square wave
```

with the parameters PWM output channel (*channel*), GPIO pin to output square wave (*wavePin*), square wave frequency (*freq*), duty cycle (*duty*), and PWM resolution (*resolution*). The resolution of the ESP32 microcontroller in Table 16-1 was set to 10, to equal the ESP8266 microcontroller resolution. If LEDs, with 220 Ω resistors, are attached to each *wavePin*, then the square wave with the greater duty cycle will result in a brighter LED.

Table 16-1. *PWM with ESP8266 and ESP32 microcontrollers*

ESP8266 Microcontroller	ESP32 Microcontroller
int wave1Pin = D1, wave2Pin = D2;	int wave1Pin = 25, wave2Pin = 26;
int freq1 = 10000, freq2 = 2000;	int freq1 = 10000, freq2 = 2000;
float duty1, duty2;	float duty1, duty2;
	int channel1 = 1, channel2 = 2;
	int resolution = 10;
void setup()	void setup()
{	{
pinMode(wave1Pin, OUTPUT);	pinMode(wave1Pin, OUTPUT);
pinMode(wave2Pin, OUTPUT);	pinMode(wave2Pin, OUTPUT);
	ledcAttachPin(wave1Pin, channel1);
	ledcAttachPin(wave2Pin, channel2);
	ledcSetup(channel1, freq1, resolution);
	ledcSetup(channel2, freq2, resolution);
duty1 = 0.8*1023;	duty1 = 0.8*1023;
duty2 = 0.4*1023;	duty2 = 0.4*1023;
}	}
void loop()	void loop()
{	{
analogWriteFreq(freq1);	

(continued)

Table 16-1. (*continued*)

ESP8266 Microcontroller	ESP32 Microcontroller
analogWrite(wave1Pin, duty1);	ledcWrite(channel1, duty1);
analogWriteFreq(freq2);	
analogWrite(wave2Pin, duty2);	ledcWrite(channel2, duty2);
}	}

The PWM output voltage oscillating between *HIGH* and *LOW* states has an average voltage of $V_{IN} \times$ *duty cycle*, where V_{IN} is the input voltage and *duty cycle* is the percentage of time that the square wave is *HIGH*. For example, a PWM 5 V supply voltage with 20% or 70% duty cycle has an average voltage of 1 V or 3.5 V, respectively, resulting in a faster motor speed when the motor is powered by the square wave with the 70% duty cycle.

A continuous sine wave of a given frequency generates a sound, which is approximated by a square wave (see Figure 16-3). A Piezo transducer, connected to an ESP8266 or ESP32 microcontroller pin producing a square wave with frequency 440 Hz, approximates the musical note A above middle C. Instructions for an ESP8266 microcontroller are

```
analogWriteFreq(440);       // define square wave frequency
analogWrite(wavePin, 512);  // square wave, 50% duty cycle
```

and the corresponding instructions, with 10-bit resolution, for an ESP32 microcontroller are

```
ledcSetup(channel, 440, 10)
ledcWrite(channel, 512)
```

A square wave with frequency 440 Hz and a 50% duty cycle is *HIGH* or *LOW* for 1136 μs, equal to $(2 \times frequency)^{-1} = 1136 \times 10^{-6}$ s. The sound is alternatively generated with the ESP8266 and ESP32 microcontroller instructions

```
digitalWrite(wavePin, !digitalRead(wavePin));
delayMicroseconds(1136);
```

Note the exclamation mark is a logical *NOT*, which results in the value *false* or *LOW* if the `digitalRead(wavePin)` is *HIGH*.

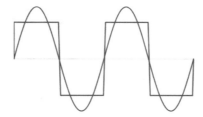

Figure 16-3. *Square wave approximating a sine wave*

Alternatively, digital information about a sound is used to generate the analog signal and reproduce the sound directly, rather than approximating the sine wave of a sound with a square wave of the same frequency.

Signal generation

One method to produce a sine or triangular wave with frequencies from 1 Hz to multiples of MHz is with an *AD9833* waveform generator module (see Figure 16-4 and Table 16-2). The *MD_AD9833* library by Marco Colli is available in the Arduino IDE. The *AD9833* module has two channels to specify two signal shapes and frequencies, but one output channel. The *AD9833* module communicates by hardware SPI (Serial Peripheral Interface) MOSI (Main-Out Secondary-In) or DATA and clock (CLK) pins with the instruction `MD_AD9833 AD(FSYNC)`, where *FSYNC* is the data signal synchronization pin. The *AD9833* module analog (AGND) and digital (DGND) GND pins are pre-connected. For sine and triangle waves, the *AD9833* module VCC pin is connected to 3.3 V (as in Figure 16-4).

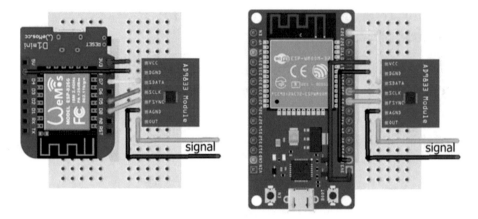

Figure 16-4. *AD9833 signal generator for a sine or triangle wave*

Table 16-2. *AD9833 signal generator module*

Component	ESP8266 Connections	ESP32 Connections
AD9833 VCC	3.3V	3.3V
AD9833 DGND	GND	GND
AD9833 SDATA (SPI MOSI)	D7	GPIO 23
AD9833 SCLK (SPI CLK)	D5	GPIO 18
AD9833 FSYNC	D0	GPIO 5
AD9833 AGND	Signal GND	Signal GND
AD9833 OUT	Signal out	Signal out

The sketch in Listing 16-1 alternately displays, for five seconds, a sine wave and a triangle wave with frequencies of 30 kHz and 20 kHz, respectively (see Figure 16-5). The instruction AD.setActiveFrequency(chan) sets the signal channel. The wave mode is defined as MODE_SINE or MODE_TRIANGLE and set with the instruction AD.setMode(mode). Signal generation starts with the instruction AD.setFrequency(chan, freq). The data synchronization pin in Listing 16-1 is defined for an ESP8266 microcontroller and is changed to 5 for the ESP32 microcontroller (see Table 16-2).

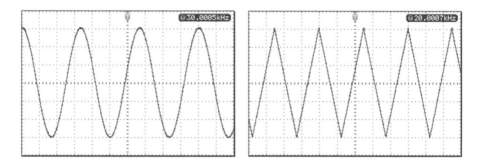

Figure 16-5. *AD9833-generated sine and triangle waves*

Listing 16-1. AD9833 sine and triangle wave generator

```
#include <SPI.h>                    // include SPI library
#include <MD_AD9833.h>              // include MD-AD9833 library
int FSYNC = D0;                     // define data synchronisation pin
MD_AD9833 AD(FSYNC);
MD_AD9833::channel_t chan;          // library channel variable
MD_AD9833::mode_t mode;             // library signal mode variable
unsigned long freq;

void setup()
{
  AD.begin();                       // initialise library
  chan = MD_AD9833::CHAN_0;         // set channel as 0 or 1
  AD.setActiveFrequency(chan);      // activate signal generator
}
```

```
void loop()
{
  wave('s', 30000, 5000);              // call sine and triangle
  wave('t', 20000, 5000);              // wave display function
}

void wave(char shape, unsigned long freq, int timeint)
{                                      // sine wave
  if(shape == 's') mode = MD_AD9833::MODE_SINE;
  else if(shape == 't') mode = MD_AD9833::MODE_TRIANGLE;
                                       // triangle wave
  AD.setMode(mode);                    // set the wave form
  AD.setFrequency(chan, freq);         // set signal frequency for channel
  delay(timeint);                      // time to generate signal
  clear();                             // call clear function
}

void clear()                          // function to clear signal
{
  mode = MD_AD9833::MODE_OFF;          // set wave mode to off
  AD.setMode(mode);                    // turn off wave generation
  delay(500);                          // time with no signal
}
```

Digital to analog converter

A digital to analog converter (DAC) converts a digital value into an analog signal. The DAC converts a number from decimal format to binary format with the DAC output voltage equal to the sum of the voltages for each bit, with the voltages reducing by half from the most significant bit (MSB) to the least significant bit (LSB). For example, the number 50 in 8-bit binary format is B00110010, and the DAC voltage is $(1 \times 2^5 + 1 \times 2^4 + 1 \times 2^1) \times$ VCC/$2^8 = 50 \times$ VCC/2^8 equal to $0.195 \times$ VCC. An 8-bit DAC with a pin voltage of VCC converts the digital value N to an analog voltage of $N \times$ VCC/2^8. The ESP32 microcontroller includes two DACs, each with 8-bit resolution, which are described later in the chapter. The ESP8266 microcontroller does not include a DAC, and in this section, a DAC is built with an ESP8266 microcontroller.

A voltage divider is the mechanism to reduce the voltage by half for each bit of the DAC. A voltage divider with an input voltage, V_{IN}, and two resistors, R1 and R2, has an output voltage, V_{OUT}, at the junction of the two resistors of $V_{IN} \times \left(\dfrac{R2}{R1 + R2} \right)$ (see Figure 16-6). If the two resistors have equal values, then the output voltage is half the input voltage. For illustrative purposes, a DAC is built with a voltage divider ladder to generate voltages, corresponding to the bit positions between the MSB and the LSB of the binary-formatted digital value.

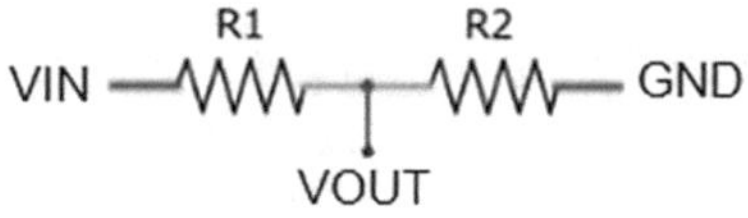

Figure 16-6. *Voltage divider*

A voltage divider ladder is built as an R-2R resistor ladder 8-bit DAC consisting of eight pairs of R and 2R resistors, with R equal to 1 kΩ (see Figure 16-7 and Table 16-3 for connections). The 2 kΩ resistor on the right side represents the MSB of the R-2R ladder 8-bit DAC. The voltage divider formed by the left pair of 2 kΩ resistors, representing the LSB, reduces the voltage at the junction to 0.5 V_{IN}. The left pair of 2 kΩ resistors are in parallel when there is no voltage on either resistor. The net resistance of two resistors, R1 and R2, in parallel is $\dfrac{1}{net\ R} = \dfrac{1}{R1} + \dfrac{1}{R2} = \dfrac{R1 + R2}{R1 \times R2}$. Therefore, when in parallel, the left pair of 2 kΩ resistors have a net resistance of 1 kΩ and are in series with resistor A, with value 1 kΩ, so the pair of 2 kΩ resistors and the 1 kΩ resistor have a combined resistance of 2 kΩ. The combination of the left pair of 2 kΩ resistors and resistor A with resistor B forms a second voltage divider, which again reduces the voltage at the junction by half. The third voltage divider is formed by grouping the left pair of 2 kΩ resistors and resistors A, B, and C with resistor D. At each stage, the voltage at the junction of the voltage divider is halved, so a *HIGH* bit value for the LSB corresponds to a voltage of $V_{IN}/2^8$, as there are effectively eight voltage dividers.

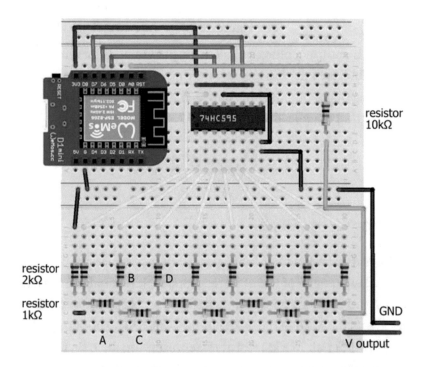

Figure 16-7. R-2R digital to analog converter with LOLIN (WeMos) D1 mini

The output voltage from the R-2R ladder 8-bit DAC corresponding to a digital value is generated by effectively using the binary format of the digital value, to set the eight voltage divider states to *HIGH* or *LOW*. For example, the 8-bit binary format of 156 is B10011100; and states of voltage dividers 1, 4, 5, and 6 (numbered from right to left) are set to *HIGH* with the DAC voltage equal to $(1/2^1 + 1/2^4 + 1/2^5 + 1/2^6) \times$ VCC or $(1 \times 2^7 + 1 \times 2^4 + 1 \times 2^3 + 1 \times 2^2) \times$ VCC$/2^8 = 156 \times$ VCC$/2^8 = 0.6094 \times$ VCC.

There are eight digital pins on the ESP8266 development board, but pins D3, D4, and D8, have built-in pull-up or pull-down resistors to maintain pin states during the ESP8266 microcontroller boot process. Instead of setting the R-2R ladder 8-bit DAC pin states with the ESP8266 microcontroller, pin states are set with a serial-in parallel-out shift register. A 74HC595 shift register loads a byte of data, consisting of 8 bits of data, one bit at a time. While the shift register clock (SRCLK) state is set *LOW*, data bits are loaded to the shift register through the serial input data (SER) pin, controlled by the storage register clock (RCLK). After all 8 bits are loaded, the shift register clock state is set *HIGH*. Instructions to pass data through a shift register are

```
digitalWrite(latchPin, LOW);                    // set the latch to LOW
shiftOut(dataPin, clockPin, MSBFIRST, number)
                                                // load number as a byte
digitalWrite(latchPin, HIGH)                    // set latch to HIGH
```

MSBFIRST indicates that the most significant bit (MSB) is loaded first, which is the state of the voltage divider on the right side of Figure 16-7.

The 74HC595 shift register pins are numbered 1–16, with the cut-out or dot at the end of the shift register indicating the end with pins 1 and 16. Connections to the 74HC595 shift register are shown in Table 16-3, with the over-line on $\overline{\text{SRCLR}}$ (clear the register) and $\overline{\text{OE}}$ (output enabled) indicating that the pin is active *LOW*. The 3.3V pin of the ESP8266 development board powers the shift register, which has an operating voltage of 2–6 V.

Table 16-3. *R-2R digital to analog converter with the ESP8266*
development board

Component	Connect to	And to
Left-hand 2 kΩ resistor (LSB)	Second 2 kΩ resistor	ESP8266 GND
7 × 2 kΩ resistors	74HC595 pins 15, 1–6 QA-QG	1 kΩ resistors
Right 2 kΩ resistor (MSB)	74HC595 pin 7 QH	
Right 2 kΩ resistor (MSB)	ESP8266 A0	Voltage output
74HC595 pin 8 GND	ESP8266 GND	
74HC595 pin 9 QH'	Not connected	
74HC595 pin 10 $\overline{\text{SRCLR}}$	ESP8266 3V3	
74HC595 pin 11 SRCLK	ESP8266 D7	
74HC595 pin 12 RCLK	ESP8266 D6	
74HC595 pin 13 $\overline{\text{OE}}$	ESP8266 GND	
74HC595 pin 14 SER	ESP8266 D5	
74HC595 pin 16 VCC	ESP8266 3V3	

The ESP8266 microcontroller 10-bit analog to digital converter (ADC)
functionality converts a voltage, between 0 and 3.2 V, on analog input pin
A0, to a digital value between 0 and 1023. The instruction analogRead(A0)
reads the voltage on the analog input pin. The reference voltage of the
ESP8266 microcontroller ADC is 1 volt; and an internal voltage divider,
consisting of 220 kΩ and 100 kΩ resistors (see Figure 16-8), increases the
maximum voltage on the analog input pin to 3.2 V. Given a voltage, V_{IN}, on
the ESP8266 development board analog input pin, the corresponding ADC
value is $V_{IN} \times \dfrac{100k\Omega}{(220+100)k\Omega} \times 1024$.

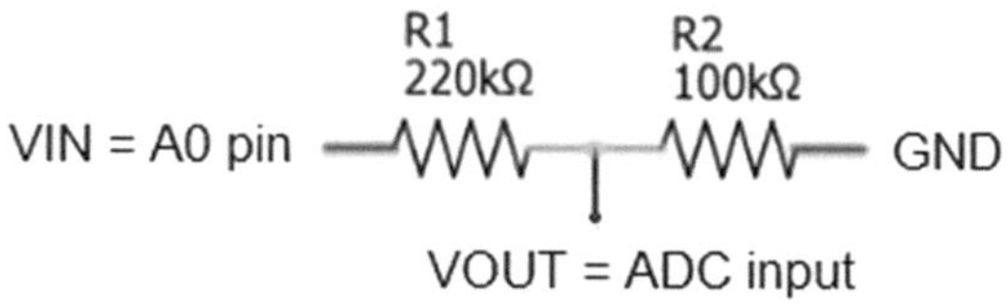

R1
220kΩ

R2
100kΩ

VIN = A0 pin —◁◁◁— —◁◁◁— GND

↓

VOUT = ADC input

Figure 16-8. *Analog to digital converter*

ADC values for input voltages between 3.2 V and 3.3 V are constrained to 1023. A 10 kΩ resistor connected between the input voltage and the ESP8266 development board analog input pin increases the limit of 3.2 V on the analog input pin to 3.3 V. An input voltage, V_{IN}, produces an ADC reading of $V_{IN} \times \dfrac{100\,k\Omega}{(10+220+100)\,k\Omega} \times 1024$. The predicted output voltage by the R-2R ladder 8-bit DAC corresponding to the digital value N is $N \times 3.3$

$V/2^8$, as the ESP8266 microcontroller has an operating voltage of 3.3 V.

Listing 16-2 illustrates using an R-2R resistor ladder 8-bit DAC to convert digital values from 0 to 255 to voltages. The 74HC595 shift register sets the eight voltage divider states, based on the binary format of the digital value, and the output voltage of the R-2R ladder 8-bit DAC is read on ESP8266 development board analog pin *A0*.

The built-in voltage divider of the ESP8266 microcontroller and the in-series 10 kΩ resistor reduce the input voltage to the ESP8266 development board analog input pin, which has a maximum voltage input of 1 volt. The output voltage from the R-2R ladder 8-bit DAC is the ADC reading of the ESP8266 microcontroller scaled by $\dfrac{(10+220+100)\,k\Omega}{100\,k\Omega} \times \dfrac{1}{1024}$.

Listing 16-2. R-2R digital to analog converter

```
int dataPin = D5;                    // shift register data
int latchPin = D6;                   // latch and clock pins
int clockPin = D7;
int Vin;                             // voltage on analog pin
float voltage, predict;              // voltage divider effect and
```

```
float voltDivid = 1000.0*(10+220+100)/100;    // adjustment to mV

void setup()
{
  Serial.begin(115200);                    // Serial Monitor baud rate
  Serial.println();
  pinMode(dataPin, OUTPUT);                // shift register pins as output
  pinMode(latchPin, OUTPUT);
  pinMode(clockPin, OUTPUT);
}

void loop()
{
  for (int i=0; i<256; i=i+50)             // incremental increases
  {
    digitalWrite(latchPin, LOW);           // start loading shift register
    shiftOut(dataPin, clockPin, MSBFIRST, i);
                                           // load 8-bit number
    digitalWrite(latchPin, HIGH);          // end loading shift register
    Vin = analogRead(A0);                  // read R-2R ladder voltage
    voltage = Vin * voltDivid / 1024.0;  // scaled R-2R ladder voltage
    predict = i * 3300.0 / 256;            // predicted output voltage
    Serial.print(i);Serial.print("\t");
    Serial.print(Vin);Serial.print("\t");          // display results
    Serial.print(voltage,0);Serial.print("\t");
    Serial.println(predict,0);
    delay(200);
  }
}
```

The maximum voltage of an R-2R ladder 8-bit DAC is $VCC \times \sum_{i=1}^{8} 1/2^i$ = 0.996×VCC = 3.287 V that corresponds to a digital value of 255 and an analog reading of 1020. An output voltage of 3.2999 V requires an R-2R ladder 16-bit DAC that corresponds to an analog reading of 1023.

Generating waves

Sine, square, triangular, and sawtooth waves are also generated with the R-2R ladder 8-bit DAC. Values of a sine wave are not always positive, as angles 90° and 270° are 1 and -1, respectively. Therefore, sine wave values are scaled by 120, and a constant of 128 is added to shift the scaled range from (-120, 120) to (8, 248) that is within the 8-bit DAC range of (0, 255). A scalar of 128 cannot be used, as the value of 256 requires a 9-bit DAC. The scaled value is converted to binary format, with the voltage divider states set to the corresponding bit of the binary-formatted number. The R-2R ladder 8-bit DAC, consisting of eight voltage dividers, generates voltages on each *rung* of the ladder. The sum of voltages from each *rung* of the R-2R ladder 8-bit DAC is the required analog voltage. For example, the scaled sine wave at 45° has the value of $212 = 128 + 120 \times \sqrt{0.5}$, which has binary format B11010100 and DAC voltage of $(1 \times 2^7 + 1 \times 2^6 + 1 \times 2^4 + 1 \times 2^2) \times VCC/2^8 = 0.828 \times VCC$.

When the R-2R ladder 8-bit DAC output is connected to a mini-loudspeaker, the sound corresponding to the scaled sine wave is heard. The frequency of the sound depends on the time taken by the ESP8266 microcontroller to generate the scaled sine wave values and convert them to binary format for the R-2R ladder 8-bit DAC. An ESP8266 microcontroller takes 15.5 ms to generate and upload, to the shift register, the scaled sine wave values for one cycle of 360 degrees with one-degree intervals, corresponding to a frequency of 64 Hz.

Different frequencies are generated by multiplying the angle of the sine wave by a constant, which increases the number of cycles in a time period, but with higher values of the multiplier, the resolution of the sine wave decreases. A potentiometer reading sets the multiplier (see Figure 16-9), and the instruction `mult = 20.0*analogRead(potPin)/1023.0` scales the potentiometer reading to an arbitrary maximum of 20, with a resultant maximum sine wave frequency of 1.28 kHz. Potentiometer connections are given in Table 16-4.

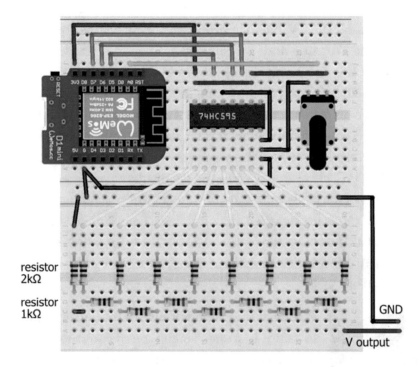

Figure 16-9. *R-2R ladder 8-bit DAC, shift register, and LOLIN (WeMos) D1 mini*

Table 16-4. *Potentiometer connections for wave generation*

Component	Connect to
Potentiometer VCC	ESP8266 VCC
Potentiometer signal (middle)	ESP8266 A0
Potentiometer GND	ESP8266 GND

The sketch in Listing 16-3 changes the multiplier of the sine wave angle to change the frequency, with corresponding sound generated by the output voltage of an R-2R ladder 8-bit DAC. In the *loop* function, the multiplier for the sine wave angle is the scaled potentiometer reading. The cycle time and the sine wave frequency are displayed every 1000 cycles. Calculation of a sine wave requires the angle to be defined in radians, and the angle in degrees is converted to radians with the formula radian = angle $\times$ π/180. In Listing 16-3, the value of the *PI* variable is predefined as 3.14159, within the Arduino IDE.

Listing 16-3. Generating a sine wave with R-2R ladder 8-bit DAC

```
int dataPin = D5;                    // shift register data
int latchPin = D6;                   // latch and clock pins
int clockPin = D7;
int count = 0;
float sum, angle, Hz;
unsigned long lastTime;
int val, sign, mult, cycleTime;

void setup()
{
  Serial.begin(115200);              // Serial Monitor baud rate
  pinMode(dataPin, OUTPUT);          // shift register pins as output
```

```
  pinMode(latchPin, OUTPUT);
  pinMode(clockPin, OUTPUT);
}

void loop()
{
  mult = 20.0*analogRead(A0)/1023.0;   // scale potentiometer value
  for (int deg=0; deg<360; deg=deg+mult)      // cycle through 360°
  {
    angle = deg*PI/180.0;                     // convert degrees to radians
    sum = sin(angle);
    val = round(128+120.0*sum);               // scaled sine wave value
    digitalWrite(latchPin, LOW);         // start loading shift register
    shiftOut(dataPin, clockPin, MSBFIRST, val);
                                              // load 8-bit number
    digitalWrite(latchPin, HIGH);            // end loading shift register
  }
  count ++;
  if(count > 999)                           // display every 1000 cycles
  {
    cycleTime = millis() - lastTime;   // time (ms) for cycle
    Hz = 1000.0 * count / cycleTime;   // frequency (Hz)
    Serial.print(mult);Serial.print("\t");
    Serial.print(Hz);Serial.print("Hz\t");
    Serial.print(1.0*cycleTime/count);Serial.println("ms");
    count = 0;                               // reset counter
    lastTime = millis();                     // reset timer
  }
}
```

In Listing 16-3, the sine wave value for an angle was calculated with the instruction sum = sin(angle).

A square wave is constructed from six odd-integer harmonics or component sine waves, as a Fourier series, with the instructions

```
sum = 0;
for (int i=1; i<12; i=i+2) sum = sum + sin(i*angle)/i;
```

A triangular wave is constructed with the same odd harmonics as a square wave, but with alternating signs and a divisor of the harmonic number squared. The instructions are

```
sum = 0;
sign = -1;
for (int i=1; i<12; i=i+2)
{
  sign = -sign;
  sum = sum + sign*sin(i*angle)/(i*i);
}
sum = sum/2;
```

A sawtooth wave is constructed with all the harmonics, but with alternate signs. Using the first nine harmonics, the instructions are

```
sum = 0;
sign = -1;
for (int i=1; i<10; i++)
{
  sign = -sign;
  sum = sum + sign*sin(i*angle)/i;
}
sum = sum/2;
```

A right-angle triangle wave is simply generated by replacing the `for (int deg=0; deg<360; deg=deg+mult) {...}` instructions, with the instructions

```
for (int i=0; i<256; i++)
{
  digitalWrite(latchPin, LOW);
  shiftOut(dataPin, clockPin, MSBFIRST, i);
  digitalWrite(latchPin, HIGH);
}
```

and a triangular wave is produced by adding the instructions

```
for (int i=1; i<255; i++)
{
  digitalWrite(latchPin, LOW);
  shiftOut(dataPin, clockPin, MSBFIRST, 255-i);
  digitalWrite(latchPin, HIGH);
}
```

The sine wave in Figure 16-10 illustrates the resolution of an R-2R ladder 8-bit DAC. When the binary-formatted number is represented with 8 bits, an essentially continuous sine wave is obtained with a step size of one. As the number of bits reduces, the step size increases, and the resolution reduces. Sine wave approximations produced by an R-2R ladder DAC with all 8 bits and with the three and two most significant bits demonstrate the rapid improvement in resolution with increasing bit number.

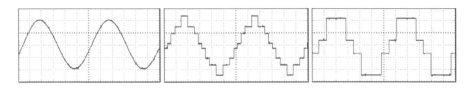

Figure 16-10. *Sine wave approximations with 8 bits and three and two most significant bits*

ESP32 8-bit DAC

The ESP32 microcontroller includes two 8-bit DACs referenced as DAC1 and DAC2 on GPIO 25 and GPIO 26. The instruction dacWrite(DACpin, value) generates a voltage of *value* × VCC/2^8, where VCC is the operating voltage of the ESP32 microcontroller. The sketch in Listing 16-4 generates the sine wave of Listing 16-3 with fewer instructions, as no R-2R ladder DAC and shift register are required, resulting in a higher sine wave frequency. The frequency is increased by including a multiplier, as in Listing 16-3.

Listing 16-4. Generating a sine wave with ESP32 DAC

```
int DACpin = DAC1;                      // DAC pin on GPIO 25
float angle;
int val;

void setup()                            // nothing in setup function
{}

void loop()
{
  for (int deg=0; deg<360; deg++)       // cycle through 360°
  {
    angle = deg*PI/180.0;               // convert degrees to radians
    val = round(128+120.0*sin(angle));  // scaled sine wave value
    dacWrite(DACpin, val);              // output voltage
  }
}
```

12-bit DAC

The MCP4725 12-bit DAC module (see Figure 16-11 with connections in Table 16-5) is an alternative to the R-2R ladder 8-bit DAC. The MCP4725 module communicates with I2C (Inter-Integrated Circuit) and has an I2C address of *0x60* to *0x67*, depending on the module version.

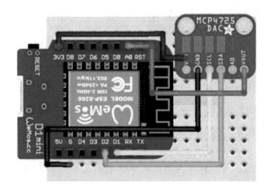

Figure 16-11. *MCP4725 12-bit DAC module and LOLIN (WeMos) D1 mini*

Table 16-5. *MCP4725 12-bit DAC module and the ESP8266 development board*

Component	Connect to
MCP4725 VOUT	ESP8266 A0
MCP4725 GND	ESP8266 GND
MCP4725 SCL	ESP8266 D1
MCP4725 SDA	ESP8266 D2
MCP4725 VCC	ESP8266 3.3V

The I2C address is obtained with the I2C scanning sketch in Listing 16-5. On transmitting to an I2C device, the device returns a *0*, indicating a successful transmission. The I2C addresses *0x00* to *0x07* and *0x78* to *0x7F* are reserved and are not scanned. I2C addresses of sensors and modules are available at learn.adafruit.com/i2c-addresses/the-list.

Listing 16-5. I2C scanner

```
#include <Wire.h>                    // include Wire library
int device = 0;                      // set device counter

void setup()
{
  Serial.begin (115200);             // Serial Monitor baud rate
  Serial.println();
  Wire.begin();                      // start I2C bus
  for (int i=8; i<127; i++)          // scan through channels 8 to 126
  {
    Wire.beginTransmission (i);      // transmit to device at address i
    if (Wire.endTransmission () == 0)
    {                                // device response to transmission
      Serial.print("Address 0x");
      Serial.println(i, HEX);        // display I2C address in HEX
      device++;                      // increment device count
      delay(10);
    }
  }
  Serial.print(device);              // display device count
  Serial.println(" device found");
}

void loop()                          // nothing in loop function
{}
```

The *Adafruit MCP4725* library instruction setVoltage(value, false) outputs a voltage of $VCC \times value/2^{12}$, where VCC is the MCP4725 module voltage supply of 3.3–5 V that is also the reference output voltage. The output voltage of the MCP4725 12-bit DAC module is confirmed by connecting the module *VOUT* pin to the ESP8266 microcontroller analog input pin *A0* with the output voltage equal to VCC*analogRead(A0)/1024, where VCC is the microcontroller operating voltage.

A sketch to generate a range of voltages and a sine wave with the MCP4725 12-bit DAC module is given in Listing 16-6. When generating the sine wave, the angle is defined in radians, so the angle, measured in degrees, is converted to radians by the formula radian = angle × π/180. One is added to the sine value, to obtain a positive number to generate the output voltage. A multiplier of 2047 for the sine value plus one is used, rather than 2048, as the instruction dac.setVoltage(4096, false) results in an output voltage of 0 volt. Different frequencies are generated by multiplying the angle of the sine wave by a constant, which increases the number of cycles in a time period, but with higher values of the multiplier, the resolution of the sine wave reduces.

Listing 16-6. Sine wave with MCP4725 12-bit DAC module

```
#include <Adafruit_MCP4725.h>      // include Adafruit MCP4725 lib
Adafruit_MCP4725 dac;              // associate dac and MCP4725 lib
float voltDivid = 3200;           // voltage divider adjustment
float VCC = 3300;                 // operating voltage
int flag = 0;                     // flag to switch to sine wave
float predict, voltage, value;
int Vin;
```

```
void setup()
{
  Serial.begin(115200);                  // Serial Monitor baud rate
  dac.begin(0x60);                       // I2C address of MCP4725
}

void loop()
{
  if(flag < 1)
  {
    for(int i=0; i<4096; i=i+50)
    {
      dac.setVoltage(i, false);             // set output voltage
      Vin = analogRead(A0);                 // read DAC voltage
      voltage = Vin * voltDivid /1024.0;    // scaled output voltage
      predict = i * VCC / 4096.0;           // predicted output voltage
      Serial.print(voltage);Serial.print("\t");
      Serial.println(predict);              // display voltages
    }
    delay(2000);
    flag = 1;                             // switch to sine wave only
  }
  for (int deg=0; deg<360; deg++)         // generate sine wave
  {
    value = 2047.0*(sin(deg*PI/180.0)+1); // scaled sine wave value
    dac.setVoltage(value, false);         // set output voltage
  }
}
```

Reading the sine wave values from a lookup table reduces processing time, relative to calculating values of the sine wave, which increases the number of cycles in a time period and so the frequency of the sine wave. The ESP8266 microcontroller has 4 MB flash memory and 50 kB SRAM (static random access memory), so the lookup table is stored in flash or programmable memory, *PROGMEM*, where the sketch is stored, rather than in SRAM, where variables are created and manipulated in a sketch. The instruction to store an array in flash memory is const type arrayname[] PROGMEM = {array values}, and the ith value of the array is accessed with the instruction pgm_read_type(arrayname + i). Character or integer data is stored in flash memory with the variable type defined as unsigned char or uint16_t and accessed with pgm_read_byte or pgm_read_word, respectively.

In Listing 16-7, sine wave values at intervals of 10° are stored in flash memory. For example, the time to generate 500 sine waves is measured to determine the frequency of the generated sine wave. The sine wave is also generated by directly calculating values of the sine wave to compare the gain in wave frequency by storing values in flash memory.

Listing 16-7. Storing sine wave values in flash memory

```
#include <Adafruit_MCP4725.h>      // include Adafruit MCP4725 lib
Adafruit_MCP4725 dac;              // associate dac and MCP4725 lib
const uint16_t lookup[] PROGMEM = {    // sine wave in flash memory
2047,2402,2747,3071,3363,3615,3820,3971,4063,4094,
4063,3971,3820,3615,3363,3071,2747,2402,2047,1692,
1347,1024, 731, 479, 274, 123,  31,   0,  31, 123,
 274, 479, 731,1024,1347,1692      // 2047×(sin(x°×π/180) + 1)
};
```

```
int value, cycle;
unsigned long lastTime = 0;
float freq;

void setup()
{
  Serial.begin(115200);                // Serial Monitor baud rate
  Serial.println();
  dac.begin(0x60);                     // I2C address of MCP4725
}

void loop()
{
  lastTime = millis();                 // start timer
  while (cycle < 500)                  // sine wave for 500 cycles
  {
    for (int i=0; i<36; i++)
    {
      value = pgm_read_word(lookup+i);  // values from flash memory
      dac.setVoltage(value, false);     // set output voltage
    }
    cycle++;
    yield();                            // required to prevent timeout
  }
  freq = 1000 * 500.0/(millis() - lastTime);     // wave frequency
  Serial.print("lookup ");Serial.print(freq);
  cycle = 0;

  lastTime = millis();
  while (cycle < 500)
  {
```

```
  for (int deg=0; deg<360; deg=deg+10)   // generate sine wave
  {                                      // scaled sine wave value
    value = 2047.0*(sin(deg*PI/180.0)+1);
    dac.setVoltage(value, false);              // set output voltage
  }
  cycle++;
  yield();
  }
  freq = 1000 * 500.0/(millis()-lastTime);
  Serial.print("\tcalc   ");Serial.println(freq);
  cycle = 0;
}
```

The sine wave frequencies from different methods of generating a sine wave, with sine values at 10° intervals, are summarized in Table 16-6. Sine waves were generated by the ESP32 microcontroller 8-bit DAC and by an ESP8266 microcontroller with an R-2R resistor ladder 8-bit DAC and an MCP4725 12-bit DAC. The frequency of the sine wave generated by the ESP32 microcontroller was double that of the ESP8266 microcontroller with the R-2R ladder 8-bit DAC, but 20 times greater than with the MCP4725 12-bit DAC module. The higher resolution of the 12-bit MCP4725 DAC module compared to the R-2R ladder 8-bit DAC was offset by slower sine wave generation. For the 12-bit MCP4725 DAC module, storing sine wave values in flash memory produced marginally higher sine wave frequency than when sine wave values were calculated. The *AD9833* module is the most powerful method generating a sine wave.

Table 16-6. *Sine wave generation methods and frequencies*

Generation Method with Values at 10° Intervals	Frequency (Hz) of Sine Wave
AD9833 module	To MHz
ESP32 8-bit DAC	1467
ESP8266 R-2R resistor ladder 8-bit DAC	647
ESP8266 MCP4725 12-bit DAC	66
With lookup table	71

Summary

Square waves with variable duty cycle were produced by the ESP8266 and ESP32 microcontrollers to control external devices. The digital to analog converter (DAC) with an R-2R resistor ladder was described for an ESP8266 microcontroller. Sine, square, triangular, and sawtooth waves were generated by combining harmonics as a Fourier series. A variety of sounds were produced from the output voltage of an R-2R ladder 8-bit DAC by changing the frequency of the sine wave. Output voltages were also generated with the MCP4725 12-bit DAC module. The AD9833 module produced sine and triangle waves with MHz frequencies. The ESP32 microcontroller 8-bit DAC produced sine waves with double the frequency of the sine waves generated by the ESP8266 microcontroller.

Components List

- ESP8266 microcontroller: LOLIN (WeMos) D1 mini or NodeMCU board

- ESP32 microcontroller: DEVKIT DOIT or NodeMCU board

- MCP4725 12-bit DAC module

- AD9833 waveform generator module

- 74HC595 shift register

- Potentiometer: 10 kΩ

- Resistors: 7× 1 kΩ, 9× 2 kΩ

CHAPTER 17

Signal generation with 555 timer IC

In Chapter 16 (Signal generation), an ESP8266 or ESP32 microcontroller generated square wave signals with variable duty cycle or generated sine and triangular wave signals when combined with an AD9833 waveform generator module. Sine waves were also generated with the addition of an external DAC (digital to analog converter) MCP4725 module to the ESP8266 microcontroller or with the built-in DAC of the ESP32 microcontroller. In Chapter 5 (MP3 player), a microcontroller signaled an MP3 player module to play a track when movement triggered a passive infrared (PIR) sensor. Even though the signaling sketches often contained fewer than 20 lines of code, signal generation always required a microcontroller. Signal generation with a 555 timer integrated circuit (IC) is an alternative to requiring a microcontroller and provides insight into combining electronic components for an application. The 555 timer IC is incorporated in timer and signal generation applications ranging from pulse and sound generation, clocks, timers and alarm triggering, power control with PWM (pulse width modulation), or any application requiring time control. This chapter describes signal generation with the 555 timer IC to complement Chapter 16 (Signal generation). As an illustrative application, the MP3 player and PIR sensor example from Chapter 5 (MP3 player) is developed with the 555 timer IC.

© Neil Cameron 2021
N. Cameron, *Electronics Projects with the ESP8266 and ESP32*,
https://doi.org/10.1007/978-1-4842-6336-5_17

555 timer IC

The 555 timer IC has eight pins, with the pin labels given in Figure 17-1
(left side). However, representing the 555 timer IC as in Figure 17-2, with
the *Threshold, Trigger,* and *Control* pins grouped together and the *Output*
and *Discharge* pins grouped together, aids interpretation of schematics
with the 555 timer IC. For circuit layouts, the 555 timer IC is represented
as in Figure 17-1 (right side) to minimize overlap of connections to the 555
timer IC.

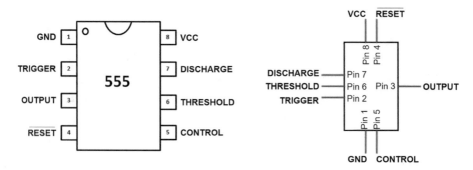

Figure 17-1. *555 timer IC pin layouts*

The 555 timer IC incorporates two voltage comparators, represented by
triangles in Figure 17-2, with reference voltages of $\frac{2}{3}$ VCC and $\frac{1}{3}$ VCC, which
are generated by two voltage dividers, formed with three 5 kΩ resistors. The
555 timer IC is primarily controlled by voltages on the *Threshold* and *Trigger*
pins. When the voltage on the *Threshold* pin is greater than $\frac{2}{3}$ VCC, the Flip-
Flop, represented by the *Reset/Set* box in Figure 17-2, is reset, the *Output* pin
state changes from *HIGH* to *LOW,* and the NPN (negative-positive-negative)
discharge transistor is turned on to create a low-impedance connection
between the *Discharge* pin and GND. Conversely, when the voltage on

the *Trigger* pin is less than $\frac{1}{3}$ VCC, the Flip-Flop is set, the *Output* pin state changes from *LOW* to *HIGH,* and the NPN discharge transistor is turned off to disconnect the *Discharge* pin from GND.

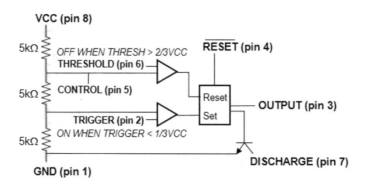

Figure 17-2. *555 timer diagram*

To control the time that voltages on the *Trigger* and *Threshold* pins are within the range of $\frac{1}{3}$ VCC and $\frac{2}{3}$ VCC, a resistor-capacitor (RC) combination is connected to the 555 timer IC. The voltage across the capacitor at *t* seconds of charging or discharging is $V(1 - e^{-t/RC})$ or $V(e^{-t/RC})$, where *V* is the supply voltage. The higher the RC value, the longer the time interval between changes in both the Flip-Flop state and the *Output* voltage. A detailed description is given in the following "*Astable mode*" section. Briefly, while the capacitor charges, the *Output* pin is *HIGH,* and the increasing capacitor voltage is the input to the *Threshold* pin. When the voltage reaches $\frac{2}{3}$ VCC, the *Output* pin state changes from *HIGH* to *LOW,* and the capacitor discharges through the *Discharge* pin. As the capacitor discharges, the decreasing capacitor voltage is the input to the *Trigger* pin; and when the voltage reaches $\frac{1}{3}$ VCC, the *OUTPUT* pin state changes from *LOW* to *HIGH,* and the capacitor starts to charge again.

The 555 timer IC has three operating modes: monostable, bistable, and astable. In monostable mode, triggering the 555 timer IC produces a *HIGH* pulse for a fixed time, which then returns to the *LOW* state until retriggered. Applications of the monostable mode include time delays. In bistable mode, the *HIGH* or *LOW* state is triggered with a switch for use in switch debouncing. In astable mode, the 555 timer IC generates square waves of fixed frequency and duty cycle determined by the value of the resistor-capacitor combination. Applications of the astable mode include pulse width modulation control of motors or lights, tone and sound generation, clock timing, and square waves and triangular and sine waves when the 555 timer IC is combined with a resistor-capacitor and an inductor-capacitor (LC), respectively.

The *Reset* pin is active *LOW*, indicated in Figure 17-2 by $\overline{RESET}$, and is inactivated by connecting the *Reset* pin to VCC. A voltage on the *Control* pin replaces the voltage comparator reference voltages of $\frac{2}{3}$ VCC and $\frac{1}{3}$ VCC with the *Control* pin voltage and half of the *Control* pin voltage, respectively. The *Control* pin is inactivated by connecting the *Control* pin to GND through a 10 nF (equal to 0.01 µF) capacitor to eliminate noise.

The CMOS (Complementary Metal Oxide Semiconductor) version of the 555 timer IC, such as the TLC555, includes MOSFETs (Metal Oxide Semiconductor Field Effect Transistors) for switching rather than BJTs (bipolar junction transistors), which are included in the standard 555 timer IC, such as the NE555. The CMOS 555 timer IC requires less power and has no voltage spikes with changing *Output* pin states, but has lower output current than the standard 555 timer IC. The CMOS 555 timer IC VCC pin supports 2–15 V, and the *Output* pin sinks 100 mA, but only sources 10 mA, while the standard 555 timer IC VCC pin supports 5–15 V with the *Output* pin sinking or sourcing up to 200 mA. Voltage spikes that occur when changing *Output* pin states with the standard 555 timer IC are eliminated by fitting a 0.1 µF capacitor across the VCC and GND pins of the 555 timer IC.

This chapter uses a CMOS 555 timer IC, except in the "Square wave to sine wave" section, which uses the standard 555 timer IC.

Monostable mode

In monostable mode for the 555 timer IC (see Figure 17-3 with connections in Table 17-1), closing the switch results in the LED turning on for one pulse length and then turning off. When the switch is open, the *Trigger* pin is connected to VCC through the pull-up resistor R_2, and the *Threshold* pin is connected to GND through the *Discharge* pin, so the *Output* pin is *LOW* and the LED is turned off. When the switch is momentarily closed, the *Trigger* pin is connected to GND, and the voltage on the *Trigger* pin is 0 V, which is less than $\frac{1}{3}$ VCC, so the Flip-Flop is set, the *Output* pin changes from *LOW* to *HIGH,* the LED is turned on, and the NPN discharge transistor is turned off to disconnect the *Discharge* pin from GND.

The capacitor C_1 starts charging through resistor R_1, as the capacitor is no longer connected to GND, and the voltage on the *Threshold* pin increases. When the voltage on the *Threshold* pin is greater than $\frac{2}{3}$ VCC, the Flip-Flop is reset, the *Output* pin changes from *HIGH* to *LOW*, the LED is turned off, and the NPN discharge transistor is turned on to create a low-impedance connection between the *Discharge* pin and GND. The capacitor now discharges through the *Discharge* pin, and the *Threshold* pin is again connected to GND and the *Trigger* pin to VCC. The cycle repeats only when the switch is next closed.

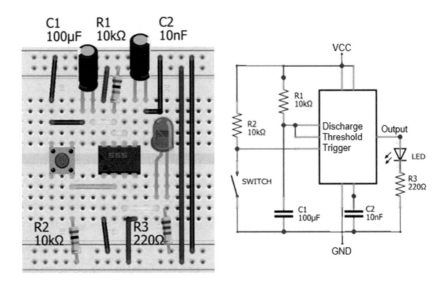

Figure 17-3. *555 monostable mode*

Table 17-1. *555 monostable mode*

Component	Connect to	Then to
555 GND (pin 1)	GND	
555 Trigger (pin 2)	Switch (right side)	
555 Output (pin 3)	LED long leg	
555 Reset (pin 4)	VCC	
555 Control (pin 5)	10 nF capacitor positive	GND
555 Threshold (pin 6)	555 Discharge (pin 7)	
555 Discharge (pin 7)	10 kΩ resistor	VCC
555 Discharge (pin 7)	100 µF capacitor positive	GND
555 VCC (pin 8)	VCC	
LED short leg	220 Ω resistor	GND
Switch (right side)	10 kΩ resistor	VCC
Switch (left side)	GND	

The time that the capacitor charges from 0 V to $\frac{2}{3}$VCC depends on the value of the resistor-capacitor pair, R_1 and C_1, in Figure 17-3. Solving $\frac{2}{3}VCC = VCC\left(1 - e^{-t/RC}\right)$ for time t has the solution $t = \ln(3) \times RC$ or approximately 1.1 × RC. For example, the actual time of 1246 ms that the *Output* pin remained *HIGH* after the switch was closed, with a 9.97 kΩ resistor and a 110 µF capacitor, was comparable with the expected time of 1205 ms (see Figure 17-4).

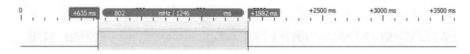

Figure 17-4. *555 monostable signal*

The resistance of a light-dependent resistor (LDR) or photoresistor decreases with increasing incident light. A night light is built by replacing the switch and pull-up resistor, R_2, in Figure 17-3, with a pull-down resistor and an LDR, respectively. The LDR resistance is between 3 kΩ and 5 kΩ in average daylight, so a 4.7 kΩ resistor provides a balanced resistance for a voltage divider with the LDR. As the incident light on the LDR reduces, the LDR resistance increases, which decreases the output voltage of the voltage divider. The *Trigger* pin is connected to the voltage divider output, and as the incident light reduces, the *Trigger* pin voltage decreases; and when it is below $\frac{1}{3}$VCC, the Flip-Flop is set, the *Output* pin changes from *LOW* to *HIGH,* and the night-light LED is turned on.

Bistable mode

In bistable mode for the 555 timer IC (see Figure 17-5 with connections in Table 17-2), closing the *ON* or *OFF* switch results in the LED being turned on or off. When the *ON* or *OFF* switch is open, the *Trigger* and *Reset* pins are connected to VCC, through pull-up resistors R_1 and R_2, so the *Output* pin is *LOW* and the LED is turned off. Note that the *Reset* pin is active *LOW*. When the *ON* switch is momentarily closed, the *Trigger* pin is connected to GND, and the voltage on the *Trigger* pin is 0 V, which is less than $\frac{1}{3}$ VCC, so the Flip-Flop is set, the *Output* pin changes from *LOW* to *HIGH,* and the LED is turned on. When the *OFF* switch is closed, the 555 timer IC is reset, the *Output* pin is *LOW,* and the LED is turned off. The 555 timer IC in bistable mode debounces the *ON* and *OFF* switches.

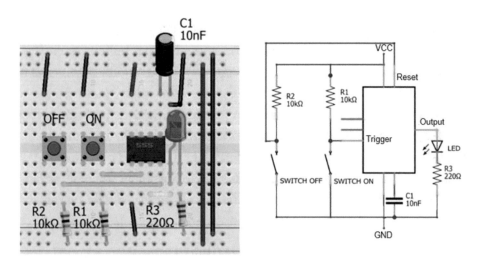

Figure 17-5. *555 bistable mode*

Table 17-2. *555 bistable mode*

Component	Connect to	Then to
555 GND (pin 1)	GND	
555 Trigger (pin 2)	Switch ON (right side)	
555 Output (pin 3)	LED long leg	
555 Reset (pin 4)	Switch OFF (right side)	
555 Control (pin 5)	10 nF capacitor positive	GND
555 VCC (pin 8)	VCC	
LED short leg	220 Ω resistor	GND
Switch ON or OFF (right side)	10 kΩ resistor	VCC
Switch ON or OFF (left side)	GND	

Astable mode

In astable mode for the 555 timer IC (see Figure 17-6 with connections in Table 17-3), a square wave is generated, as illustrated by the two LEDs being turned on and off alternately. The square wave duty cycle and frequency, which is the inverse of the length of the square wave, are determined by the values of the charging capacitor, C_1, and two resistors, R_1 and R_2. The LED connected between the *Output* pin and GND sources current from the *Output* pin, while the LED connected between VCC and the *Output* pin sinks current to the *Output* pin. When the *Output* pin is *HIGH*, the LED sourcing current is turned on, and the LED sinking current is turned off. Conversely, when the *Output* pin is *LOW*, the LED sourcing current is turned off, and the LED sinking current is turned on.

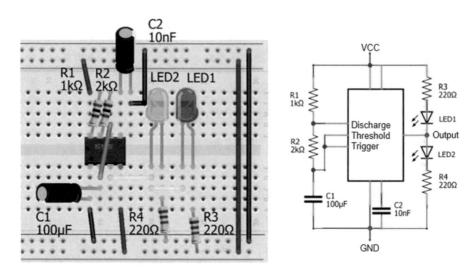

Figure 17-6. *555 astable mode*

Table 17-3. *555 astable mode*

Component	Connect to	Then to
555 GND (pin 1)	GND	
555 Trigger (pin 2)	555 Threshold (pin 6)	
555 Output (pin 3)	LED2 long leg	LED1 short leg
555 Reset (pin 4)	VCC	
555 Control (pin 5)	10 nF capacitor positive	GND
555 Threshold (pin 6)	2 kΩ resistor	555 Discharge (pin 7)
555 Discharge (pin 7)	1 kΩ resistor	VCC
555 VCC (pin 8)	VCC	
LED1 long leg	220 Ω resistor	VCC
LED2 short leg	220 Ω resistor	GND
100 μF capacitor positive	555 Trigger (pin 2)	
100 μF capacitor negative	555 Trigger (pin 1)	

The capacitor, C_1, charges through the two resistors, R_1 and R_2, and the voltage on the *Threshold* pin increases. When the voltage on the capacitor and the *Threshold* pin is greater than $\frac{2}{3}$ VCC, the Flip-Flop is reset, the *Output* pin changes from *HIGH* to *LOW*, the LED sourcing current LED_2 is turned off, the LED sinking current LED_1 is turned on, and the NPN discharge transistor is turned on to create a low-impedance connection between the *Discharge* pin and GND. The capacitor now discharges through resistor R_2 and the *Discharge* pin.

When the voltage on the discharging capacitor and the *Trigger* pin is less than $\frac{1}{3}$ VCC, the Flip-Flop is set, the *Output* pin changes from *LOW* to *HIGH*, the LED sourcing current LED_2 is turned on, the LED sinking current LED_1 is turned off, and the NPN discharge transistor is turned off to disconnect the *Discharge* pin from GND. The capacitor now charges through the two resistors, R_1 and R_2, and the cycle repeats.

Resistor values, R_1 and R_2, and the capacitor, C_1, determine the time that the capacitor charges from $\frac{1}{3}$ VCC to $\frac{2}{3}$ VCC, but the discharge time is defined only by resistor R_1 and the capacitor. The time required to increase capacitor voltage from $\frac{1}{3}$ VCC to $\frac{2}{3}$ VCC is the difference in times between charging from 0 V to $\frac{2}{3}$ VCC and from 0 V to $\frac{1}{3}$ VCC. The voltage across a capacitor at t seconds of charging is $VCC(1 - e^{-t/RC})$. The two equations $\frac{2}{3}VCC = VCC\left(1 - e^{-t2/RC}\right)$ and $\frac{1}{3}VCC = VCC\left(1 - e^{-t1/RC}\right)$ are solved for t_1 and t_2, the two charging times. The difference between the charging times, $t_2 - t_1$, is $\ln(2) \times (R_1 + R_2) \times C_1$ or $0.693 \times (R_1 + R_2) \times C_1$ seconds. The equation for the voltage across a capacitor at t seconds of discharging is $Ve^{-t/RC}$. The time that the capacitor is discharging from $\frac{2}{3}$ VCC to $\frac{1}{3}$ VCC is similarly calculated as $\ln(2) \times R_2C_1$ seconds.

The length of the square wave is $\ln(2) \times (R_1 + 2R_2) \times C_1$ seconds, and the duty cycle is $(R_1 + R_2)/(R_1 + 2R_2)$. The frequency of the square wave is the inverse of the square wave length and is often written as $1.44/[(R_1 + 2R_2) \times C_1]$, as $\ln(2)^{-1} = 1.44$. For example, with resistor values of 986 Ω and 1981 Ω and a 110 μF capacitor, the actual capacitor charging and discharging times of 220 ms and 152 ms, respectively, with a duty cycle of 59%, a wavelength of 372 ms, and a frequency of 2.69 Hz were similar to the expected capacitor charging and discharging times of 226 ms and 151 ms with a duty cycle of 60%, a wavelength of 377 ms, and a frequency of 2.65 Hz (see Figure 17-7).

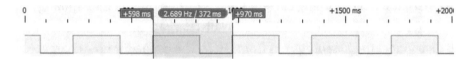

Figure 17-7. *555 astable square wave signal*

With fixed values for resistor R_1 and capacitor C, the value of resistor R_2 is chosen to generate a square wave with frequency $[\ln(2) \times (R_1 + 2R_2) \times C]^{-1}$ Hz. An electronic piano is built by connecting several pairs of switches and R_2 resistors to the 555 timer IC, with fixed values for the R_1 resistor (1 kΩ) and capacitor (1 μF) (see Figure 17-8 with connections in Table 17-5). Pressing a switch connects the series of R_2 resistors to the *Trigger* and *Discharge* pins, and the capacitor starts to charge and then discharge, which produces a square wave as long as the switch is pressed. For example, the note G4 with frequency 392 Hz requires a total resistance of 1340 Ω. The R_2 resistors are in series with the total resistance equal to the sum of the resistors. The R_2 resistors for notes C5, B4, and A4, which precede the resistor for note G4, total 1130 Ω, so the required R_2 resistor for the note G4 is 210 Ω and a 200 Ω resistor is included, as it is a readily available resistor value. In practice, frequencies of the generated sounds were within 7 Hz of the true frequencies (see Table 17-4).

Table 17-4. *Electronic piano resistor combinations*

Note	C4	D4	E4	F4	G4	A4	B4	C5
True frequency (Hz)	262	294	330	349	392	440	494	523
Resistor (Ω)	330	220	150	220	200	150	100	880
Cumulative resistance (Ω)	2250	1920	1700	1550	1330	1130	980	880
Project frequency (Hz)	262	298	328	352	394	443	487	523

A speaker is connected to the *Output* pin, through a 10 µF capacitor.

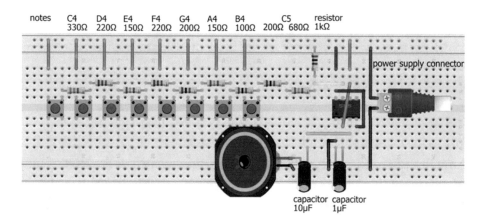

Figure 17-8. *555 timer IC and electronic piano*

Table 17-5. *555 timer IC and electronic piano*

Component	Connect to	Then to
555 GND (pin 1)	GND	
555 Trigger (pin 2)	555 Threshold (pin 6)	
555 Output (pin 3)	10 µF capacitor positive	Speaker positive
555 Reset (pin 4)	VCC	
555 Threshold (pin 6)	Switches (left side)	
555 Discharge (pin 7)	Resistors	Switches (right side)
555 VCC (pin 8)	VCC	
1 µF capacitor positive	555 Trigger (pin 2)	
1 µF capacitor negative	555 Trigger (pin 1)	
Speaker negative	GND	

Variable duty cycle

The square wave duty cycle with astable mode is always greater than 50% as the capacitor charges through resistors R_1 and R_2, but discharges through resistor R_2 (see Figure 17-6). If two diodes, such as the IN4001, are incorporated (see Figure 17-9 with connections in Table 17-6), then the capacitor charges through resistor R_1 only and discharges through resistor R_2 only.

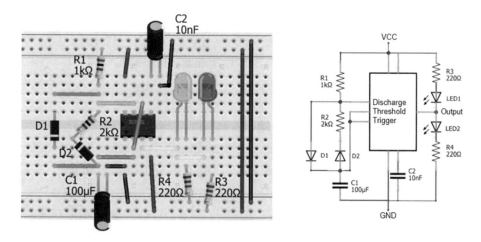

Figure 17-9. *555 astable mode with full duty cycle range*

Table 17-6. *555 astable mode with full duty cycle range*

Component	Connect to	Then to
555 GND (pin 1)	GND	
555 Trigger (pin 2)	555 Threshold (pin 6)	
555 Trigger (pin 2)	Diode (D1) cathode (negative)	
555 Trigger (pin 2)	Diode (D2) anode (positive)	2 kΩ resistor
555 Output (pin 3)	LED2 long leg	LED1 short leg
555 Reset (pin 4)	VCC	
555 Control (pin 5)	10 nF capacitor positive	GND
555 Discharge (pin 7)	1 kΩ resistor	VCC
555 VCC (pin 8)	VCC	
LED1 long leg	220 Ω resistor	VCC
LED2 short leg	220 Ω resistor	GND
100 µF capacitor positive	555 Trigger (pin 2)	
100 µF capacitor negative	555 Trigger (pin 1)	

The forward voltage drop of the diodes results in longer charge and discharge times, which are increased from $\ln(2) \times R_1C_1$ and $\ln(2) \times R_2C_1$ seconds to $\alpha \times R_1C_1$ and $\alpha \times R_2C_1$, with the constant α equal to $\ln\left[1 + \dfrac{VCC}{VCC - 3V_d}\right]$, where V_d is the forward voltage of the diode. For example, if VCC is 5 V and the diode forward voltage is 0.6 V, then the discharge time is $\ln(2.56) \times R_2C_1$ rather than $\ln(2) \times R_2C_1$ when no diode is included in the circuit. The square wave duty cycle is unaffected by inclusion of the two diodes and is less than or greater than 50% when resistor R_1 is less than or greater than resistor R_2. For example, with resistor values of 986 Ω and 1981 Ω and a 110 μF capacitor, the actual capacitor charging and discharging times of 99 ms and 203 ms, respectively, with a duty cycle of 33% were similar to the expected capacitor charging and discharging times of 102 ms and 205 ms (see Figure 17-10).

Figure 17-10. *Variable duty cycle with astable mode*

The voltage across a capacitor charging or discharging through a resistor of RΩ is $V_t = V_S + (V_0 - V_S)e^{-t/RC}$, where V_0 is the initial voltage across the capacitor with capacitance C and V_S is the supply voltage. If the capacitor is fully discharged with $V_0 = 0$, the supply voltage is V; then the equation reduces to the usual formula for a charging capacitor of $V(1 - e^{-t/RC})$. Similarly for a discharging capacitor with $V_0 = V$, then the supply voltage is $V_s = 0$ with the usual formula for a discharging capacitor of $Ve^{-t/RC}$.

When a diode, with forward voltage V_d, is included in series with the charging resistor R_1 and the capacitor charges from $\frac{1}{3}$ VCC to $\frac{2}{3}$ VCC, the charging time is $R_1 C_1 \times \ln\left[1 + \dfrac{VCC}{VCC - 3V_d}\right]$ for a supply voltage $V_S = VCC - V_d$, $V_0 = \frac{1}{3} VCC$, and $V_t = \frac{2}{3}$ VCC. Likewise when a diode is included in series with the discharging resistor R_2 and the capacitor discharges from $\frac{2}{3}$ VCC to $\frac{1}{3} VCC$, the discharging time is $R_2 C_1 \times \ln\left[1 + \dfrac{VCC}{VCC - 3V_d}\right]$ for a supply voltage $V_S = V_d$, $V_0 = \frac{2}{3}$ VCC, and $V_t = \frac{1}{3}$ VCC. Note than when the diode forward voltage, V_d, is set to zero in the formulae, the charging and discharging times are $\ln(2) \times R_1 C_1$ and $\ln(2) \times R_2 C_1$, as before.

50% duty cycle

If the capacitor charges and discharges through the same resistor, then the duty cycle is close to 50%, irrespective of the value of the resistor or capacitor. The resistor is connected between the *Output* pin and the *Trigger* and *Threshold* pins (see Figure 17-11 with connections in Table 17-7).

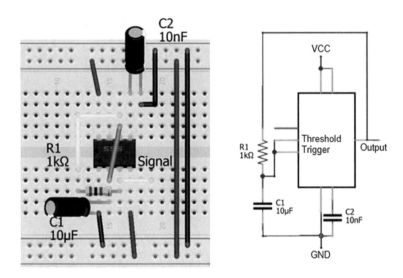

Figure 17-11. *555 astable mode with 50% duty cycle*

Table 17-7. *555 astable mode with full duty cycle range*

Component	Connect to	Then to
555 GND (pin 1)	GND	
555 Trigger (pin 2)	555 Threshold (pin 6)	
555 Output (pin 3)	Signal	
555 Output (pin 3)	1 kΩ resistor	555 Threshold (pin 6)
555 Reset (pin 4)	VCC	
555 Control (pin 5)	10 nF capacitor positive	GND
555 VCC (pin 8)	VCC	
10 μF capacitor positive	555 Trigger (pin 2)	
10 μF capacitor negative	555 Trigger (pin 1)	

(continued)

Table 17-7. (*continued*)

Component	Connect to	Then to
NPN BJT collector	220 Ω resistor	LED short leg
NPN BJT base	10 kΩ resistor	555 Output (pin 3)
NPN BJT emitter	GND	
LED long leg	VCC	

The capacitor charges through resistor R_1, and the voltage on the *Threshold* pin increases. When the voltage on the capacitor and the *Threshold* pin is greater than $\frac{2}{3}$ VCC, the Flip-Flop is reset, the *Output* pin changes from *HIGH* to *LOW*. The capacitor now discharges through resistor R_1 and the *Output* pin. When the voltage on the discharging capacitor and the *Trigger* pin is less than $\frac{1}{3}$ VCC, the Flip-Flop is set, the *Output* pin changes from *LOW* to *HIGH*. The capacitor now charges through the resistor R_1, and the cycle repeats.

The length of the square wave is $\ln(2) \times 2R_1C_1$ seconds. For example, with resistor and capacitor values of 986 Ω and 110 µF, the square wave frequency of 6.55 Hz was similar to the expected frequency of 6.65 Hz (see Figure 17-12).

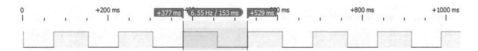

Figure 17-12. *Square wave with 50% duty cycle*

When a load is applied to the *Output* pin, even just an LED, then the square wave *HIGH* pulse length increases, the duty cycle increases, and the frequency decreases. If a load is to be controlled, then the base of a transistor is connected to the *Output* pin, with the load powered through the transistor (see Figure 17-13 with connections in Table 17-7). A BC548 or 2N2222 transistor is suitable with a 10 kΩ resistor between the *Output* and transistor base pins, to limit the current on the transistor base pin.

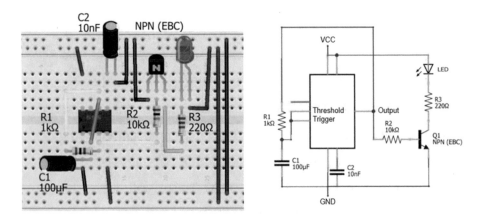

Figure 17-13. *555 astable mode with 50% duty cycle and load*

The square wave frequency is controlled interactively by connecting a potentiometer in series with resistor R_1. Retaining the 1 kΩ resistor maintains a time lag for the discharging capacitor when the potentiometer is turned to zero resistance.

PWM mode

Pulse width modulation (PWM) of the square wave is interactively controlled by replacing resistor R_1 in Figure 17-13 with a potentiometer of resistance PΩ and two diodes, such as the IN4001 (see Figure 17-14 with connections in Table 17-8). The capacitor charges and discharges through the resistances on each side of the potentiometer, $\beta \times P\Omega$ and $(1 - \beta) \times P\Omega$, so the sum of the charging and discharging times is constant. Inclusion of the diodes increases the square wave length from $\ln(2) \times 2R_1C_1$ seconds to $\ln\left[1 + \dfrac{VCC}{VCC - 3V_d}\right] \times PC_1$ seconds, as described in the *"Variable duty cycle"* section of the chapter. For example, a 10 kΩ potentiometer and a 100 µF capacitor result in a square wave frequency of 1.06 Hz with a duty cycle ranging from 10% to 90%.

To control a load with PWM, the *Output* pin is connected to the base of a transistor, with the load then powered through the transistor, such as a 2N2222 (see Figure 17-14). For example, a servo motor is controlled with the 555 timer IC by connecting the *Output* pin directly to the servo motor signal pin. A servo motor rotates to angles 0° and 180° with a square wave of 50 Hz and pulse widths of 0.5 ms and 2.5 ms. A square wave of 50.6 Hz is produced by a 555 timer IC in astable mode with a 10 kΩ potentiometer and a 2.1 µF capacitor (C_1).

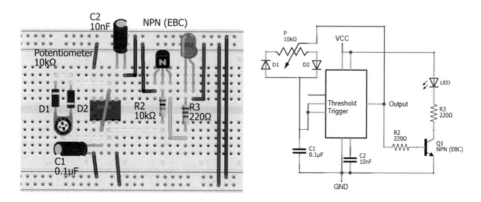

Figure 17-14. *555 astable mode with PWM*

Table 17-8. *555 astable mode with PWM*

Component	Connect to	Then to
555 GND (pin 1)	GND	
555 Trigger (pin 2)	555 Threshold (pin 6)	
555 Output (pin 3)	Potentiometer center pin	
555 Reset (pin 4)	VCC	
555 Control (pin 5)	10 nF capacitor positive	GND
555 Threshold (pin 6)	Diode (D1) cathode (negative)	Potentiometer
555 Threshold (pin 6)	Diode (D2) anode (positive)	Potentiometer
555 VCC (pin 8)	VCC	
Transistor collector	220 Ω resistor	LED short leg
Transistor base	10 kΩ resistor	555 Output (pin 3)
Transistor emitter	GND	
LED long leg	VCC	
0.1 µF capacitor positive	555 Trigger (pin 2)	
0.1 µF capacitor negative	555 Trigger (pin 1)	

Function generator

A square wave describes a non-sinusoidal, periodic oscillation, with instantaneous changes from a minimum to a maximum value, which has applications in switching and signal processing. In contrast, a sine wave describes a smooth, periodic oscillation, which has applications in describing mechanical, electrical, and sound patterns. For example, a sound is described as a combination of sine waves with different frequencies and amplitudes. While the 555 timer IC produces square waves, there are several applications that require generation of a sine wave.

A square wave with frequency f is represented as a Fourier series of sine waves over time t as

$$x(t) = \frac{4}{\pi}\left\{ \sin(2\pi ft) + \frac{1}{3}\sin(3 \times 2\pi ft) + \frac{1}{5}\sin(5 \times 2\pi ft) + \ldots \right\}$$

with the Fourier series consisting of odd-integer harmonics. Figure 17-15 illustrates a sine wave with a frequency of 2 Hz and a Fourier series approximation of a square wave by summing the first ten odd-integer harmonics.

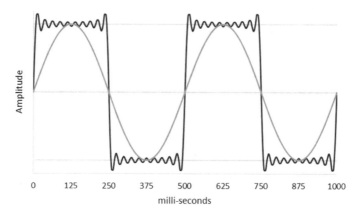

Figure 17-15. *Sine wave and odd-integer harmonics*

The base sine wave of a square wave is obtained by filtering the higher harmonics with a low-pass filter. A low-pass filter allows low-frequency signals to pass through the filter, while a high-pass filter attenuates low-frequency signals. Using the layout of a voltage divider, a resistor-capacitor (RC) combination forms an RC low-pass filter, with the capacitor passing high frequencies to GND and the lower frequencies available at *VOUT* (see Figure 17-16). The cutoff frequency of a low-pass filter is $(2\pi RC)^{-1}$Hz.

Figure 17-16. *Voltage divider and resistor-capacitor low-pass filter*

The resistor value of an RC low-pass filter is selected, based on the load of the low-pass filter, and then the capacitor value is determined. For example, a square wave with frequency of 153 Hz and 50% duty cycle is generated by the 555 timer IC with a 4.7 kΩ resistor and a 1 µF capacitor. To obtain the base sine wave with an RC low-pass filter, the resistor value for the RC low-pass filter is chosen as 1 kΩ; and to obtain a cutoff frequency, *fcut*, of 153 Hz, the required capacitor value is 1.04 µF, equal to $(2\pi R f_{cut})^{-1}$F. With a 1 kΩ resistor and a 1 µF capacitor, the actual cutoff frequency of the RC low-pass filter is 159 Hz. An RC low-pass filter is shown in Figure 17-17 with connections in Table 17-9.

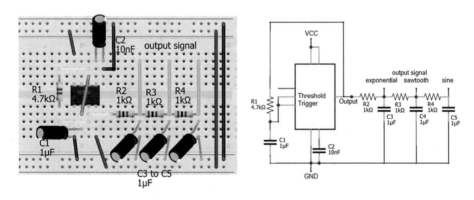

Figure 17-17. *555 timer IC and RC low-pass filters*

Table 17-9. *555 timer IC and RC low-pass filters*

Component	Connect to	Then to
555 GND (pin 1)	GND	
555 Trigger (pin 2)	555 Threshold (pin 6)	
555 Output (pin 3)	4.7 kΩ resistor	555 Threshold (pin 6)
555 Reset (pin 4)	VCC	
555 Control (pin 5)	10 nF capacitor positive	GND
555 VCC (pin 8)	VCC	
1 kΩ resistor (R2)	555 Output (pin 3)	Exponential signal
1 kΩ resistors (R3 and R4)	1 kΩ resistor (R2 and R3)	Sawtooth and sine signal
3×1 µF capacitor positive	1 kΩ resistors	
3×1 µF capacitor negative	GND	
1 µF capacitor positive	555 Trigger (pin 2)	
1 µF capacitor negative	555 Trigger (pin 1)	

The output signal from the RC low-pass filter is the same form as for a charging and discharging capacitor (see Figure 17-18, top graph). If the output from the RC low-pass filter is the input to a second low-pass filter with the same resistor and capacitor values of 1 kΩ and 1 µF, then the output signal of the second low-pass filter is a triangular wave (see Figure 17-18, middle graph). Adding a third low-pass filter converts the triangular wave to a sine wave with same frequency as the square wave (see Figure 17-18, bottom graph). The 555 timer IC and the three RC low-pass filters form a function generator to produce square waves, triangular waves, and sine waves.

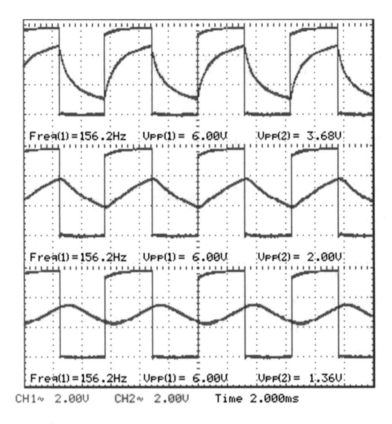

Figure 17-18. *Output waveforms from RC low-pass filters*

In Figure 17-18, the output signals from the three RC low-pass filters are shown relative to the square wave signal generated by the same 555 timer IC. The three waves have the required waveform, but the signal amplitudes decline with each RC filter, which is, to an extent, expected. An RC low-pass filter has a cutoff frequency of $(2\pi RC)^{-1}$Hz, and the capacitor has a reactance of Xc equal to $(2\pi Cf)^{-1}\Omega$, which is the capacitor opposition to a change in voltage for a signal with frequency f. If a sine wave with amplitude V volts is input to an RC low-pass filter, then the output wave amplitude is reduced to $V \times X_C / \sqrt{R^2 + X_C^2}$ volts. When the capacitor value is equal to $(2\pi Rf_{cut})^{-1}$F, then the capacitor reactance equals the resistor value, R, and the equation for the output wave amplitude simplifies to $V / \sqrt{2}$. The amplitude of sine wave signals at the output of the first, second, and third RC low-pass filters is $V / \sqrt{2}$, $V/2$, and $V / 2\sqrt{2}$ volts, respectively. The amplitudes of signals from the three RC low-pass filters, given the initial square wave signal, also decline in a systematic manner.

Square wave to sine wave

An inductor-capacitor (LC) filter is an alternative to a series of RC low-pass filters to convert a square wave to a sine wave. The LC filter and LC circuit is described in Chapter 18 (Measuring electricity). Using the layout of a voltage divider, the LC circuit is also a low-pass filter as the inductor blocks high frequencies and the capacitor blocks low frequencies, resulting in low frequencies at *VOUT* (see Figure 17-19).

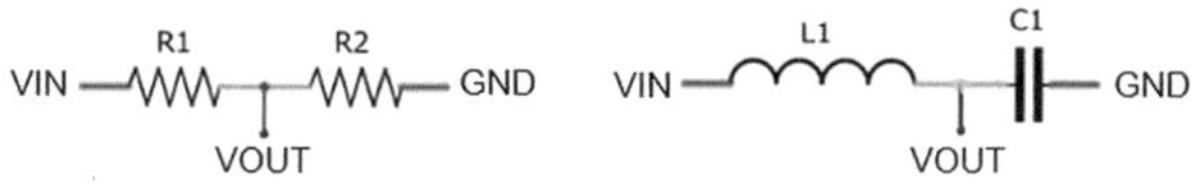

Figure 17-19. Voltage divider and inductor-capacitor low-pass filter

The LC circuit resonates at a frequency of $\left(2\pi\sqrt{LC}\right)^{-1}$ Hz. If the 555 timer IC generates a 50% duty cycle square wave at the resonance frequency of the LC circuit, then the output of the LC circuit is a sine wave (see Figure 17-21). For example, an LC circuit with a 470 µH inductor and 1 µF capacitor has a resonant frequency of 7.3 kHz, and a 555 timer IC with a 1 kΩ resistor and a 0.1 µF capacitor generates a 50% duty cycle square wave with frequency of 7.2 kHz. The standard 555 timer IC, such as the NE555, is used to generate the square wave for the LC circuit. Voltage spikes that occur when changing *Output* pin states with the standard 555 timer IC are eliminated by fitting a 0.1 µF capacitor across the VCC and GND pins of the 555 timer IC (see Figure 17-20 with connections in Table 17-10).

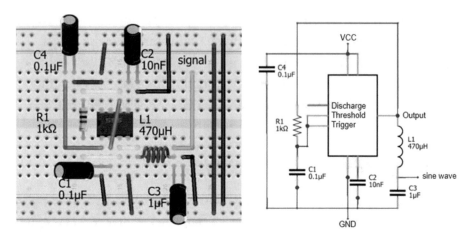

Figure 17-20. *555 and inductor-capacitor low-pass filter*

Table 17-10. *555 and inductor-capacitor low-pass filter*

Component	Connect to	Then to
555 GND (pin 1)	GND	
555 Trigger (pin 2)	555 Threshold (pin 6)	
555 Output (pin 3)	1 kΩ resistor	555 Threshold (pin 6)
555 Reset (pin 4)	VCC	
555 Control (pin 5)	10 nF capacitor positive	GND
555 VCC (pin 8)	VCC	
Inductor	555 Output (pin 3)	
Inductor	Sine signal	1 µF capacitor positive
1 µF capacitor negative	GND	
0.1 µF capacitor (C4) positive	VCC	
0.1 µF capacitor (C1) positive	555 Trigger (pin 2)	
0.1 µF capacitors negative	GND	

In practice, the square wave duty cycle and frequency generated by a standard 555 timer IC powered at 6 V with a 1 kΩ resistor and a 0.1 µF capacitor were 66.7% and 5.6 kHz. The resultant *sine* wave produced by the LC circuit had a frequency of 5.0 kHz (see Figure 17-21).

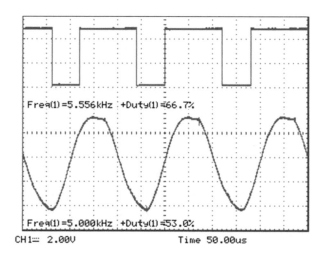

Figure 17-21. *Square wave from 555 timer IC and sine wave from LC filter*

Bipolar junction transistor as a switch

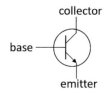

In the "*50% duty cycle*" and "*PWM mode*" sections of the chapter, an NPN (negative-positive-negative) bipolar junction transistor (BJT) functioned as a switch to turn on or off the power to a load, which was an LED. When the 555 timer IC *Output* pin state was *HIGH*, the BJT turned on power to the load; and conversely, no power was available to the load when the *Output* pin state was *LOW*. A detailed description of an NPN BJT is out of the scope of the chapter, but practical aspects of using an NPN BJT as a switch are described.

The BJT has three pins: emitter (E), base (B), and collector (C). The pin layout of a BJT is specific to the model, with differences in layout even between manufactures of the same model. The BJT pin layout is available from the manufacturer's datasheet or is determined with a multimeter by connecting the positive multimeter lead to one pin and measuring the voltage on the other BJT pins. When a voltage is detected on both of the other pins, relative to the pin connected to the positive multimeter lead, then the multimeter positive lead is connected to the NPN BJT base pin. To differentiate between the emitter and collector pins, the NPN BJT emitter pin has a marginally higher voltage than the NPN BJT collector pin.

When an NPN BJT is functioning as an amplifier and a small current is applied to the base pin, then a larger current flows between the collector and emitter pins. The ratio of the current between the BJT collector and emitter pins relative to the current on the BJT base is termed the *DC (direct current) gain* and denoted β, but also termed h_{FE} on datasheets. A change in the base current, Δ, is reflected by a change in the collector to emitter current of $\beta \times \Delta$. The BJT gain is determined from the manufacturer's datasheet or by measuring the current at the BJT base and collector pins. For example, with the 2N2222 BJT in Figure 17-22 (left side), the currents at the base and collector pins were 255 µA and 25.4 mA, respectively, giving a BJT gain of 100.

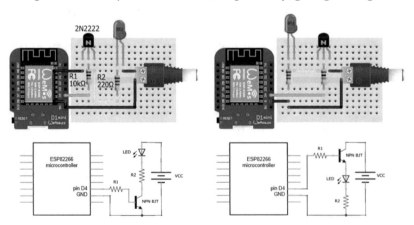

Figure 17-22. *Bipolar junction transistor as a LOW-side or HIGH-side switch*

In contrast, when the BJT is functioning as a switch, the base current is sufficiently high that an increase in the base current does not result in an increase in the collector to emitter current, as the BJT is *saturated*. In saturation mode, the collector to emitter current is either switched on or off.

For an NPN BJT to function as a switch, the BJT emitter is connected to GND, and the NPN BJT is termed a *LOW*-side switch (see Figure 17-22, left side). To illustrate an NPN BJT functioning as a switch to turn on or off power to a load, the base pin of a 2N2222 BJT in a TO-92 package is connected to an ESP8266 development board pin *D4*, and the collector pin is connected to the LED resistor and the emitter pin to GND. When the ESP8266 *D4* pin state is *HIGH*, the current on the BJT base enables current to flow between the BJT collector and emitter. Current now flows from the external 5 V power source, through the LED and resistor, to the BJT and to GND; and the LED turns on.

For the example layout in Figure 17-22 (left side), when the ESP8266 *D4* pin state is *HIGH*, the BJT base current is 260 μA = (3.3 -0.7) V/10 kΩ as an NPN BJT has a voltage drop of 0.7 V between the base and emitter. Given the BJT gain of 100, the collector to emitter current is 26 mA = 100 × 260 μA, which is the current through the LED. The red LED used in this chapter has a forward voltage drop of 2.12 V at 26 mA, and the voltage across the LED resistor of 2.6 V = 26 mA × 100 Ω results in a voltage of 280 mV across the BJT collector and emitter pins.

In the Figure 17-22 (right side) schematic, the NPN BJT is connected to VCC and is termed a *HIGH*-side switch. The *HIGH*-side switch is not recommended as the current through the LED is constrained, even though the components are identical in the two schematics of Figure 17-22. In practice, the BJT base current of 34 μA results in a voltage across the base resistor of 338 mV = 34 μA × 10 kΩ. The voltage drops of the LED and base-emitter of 1.92 V and 0.7 V, respectively, leave a voltage across the LED resistor of 342 mV, which equates to a current of 3.4 mA – one-eigth of the current through the LED with the BJT as a *LOW*-side switch. Note the lower forward voltage of the LED at a lower current. The essential difference between the NPN BJT functioning as a *LOW*-side and a *HIGH*-side switch is the lower voltage (280 mV relative to 2.74 V) across the BJT collector and emitter pins with the *LOW*-side switch.

When the BJT functions as an amplifier, the BJT base resistor value is determined from the BJT gain, β, and the required current through the load, I_L. The base current is I_L/β, and after subtracting the base-emitter voltage drop of 0.7 V from the base voltage, V_B, the base resistor value is $(V_B - 0.7) \times \beta/I_L$. For example, the base resistor, R_{BASE}, for the BJT *LOW*-side switch to supply the LED with 20 mA from the 5 V power source in Figure 17-22 (left side) is equal to (3.3-0.7)V $\times$ 100/0.02 A = 13 kΩ. However, when the BJT functions as a switch, a lower value base resistor, such as $R_{BASE}/2$ or 6.8 kΩ, ensures that the BJT is in saturation mode.

MP3 player and PIR sensor application

This chapter demonstrated signal generation by the 555 timer IC with applications in switch control, in timing, in sound generation, in appliance control with PWM, and as a function generator of square, triangular, and sine waves. The 555 timer IC is also used to transform the signal from one device into the required format for another device. In Chapter 5 (MP3 player), when a passive infrared (PIR) sensor detects movement, the PIR sensor sends a *HIGH* signal for 5 s that is read by a microcontroller, which transfers a command sequence to the MP3 player to play a soundtrack. If a short *LOW* signal is received on the MP3 player *IO2* pin, then the next track is played. However, if a long *LOW* signal is received on the MP3 player pin, then the volume is increased. To replace the microcontroller, the *HIGH* PIR signal lasting 5 s must be converted to a *LOW* signal lasting only 0.5 s.

The 555 timer IC in monostable mode, with a specific resistor-capacitor combination, generates a 0.5 s *HIGH* signal, when the *Trigger* pin is connected to GND. Therefore, a process is required to invert the PIR long

HIGH signal and trigger the 555 timer IC in monostable mode to generate a short *HIGH* signal that is inverted and sent to the MP3 player *IO2* pin.

A signal is inverted with a bipolar junction transistor (BJT), such as the BC548 or 2N2222 transistor. To illustrate signal inversion, two LEDs are turned on and off alternately. With the Arduino IDE example *Blink* sketch, the red LED reflects the ESP8266 microcontroller signal, and the blue LED indicates the inverted microcontroller signal (see Figure 17-23). Both the red LED and the BJT base pin are connected to the ESP8266 development board signal pin. When the signal pin state is *LOW*, there is no current on the BJT base nor across the BJT collector and emitter pins, so the current flows through the blue LED. Conversely, when the signal pin state is *HIGH*, the resultant current on the BJT base enables current to flow between the BJT collector and emitter. The blue LED resistance is greater than the collector-emitter resistance, so the BJT effectively shorts out the LED and the blue LED is turned off.

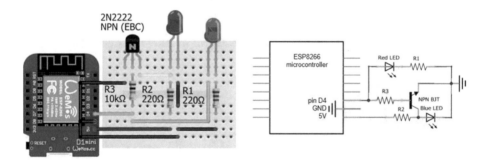

Figure 17-23. *Signal inversion with bipolar junction transistor*

The schematic for the PIR sensor to trigger the MP3 player to play the next soundtrack is shown in Figure 17-24, with connections in Table 17-11. When movement is detected by the PIR senor, the PIR sensor outputs a *HIGH* signal for five seconds. An NPN BJT could invert the long *HIGH* PIR signal, with the subsequent *LOW* signal triggering the 555 timer IC in monostable mode to generate a short *HIGH* signal, to be inverted by a

second NPN BJT, to produce a short *LOW* signal as required by the MP3
player to play the next soundtrack.

If the inverted long *HIGH* PIR signal is sent to the *Trigger* pin of the 555
timer IC in monostable mode, then the long *LOW* signal would repeatedly
trigger the 555 timer IC during the five-second duration of the *LOW* signal.
A resistor (R_2)–capacitor (C_3) combination is incorporated to generate a
short *LOW* signal for the 555 timer IC *Trigger* pin. The resistor R_4 reduces
the voltage due to the *HIGH* PIR signal to a small current on the base pin
of the NPN BJT, which enables current to flow from the BJT collector pin
to the emitter pin. The capacitor C_3 and the 555 timer IC *Trigger* pin are
connected to GND, as the capacitor partially discharges; then capacitor
C_3 recharges through resistor R_2, and the 555 timer IC *Trigger* pin is again
connected to VCC.

The 555 timer IC *Trigger* pin is *LOW* for 41 ms, which is sufficient
to trigger the 555 timer IC in monostable mode, which sets the *Output*
pin *HIGH* for $\ln(3) \times R_1C_1$, equal to 0.55 second with a 5.1 kΩ and 10 μF
resistor-capacitor combination. A second NPN BJT inverts the 555 timer IC
signal, which is sent to the MP3 player *IO2* pin to play the next soundtrack.

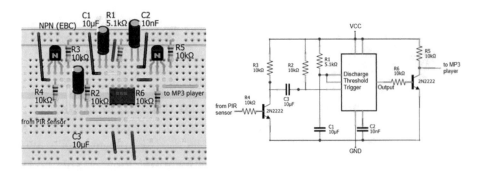

Figure 17-24. *PIR sensor and MP3 player*

Table 17-11. *PIR sensor and MP3 player*

Component	Connect to	Then to
555 GND (pin 1)	GND	
555 Trigger (pin 2)	10 kΩ resistor R2	10 μF capacitor C3
555 Reset (pin 4)	VCC	
555 Control (pin 5)	10 nF capacitor C2 positive	GND
555 Threshold (pin 6)	555 Discharge (pin 7)	
555 Discharge (pin 7)	5.1 kΩ resistor R1	VCC
555 Discharge (pin 7)	10 μF capacitor C1 positive	GND
555 VCC (pin 8)	VCC	
Transistor (from PIR) collector	10 kΩ resistor R3	10 μF capacitor C3 negative
Transistor (from PIR) base	10 kΩ resistor R4	From PIR sensor
Transistor (to MP3) collector	10 kΩ resistor R5	To MP3 player
Transistor base	10 kΩ resistor R6	555 Output (pin 3)
Transistor emitter	GND	
Capacitor C1, C2 negative	GND	

The signal sequence is shown in Figure 17-25 starting with the PIR sensor output of a long *HIGH* signal, which is inverted by an NPN BJT causing capacitor C_3 to partially discharge and then recharge, which triggers the 555 timer IC to generate a short *HIGH* signal that is inverted by the second NPN BJT to a short *LOW* signal for input to the MP3 player.

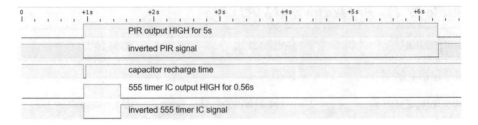

Figure 17-25. *PIR sensor and MP3 player signal sequence*

Summary

The functionality of the 555 timer IC is described with examples of the 555 timer IC in monostable, bistable, and astable modes. Examples included monostable mode with an incident light used to trigger a time delay, astable mode with an electronic piano, generation of a square wave with fixed frequency and variable duty cycle to control a servo motor or a square wave with fixed duty cycle and variable frequency. The 555 timer IC and resistor-capacitor low-pass filters formed a function generator to produce square waves, triangular waves, and sine waves. The 555 timer IC and an inductor-capacitor filter converted a square wave to a sine wave. Signal transformation by a 555 timer IC and transistors enabled movement detected by a PIR sensor to trigger an MP3 player to play a soundtrack, without requiring a microcontroller.

Components List

- 555 timer IC: Standard NE555 and CMOS TLC555

- Resistor: 2× 220 Ω, 3× 1 kΩ, 2 kΩ, 4.7 kΩ, 2× 10 kΩ, 20 kΩ

- Capacitor: 10 nF, 0.1 μF, 4× 1 μF, 47 μF, 100 μF

- Inductor: 470 μH

- Switch tactile: 2×

- LED: 2×

- Diode: 2× IN4001

- Potentiometer: 10 kΩ

- NPN transistor: BC548 or 2N2222

CHAPTER 18

Measuring electricity

Voltage, current, resistance, and capacitance are measured with a
multimeter. Understanding the required circuitry and programming an
ESP8266 or ESP32 microcontroller to measure voltage, current, resistance,
capacitance, and inductance is a valuable exercise when studying
electronics. A voltage divider and an analog to digital converter (ADC)
are essential to measuring voltage, current, resistance, capacitance, and
inductance, which are described prior to the measurement projects. For
each project, connection of all components to a common ground defines
the voltage reference point. If a project gives unusual results, then check
that a common ground has been established.

Voltage divider

A voltage divider reduces an input voltage to a lower output voltage.
A voltage divider consists of an input voltage, V_{IN}, and two resistors,
R1 and R2, with the output voltage measured at the junction of the two
resistors (see Figure 18-1). The output voltage, V_{OUT}, of the voltage divider
is $V_{IN} \times \left(\dfrac{R2}{R1 + R2} \right)$. For example, if the two resistors have equal value, then
the output voltage is half of the input voltage. Conversely, given the input
voltage, the required output voltage, and the value of resistor R1, the value
of resistor R1 is $R2 \times \left(\dfrac{V_{OUT}}{V_{IN} - V_{OUT}} \right)$. For example, the maximum possible

© Neil Cameron 2021
N. Cameron, *Electronics Projects with the ESP8266 and ESP32*,
https://doi.org/10.1007/978-1-4842-6336-5_18

input voltage of 12 V is too high to read on the analog pin of an ESP8266 microcontroller, and a voltage divider is required to reduce the maximum voltage to 3.2 V. Given the value of 100 kΩ for resistor R1, the value of resistor R2 is 36.4 kΩ.

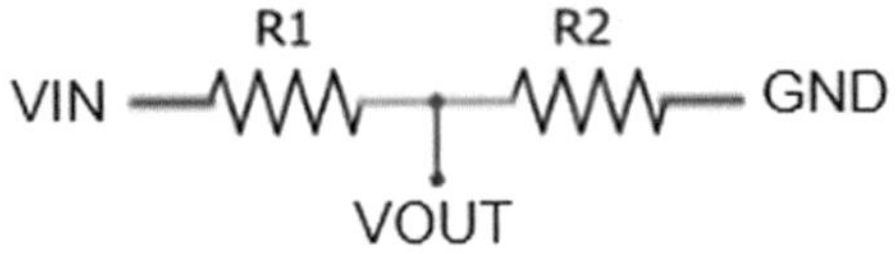

Figure 18-1. *Voltage divider*

A voltage divider consisting of the resistor pair 1 kΩ and 2 kΩ reduces the input voltage by a third, as does the resistor pair 10 kΩ and 20 kΩ. The difference between the two resistor pairs is that lower power is used and less heat is produced by the 10 kΩ and 20 kΩ resistor pair. Power is the product of voltage and current, equal to $\dfrac{V_{IN}^2}{R1+R2}$. For an input voltage of 5 V, the power used by voltage dividers with the 1 kΩ and 2 kΩ resistor pair and with the 10 kΩ and 20 kΩ resistor pair is 8.33 mW and 0.83 mW, respectively. Therefore, resistors of high resistance are used in a voltage divider to reduce power requirements and heat dissipation by the resistors.

The ESP8266 development board contains an internal voltage divider, consisting of 100 kΩ and 220 kΩ resistors (see Figure 18-2), which increases the maximum voltage on the analog input pin, from the reference voltage of 1 volt to 3.2 V. The ESP8266 microcontroller 10-bit analog to digital converter (ADC) functionality converts a voltage, between 0 and 3.2 V, on the analog input pin *A0* to a digital value between 0 and 1023, equal to $2^{10} - 1$. Given a voltage, V_{IN}, on the ESP8266 development board analog input pin, the corresponding ADC value is

$$V_{IN} \times \frac{100\,k\Omega}{(220+100)\,k\Omega} \times 1024.$$

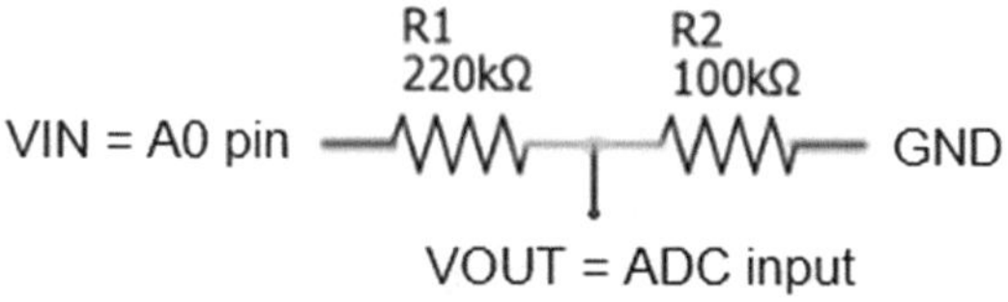

```
              R1              R2
            220kΩ           100kΩ
VIN = A0 pin ──WW──┬──WW── GND
                   │
              VOUT = ADC input
```

Figure 18-2. *Analog to digital converter*

ADC values for input voltages between 3.2 V and 3.3 V are constrained to 1023. A 10 kΩ resistor connected between the input voltage and the ESP8266 development board analog input pin increases the limit of 3.2 V on the analog input pin to 3.3 V.

The 12-bit analog to digital converter (ADC) functionality of the ESP32 microcontroller converts a voltage, between 0 and 3.3 V, on an analog input pin to a digital value between 0 and 4095, equal to $2^{12} - 1$.

Analog to digital converter

Several projects in this chapter use the Successive Approximation Register analog to digital converter (SAR ADC) module of the ESP8266 or ESP32 microcontroller. The 10-bit (ESP8266) or 12-bit (ESP32) ADC converts a voltage, V_{IN}, on an analog input pin to a digital value between 0 and $1023 = 2^{10} - 1$ or $4095 = 2^{12} - 1$, relative to a reference voltage, V_{REF}. Changing the ESP32 microcontroller ADC resolution is described in Chapter 21 (Microcontrollers). For each of 10 (ESP8266) or 12 (ESP32) successive comparisons, V_{IN} is compared to a set voltage, $V_{SET(N)}$, defined by the microcontroller conversion logic module and generated by the microcontroller digital to analog converter (DAC). Comparison of V_{IN} with the first set voltage, equal to $V_{SET(1)} = V_{REF}/2$, determines the most significant bit (MSB) of the output ADC digital value. Successive comparisons with set voltages $V_{SET(N)}$ equal to $V_{SET(N-1)} \pm V_{REF}/2^N$, with $V_{SET(N)}$ higher than $V_{SET(N-1)}$ if V_{IN} is greater than $V_{SET(N-1)}$, provide the subsequent bits of the output ADC digital value.

The ADC process is illustrated with an ESP8266 microcontroller. For an input voltage of 1.28 V that is reduced to 0.40 V by the internal voltage divider of the ESP8266 microcontroller, the first set voltage, $V_{SET(1)}$, is $V_{REF}/2 = 0.5$ V. As V_{IN} of 0.4 V is lower than $V_{SET(1)}$, then the MSB of the ADC digital value is set to zero. In the second comparison, $V_{SET(2)} = V_{SET(1)} - 1$ V/$2^2 = 0.25$ V, and as V_{IN} is greater than $V_{SET(2)}$, then the second bit of the ADC digital value is set to one and the third set voltage is $V_{SET(3)} = V_{SET(2)} + 1$ V/$2^3 = 0.375$ V. The ten successive comparisons result in the 10-bit binary value B0110011001 corresponding to the ADC digital output, which has a decimal value of 409. To confirm the ADC digital output, an input voltage of 1.28 V on the ESP8266 development board A0 pin is reduced to 0.4 V, by the internal voltage divider, and scaled by 1024, which results in the integer part of $(1024 \times 0.4\ \text{V}/1\ \text{V}) = 409$.

Converting an analog voltage to a digital value takes the ESP8266 microcontroller 135 μs, by which time V_{IN} may have changed. The ADC includes a Sample and Hold module that includes a MOSFET switch, which is opened after the ADC process has started, and a capacitor, on which V_{IN} is held constant (see Figure 18-3). For a 10-bit ADC, there are 1024 voltage classes with levels 0–1023; and given the interval voltage divider and a reference voltage of 1 V, an ADC voltage class spans 3.125 mV. ADC values of 0, 1, and 1023 correspond to V_{IN} values of from 0 V to less than 3.125 mV, from 3.125 mV to less than 6.25 mV, and from 3.197 V to less than 3.2 V, respectively. In the preceding example, the input voltage of 1.28 V is contained in the 410th voltage class of 1.278 V to less than 1.281 V.

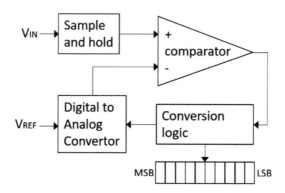

Figure 18-3. *Analog to digital converter*

Voltage meter

A battery voltage is measured with the ESP8266 or ESP32 microcontroller ADC. Although the ESP8266 microcontroller internal voltage divider of 100 kΩ and 220 kΩ resistors increases the maximum input voltage to 3.2 V, an additional voltage divider further reduces the battery voltage on the analog input pin. Voltage divider resistors of 22 kΩ and 10 kΩ enable measurement of a maximum battery voltage of 10.24 V, equal to $3.2\,V\,/\left(\dfrac{10k}{22k+10k}\right)$. The measured battery voltage is the 10-bit ADC output value multiplied by

$10.24\,V/2^{10}$, which is displayed on a 128 × 32–pixel OLED screen (see Figure 18-4 with connections in Table 18-1). Instead of the external voltage divider, resistors summing to 702 kΩ and connected in series with the internal voltage divider, also increase the maximum voltage on the ESP8266 microcontroller analog input pin to 10.24 V.

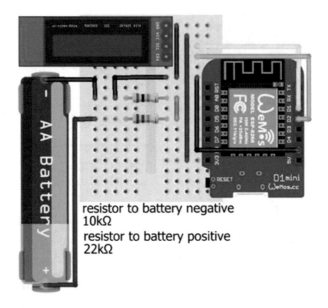

resistor to battery negative
10kΩ
resistor to battery positive
22kΩ

Figure 18-4. *Battery voltage measurement with LOLIN (WeMos) D1 mini*

Table 18-1. *Battery voltage measurement with the ESP8266 development board*

Component	Connect to ESP8266	And to
Battery positive	22 kΩ resistor	A0
Battery negative	10 kΩ resistor	A0
Battery negative	GND	OLED GND
OLED VCC	3V3	
OLED SDA	D2	
OLED SCL	D1	

In Listing 18-1, the battery voltage is displayed on an OLED display with a battery graphic illustrating the battery voltage. The battery frame is drawn as a solid rectangle of 45 × 12 pixels, starting at position *(0, 20)* on the OLED screen with the instruction oled.fillRect(0, 20, 45, 12, WHITE). The empty battery section is an overlaid black rectangle. The length of the empty battery section is the complement of the measured battery voltage divided by the maximum battery voltage and scaled by 41, the length of the battery frame of 45 pixels minus twice the width of the battery frame of 2 pixels. A battery cap is added as another filled rectangle. The *Adafruit SSD1306* library references the *Adafruit GFX* and *Wire* libraries, so the #include <Adafruit_GFX.h> and #include <Wire.h> instructions are not required.

Listing 18-1 is for an ESP8266 microcontroller. The only changes to the sketch, when using an ESP32 microcontroller, are definition of the analog input pin, as the ESP32 development board has six analog input pins (see Chapter 21 (Microcontrollers)), inclusion of the instruction pinMode(ADCpin, INPUT), and replacing the divisor 1024 by 4096, in the instruction

```
voltage = analogRead(ADCpin)*maxVolt/1024.0;
                                        // calculate battery voltage
```

Listing 18-1. Battery voltage measurement

```
#include <Adafruit_SSD1306.h>          // Adafruit SSD1306 library
int width = 128;                       // OLED screen size
int height = 32;                       // associate oled with SSD1306
Adafruit_SSD1306 oled(width, height, &Wire, -1);
int ADCpin = A0;                       // define analog input pin
float maxVolt = 10.24;                 // maximum battery voltage
float voltage;
int battery;
```

```
void setup()
{                                   // OLED display and I2C address
  oled.begin(SSD1306_SWITCHCAPVCC, 0x3C);
  oled.clearDisplay();              // clear OLED display
  oled.setTextColor(WHITE);         // set font color
  oled.setTextSize(2);              // set font size (1, 2, 3 or 4)
  oled.display();                   // start display instructions
}

void loop()
{                                   // calculate battery voltage
  voltage = analogRead(ADCpin)*maxVolt/1024.0;
  oled.clearDisplay();
  oled.setCursor(0,0);              // position cursor at (0, 0)
  oled.print(voltage);
  oled.print("V");                  // display battery voltage
  oled.fillRect(0, 20, 45, 12, WHITE);  // battery frame 2 pixels width
  battery = 41*voltage/maxVolt;     // full battery section
  battery = constrain(battery, 0, 41);
  oled.fillRect(2+battery, 22, 41-battery, 8, BLACK);
                                    // empty battery section
  oled.fillRect(45, 23, 3, 6, WHITE);  // battery top
  oled.display();
  delay(2000);                      // delay 2s between readings
}
```

In practice, voltages measured by the ESP8266 and ESP32 microcontrollers used in this chapter overestimated and underestimated supplied voltages, in the range of 1–3 V, by 3% and -16%, respectively. For comparison, the estimated voltage was not biased when measured with the ATmega328P microcontroller of an Arduino Uno. A biased estimate of *N*% is corrected by adjusting the measured voltage with the instruction voltage = voltage /(1+N/100), with N negative when the measured voltage is an underestimate.

Voltage meter with a load

A battery is measured with and without a load using a bipolar junction transistor (BJT) 2N2222 to turn on or off the battery current to a load, consisting of a low-value

10 Ω resistor (see Figure 18-5). The method is adapted from the battery tester of Andreas Spiess. With the BJT off, the battery voltage is measured on the BJT collector pin, *collPin*. The BJT base pin, *basePin*, is set *HIGH* to turn on the BJT, with the battery now providing power to the load. The voltage across the load and the BJT is again measured on the BJT collector pin. Schematics for the ESP8266 and ESP32 development boards are shown in Figures 18-6 and 18-7, with connections in Table 18-2.

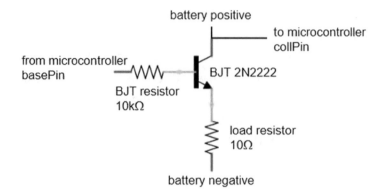

Figure 18-5. *Battery voltage measurement with and without a load*

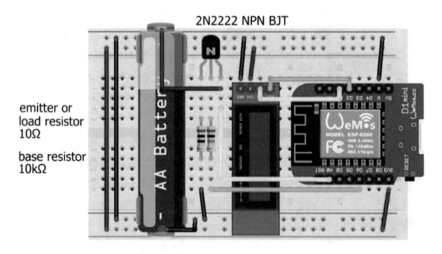

Figure 18-6. *Battery voltage tester with LOLIN (WeMos) D1 mini*

Table 18-2. *Battery voltage tester with ESP8266 and ESP32 development boards*

Component	ESP8266	And to	ESP32	And to
BJT emitter	10 Ω resistor	GND	10 Ω resistor	GND
BJT base	10 kΩ resistor	D6	10 kΩ resistor	GPIO 25
BJT collector	A0	Battery positive	GPIO 35	Battery positive
OLED VCC	3V3		3V3	
OLED GND	GND		GND	
OLED SDA	D2		GPIO 21	
OLED SCL	D1		GPIO 22	
Battery negative	GND		GND	

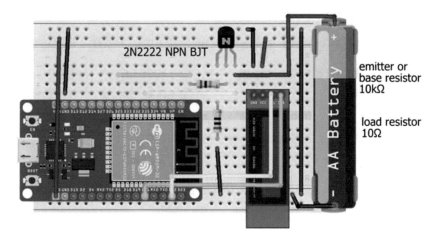

Figure 18-7. *Battery voltage tester with the ESP32 DEVKIT DOIT development board*

The sketch in Listing 18-2 measures the battery voltage at two-second intervals and displays the battery voltage, with and without the load, on the OLED screen. Repeat measurements of the battery voltage are made in the *readings* function, with the average ADC reading scaled by the reference voltage.

Listing 18-2 is for an ESP8266 microcontroller. When using an ESP32 microcontroller, the GPIO pin numbers for the BJT base and collector pins are changed (see Table 18-2), the value of *maxVolt* is increased to 3.3 V, and the instruction pinMode(collPin, INPUT) is included in the setup function. The divisors of 1024 in the *loop* function are changed to 4096, as the ESP32 microcontroller has a 12-bit ADC compared to the 10-bit ADC of the ESP8266 microcontroller. Subsequent schematics and sketches are demonstrated with a LOLIN (WeMos) D1 mini development board and sketches for an ESP8266 microcontroller. Connections to an ESP32 development board and required changes to the ESP32 microcontroller sketch are similar to those just described.

Listing 18-2. Battery voltage with and without load measurement

```
#include <Adafruit_SSD1306.h>      // SSD1306 library for OLED
int width = 128;                    // OLED screen size
int height = 32;                    // associate oled with SSD1306
Adafruit_SSD1306 oled(width, height, &Wire, -1);
int basePin = D6;                   // BJT base pin
int collPin = A0;                   // BJT collector pin
unsigned long sum;
int reps = 10;                      // number of repeat measurements
float maxVolt = 3.2;                // 3.2V maximum voltage
float Vbatt, Vload;
```

```
void setup()
{
  pinMode(basePin, OUTPUT);          // define basePin as OUTPUT
  oled.begin(SSD1306_SWITCHCAPVCC, 0x3C);     // OLED I2C address
  oled.clearDisplay();               // clear OLED display
  oled.setTextColor(WHITE);          // OLED font color
  oled.setTextSize(1);               // font size 1 character 6×8 pixels
  oled.display();                    // start display instructions
}

void loop()
{
  readings(LOW);                     // read BJT collector pin, BJT off
  Vbatt = maxVolt*sum/(reps*1024.0);              // battery voltage
  if(Vbatt > 0.1)
  {
    readings(HIGH);                  // read BJT collector pin, BJT on
    Vload = maxVolt*sum/(reps*1024.0);   // battery voltage with load
    screen();                        // call screen function
  }
  else
  {
    oled.clearDisplay();             // clear OLED when
    oled.display();                  // no battery voltage
  }
  delay(2000);                       // delay between measurements
}
```

```
void readings(int pinState)          // function to measure BJT pin
{
  digitalWrite(basePin, pinState);   // BJT base pin turned on or off
  sum = 0;
  for (int i=0; i<reps; i++)         // repeat voltage measurements
  {                                  // sum of voltage measurements
    sum = sum + analogRead(collPin);
    delay(5);
  }
  digitalWrite(basePin, LOW);        // turn off BJT base pin
}
void screen()                        // function for OLED display
{
  oled.clearDisplay();               // clear OLED display
  oled.setCursor(0,0);               // move cursor to position (0,0)
  oled.print("battery ");oled.print(Vbatt,3);oled.println("V");
  oled.setCursor(0, 12);
  oled.print("+load    ");oled.print(Vload,3);oled.print("V");
  oled.setCursor(0, 24);
  oled.print("perform ");oled.print(100.0*Vload/Vbatt,0);
  oled.print("%");
  oled.display();
}
```

Resistance meter (ohmmeter)

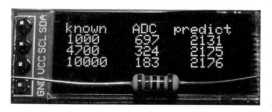

The value of an unknown resistor is determined with a voltage divider. Given an input voltage, V_{IN}, the corresponding ADC output value of the voltage divider is $\dfrac{V_{IN}}{V_{REF}} \times \dfrac{R2}{R1+R2} \times 1024$, where V_{REF} is the ADC reference voltage for a microcontroller with a 10-bit ADC, as $1024 = 2^{10}$. If the input and reference voltages are the same, then rearranging the formula gives $R2 = \dfrac{R1 \times ADC}{1024 - ADC}\ \Omega$.

Rather than using a known resistor with one value in the voltage divider, resistors with several values provide a range of known resistances to reference the unknown resistor. Specific values of the known resistors are arbitrary, but they could span a range such as 1 kΩ, 4.7 kΩ, and 10 kΩ, which enables reliable measurement of resistance values between 1 kΩ and 10 kΩ. The layout is shown in Figure 18-8 with connections given in Table 18-3.

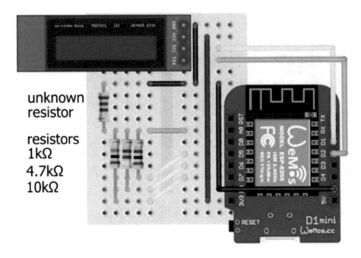

Figure 18-8. *Resistor meter (ohmmeter) with LOLIN (WeMos) D1 mini*

Table 18-3. *Resistor meter (ohmmeter) with the ESP8266 development board*

Component	Connect to ESP8266	And to
Known resistors	D5, D6, D7	A0
Unknown resistor	A0	GND
OLED VCC	3V3	
OLED GND	GND	
OLED SDA	D2	
OLED SCL	D1	

In Listing 18-3, prior to obtaining the ADC readings, the known resistor pins are set to *INPUT*, so that no current flows, which is equivalent to connecting a 100 MΩ resistor to each pin. Each known resistor pin is sequentially set to *OUTPUT*, with a *HIGH* signal, which sets the voltage on the known resistor pin to the voltage divider input voltage. The unknown resistor value is determined, with a constraint on the ADC reading to avoid extreme values, and the known resistor pin is again set to *INPUT*. In Figure 18-8, the known resistor with the lowest value is connected to the lowest of the ESP8266 development board pin numbers: D5, D6, and D7.

Listing 18-3. Resistance meter (ohmmeter)

```
#include <Adafruit_SSD1306.h>        // Adafruit SSD1306 library
int width = 128;                     // OLED screen size
int height = 32;                     // associate oled with SSD1306
Adafruit_SSD1306 oled(width, height, &Wire, -1);
int resistPin = A0;                  // analog input pin
int pin[] = {D5, D6, D7};            // pins for known resistor
float known[] = {1000.0, 4700.0, 10000.0};   // known resistor values
float resist, reading;

void setup()
{                                    // OLED display and I2C address
  oled.begin(SSD1306_SWITCHCAPVCC, 0x3C);
  oled.clearDisplay();               // clear OLED display
  oled.setTextColor(WHITE);          // set font color
  oled.setTextSize(1);               // set font size (1, 2, 3 or 4)
  oled.display();                    // update display instructions
  for (int i=0; i<3; i++) pinMode(pin[i], INPUT);
}                                    // set known resistor pins to INPUT

void loop()
{
  oled.clearDisplay();               // clear OLED display
  oled.setCursor(0,0);
```

```
oled.print("known   ADC  predict");   // header on OLED screen
for (int i=0; i<3; i++)                // for each known resistor
{
   pinMode(pin[i], OUTPUT);            // set known resistor pin
   digitalWrite(pin[i], HIGH);         // to OUTPUT and to HIGH
   reading = analogRead(resistPin);    // voltage divider reading
   if(reading < 10 || reading > 1013) reading = 0;
                                       // constrain ADC reading
   resist = known[i]*reading/(1024.0-reading);
                                       // calculate resistance
   pinMode(pin[i], INPUT);        // reset known resistor pin to INPUT
   oled.setCursor(1, (i+1)*8); // OLED column 1, row 8, 16, 24
   oled.print(known[i],0);      // display known resistor
   oled.setCursor(50, (i+1)*8);
   oled.print(reading,0);       // display ADC reading
   oled.setCursor(90, (i+1)*8);
   oled.print(resist,0);        // display calculated resistance
   oled.display();
}
delay(5000);
}
```

Capacitance meter

The capacitance of a capacitor is measured from the charging time of the capacitor. When a resistor, R, is connected in series with a capacitor, C, the capacitor will charge through the resistor until the voltage across the capacitor equals the reference voltage, V_{REF} (see Figure 18-9). The voltage across the capacitor after t seconds of charging is $V_{REF}(1 - e^{-t/RC})$. After RC seconds of charging, the voltage across the capacitor is 0.632 V_{REF}, as $(1 - e^{-1}) = 0.632$. The value of RC is determined when the analog to digital converter (ADC) reading for the voltage across the capacitor exceeds 647.3 = 0.632×1024, as the ADC equates 0 V to 0 and V_{REF} to 1023. The parameter RC is also written as τ, the Greek letter tau.

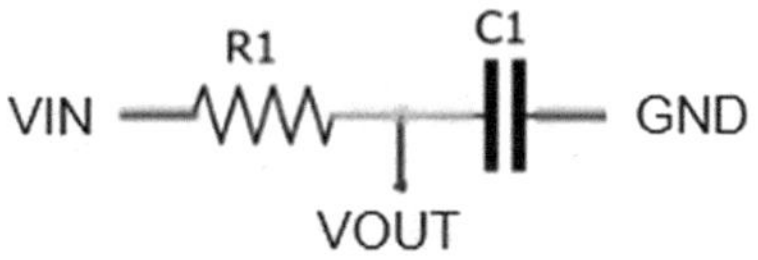

Figure 18-9. *Resistor-capacitor combination*

Electrolytic capacitors are polarized, and the anode must be at a higher voltage than the cathode (negative leg). The cathode has a minus sign marking and a colored stripe on the side of the capacitor. The long leg of an electrolytic capacitor is the anode or positive leg (see Figure 18-10 and Table 18-4). If the capacitor charging time is too short, then the 10 kΩ charging resistor is replaced with a higher value; and, conversely, the 10 kΩ resistor is replaced with a lower value if the capacitor charging time is too long. Higher values of the charging resistor extend the capacitor charging time for more precise capacitance estimates. In contrast, a low value of the discharge resistor results in a rapid capacitor discharge.

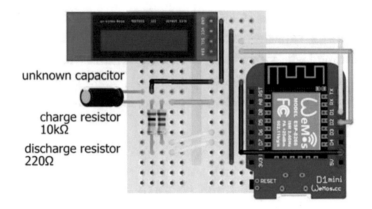

Figure 18-10. *Capacitance meter with LOLIN (WeMos) D1 mini*

Table 18-4. *Capacitance meter with the ESP8266 development board*

Component	Connect to ESP8266	And to
Charge resistor	D7	A0
Discharge resistor	D6	A0
Unknown capacitor positive	A0	
Unknown capacitor negative	GND	OLED GND
OLED VCC	3V3	
OLED SDA	D2	
OLED SCL	D1	

In Listing 18-4, the capacitor charge pin is set *HIGH,* and the timing of the charging capacitor starts. When the ADC value for the voltage across the capacitor reaches 648, the timing stops, and the capacitance is calculated from the charging time and the resistor value. Both the capacitor charge and discharge pins are then set *LOW* to allow the capacitor to discharge, after which the capacitor discharge pin is set to *INPUT,* so that no current flows through the discharge pin, and the cycle repeats. Setting a pin to *INPUT* is equivalent to connecting a 100 MΩ resistor in series with the pin. A lower limit to the estimated capacitance value is set at 10 nF. The sketch in Listing 18-4 was developed from the sketch at www.arduino.cc/en/Tutorial/CapacitanceMeter.

Listing 18-4. Capacitance meter

```
#include <Adafruit_SSD1306.h>        // Adafruit SSD1306 library
int width = 128;                     // OLED screen size
int height = 32;                     // associate oled with SSD1306
Adafruit_SSD1306 oled(width, height, &Wire, -1);
int capPin = A0;                     // capacitor positive pin
int chargePin = D7;                  // pin with 10kΩ charge resistor
int dischargePin = D6;               // 220Ω discharge resistor pin
float resistor = 10000.0;            // 10kΩ charge resistor
unsigned long startTime;
float mF, uF, nF;                    // uF for microF (Greek letter μ)

void setup()
{                                    // OLED display and I2C address
  oled.begin(SSD1306_SWITCHCAPVCC, 0x3C);
  oled.clearDisplay();               // clear OLED display
  oled.setTextColor(WHITE);          // set font color
  oled.setTextSize(2);               // set font size (1, 2, 3 or 4)
  oled.display();                    // update display instructions
  pinMode(chargePin, OUTPUT);        // set charge pin
  digitalWrite(chargePin, LOW);      // as OUTPUT and to 0V
}

void loop()
{
  oled.clearDisplay();
  oled.setCursor(0,0);
```

```
digitalWrite(chargePin, HIGH);     // charge pin to reference voltage
startTime = millis();              // start timing charging capacitor
while(analogRead(capPin) < 648) {} // do nothing while ADC < 648
mF = (millis() - startTime) / resistor;
                                   // calculate capacitance = time/R
uF = 1000.0 * mF;                  // change millifarad to microfarad
if (uF > 1)
{
  if (uF < 10) oled.print(uF, 1); // display capacitance with 1DP
  else oled.print(uF, 0);         // or 0DP depending on value
  oled.print(" uF");
}
else
{
  nF = 1000.0 * uF;               // convert to nanofarad
  if (nF > 10)                    // only display if value > 10nF
  {
    oled.print(nF, 0);            // display capacitance
    oled.print(" nF");
  }
}
digitalWrite(chargePin, LOW);     // set charge pin to 0V
pinMode(dischargePin, OUTPUT);    // set discharge pin
digitalWrite(dischargePin, LOW);  // to OUTPUT and 0V
while(analogRead(capPin) > 0) {}  // do nothing while capacitor
                                  // discharges
pinMode(dischargePin, INPUT);     // set discharge pin to INPUT
oled.display();
delay(2000);                      // to ensure no current flows
}
```

More significant figures for capacitors with low values are obtained by replacing the *millis* function with the *micros* function to measure the time interval in microseconds, rather than milliseconds, and dividing (`micros()-startTime`) by 1000. The 32-bit timer counts to $2^{32} - 1$ and then resets, so the *millis* and *micros* functions reset after 49.7 days and 71.58 minutes, respectively.

Current meter (ammeter)

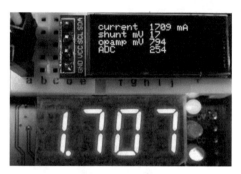

Current (I) in a circuit is measured from the voltage (V) across a known resistor (R) that is specifically included in the circuit, as $I = V/R$. The resistor must have low resistance, so that the circuit voltage is not significantly decreased by the resistor. A 0.01 Ω current shunt is a resistor defined by the maximum allowable current and the voltage drop at that current, such as 100 mV at 10 A. The power through a low-value resistor, V^2/R, is high, but a current shunt resistor is designed to distribute the generated heat.

The expected voltage across a 0.01 Ω shunt resistor is 10 mV per amp of current, so measuring current with a shunt resistor alone has low resolution (e.g., as in Figure 18-11). With the ESP8266 microcontroller 10-bit analog to digital converter (ADC), a current increase of 1 amp increases the ADC value by $3.2 = 10\ mV \times 2^{10}/V_{REF}$, given the ESP8266 microcontroller reference voltage of 3.2 V. Conversely, a unit increase in the ADC value corresponds to an increased voltage of 3.125 mV or $3.2\ V/2^{10}$ across the 0.01 Ω shunt resistor and to an increased current of 312 mA.

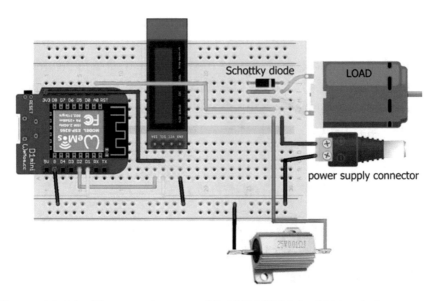

Figure 18-11. *Shunt resistor and LOLIN (WeMos) D1 mini*

An operational amplifier, such as an LM358, or an instrumental amplifier, such as an AD623, amplifies the voltage from the shunt resistor to increase resolution of the current measurement. The amplification gain of the LM358 operational amplifier, $1 + \dfrac{R_{feedback}}{R_{GND}}$, is determined by the feedback and ground (GND) resistors (see Figure 18-12). The non-inverting operational amplifier connected to the two resistors, R_{GND} and $R_{feedback}$, forms a voltage divider. Voltages on the operational amplifier output and the inverting input terminals are equivalent to the voltage divider input and output voltages. The output voltage, V_{OUT}, of a voltage divider is $V_{IN} \times \left(\dfrac{R2}{R1 + R2}\right)$. Incorporating the resistor values in the formula gives $V_{op\ amp\ IN} = V_{op\ amp\ OUT} \times \left(\dfrac{R_{GND}}{R_{feedback} + R_{GND}}\right)$ and the operational amplifier gain of $\dfrac{V_{op\ amp\ OUT}}{V_{op\ amp\ IN}} = 1 + \dfrac{R_{feedback}}{R_{GND}}$. For example, an amplification gain of 46 is obtained with a 100 kΩ and 2.2 kΩ resistor pair. A 0.1 uF capacitor is connected to the operational amplifier output to reduce noise.

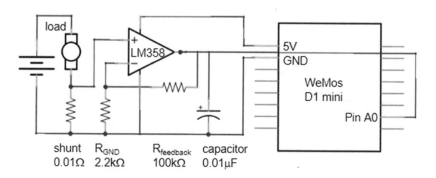

Figure 18-12. *Non-inverting operational amplifier*

The operational amplifier gain in voltage increases the resolution of the current meter. For example, given a current of 1 A, the 100 kΩ and 2.2 kΩ resistor pair increases the LM358 operational amplifier output voltage from 10 mV to 465 mV, producing an ADC value of 149 = $gain \times 10$ mV $\times 1024/V_{REF}$ that is substantially higher than the ADC value of 3 without amplification. Likewise, a unit change in the ADC value corresponds to a shunt voltage change of 0.067 mV = $V_{REF}/(1024 \times gain)$, mapping to a current differential of only 6.7 mA.

In Figure 18-13, an LM358 operational amplifier is added to the schematic in Figure 18-11 to amplify the voltage from the shunt resistor to both increase the ADC value and the resolution of the current meter. Connections are given in Table 18-5.

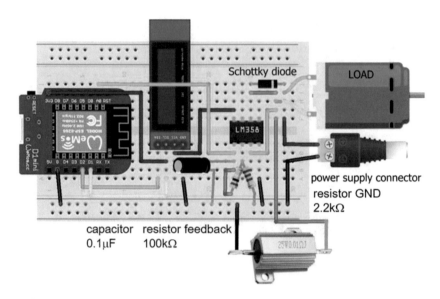

Figure 18-13. Operational amplifier, shunt resistor, and LOLIN (WeMos) D1 mini

If the load is a DC motor, then the motor, which is partially an inductor, will generate a voltage to maintain current when power to the motor is switched off. Fitting a diode across the motor prevents a voltage spike and dissipates energy through the motor when power is switched off. A Schottky diode, which is a fast-switching diode with a low forward voltage drop, is recommended.

Table 18-5. *Operational amplifier, shunt resistor, and ESP8266 development board*

Component	Connect to	And to
LM358 output (pin 1)	ESP8266 A0	
LM358 output (pin 1)	Capacitor	ESP8266 GND
LM358 inverting input (pin 2)	Feedback resistor	LM358 output (pin 1)
LM358 inverting input (pin 2)	GND resistor	ESP8266 GND
LM358 non-inverting input (pin 3)	Load negative	
LM358 GND (pin 4)	ESP8266 GND	
LM358 VCC (pin 8)	ESP8266 3V3	
Load positive	Schottky diode cathode (stripe)	Battery positive
Load negative	Schottky diode anode	Shunt resistor 0.01 Ω
ESP8266 GND	Shunt resistor 0.01 Ω	Battery negative
OLED VCC	ESP8266 3V3	
OLED GND	ESP8266 GND	
OLED SDA	ESP8266 D2	
OLED SCL	ESP8266 D1	

The sketch (see Listing 18-5) converts the ADC reading to the operational amplifier voltage output, which is converted to a voltage across the shunt, according to the specification of the current shunt and the operational amplifier gain, and then to the current through the load. Repeated ADC readings are averaged to reduce noise.

Listing 18-5. Ammeter with shunt resistor

```
#include <Adafruit_SSD1306.h>        // Adafruit SSD1306 library
int width = 128;                     // OLED screen size
int height = 32;                     // associate oled with SSD1306
Adafruit_SSD1306 oled(width, height, &Wire, -1);
int ADCpin = A0;
unsigned long ADC;
int Rfeedback = 100000;              // feedback resistor value
int RGND = 2200;                     // resistor GND value
float current, opAmpmV, shuntmV, gain;

void setup()
{
  Serial.begin(115200);
  oled.begin(SSD1306_SWITCHCAPVCC, 0x3C);
                            // OLED display and I2C address
  oled.clearDisplay();               // clear OLED display
  oled.setTextColor(WHITE);          // set font color
  oled.setTextSize(1);               // set font size (1, 2, 3 or 4)
  oled.display();                    // update display instructions
  gain = 1.0 + Rfeedback/RGND;       // calculate op amp gain
}

void loop()
{
  ADC = 0;
  for (int i=0; i<100; i++)          // repeated analog readings
  {
    ADC = ADC + analogRead(ADCpin);
    delay(10);
  }
  ADC = ADC/100;                     // average of analog readings
  opAmpmV = ADC*3200.0/1024;         // op amp output voltage
```

```
shuntmV = opAmpmV / gain;          // voltage on shunt
current = 100.0 * shuntmV;         // shunt mV to current in mA
oled.clearDisplay();
oled.setCursor(0,0);                    // display results on OLED
oled.print("current");oled.print(current,0);
oled.println(" mA");
oled.print("shunt mV ");oled.println(shuntmV,0);
oled.print("opamp mV ");oled.println(opAmpmV,0);
oled.print("ADC      ");oled.println(ADC);
oled.display();
delay(1000);
}
```

Figure 18-14 illustrates current measurement with a multimeter and by an ammeter with an LED display. In both cases, the meter is inserted in series with the load, although the circuit layout with the shunt resistor and the operational amplifier in Figure 18-13 is not as obvious. The ammeter with an LED display has a 0.05 Ω (R050) shunt resistor and is externally powered.

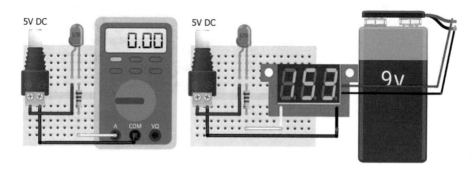

Figure 18-14. *Current meter (ammeter)*

Current sensor

Current is measured by the MAX471 module, with an upper limit of 3 A. The load positive is connected to the MAX471 RS- pin and the load negative to GND, with the load power supply positive connected to the MAX471 RS+ pin (see Figure 18-15 with connections in Table 18-6). The default resolution of the MAX471 module is 3.125 mA, equal to 3.2 A/2^{10}, given the 10-bit ADC of the ESP8266 microcontroller. The voltage on the MAX471 *OUT* pin is ideally equivalent to 1 volt per amp of current. The MAX471 *SIGN* pin indicates a discharging or charging battery, with an analog reading greater than 50 or near zero, respectively.

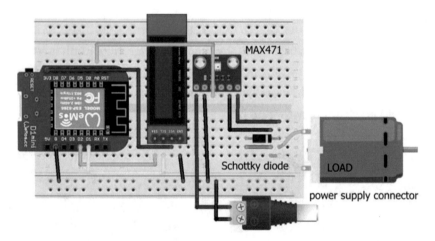

Figure 18-15. *Current sensor MAX471 with LOLIN (WeMos) D1 mini*

Table 18-6. *Current sensor MAX471 and ESP8266 development board*

Component	Connect to	And to
MAX471 RS+	Battery positive	
MAX471 GND	Battery negative	ESP8266 GND
MAX471 OUT	ESP8266 A0	
MAX471 SIGN		
MAX471 GND	Load negative	
MAX471 RS-	Load positive	
OLED VCC	ESP8266 3V3	
OLED GND	ESP8266 GND	
OLED SDA	ESP8266 D2	
OLED SCL	ESP8266 D1	

In the sketch (see Listing 18-6), the current for a load is measured with the MAX471 module, with measurements displayed every five seconds.

Listing 18-6. Current sensor MAX471 and ESP8266 development board

```
#include <Adafruit_SSD1306.h>        // Adafruit SSD1306 library
int width = 128;                      // OLED screen size
int height = 32;                      // associate oled with SSD1306
Adafruit_SSD1306 oled(width, height, &Wire, -1);
int currentPin = A0;                  // analog input pin
float current;
```

```
void setup()
{
  oled.begin(SSD1306_SWITCHCAPVCC, 0x3C);    // OLED I2C address
  oled.clearDisplay();                        // clear OLED display
  oled.setTextColor(WHITE);                   // set font color
  oled.setTextSize(3);                        // set font size (1, 2, 3 or 4)
  oled.display();                             // update display instructions
}

void loop()
{
  current = analogRead(currentPin);           // analog MAX471 reading
  current = 1000*current*3.2/1024;            // convert to current
  oled.clearDisplay();
  oled.setCursor(0,0);                        // position cursor
  oled.print(current,0); oled.print(" mA");   // display current
  oled.display();
  delay(5000);
}
```

Current and voltage sensor

Both current and voltage are measured with the INA219 module, which has at least two formats, from which the corresponding power and energy over time are derived. The Adafruit INA219 library instructions getShuntVoltage_mV() and getBusVoltage_V() provide the voltage across the INA219 0.1 Ω (R100) shunt resistor and across the load pins, equal to the supply voltage minus the shunt voltage. The power measurement is obtained with the instruction getPower_mW() or calculated as the product of voltage and current (see Figure 18-16 with connections in Table 18-7).

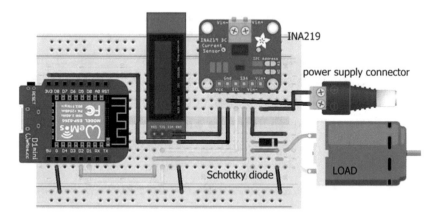

Figure 18-16. *Current sensor (INA219) and LOLIN (WeMos) D1 mini*

The INA219 module measures the voltage across a 0.1 Ω shunt resistor with a maximum voltage input of 320 mV. The maximum current that the INA219 module measures is 3.2 A, equal to 320 mV/0.1 Ω. The default resolution of the INA219 module is 0.8 mA, equal to $3.2 A/2^{12} = 3.2 A/4096$, given the INA219 12-bit analog to digital converter (ADC). The resolution is increased to 0.1 mA, equal to $400 mA/2^{12}$, by reducing the INA219 amplifier gain by a factor of eight, resulting in a maximum voltage input of 40 mV and maximum current of 400 mA. Instructions for the default and high resolution settings are setCalibration_32V_2A() and setCalibration_16V_400mA(), respectively. An intermediate resolution option is available with the setCalibration_32V_1A() instruction.

The INA219 module uses I2C (Inter-Integrated Circuit) for communication with the ESP8266 or ESP32 microcontroller, and the *Adafruit INA219* library references the *Wire* library, so the #include <Wire.h> instruction is not required. The default I2C address of the INA219 module is *0x40,* which is changed to *0x41, 0x44,* or *0x45* by bridging the module *A0* jumper, the *A1* jumper, or both the *A0* and *A1* jumpers, respectively. For example, the I2C address is defined as *0x41*, with the instruction Adafruit_INA219 ina219(0x41). Note that if the default I2C address is used, then the instruction Adafruit_INA219 ina219 is sufficient.

If the load is a DC motor, then the motor, which is partially an inductor, will generate voltage to maintain current when power to the motor is switched off. Fitting a diode across the motor will prevent a voltage spike and dissipate energy through the motor when power is switched off. A Schottky diode, which is a fast-switching diode, is recommended.

Table 18-7. *Current sensor (INA219) with the ESP8266 development board*

Component	Connect to ESP8266	And to
INA219 VCC	3V3	
INA219 GND	GND	Battery negative
INA219 SCL	D1	
INA219 SDA	D2	
INA219 VIN-	Load positive	
INA219 VIN+	Battery positive	
Schottky diode cathode (stripe)	Load positive	
Schottky diode anode	Load negative	INA219 GND
OLED VCC	3V3	
OLED GND	GND	
OLED SDA	D2	
OLED SCL	D1	

Listing 18-7 measures the current, power, and cumulative energy for a load with the INA219 module, with measurements displayed every five seconds. The second OLED screen displays the supply and load voltages. The high precision option is selected with the maximum current of 400 mA.

Listing 18-7. Current sensor (INA219)

```
#include <Adafruit_INA219.h>    // define Adafruit_INA219 lib
Adafruit_INA219 ina219;         // default I2C, associate ina219 with lib
#include <Adafruit_SSD1306.h>   // Adafruit SSD1306 library
int width = 128;                // OLED screen size
int height = 32;                // associate oled with SSD1306
Adafruit_SSD1306 oled(width, height, &Wire, -1);
float shunt, load, supply, current, power;
float energy = 0;

void setup()
{
  ina219.begin();
//  ina219.setCalibration_32V_2A();    // default precision option
//  ina219.setCalibration_32V_1A();    // intermediate option
  ina219.setCalibration_16V_400mA();   // high precision option
  oled.begin(SSD1306_SWITCHCAPVCC, 0x3C);    // OLED I2C address
  oled.clearDisplay();                 // clear OLED display
  oled.setTextColor(WHITE);            // set font color
  oled.setTextSize(1);                 // set font size (1, 2, 3 or 4)
  oled.display();                      // update display instructions
}
```

```
void loop()
{
  shunt = ina219.getShuntVoltage_mV();        // shunt voltage in mV
  load = ina219.getBusVoltage_V();            // load voltage in V
  supply = load + shunt / 1000.0;             // supply voltage in V
  current = ina219.getCurrent_mA();           // current in mA
  power = ina219.getPower_mW();                // power in mW
  energy = energy + power / 3600.0;           // energy in mAh
  oled.clearDisplay();
  oled.setCursor(0,0);                        // display results
  oled.print("current ");oled.print(current,0);
  oled.println(" mA");
  oled.print("shunt    ");oled.print(shunt,0); oled.println(" mV");
  oled.print("power    ");oled.print(power,0); oled.println(" mW");
  oled.print("energy   ");oled.print(energy,0); oled.print(" mAh");
  oled.display();
  delay(5000);
  oled.clearDisplay();
  oled.setCursor(0,0);                        // display supply and load V
  oled.print("supply ");oled.print(supply); oled.println(" V");
  oled.print("load   ");oled.print(load); oled.println(" V");
  oled.display();
  delay(5000);
}
```

Solar panel and battery meter

A current and voltage measurement application is monitoring the net battery charge or discharge current of a battery providing power to a load and charging through a solar panel. The solar panel and battery output currents and the battery voltage are displayed graphically on an ST7735 TFT LCD screen with the minimum, present, and maximum battery output currents, the present battery voltage, and the cumulative battery energy output (see Figure 18-17). The graph displays the battery current output with positive values for a discharging battery and negative values for a charging battery.

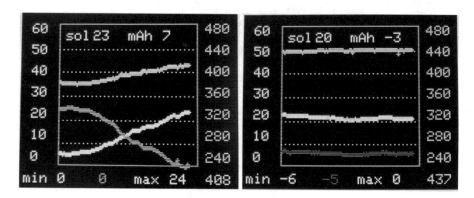

Figure 18-17. *Solar panel current with battery current and voltage display*

Time is on the X-axis with the solar panel and battery current output on the left Y-axis and battery voltage on the right Y-axis. Figure 18-17 (left graph) demonstrates the combination of a solar panel and battery providing power for an LED. As the solar panel current (white line on the left axis) increased from 5 mA with increasing sunshine, the battery current output (green line on the left axis) decreased, and the battery voltage increased to 4.08 V (value below and yellow line on the right axis) with the present solar panel current output of 23 mA (*sol 23*). The minimum, present, and maximum battery current outputs are displayed below the graph. Over the time period, the battery energy output was 7 mAh (see Figure 18-18 for screen layout).

When the LED was removed (Figure 18-17, right graph), the solar panel current output (white line on the left axis) was 20 mA, the battery current output of -5 mA indicated the battery was charging (red line on the left axis), and the total energy provided to the battery was 3 mAh. The battery voltage was maintained at 4.4 V (yellow line on the right axis).

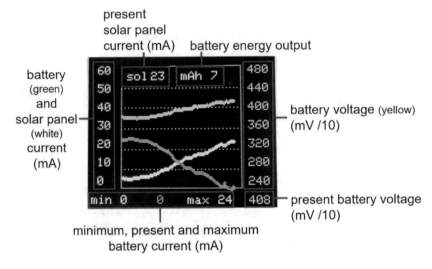

Figure 18-18. *Explanation of screen display*

The solar panel charges a 3.7 V lithium battery through the TP4056 battery protection module (see Figure 18-19). The TP4056 battery protection module terminal pair *IN-* and *OUT-* are internally connected, as are the terminal pair *OUT+* and *B(battery)+*. In contrast, the terminal pair *B-* and *OUT-* are internally connected only when there is a voltage on the *B+* terminal. Further details of the TP4056 battery protection are given in Chapter 6 (Bluetooth speaker). An MT3608 DC to DC step-up boost converter power supply module increases the 3.7 V lithium battery output voltage to 5 V, as required by the load. The MT3608 boost converter terminals *VIN-* and *VOUT-* are internally connected. Solar panel and battery output currents are measured with INA219 modules. The graph scale for current output is changed from 0–60 mA to 0–300 mA by an interrupt service routine (ISR) that defines the graph maximum value, with the ISR triggered by a switch. The maximum voltage on the ESP8266 microcontroller analog input pin is 3.2 V; and a voltage divider consisting of two 10 kΩ resistors reduces, by half, the battery voltage on the analog input pin. Component connections are given in Table 18-8.

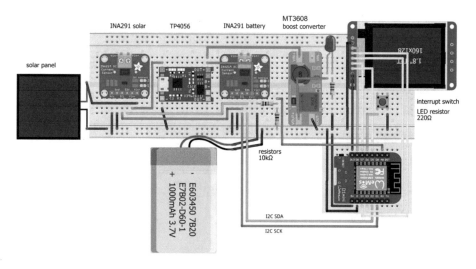

Figure 18-19. *Solar panel and battery current meter*

Table 18-8. *Solar panel and battery current meter*

Component	Connect to	And to
Solar INA219 VIN+	Solar panel positive	
Solar INA219 VIN-	TP4056 (IN) +	
Battery INA219 VIN+	Battery positive	
Battery INA219 VIN-	TP4056 OUT+/B+	
Boost converter VIN+	TP4056 OUT+/B+	
Boost converter VOUT+	Load positive	
ESP8266 D2 (SDA)	Solar INA219 SDA	Battery INA219 SDA
ESP8266 D1 (SCL)	Solar INA219 SCL	Battery INA219 SCL
ESP8266 A0	10 kΩ resistor voltage divider	Battery positive
ST7735 TFT LCD GND	ESP8266 GND	

(*continued*)

Table 18-8. (*continued*)

Component	Connect to	And to
ST7735 TFT LCD CS	ESP8266 D8 (SPI CS)	
ST7735 TFT LCD RESET	ESP8266 D4	
ST7735 TFT LCD A0 or DC	ESP8266 D3	
ST7735 TFT LCD SDA	ESP8266 D7 (SPI MOSI)	
ST7735 TFT LCD SCK	ESP8266 D5 (SPI SCL)	
ST7735 TFT LCD LED	ESP8266 3V3	
Switch	ESP8266 D6	ESP8266 GND
ESP8266 5V	Solar INA219 VCC	Battery INA219 VCC
ESP8266 GND	Solar INA219 GND	Battery INA219 GND
ESP8266 GND	Solar panel negative	TP4056 (IN) -
ESP8266 GND	Boost converter VOUT-	Load negative
ESP8266 GND	Battery negative	

The first section of the sketch, in Listing 18-8, defines libraries and variables, with the *setup* function initializing the INA219 modules, the ST7735 TFT LCD screen, and the interrupt. The *graph* function creates the graph display, with data points plotted and graph updates drawn by the *screenVal* and *detail* functions, respectively. The *screenVal* function displays minimum, present, and maximum battery current outputs, below the graph. The *detail* function calculates cumulative energy output by the battery that is displayed along with the solar panel current output. In both the *screenVal* and *detail* functions, black rectangles over-print the previous text and values, as the displayed text and values may require fewer characters. The instruction setTextColor(color, BLACK) over-prints existing text only. HEX codes for colors are defined in the *Adafruit_ST77xx.h* file in the *Adafruit_ST7735_and_ST7789* library.

In the *loop* function, the battery and solar panel current outputs and the battery voltage are measured and plotted, with the *screenVal* function called to display values. To differentiate between a discharging and a charging battery, the color of a displayed value and the graph data points change from green to red, with a negative (charging) graph point plotted by changing the sign of the charging battery current. The baseline of the graph is on row 110 of the ST7735 TFT LCD screen, and with a graph height of 100, a point corresponding to the battery current is plotted on row *110 – 100 × (current/maximum value)*. For example, if the maximum value of the current axis is 60 mA, then a battery output current of 18 mA is plotted on row 80 = *110 – 100 × 18/60*. The *graph* function displays the graph boundary using the library *fillRect* and *drawRect* functions, calculates and displays the Y-axis labels for the battery current and battery voltage, and prints five dotted lines across the graph to aid interpretation of the graph. The interrupt service routine (ISR), *scale*, changes the maximum value of the battery current axis on the graph.

With two INA219 modules, two I2C addresses are required to differentiate between the modules. The default I2C address of *0x40* is used by the solar panel INA219 module, and the battery INA219 module has an I2C address of *0x41*, with the instruction `Adafruit_INA219 inaBatt(0x41)` with the module *A0* jumper bridged. The ST7735 TFT LCD screen communicates with Serial Peripheral Interface (SPI), although the ST7735 TFT LCD screen MOSI pin is labeled SDA. The *Adafruit ST7735* library references the *Adafruit_GFX* library, so the `#include <Adafruit_GFX.h>` instruction is not required. The ST7735 TFT LCD screen orientation is set to either portrait or landscape by the `setRotation(N)` instruction with value of 0 or 1, respectively, or with 2 or 3 to rotate the image by 180° for portrait or landscape, respectively.

Listing 18-8. Solar panel and battery meter

```
#include <Adafruit_INA219.h>        // define Adafruit INA219 library
Adafruit_INA219 inaSolar;        // associate inaSolar and inaBatt with lib
Adafruit_INA219 inaBatt(0x41);     // I2C address 0x41, 0x40 is default
#include <Adafruit_ST7735.h>       // include the ST7735 library
int TFT_CS = D8;                   // ST7735 screen chip select pin
int DCpin = D3;                    // ST7725 screen DC pin
int RSTpin = D4;                   // ST7735 screen reset pin
                            // associate tft with Adafruit_ST7735 lib
Adafruit_ST7735 tft = Adafruit_ST7735(TFT_CS, DCpin, RSTpin);
int batVPin = A0;                  // battery voltage reading pin
int scalePin = D6;                 // scale pin for interrupt
unsigned int BLACK = 0x0000;
unsigned int YELLOW = 0xFFE0;
unsigned int GREEN = 0x07E0;       // HEX codes for colors
unsigned int RED = 0xF800;
unsigned int WHITE = 0xFFFF;
int maxRead = 99;                  // maximum readings per screen
int n = 0;                         // reading number
int maxVal = 0;                    // initial maximum and minimum
int minVal = 1000;                 // for battery output
int initialY = 60;                 // initial maximum of Y axis
int alterY = 300;                  // alternative maximum of Y axis
volatile int maxY;                 // actual maximum Y axis
float maxV = 4.80;                 // maximum and minimum value
float minV = 2.40;                 // for battery voltage
float labelV = (maxV-minV)/6.0;    // 6 labels on battery voltage axis
int delayTime = 5;                 // delay (s) between readings
float energy = 0;                  // cumulative energy output
float batt, solar;                 // battery and solar current
```

```
float battV;                        // battery voltage
float battS, solarS, battVS;        // scaled values for graph
int labelY, newmaxY, batDirect;

void setup()
{
  inaSolar.begin();                 // initialise INA219 modules
  inaBatt.begin();
  inaSolar.setCalibration_16V_400mA();        // 16V, 400mA range
  inaBatt.setCalibration_16V_400mA();
  tft.initR(INITR_BLACKTAB);        // initialise ST7735 screen
  tft.fillScreen(BLACK);            // clear screen
  tft.setRotation(3);               // orientate ST7735 screen
  tft.drawRect(0,0,160,128,WHITE);          // draw white frame line
  tft.drawRect(1,1,158,126,WHITE);          // and second frame line
  maxY = initialY;                  // set graph axes
  newmaxY = initialY;
  graph();                          // call graph function
  pinMode(scalePin, INPUT_PULLUP);          // set pin state HIGH
  attachInterrupt(digitalPinToInterrupt(scalePin), scale,
  FALLING);
}

void loop()
{
  if(newmaxY != maxY)               // change graph Y axis
  {
    newmaxY = maxY;
    graph();                        // call graph function
    n = 0;                          // set number of readings to zero
  }
```

```
n++;                                   // increment reading number
if(n > maxRead)
{                                      // new screen if n > maximum
   graph();
   n = 0;
}
batt = inaBatt.getCurrent_mA();        // battery current output
if(batt < minVal) minVal = batt;       // update minimum and
if(batt > maxVal) maxVal = batt;       // maximum battery current
screenVal(WHITE, minVal, 5, "min");    // display minimum and
screenVal(WHITE, maxVal, 85, "max");   // maximum battery current
solar = inaSolar.getCurrent_mA();      // solar panel current reading
solarS = 110-100.0*solar/maxY;         // scale solar panel reading
tft.fillCircle(25+n, solarS, 1, WHITE);
                                       // plot scaled solar panel reading
if(batt < 0)
{                                      // when battery charging
   screenVal(RED, batt, 35, "");       // change line color to RED
   battS = 110+100.0*batt/maxY;        // scale battery reading
   tft.fillCircle(25+n, battS, 1, RED);
}                                      // plot scaled battery reading
else
{                                      // when battery discharging
   screenVal(GREEN, batt, 35, "");    // change line color to GREEN
   battS = 110-100.0*batt/maxY;
   tft.fillCircle(25+n, battS, 1, GREEN);
}                                      // double battery reading
battV = 2.0*analogRead(batVPin);       // due to voltage divider
battV = 3.2 * battV /1024.0;           // battery voltage
```

```
  screenVal(YELLOW, battV*100, 105, "");
                                          // change color to YELLOW
  battVS = 110-100.0*(battV-minV)/(maxV-minV);
                                          // scale battery voltage
  tft.fillCircle(25+n, battVS, 1, YELLOW);
                                          // plot scaled battery voltage
  detail();                               // function for solar and energy
  delay(delayTime * 1000);                // delay (s) between readings
}

void graph()                              // function to draw graph
{
  labelY = maxY/6;                        // 7 labels on each Y axis
  tft.fillRect(2,2,156,124,BLACK);        // fill screen in BLACK
  tft.drawRect(25,10,100,100,GREEN);      // graph rectangle in GREEN
  for (int i=0; i<7; i++)                 // label y axis
  {
    tft.setCursor(5,10+i*(100/6-1));      // position labels
    tft.setTextColor(WHITE, BLACK);
    tft.print(maxY-i*labelY);             // left side Y axis value
    tft.setCursor(130,10+i*(100/6-1));
    tft.setTextColor(YELLOW, BLACK);
    tft.print(maxV-i*labelV,2);           // right side Y axis value
  }
  for (int j=0; j<5; j++)                 // draw 5 dashed lines on graph
  for (int i=0; i<33; i++) tft.drawPixel(25+3*i, 28+j*100/6,
  YELLOW);
  tft.setTextColor(WHITE, BLACK);
  tft.setCursor(30, 15);                  // headings for solar and energy
  tft.print("sol");
  tft.setCursor(75, 15);
  tft.print("mAh");
}
```

```
void screenVal(unsigned int color, int val, int x, String text)
{                               // function to display text and value below graph
  tft.setTextSize(1);
  tft.setTextColor(color, BLACK);
  tft.setCursor(x, 115);                    // row number 115
  tft.print(text);
  tft.setCursor(x + 25, 115);               // position in row
  if(x == 5) tft.fillRect(30,115,20,8,BLACK);
                                            // over-write previous value
  else if(x == 35) tft.fillRect(60,115,20,8,BLACK);
  else if(x == 85) tft.fillRect(110,115,20,8,BLACK);
  tft.setTextColor(color, BLACK);
  if(x != 105) tft.print(val);              // print new value
  else tft.print(val/100.0,2);              // 2DP for battery voltage
}

IRAM_ATTR void scale()                      // ISR to change Y axis scale
{
  if(newmaxY == alterY) maxY = initialY;
  else maxY = alterY;
}

void detail()
{                                           // battery energy output
  energy = energy + battV * delayTime * batt /3600.0;
                                            // energy (mAh)
  tft.setTextColor(WHITE, BLACK);
  tft.fillRect(50,15,15,8,BLACK);           // overlay if fewer digits
  tft.setCursor(50,15);
  tft.print(solar,0);                       // solar panel current output
```

```
tft.fillRect(100,15,20,8,BLACK);
tft.setCursor(100,15);
tft.print(energy,0);                          // battery current output
}
```

Inductance meter

Resistor-capacitor (RC) filters block particular frequencies of a signal, with low-pass and high-pass filters blocking high and low frequencies, respectively. For a low-pass filter, the capacitor passes the high frequencies to GND with the lower frequencies available at *VOUT* (see Figure 18-20). In the high-pass filter, low frequencies are blocked by the capacitor, with the higher frequencies available at *VOUT*. The inductor-capacitor (LC) filter is also a low-pass filter as the inductor blocks high frequencies and the capacitor passes the high frequencies to GND resulting in low frequencies at *VOUT*.

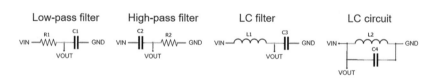

Figure 18-20. *Filters and inductor-capacitor circuit*

Inductors, denoted *L* in honor of Emil Lenz, are used in inductor-capacitor (LC) circuits (see Figure 18-20) for either generating signals with a specific frequency or filtering a signal to retain a particular frequency. The capacitor stores energy in the electric field across its plates, while the inductor stores energy as a magnetic field. When an inductor is connected across a charged capacitor, the voltage across the capacitor generates a current through the inductor and increases its magnetic field. When the voltage across the capacitor drops to zero, the energy stored in the inductor magnetic field induces a voltage across the inductor, and the current recharges the capacitor. The cycle of *capacitor discharge* to *inductor charge* to *inductor discharge* to *capacitor charge* repeats at a frequency of $\left(2\pi\sqrt{LC}\right)^{-1}$ Hz.

When a voltage burst is applied to the LC circuit, the circuit starts to resonate at a specific frequency, but due to the components' internal resistance, the oscillation will dampen over time (see Figure 18-21). When connected across the output of the LC circuit, a voltage comparator generates a square wave with the same frequency as the LC circuit. The value of an unknown inductor is determined from the square wave frequency of the voltage comparator and the known capacitor value. In practice, the square wave pulse width is measured; and as frequency equals $(2 \times pulse\ width)^{-1}$Hz, then the inductance is derived directly from *pulse width* $= \pi\sqrt{LC}$. The measurement unit of inductance is henry, *H*, in honor of Joseph Henry, who discovered inductance.

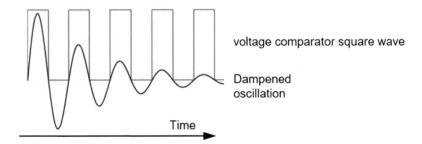

Figure 18-21. *LC circuit oscillation*

The voltage comparator output voltage is the supply voltage when the voltage at the plus (+) input pin is greater than the voltage at the negative (–) input pin. The LM393 voltage comparator generates a square wave with the same frequency as the damped oscillation from the LC circuit. The LM393 comparator output pin is pulled up to a *HIGH* state by the 1 kΩ resistor across the LM393 output and VCC pins. The schematic and connections are shown in Figure 18-22 and Table 18-9, respectively.

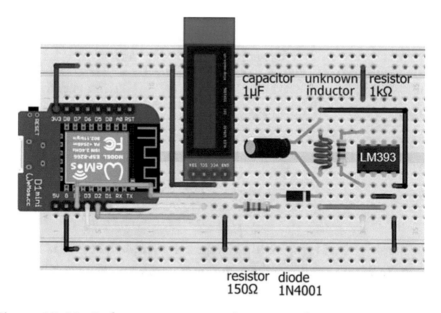

Figure 18-22. *Inductance meter and LM393 voltage comparator*

Table 18-9. *Inductance meter and LM393 voltage comparator*

Component	Connect to	And to
LM393 output (pin 1)	ESP8266 D3	Resistor 1 kΩ
LM393 input (-) (pin 2)	ESP8266 GND	
LM393 input (+) (pin 3)	Inductor	
LM393 input (+) (pin 3)	Diode cathode (stripe)	Capacitor (positive)
LM393 GND (pin 4)	ESP8266 GND	
LM393 VCC (pin 8)	ESP8266 3V3	Resistor 1 kΩ
ESP8266 D0	Resistor 150 Ω	
Diode anode	Resistor 150 Ω	

(*continued*)

Table 18-9. (*continued*)

Component	Connect to	And to
ESP8266 GND	Inductor	Capacitor (negative)
OLED VCC	ESP8266 3V3	
OLED GND	ESP8266 GND	
OLED SDA	ESP8266 D2	
OLED SCL	ESP8266 D1	

In the sketch in Listing 18-9, a voltage burst is applied to the LC circuit, and the *HIGH* pulse width of the resulting square wave generated by the LM393 voltage comparator is measured with the instruction pulse = pulseIn(LM393pin, HIGH, timeout). If signal is *HIGH*, then the *pulseIn* function waits until the signal is *LOW*, starts timing when the signal goes *HIGH*, and stops timing when the signal goes *LOW*. If a *HIGH* pulse is not detected before *timeout* microseconds, then a zero value is returned. The square wave frequency is $10^6 \times (2 \times pulse\ width)^{-1}$ Hz, as the pulse width is measured in microseconds, and the inductor value is $\dfrac{pulse\ width^2}{\pi^2 \times capacitor}$. The inductor meter is reasonably accurate for inductances of 50 µH and above. For example, the estimated inductance for a 470 µH inductor with a 1 µF electrolytic or ceramic capacitor was 462 µH or 415 µH, respectively. Pulse length with a ceramic capacitor is generally 2–3 µs lower than with an electrolytic capacitor (see Figure 18-23).

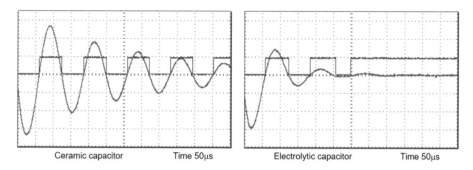

| Ceramic capacitor | Time 50µs | Electrolytic capacitor | Time 50µs |

Figure 18-23. *Inductor-capacitor oscillation with ceramic or electrolytic capacitor*

A ceramic capacitor fitted across the inductor prolongs the inductor-capacitor oscillation to a greater extent than an electrolytic capacitor (see Figure 18-23). An electrolytic capacitor is less effective at higher frequencies than a ceramic capacitor, due to the higher equivalent series resistance (ESR) and inductance (ESL), resulting in longer charging and discharging times. For example, the pulse length of a 1 µF capacitor and a 470 µH inductor pair is a constant 64 µs with a ceramic capacitor, but only the first two pulses of 65 µs and 70 µs are detectable when an electrolytic capacitor is used (see Figure 18-23). With an inductor of less than 50 µH, no pulses are detectable when an electrolytic capacitor is used, given the high oscillation frequency of 25 kHz.

Listing 18-9. Inductor meter

```
#include <Adafruit_SSD1306.h>            // Adafruit SSD1306 library
int width = 128;                         // OLED screen size
int height = 32;                         // associate oled with SSD1306
Adafruit_SSD1306 oled(width, height, &Wire, -1);
int voltPin = D0;                        // voltage burst pin
int LM393pin = D3;                       // LM393 output pin
float capacitor = 1.0;                   // measured in µF
int timeout = 1000;                      // timeout limit in µs
```

```
float pulse, pulse1, pulse2, frequency, inductance;

void setup()
{
  pinMode(voltPin, OUTPUT);              // define voltPin as output
  oled.begin(SSD1306_SWITCHCAPVCC, 0x3C);     // OLED I2C address
  oled.clearDisplay();                   // clear OLED display
  oled.setTextColor(WHITE);              // set font color
  oled.setTextSize(1);                   // set font size (1, 2, 3 or 4)
  oled.display();                        // update display instructions

}
void loop()
{
  digitalWrite(voltPin, HIGH);           // apply 3.2V on voltPin
  delay(5);                              // time to charge the inductor
  digitalWrite(voltPin,LOW);             // end of voltage burst
  pulse1 = pulseIn(LM393pin, HIGH, timeout);
                                         // measure HIGH pulse duration
  pulse2 = pulseIn(LM393pin, HIGH, timeout);
  if(pulse2 > 0) pulse = (pulse1+pulse2)/2.0;
                                         // average pulse length
  else pulse = pulse1;
  if(pulse > 0)
  {
    frequency = 1E6/(2.0*pulse);    // shorthand for 10 to the power 6
    inductance = pulse*pulse/(PI*PI*capacitor);
                                         // calculate inductance
    oled.clearDisplay();
    oled.setCursor(0,0);                 // display results
    oled.print("inductance uH ");oled.println(inductance,0);
```

```
    oled.print("frequency Hz  ");oled.println(frequency,0);
    oled.print("high time us  ");oled.print(pulse,0);
    oled.display();
  }
  delay(1000);
}
```

Summary

Voltage across a load, resistance of a load, and current through a load were measured using an ESP8366 or ESP32 microcontroller analog to digital converter (ADC). Voltage, resistance, and current were determined from the voltage across the load or the voltage across a shunt resistor to derive current through the load. The charging time of a capacitor defined its capacitance. An INA219 current and voltage measurement module quantified the power and cumulative energy used by a load. The net battery charge or discharge current of a battery providing power to a load and charging through a solar panel was measured with two INA219 modules, with the information over time displayed on an ST7735 TFT LCD screen. Inductance was measured by applying a voltage burst to an inductor-capacitor circuit. The frequency that the inductor-capacitor circuit resonated was related to the inductance. The oscillating sine wave was converted to a square wave by a voltage comparator and the inductance derived from the square wave frequency.

Components List

- ESP8266 microcontroller: LOLIN (WeMos) D1 mini or NodeMCU board

- ESP32 microcontroller: DEVKIT DOIT or NodeMCU board

- OLED display: 128 × 32 pixels

- Battery: 5 V or 9 V

- Resistor: 150 Ω, 220 Ω, 2× 1 kΩ, 2.2 kΩ, 10 kΩ, 22 kΩ, and 47 kΩ

- LED

- Shunt resistor: 0.01 Ω

- Operational amplifier: LM358

- Current sensor: 2× INA219

- Solar panel: 5 V output

- Lithium battery: 3.7 V

- Lithium battery charging module: TP4056

- DC-DC adjustable step-up (boost) converter: MT3608

- TFT LCD screen: ST7735, 1.8 inches, 128 × 160 pixels

- Tactile switch

- Voltage comparator: LM393

- Capacitor: 0.1 µF, 1 µF ceramic or electrolytic

- Diode: IN4001

CHAPTER 19

Rotary encoder control

A rotary encoder detects rotation of the center shaft and is used to control machinery position and motor speed, audio volume, the cursor position on an LCD (Liquid Crystal Display) screen, or simply LED brightness. For example, in Chapter 1 (Internet radio), the radio station and volume were selected by turning a rotary encoder. The incremental rotary encoder has 20 positions, and the rotor is continuously rotated clockwise or anti-clockwise to increase or decrease a control variable. The rotary encoder has two pins, termed A or CLK (clock) and B or DT (data), and a common pin. As the rotary encoder rotor is turned, pins A and B each make contact with the common pin, which generates square waves, but as the pins are offset, the square waves are 90° out of phase (see Figure 19-1). The number of square wave pulses indicates the extent of the rotation, which is measured on either pin A or pin B.

© Neil Cameron 2021
N. Cameron, *Electronics Projects with the ESP8266 and ESP32*,
https://doi.org/10.1007/978-1-4842-6336-5_19

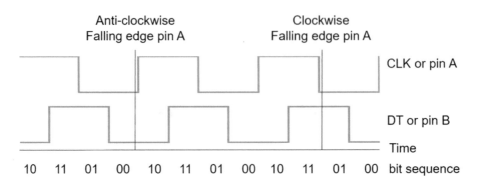

Figure 19-1. *Rotary encoder square waves*

The square wave states at a given time indicate the direction of rotation. If the direction is clockwise, then pin A makes contact with the common pin before pin B makes contact. When pin A disconnects from the common pin, the pin A square wave state changes from *HIGH* to *LOW*, but the pin B square wave is still *HIGH* (read Figure 19-1 from left to right). The position that a square wave changes from *HIGH* to *LOW* or from *LOW* to *HIGH* is the falling edge or rising edge, respectively. In contrast, when the direction of rotation is anti-clockwise, the pin B square wave state is *LOW* at the falling edge of the pin A square wave (read Figure 19-1 from right to left). The direction of rotation is determined by reading the pin B square wave state at a falling edge of the pin A square wave. If the pin B square wave is *HIGH*, then rotation is clockwise, but anti-clockwise if the pin B square wave is *LOW* at the falling edge of the pin A square wave.

The sketch in Listing 19-1 demonstrates the rotary encoder generating square waves, to control two LEDs (see Figure 19-2). The pin A square wave state is monitored, and when a falling edge is detected, the pin B square wave state is read. The *LED* function turns on the red or green LED, displays the rotation direction, and increases or decreases the count of encoder increments. Note that the rotary encoder must be turned two increments to detect the rotation direction. For Listing 19-1, the resistor and capacitor pairs in Figure 19-2 are not connected.

To illustrate that a solution for one microcontroller is not necessarily appropriate for a microcontroller with a higher CPU frequency, the sketch in Listing 19-1 is run on both an Arduino Nano and an ESP8266 microcontroller. With the ATmega328P microcontroller of the Arduino Nano, the number and direction of rotary encoder turns are detected reasonably correctly, provided the rotary encoder is not turned quickly. In contrast, there are substantial errors in rotary encoder turn detection by an ESP8266 microcontroller, which has a higher CPU frequency, 160 MHz compared to 16 MHz of the ATmega328P microcontroller. Rotary encoder turn detection is worse with an ESP32 microcontroller, which has a CPU frequency of 240 MHz, as every pin bounce is detected.

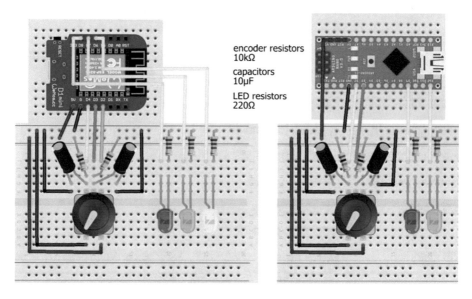

Figure 19-2. *Rotary encoder and LEDs with LOLIN (WeMos) D1 mini and Arduino Nano*

Rotary encoder and LED connections are given in Table 19-1 and shown in Figure 19-2. Listings 19-1, 19-2, and 19-3 require two LEDs, while Listing 19-5 requires three LEDs, so all three LEDs are included in Figure 19-2 to avoid repetition.

When uploading a sketch to the ESP8266 microcontroller, GPIO pins D3 and D4 must not be pulled *LOW*, so the pins are disconnected from the rotary encoder *DT* and *CLK* pins.

Table 19-1. *Rotary encoder and LEDs*

Component	Connect to	And to	And to
Rotary encoder CLK	ESP8266 D4 or Nano pin 2	Capacitor positive	
Rotary encoder CLK		10 kΩ resistor	ESP8266 or Nano 5V
Rotary encoder DT	ESP8266 D3 or Nano pin 3	Capacitor positive	
Rotary encoder DT		10 kΩ resistor	ESP8266 or Nano 5V
Rotary encoder SW	ESP8266 D2		
Rotary encoder VCC	ESP8266 or Nano 5V		
Rotary encoder GND	ESP8266 or Nano GND		
Capacitor negative	ESP8266 or Nano GND		
LED long leg	ESP8266 D8, D7, D6, or Nano pins 9 and 12		
LED short leg	220 Ω resistor	ESP8266 or Nano GND	

Listing 19-1. Rotary encoder with LEDs

```
int CLKpin = D4;                    // rotary encoder pins
int DTpin = D3;                     // CLK = pin A and DT = pin B
int redLED = D8;
int greenLED = D7;                  // define LED pins
int count = 0;
```

```
int oldCLK = LOW;
int newCLK;

void setup()
{
  Serial.begin(115200);                  // Serial Monitor baud rate
  pinMode(redLED, OUTPUT);               // set LED pins as output
  pinMode(greenLED, OUTPUT);
}

void loop()
{
  newCLK = digitalRead(CLKpin);          // state of pin A (CLK)
  if(newCLK == LOW && oldCLK == HIGH)    // falling edge of pin A
  {                                      // pin B HIGH
    if(digitalRead(DTpin) == HIGH) LED(HIGH, 1, "up");
    else LED(LOW, -1, "down ");          // pin B (DT) LOW
  }
  oldCLK = newCLK;                       // reset pin A (CLK) state
//  delay(100);                          // to confirm microcontroller
}                                        // can miss rotary encoder turns

void LED(int state, int increment, String text)
{
  digitalWrite(redLED, 1-state);         // turn on or off the LEDs
  digitalWrite(greenLED, state);
  Serial.print(text);
  count = count + increment;             // update and display count
  Serial.println(count);
}
```

Debouncing

There are two issues with the sketch in Listing 19-1. First, bouncing of the rotary encoder pin A and B connections with the common pin produces spurious changes in the detected direction and count of encoder increments. A hardware solution to debouncing the rotary encoder pins is inclusion of 10 kΩ pull-up resistors (R) and 10 μF (C) capacitors between the rotary encoder pins A and B with GND (see Figure 19-2 and Table 19-1). The resistor-capacitor combination creates a debounce delay of 69 ms, equal to RC × ln(2) seconds. Further information on capacitor changing and discharging times is given in Chapter 17 (Signal generation with 555 timer IC). Some rotary encoder modules, such as the KY-040 module, include 10 kΩ pull-up resistors on the CLK and DT connections, so only the 10 μF capacitors are required for debouncing.

The resistor-capacitor combination to debounce the rotary encoder connections for pins A and B with the common pin must ensure that sufficient time has elapsed for the connection bouncing to have stopped, without being too long to have missed rotary encoder rotations. The delay of 69 ms achieved with a 10 kΩ resistor and a 10 μF capacitor is a compromise.

Interrupts

The second issue with the sketch in Listing 19-1 is that the microcontroller is continuously reading the pin A square wave state to detect a falling edge and then reading the pin B square wave state to determine the direction of rotation. If the sketch included other actions, then the microcontroller will miss detecting falling edges of the pin A square wave. Inclusion of a short delay of 100 ms in the *loop* function of Listing 19-1 illustrates the point. The problem of not detecting the falling edges is resolved by including an interrupt to detect falling edges of the pin A square wave (see Listing 19-2). The interrupt is active on the falling edge of the pin A (CLK) square wave, and the interrupt service routine (ISR) reads the pin B (DT) square wave state to determine the direction of rotation. The variable *change* is updated in both the *loop* function and the ISR, so is defined as volatile. Only instructions referring to the interrupt are annotated in Listing 19-2, to emphasize the few differences between Listings 19-1 and 19-2.

Listing 19-2 is for an ESP8266 microcontroller. When using an ESP32 microcontroller, the rotary encoder pins are defined with the instructions

```
pinMode(CLKpin, INPUT);
pinMode(DTpin, INPUT);
```

In Listing 19-2, the ISR is defined with the instruction IRAM_ATTR void isr() for an ESP8266 or ESP32 microcontroller to store the interrupt in internal RAM (IRAM), rather than in the slower flash memory. For the Arduino Nano, the ISR is defined as void isr().

Listing 19-2. Rotary encoder with interrupt

```
int CLKpin = D4;
int DTpin = D3;
int redLED = D8;
int greenLED = D7;
int count = 0;
volatile int change;                          // variable used in ISR

void setup()
{
  Serial.begin(115200);
  pinMode(redLED, OUTPUT);
  pinMode(greenLED, OUTPUT);                   // attached interrupt
  attachInterrupt(digitalPinToInterrupt(CLKpin), isr, FALLING);
}
```

```
void loop()
{
  if(change != 0)                          // rotary encoder direction
  {
    if(change > 0) LED(HIGH, "up   "); // clockwise
    else if(change < 0) LED(LOW, "down ");         // anti-clockwise
    change = 0;
  }
}

void LED(int state, String text)          // no change to LED function
{
  digitalWrite(redLED, 1-state);
  digitalWrite(greenLED, state);
  Serial.print(text);
  count = count + change;
  Serial.println(count);
}

IRAM_ATTR void isr()                      // interrupt service routine
{
  change = 2*digitalRead(DTpin) - 1;
}                                         // determine direction of rotation
```

Including an interrupt to detect changes in the pin A square wave state and resistor-capacitor pairs to debounce the rotary encoder pins improves detection of rotary encoder turns for the ATmega328P microcontroller, but not substantially for the ESP8266 and ESP32 microcontrollers. The next section describes an effective solution to debouncing the rotary encoder.

Square wave states

Debouncing is eliminated by only counting the changes in square wave states that are consistent with a clockwise or anti-clockwise rotation. The square wave states for pins A and B are easily visualized by connecting two LEDs to rotary encoder pins A and B (see Figure 19-3 with connections in Table 19-2).

Figure 19-3. *Rotary encoder and test LEDs*

Table 19-2. *Rotary encoder and test LEDs*

Component	Connect to	And to
Rotary encoder pin A (CLK)	Red LED long leg	
Rotary encoder pin B (DT)	Green LED long leg	
Rotary encoder VCC	Battery 5V	
Rotary encoder GND	Battery GND	
LED short legs	220 Ω resistors	Battery GND

When the incremental rotary encoder is rotated slowly clockwise, the LED attached to pin A turns on; and, before the incremental rotation is completed, the LED connected to pin B turns on. If the rotary encoder is again turned slowly through one increment, the two LEDs turn off with the LED attached to pin A turning off first. The LED sequence, written as LED_A, LED_B, is 00, 10, 11, 01, and back to 00 (see Figure 19-1). The sequence, consisting of 2 bits with 1 bit for each pin, is known as Gray code, after Frank Gray, with two successive events only differing by 1 bit. The LED or 2-bit sequence when rotating the rotary encoder slowly anti-clockwise is 00, 01, 11, 10, and back to 00.

The changes in square wave states for pins A and B are written as 4-bit numbers, describing the square wave states as the incremental rotation progresses. For example, if the rotation is clockwise, the square wave states for pins A and B are *LOW, LOW,* then *HIGH, LOW,* then *HIGH, HIGH,* then *LOW, HIGH,* and finally *LOW, LOW.* Written as 4-bit numbers, the sequences are (00)(10), (10)(11), (11)(01), and (01)(00) (see Table 19-3).

Table 19-3. *Bit sequence of rotary encoder square wave states*

Initial State	Next State	4-Bit Number
LOW, LOW	*HIGH, LOW*	0010
HIGH, LOW	*HIGH, HIGH*	1011
HIGH, HIGH	*LOW, HIGH*	1101
LOW, HIGH	*LOW, LOW*	0100

A 4-bit number has 16 possible values, and each value is mapped to a directional increment of the rotary encoder (see Table 19-4). The 4-bit numbers with a zero score represent either no pin changes or two pin changes, such as 0101 or 0011, respectively.

Table 19-4. *Rotary encoder square wave states as 4-bit numbers*

4-Bit Number	Decimal	Pin A (CLK) and Pin B (DT) Previous State	Current State	Change	Direction	Score
0000	0	LOW, LOW	LOW, LOW	None		0
0001	1	LOW, LOW	LOW, HIGH		Anti-clockwise	-1
0010	2	LOW, LOW	HIGH, LOW		Clockwise	1
0011	3	LOW, LOW	HIGH, HIGH	Two pins		0
0100	4	LOW, HIGH	LOW, LOW		Clockwise	1
0101	5	LOW, HIGH	LOW, HIGH	None		0
0110	6	LOW, HIGH	HIGH, LOW	Two pins		0
0111	7	LOW, HIGH	HIGH, HIGH		Anti-clockwise	-1
1000	8	HIGH, LOW	LOW, LOW		Anti-clockwise	-1
1001	9	HIGH, LOW	LOW, HIGH	Two pins		0
1010	10	HIGH, LOW	HIGH, LOW	None		0
1011	11	HIGH, LOW	HIGH, HIGH		Clockwise	1
1100	12	HIGH, HIGH	LOW, LOW	Two pins		0
1101	13	HIGH, HIGH	LOW, HIGH		Clockwise	1
1110	14	HIGH, HIGH	HIGH, LOW		Anti-clockwise	-1
1111	15	HIGH, HIGH	HIGH, HIGH	None		0

Both square wave states must be determined whenever either square wave state changes, so two interrupts are required, one for each of the rotary encoder pins A and B. The two square wave states are converted to a 4-bit number, consisting of the previous and current states, to obtain the corresponding score. When the score is equal to +2 or -2, then the rotary encoder has rotated clockwise or anti-clockwise by one increment, as an incremental rotation of the rotary encoder has two state changes. If a more definite rotation of the rotary encoder is required, then a score of +4 or -4 requires a rotation of two increments.

The sketch in Listing 19-3 maps both square wave states to a score to determine both the direction and extent of the rotary encoder rotation. Score values are included in the vals[] array, and an ISR is activated by a change in square wave state for either pin A (CLK) or pin B (DT). The *loop* and *LED* functions are identical to those in Listing 19-2. The resistor and capacitor pairs for the rotary encoder pins are no longer required for debouncing (see Figure 19-4 with connections in Table 19-5). When the rotary encoder is turned quickly, there is no loss of accuracy in detecting rotary encoder rotations. Note that the rotary encoder rotor is only turned one increment to detect the rotation direction.

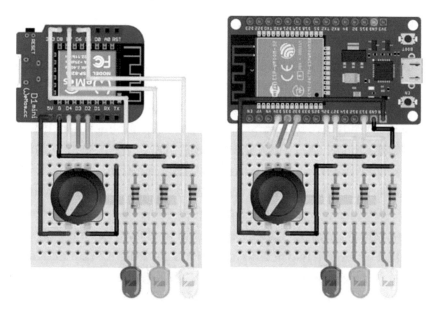

Figure 19-4. *Rotary encoder and LEDs with LOLIN (WeMos) D1 mini and ESP32 DEVKIT DOIT board*

Table 19-5. *Rotary encoder and LEDs with ESP8266 and ESP32 microcontrollers*

Component	Connect to ESP8266	Connect to ESP32
Rotary encoder CLK	D4	GPIO 34
Rotary encoder DT	D3	GPIO 35
Rotary encoder SW	D2	GPIO 32
Rotary encoder VCC	5V	VIN
Rotary encoder GND	GND	GND
LED long leg	D8, D7, D6	GPIO 26, GPIO 27, GPIO 13
LED short leg	220 Ω resistor and GND	220 Ω resistor and GND

The ISR constructs the 4-bit number from the retained previous square wave states and the current square wave states for pins A and B and then increments the score. The bit shift symbol << moves a bit with value N to position r with the instruction (N<<r). To represent the current square wave states, the 4-bit number is reduced to a 2-bit number by bit shifting two positions, equal to the remainder of the 4-bit number when divided by four, with the instruction oldState = newState % 4. For example, if the rotary encoder moves clockwise from an initial state *HIGH, HIGH* to state *LOW, LOW*, the 2-bit number sequence is 11, 01, and 00, corresponding to the two 4-bit numbers of 1101 and 0100 (see Table 19-4). The 4-bit number for the second stage of the incremental rotation of 0100 has the 2-bit value of 00, when bit shifted two positions, which is equivalent to a remainder of 0 when the decimal value 8 (4-bit value of 0100) is divided by 4. Alternatively, the instruction oldState = (digitalRead(CLKpin)<<1)+digitalRead (DTpin) would suffice, but the square wave states may have changed since the interrupt was activated.

The new square wave states are a combination of the previous states and the current states of the pin A (CLK) and pin B (DT) square waves. The new state consists of the previous square wave states for pins A and B, but shifted two positions (<<2), the current pin A square wave state shifted one position (<<1), and the current pin B square wave state.

A switch case instruction is an alternative to including the score values in an array. For example, the instruction score = score + vals[newState] in Listing 19-3 is replaced with

```
switch (newState)
{
  case 0: case 3: case 5: case 6: case 9: case 10: case 12:
  case 15:
    break;                                    // no change
  case 1: case 7: case 8: case 14:
```

```
    score = score - 1; break;                  // reduce score by one
  case 2: case 4: case 11: case 13:
    score++; break;                            // increase score by one
  default: break;
}
```

Listing 19-3. Rotary encoder with square wave states

```
int CLKpin = D4;                        // define rotary encoder pins
int DTpin = D3;
int redLED = D8;                        // define LED pins
int greenLED = D7;
int vals[] = {0,-1,1,0,1,0,0,-1,-1,0,0,1,0,1,-1,0};
                                        // array of scores
int count = 0;
volatile int score = 0;
volatile int change = 0;      // variables used in isr and loop functions
volatile int oldState = 0;

void setup()
{
  Serial.begin(115200);                 // Serial Monitor baud rate
  pinMode(redLED, OUTPUT);              // set LED pins as output
  pinMode(greenLED, OUTPUT);           // attach interrupt
  pinMode(CLKpin, INPUT);              // required by ESP32
  pinMode(DTpin, INPUT);               // required by ESP32
  attachInterrupt(digitalPinToInterrupt(CLKpin), isr, CHANGE);
  attachInterrupt(digitalPinToInterrupt(DTpin), isr, CHANGE);
}
```

```
void loop()
{
  if(change != 0)                          // rotary encoder rotated
  {
    if(change > 0) LED(HIGH, "up    ");        // clockwise
    else if(change < 0) LED(LOW, "down ");     // anti-clockwise
    change = 0;
  }
}

void LED(int state, String text)
{
  digitalWrite(redLED, 1-state);        // turn LEDs on or off
  digitalWrite(greenLED, state);
  Serial.print(text);
  count = count + change;               // update count
  Serial.println(count);
}

IRAM_ATTR void isr()                    // interrupt service routine
{                                       // construct 4-bit number
  int newState = (oldState<<2)+(digitalRead(CLKpin)<<1)+
  digitalRead(DTpin);
  score = score + vals[newState];       // allocate score from array
  oldState = newState % 4;
                      // remainder to leave new CLK and DT state
  if(score == 2 || score == -2)         // 2 steps for complete rotation
  {
    change = score/2;                   // unit change per two steps
    score = 0;                          // reset score
  }
}
```

State switching

The rotary encoder switch, activated by pressing down on the stem of the rotary encoder, is used to change the state of a binary variable, such as turning on or off an LED. Noting the time that the switch is pressed differentiates between a long and a short press, enabling the switch to control a variable with three levels rather than only two levels. In Listing 19-4, the rotary encoder switch (SW) pin uses the ESP8266 or ESP32 microcontroller internal pull-up resistor, rather than including a separate resistor in the circuit. An internal pull-up resistor is activated with the instruction `pinMode(pin, INPUT_PULLUP)`, and the pin is active *LOW* rather than *HIGH*. When the rotary encoder switch is pressed and then released, the pin state changes from *HIGH* to *LOW* and then back to *HIGH*.

Listing 19-4 defines ESP8266 development board pin *D2* as an interrupt pin, and depending on the length of time that the switch is pressed, the *changeSW* variable is allocated the character value of `'L'`, `'S'`, or `'B'` to indicate a long or short press or a switch bounce. The *changeSW* variable is not allocated the string value of *"Long"*, *"Short"*, or *"Bounce"*, as strings are not passed to an interrupt. The ISR compares the time that the switch was pressed with the time that the switch was released, relative to the predefined *longpress* and *shortpress* values, to determine if a long press or a short press or a switch bounce occurred. When the switch is released, the time between pressing and releasing the switch is displayed with the category "*long press*", "*short press*", or "*switch bounce*", with the LED state only changing after a long or short switch press.

Listing 19-4. Rotary encoder switch

```
int SWpin = D2;                       // rotary encoder switch pin
int SWled = D6;                       // LED pin
int longPress = 1000;                 // time (ms) for long or short press
int shortPress = 500;
volatile unsigned long newTime, oldTime;
volatile char changeSW;               // variables in loop and isr functions
volatile unsigned int lagTime;

void setup()
{
  Serial.begin(115200);               // Serial Monitor baud rate
  pinMode(SWled, OUTPUT);             // set LED pin as output
  pinMode(SWpin, INPUT_PULLUP);       // activate pull-up resistor
  attachInterrupt(digitalPinToInterrupt(SWpin), isr, CHANGE);
}                                     // SWpin as interrupt pin and attache ISR

void loop()
{
  if(changeSW != ' ')                 // switch released, turn on or off
  {                                   // LED if long or short press
    Serial.print(lagTime);Serial.print("\t");
                                      // display switch press time lag
    if(changeSW != 'B') digitalWrite(SWled,
    !digitalRead(SWled));
    if(changeSW == 'L') Serial.println("long press");
    else if(changeSW == 'S') Serial.println("short press");
    else Serial.println("switch bounce");
                                      // display only, no effect on LED
    changeSW = ' ';                   // reset change variable
  }
}
```

```
IRAM_ATTR void isr()
{
  newTime = millis();                    // get time ISR triggered
  if(digitalRead(SWpin) == HIGH)   // switch now released
  {
    lagTime = newTime - oldTime;   // time between switch presses
    if(lagTime > longPress) changeSW = 'L';      // L for long press
    else if(lagTime > shortPress) changeSW = 'S';
                                                 // S for short press
    else changeSW = 'B';                         // B for bounce
  }
  oldTime = newTime;                       // reset switch press/release time
}
```

Incrementing a value

While the number of square wave pulses indicates the extent of the
rotation of the rotary encoder, the switch is used to control the size of the
incremental count. For example, pressing the switch for a long or short
time changes the incremental count by ten or one. Listing 19-3 is readily
extended by including the instructions for the rotary encoder switch:

```
int SWpin = D2;                    // rotary encoder switchpin
int SWled = D6;                    // LED pin
int longPress = 1000;              // time (ms) for long press
volatile unsigned long newTime, oldTime, lagTime;
volatile int increment = 1;
```

Instructions are added for the LED, the pull-up resistor, and attaching the interrupt with ISR *isrSwitch* in the *setup* function:

```
pinMode(SWled, OUTPUT);                        // set LED pin as output
pinMode(SWpin, INPUT_PULLUP);                  // activate pull-up resistor
attachInterrupt(digitalPinToInterrupt(SWpin), isrSwitch,
CHANGE);
```

In the LED function, the count instruction is changed

```
count = count + change*increment;                    // update count
```

and an instruction is added for the LED to indicate the value of the increment:

```
digitalWrite(SWled, increment>1);      // turn on LED if increment >1
```

Instructions for the ISR to change the size of the increment are

```
IRAM_ATTR void isrSwitch()
{
  newTime = millis();                              // get time ISR triggered
  if(digitalRead(SWpin) == HIGH)                  // switch released
  {
    lagTime = newTime - oldTime;
    if(lagTime > longPress) increment = 10;  // update increment
    else if(lagTime > 100) increment = 1;    // debounce switch
  }
  oldTime = newTime;                      // reset switch press/release time
}
```

The size of the incremental count is also controlled by the rotation speed of the rotary encoder, with a high speed resulting in a larger increment than a low speed. The ISR maps changes in the pin A and B square wave states to score the rotation and calculates the rotation time from the interval between falling and rising edges of the pin A square wave. Instructions in an ISR should be as few as possible to minimize the processing time, and the ISR could be split into two ISRs. ISRs do not run in parallel, and one interrupt starts when the previous interrupt finishes. Splitting the ISR into two separate ISRs is not more efficient.

To control the incremental count by the rotation speed of the rotary encoder, Listing 19-3 is again readily adapted. Variable definitions and the LED pin are included at the start of the sketch:

```
int incLED = D6;                  // LED pin indicates when increment > 1
int rotation = 500;               // threshold rotation time (ms)
int increment = 1;
volatile unsigned long newTime, oldTime, lagTime;
volatile int newCLK;              // variables used in isr() and loop()
volatile int oldCLK = 0;
```

The LED to indicate when a large increment is activated is included in the *setup* function:

```
pinMode(incLED, OUTPUT);
```

In the LED function, the count instruction is changed

```
count = count + change*increment;         // update count
```

and an instruction is added for the LED to indicate the increment value:

```
digitalWrite(incLED, increment>1);    // turn LED on if increment > 1
```

In the existing ISR, to avoid rereading the state of the square wave of pin A (CLK), the instruction

```
int newState = (oldState<<2)+(digitalRead(CLKpin)<<1)+
digitalRead(DTpin);
```

is replaced with the instructions

```
newCLK = digitalRead(CLKpin);
int newState = (oldState<<2)+(newCLK<<1)+digitalRead(DTpin);
```

Instructions to calculate the rotary encoder rotation time and the corresponding increment are included in the existing ISR, as

```
newTime = millis();                       // get time ISR triggered
if(newCLK == HIGH && oldCLK == LOW)       // interval between falling
{                                         // and rising edge on pin A (CLK)
   lagTime = newTime - oldTime;
   if(lagTime < rotation && lagTime > 100) increment = 10;
                                          // fast rotation
   else if(lagTime > rotation) increment = 1;      // slow rotation
   oldTime = newTime;                     // reset rising/falling edge time
}
oldCLK = newCLK;                          // reset state of pin A (CLK)
```

Listing 19-5 incorporates the additions to Listing 19-3 for the incremental count to be determined by the rotary encoder rotation, with the additional instructions commented.

Listing 19-5. Control incremental count by rotary encoder rotation speed

```
int CLKpin = D4;
int DTpin = D3;
int redLED = D8;
int greenLED = D7;
int vals[] = {0,-1,1,0,1,0,0,-1,-1,0,0,1,0,1,-1,0};
int count = 0;
volatile int score = 0; volatile int change = 0;
volatile int oldState = 0;
```

```
int incLED = D6;                        // increment indicator LED pin
int rotation = 500;                     // threshold rotation time (ms)
int increment = 1;                      // default increment
volatile unsigned long newTime, oldTime, lagTime;
volatile int newCLK;                    // variables used in ISR
volatile int oldCLK = 0;

void setup()
{
  Serial.begin(115200);
  pinMode(redLED, OUTPUT);
  pinMode(greenLED, OUTPUT);
  pinMode(CLKpin, INPUT);
  pinMode(DTpin, INPUT);
  attachInterrupt(digitalPinToInterrupt(CLKpin), isr, CHANGE);
  attachInterrupt(digitalPinToInterrupt(DTpin), isr, CHANGE);
  pinMode(incLED, OUTPUT);              // increment indicator LED
}

void loop()
{
  if(change != 0)
  {
    if(change > 0) LED(HIGH, "up   ");
    else if(change < 0) LED(LOW, "down ");
    change = 0;
  }
}

void LED(int state, String text)
{
  digitalWrite(redLED, 1-state);
  digitalWrite(greenLED, state);
```

```
  Serial.print(text);
  count = count + change*increment;              // incremented count
  digitalWrite(incLED, increment>1);
                                      // turn LED on, increment = 10
  Serial.print(increment);Serial.print("\t");
                                      // display updated increment
  Serial.println(count);
}

IRAM_ATTR void isr()
{                                      // avoid re-reading the square
  newCLK = digitalRead(CLKpin);        // wave state of pin A (CLK)
  int newState = (oldState<<2)+(newCLK<<1)+digitalRead(DTpin);
  score = score + vals[newState];
  oldState = newState % 4;
  if(score == 2 || score == -2)
  {
    change = score/2;
    score = 0;
  }
  newTime = millis();                  // get time ISR triggered
  if(newCLK == HIGH && oldCLK == LOW)  // interval between falling
  {                                    // and rising edge on pin A (CLK)
    lagTime = newTime - oldTime;
    if(lagTime < rotation && lagTime > 100) increment = 10;
                                                // fast rotation
    else if(lagTime > rotation) increment = 1;  // slow rotation
    oldTime = newTime;                 // reset rising/falling edge time
  }
  oldCLK = newCLK;                     // reset state of pin A (CLK)
}
```

The advantage of using interrupts to detect rising or falling edges of a square wave, to define changes in square wave states, is that the ESP8266 or ESP32 microcontroller can process other instructions simultaneously, without missing square wave state changes. Mapping changes in square wave states to a score, to then determine both the direction and extent of the rotation of the rotary encoder, also resolves the problem of connection bouncing within the rotary encoder. Consequently, resistor and capacitor combinations are not required to create a debounce delay.

Summary

Rotary encoder control of devices by both the direction and extent of rotation was illustrated. Methods to improve measuring the direction and extent of rotation of a rotary encoder are described. Interrupts alone did not enable detection of all rotation increments. Changes in square wave states generated by the rotary encoder internal connection pins were mapped to 4-bit numbers. Implementing only the state changes with appropriate 4-bit numbers effectively debounced the rotary encoder internal connections. The incremental change in the count of the rotary encoder rotations was controlled by the rotary encoder switch or by the speed of rotation.

Components List

- ESP8266 microcontroller: LOLIN (WeMos) D1 mini or NodeMCU board

- ESP32 microcontroller: DEVKIT DOIT or NodeMCU board

- Arduino Nano

- Rotary encoder: KY-040

- LED: different colors ×3

- Resistor: 3× 220 Ω, 2× 10 kΩ

- Capacitor: 2× 10 μF

CHAPTER 20

OTA and saving data to EEPROM, SPIFFS, and Excel

The memory storage device for computers and microcontrollers is termed flash memory, which retains data when power is turned off. In contrast, data stored in RAM (random access memory) is lost when power is turned off. Flash memory is partitioned into several sections: application, OTA (over the air) updating, SPIFFS (Serial Peripheral Interface Flash File System), EEPROM (Electrically Erasable Programmable Read-Only Memory), Wi-Fi, and configuration information. A sketch is stored in application memory, and the variables created and manipulated in a sketch are stored in RAM. The opportunity to upload a sketch remotely with OTA and options for saving data in SPIFFS and EEPROM partitions of flash memory are outlined in this chapter. Saving data directly to a Microsoft Excel file, instead of using an SD card for data logging, is also described.

© Neil Cameron 2021
N. Cameron, *Electronics Projects with the ESP8266 and ESP32*,
https://doi.org/10.1007/978-1-4842-6336-5_20

OTA updating

OTA updating remotely uploads a sketch through a Wi-Fi connection with the ESP8266 or ESP32 microcontroller. The sketch is initially uploaded with a Serial connection, but subsequent uploads of the sketch use the Wi-Fi connection for OTA updating. The laptop or computer to transmit the revised sketch and the ESP8266 or ESP32 microcontroller to receive the updated sketch must be connected to the same Wi-Fi network. A requirement of the *ArduinoOTA* library, which is preinstalled in the Arduino IDE, is that *Python 3.x* is installed on the laptop or computer. *Python 3.x* is downloaded from `www.python.org/downloads`, and the option to *Add Python 3.x to PATH* must be selected (see Figure 20-1).

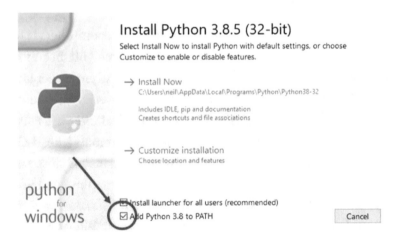

Figure 20-1.   Installation of Python 3.x

When a sketch is first uploaded, through the Serial connection, the default name and IP address of the microcontroller network port is *esp8266-[Chip identity] at IP address* or *esp3232-[MAC address] at IP address*. Naming a network port, rather than using the IP address, allows the user to identify a particular microcontroller by the user-defined *name* with the instruction `ArduinoOTA.setHostname("name")`. Similarly, a user

password to permit OTA updating is set with the instruction ArduinoOTA.
setPassword("password"), as the default is no password. If a password
has been defined, then the password is requested when the Arduino IDE
has been restarted or the password has been changed. A list of available
network ports is displayed by selecting the *Tools* menu in the Arduino IDE
and the *Port* option (see Figure 20-2). OTA updating incorporates *mDNS*
(multicast Domain Name System) to match the network port name to an
IP address for small networks, using UDP (User Datagram Protocol) to
send and receive UDP messages. Further details are available at arduino-
esp8266.readthedocs.io/en/latest/ota_updates/readme.html. For the
ESP8266 and ESP32 microcontrollers, the *ArduinoOTA* library references
the *ESP8266WiFi* and *WiFi* libraries, respectively, so the instructions
#include <ESP8266WiFi.h> and #include <WiFi.h> are not required.

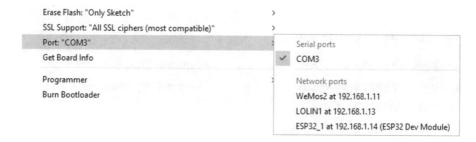

Figure 20-2. *Available network ports to OTA updating*

OTA updating is demonstrated with the sketch in Listing 20-1, which
turns on or off an LED for a fixed time. Listing 20-1 is for an ESP8266
microcontroller, but for an ESP32 microcontroller, the *mDNS* library
is installed with the instruction #include <ESPmDNS.h>. The *mDNS*
and *WiFiUdp* libraries for the ESP8266 and ESP32 microcontrollers are
effectively built-in, once the ESP8266 and ESP32 Board Managers are
installed in the Arduino IDE. When a sketch is first uploaded, through
the Serial connection, the Serial Monitor is available to print progress
messages, but the Serial Monitor is not available with OTA updating. In
the *setup* function, a Wi-Fi connection is made, and the microcontroller

network port is named. The sketch includes the *flash* function to flash the built-in LED every 500 ms while the ESP8266 or ESP32 microcontroller is connecting to the Wi-Fi network. In the *loop* function, OTA updates are monitored with the instruction ArduinoOTA.handle(), with the instruction repeated after a long delay in the sketch. There are no other changes to instructions in the *loop* function of the sketch, compared to when uploading the sketch with a USB connection.

Remote OTA updating of a revised sketch uses the named network port of the ESP8266 or ESP32 microcontroller for the Wi-Fi connection, rather than the Serial connection. With the ESP8266 or ESP32 development board now remotely powered, in the Arduino IDE *Tools* menu, select *Port* from a list of available network ports, as illustrated in Figure 20-2. Select the appropriate *Port*; make the required changes to the sketch, such as adjusting the LED delay time; and upload the sketch with OTA.

Listing 20-1. OTA updating

```
#include <ArduinoOTA.h>          // include OTA library
#include <ESP8266mDNS.h>         // and mDNS libraries
#include <WiFiUdp.h>             // include Wi-FI UDP library
char ssid[] = "xxxx";            // change xxxx to Wi-Fi ssid
char password[] = "xxxx";        // change xxxx to Wi-Fi password
int LEDpin = 2;                  // built-in LED

void setup()
{
  Serial.begin(115200);         // Serial Monitor baud rate
  pinMode(LEDpin, OUTPUT);
  WiFi.mode(WIFI_STA);          // initialise Wi-Fi
  WiFi.begin(ssid, password);
```

```
while (WiFi.status() != WL_CONNECTED)
{
  delay(500);                              // flash LED while
  flash();                                 // connecting to Wi-Fi
}
Serial.print("IP address: ");
Serial.println(WiFi.localIP());      // display network port address
ArduinoOTA.setHostname("WeMos2");         // name network port
ArduinoOTA.setPassword("admin1");         // set password
ArduinoOTA.begin();                       // initialise ArduinoOTA
}

void loop()
{
  ArduinoOTA.handle();                             // check for OTA updates
  digitalWrite(LEDpin, !digitalRead(LEDpin)); // turn on or off LED
  delay(1000);
}

void flash()                                      // function to flash LED
{
    digitalWrite(LEDpin, HIGH);
    delay(100);
    digitalWrite(LEDpin, LOW);
}
```

Saving data

Data logging sketches store data externally on an SD (Secure Digital) card using SPI (Serial Peripheral Interface) communication. The Arduino IDE built-in *SD* library provides the necessary instructions to create, open, and close files and write to and read from files on an SD card module. Storing data on an SD card for applications with either low or short-term data storage requirements is not efficient, and an alternative is to store data in the ESP8266 or ESP32 microcontroller memory. For example, storing a device setting, such as the state of a relay or the brightness of an LED, in flash memory ensures that the device state is maintained when the microcontroller is reset either after being powered off or if power was lost. Other examples include storing the ESP32 camera image files in Chapter 2 (Intranet camera) or the servo motor positions generated by an app in Chapter 10 (Build an app).

The ESP8266 and ESP32 microcontrollers have <50 kB RAM (random access memory) and 520 kB SRAM (static random access memory), respectively, where variables are created and manipulated in a sketch. RAM is volatile memory, and the contents are not accessible after the microcontroller is powered down.

In contrast, the ESP8266 and ESP32 microcontrollers have 4 MB flash memory that is non-volatile and is retained when the microcontroller is powered down. A sketch is stored in the application partition of flash memory, as are large amounts of data for a lookup table of a sketch, such as in Chapter 16 (Signal generation). An array is stored in the application partition of flash memory with the instruction `const datatype arrayname[] PROGMEM = {array values}`, and the *ith* value of the array is accessed with the instruction `pgm_read_datatype(arrayname + i)`. Character or integer data is stored with the parameter *datatype* defined as `unsigned char` or `uint16_t` and accessed with `pgm_read_byte` or `pgm_read_word`, respectively. A *string literal* containing, for example, the AJAX code of a web page is also stored in the application partition of flash memory, as in Chapters 7 (Wireless local area network), 8 (Updating a web page), 9 (WebSocket), and 12 (GPS tracking app with Google Maps).

Saving to EEPROM

EEPROM (Electrically Erasable Programmable Read-Only Memory) is non-volatile memory that retains the information when the ESP8266 or ESP32 microcontroller is turned off. EEPROM consists of up to 4096 bytes, which is one sector of flash memory, with read and write access for each byte. EEPROM has a limit of 100k write cycles at each memory location. In Chapter 2 (Intranet camera), the number of images stored on an SD card was saved in EEPROM.

Accessing data held in EEPROM uses instructions from the Arduino IDE built-in *EEPROM* library. For example, the *ith* byte in EEPROM is written to or read from with the instruction EEPROM.write(i, val) or EEPROM.read(i), respectively, where *val* has an integer value between 0 and 255 equal to $2^8 - 1$, inclusive. Numbering of EEPROM bytes starts from zero. Integers, real numbers, strings, and structures that require more than 1 byte of memory are written to or read from EEPROM with the instruction EEPROM.put(EEaddress, val) or EEPROM.get(EEaddress, val), respectively, where *EEaddress* is the EEPROM byte to start writing to or reading from and *val* is the value of an integer, real number, string, or structure. Both an integer and a real number require 4 bytes of EEPROM storage, with a string requiring 12 bytes, irrespective of the magnitude of the integer or the length of the string. When logging data with a fixed structure, the number of bytes of a record is constant, and the number of records is stored in EEPROM byte zero, with the EEPROM address of a new record equal to a multiple of the number of records plus four. For example, if there are already eight data records stored in EEPROM and a data record consists of a time (two integers), an integer, and a real number that requires 16 bytes of memory, then the EEPROM address for the ninth record is 132, equal to 8 (records) × 16 (bytes) + 4 (count at address 0).

EEPROM writing and reading instructions are prefixed with the instruction EEPROM.begin(N), where N is the number of EEPROM bytes to be accessed. For example, access of up to 1000 EEPROM bytes requires the instruction EEPROM.begin(1000). Writing to EEPROM is followed with the instruction EEPROM.commit(). The number of bytes allocated to EEPROM is obtained with the instruction EEPROM.length().

 The sketch in Listing 20-2 saves the ultraviolet sensor reading to EEPROM every five seconds and displays the saved data on the Serial Monitor. The number of records is obtained with the instruction EEPROM.get(0, records), rather than EEPROM.read(0) which is the value of the byte in address zero, as there may be more than 255 records. In the sketch, commands are entered on the Serial monitor to write data, to display data, and to reset data stored in EEPROM. When the number of bytes required by the records approaches the set EEPROM capacity, the number of records is reset to zero. The number of bytes for a record is determined with the sizeof() instruction, which can either reference the variable type or the variable itself, as illustrated in the instruction int Nbytes = sizeof(float) + sizeof(data.minuteTime) + sizeof(int).

Listing 20-2. Saving data in EEPROM

```
#include <EEPROM.h>                    // include EEPROM library
int EEaddress, records;
unsigned long seconds, nowTime, lastTime = 0;
char cmd = ' ';                        // command character

typedef struct                         // structure to hold data record
{
  float UV;                            // a real number (4 bytes) and an
  int minuteTime;                      // integer (4 bytes in EEPROM)
  int secondTime;
} dataStruct;
```

```
dataStruct data;                          // number of bytes to store data
int Nbytes = sizeof(float) + sizeof(data.minuteTime) +
sizeof(int);

void setup()
{
  Serial.begin(115200);                   // Serial Monitor baud rate
  EEPROM.begin(1000);                     // set EEPROM capacity
  EEPROM.put(0, 0);                       // set record number to zero
  EEPROM.commit();                        // write to EEPROM
  Serial.print("Enter R: record, D: display");
  Serial.println(" or Z: zero UV record");
}

void loop()
{                                         // command from Serial buffer
  if(Serial.available() > 0) cmd = Serial.read();
  nowTime = millis();                     // start of time interval
  if((nowTime - lastTime > 5000) && (cmd == 'R'))
  {                                       // collect data every 5s
    data.UV = analogRead(A0)*3200.0/1024; // convert reading to mV
    seconds = (nowTime/1000);
    data.minuteTime = seconds / 60;       // calculate elapsed minutes
    data.secondTime = seconds % 60;       // and seconds
    EEPROM.get(0, records);               // number of EEPROM records
    EEaddress = records * Nbytes + 4;     // address of new record
    if((EEaddress + Nbytes) > EEPROM.length())
    {                                     // check if exceeding the set EEPROM capacity
      records = 0;          // reset EEPROM record number
      EEaddress = 4;        // avoid over-flowing EEPROM
    }
```

```
    records++;                          // increment number of records
    EEPROM.put(0, records);             // update number of records
    EEPROM.put(EEaddress, data);        // write data to EEPROM
    EEPROM.commit();
    Serial.print("UV index ");Serial.println(data.UV);
                                        // display data
    lastTime = nowTime;                 // update time interval
  }
  if(cmd == 'D')                        // display data held on EEPROM
  {                                     // number of EEPROM records
    records = EEPROM.get(0, records);
    for (int i=0; i<records; i++)
    {
      EEaddress = i * Nbytes + 4;   // EEPROM address of ith record
      EEPROM.get(EEaddress, data); // read and display EEPROM
      Serial.print(data.minuteTime);Serial.print(":");
      Serial.print(data.secondTime);Serial.print("\t");
      Serial.println(data.UV);
    }
    cmd = ' ';                          // reset command
    Serial.print("Enter R: record, D: display");
    Serial.println(" or Z: zero UV record");
  }
  if(cmd == 'Z')                        // command to reset records
  {
    EEPROM.put(0, 0);                   // set record number to zero
    EEPROM.commit();
    cmd = ' ';
    Serial.print("Enter R: record, D: display");
    Serial.println(" or Z: zero UV record");
  }
}
```

Figure 20-3 illustrates using an ESP8266 or ESP32 microcontroller EEPROM to store measurements from an ultraviolet sensor, with connections given in Table 20-1. For an ESP32 development board, the analogRead instruction in Listing 20-2 is changed to data.UV = analogRead(N)*3300.0/4096, with the analog input pin number, N.

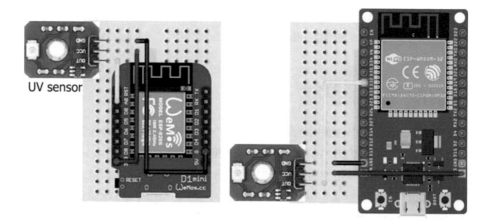

Figure 20-3. *EEPROM and ultraviolet sensor*

Table 20-1. *EEPROM and ultraviolet sensor with ESP8266 and ESP32 microcontrollers*

Component	ESP8266	ESP32
UV sensor OUT	A0	GPIO 32
UV sensor VCC	3V3	3V3
UV sensor GND	GND	GND

The number of bytes required to store a data record in EEPROM for a character, an integer, or a real number is 1, 4, or 4, respectively. When storing a string, the number of bytes depends on the string data type. The string defined as `String s = "ABCDEFGH"` requires 12 bytes of EEPROM, but the string defined as `char * s = "ABCDEFGH"` requires only 4 bytes, with s defined as a *pointer to char*, which points to an object of type *array of char* with length eight. The length of a string, s, is obtained with the instruction `s.length()` or `strlen(s)`, when the string data type is defined as `String`. or `char s[]`.

Saving to SPIFFS

SPIFFS (Serial Peripheral Interface Flash File System) is a file system for microcontrollers to write to and read from files stored in flash memory. The partition of flash memory for SPIFFS is adjusted within the Arduino IDE depending on the requirements of a sketch. For example, the default SPIFFS partition for an ESP32 microcontroller is 1472 kB. SPIFFS is used to store data files, files containing HTML and AJAX code for a web page, and image files.

The ES8266 and ESP32 microcontrollers use the *LittleFS* and *SPIFFS* libraries, respectively. The *LittleFS_esp32* library is available in the Arduino IDE, but currently Espressif supports the built-in *SPIFFS* library for the ESP32 microcontroller. Instruction parameters for accessing a file with the *LittleFS* and *SPIFFS* libraries are listed in Table 20-2. Note that double quotes around instruction parameters in Table 20-2 are required for the ESP8266 microcontroller, but not for the ESP32 microcontroller. SPIFFS has a flat structure as directories are not supported. A file with path *temp/filename.txt* creates a file called *temp/filename.txt* and not a file called *filename.txt* in the *temp* directory. The ESP8266 SPIFFS, with the *FS* library, is currently deprecated; and the *LittleFS* library, which is faster, is recommended. The only changes to instructions are replacing `#include<FS.h>` and `SPIFFS.function()` instructions with `#include<LittleFS.h>` and `LittleFS.function()` instructions. The `SPIFFS.rename()` instruction enables both the *dir* and *filename* components of */dir/filename.txt* to be changed, while `LittleFS.rename()` changes only the *filename* component. Further information is available at arduino-esp8266. readthedocs.io/en/2.7.4_a/filesystem.html.

Table 20-2. *SPIFFS instruction parameters for ESP8266 and ESP32 microcontrollers*

File Access	ESP8266 LittleFS Library	ESP32 SPIFFS Library
Read file from start	"r"	FILE_READ
Create/truncate file to write from start	"w"	FILE_WRITE
Append from end	"a"	FILE_APPEND

The sketch in Listing 20-3 demonstrates opening, writing to, reading from, renaming, and deleting a file stored in SPIFFS. Although SPIFFS has a flat structure, files are allocated to directories by prefixing the file name with a directory name, such as */temp/testfile.txt*. The *8-3* file naming convention, for the file name (eight characters) and extension (three characters), is recommended, given the limit of 31 characters for the directory and file name. The *SPIFFS* library file access parameters, "r", "w", and "a" in Table 20-2 are sufficient for applications, although the parameters "r+", "w+", and "a+" are also available.

Listing 20-3. Write to, read from, and append file with SPIFFS for the ESP8266 microcontroller

```
#include <LittleFS.h>                    // include LittleFS library
String filename = "/temp/testfile.txt"; // structure /dir/file
String newname = "/temp/newfile.txt";

void setup()
{
  Serial.begin(115200);                 // Serial Monitor baud rate
```

```
  if(LittleFS.begin()) Serial.println("initialised OK");
  dirContent("/");                        // contents of main directory
  dirContent("/temp");                    // contents of sub directory
  File file = LittleFS.open(filename, "w");     // open file to write
  file.println("ABC");
  file.println("123");                         // instead of print("xxx/n")
  file.close();
  fileContent(filename);                  // function display file content
  dirContent("/temp");
  file = LittleFS.open(filename, "a"); // append to file
  file.println("XYZ");
  file.close();
  LittleFS.rename(filename, newname);
                                    // change filename not directory
  fileContent(newname);
  dirContent("/temp");
  if(LittleFS.exists(filename)) LittleFS.remove(filename);
}                                            // delete file

void dirContent(String dname) // function to display directory content
{
  Serial.print(dname);Serial.println(" content");
  Dir dir = LittleFS.openDir(dname);
  while(dir.next())
  {
    File file = dir.openFile("r");         // read file
    Serial.print("file ");Serial.print(file.name());Serial.
    print("\t");
    Serial.print("size ");Serial.println(file.size()); // filesize
  }
}
```

```
void fileContent(String fname)        // function to display file content
{
  File file = LittleFS.open(fname, "r");
  while(file.available()) Serial.write(file.read());
  file.close();
}

void loop()                                  // nothing in loop function
{}
```

For the ESP32 microcontroller, other than changing the library from
LittleFS to *SPIFFS* and the file access parameters, the corresponding sketch
only differs from Listing 20-2 in the function to list files in a directory (see
Listing 20-4). The SPIFFS.rename() instruction enables both the *dir* and
filename components of */dir/filename.txt* to be changed, similar to the *FS*
library for the ESP8266 microcontroller.

Listing 20-4. List directory files with SPIFFS for the ESP32
microcontroller

```
void dirContent(String dname)
{
  Serial.print(dname);Serial.println(" content");
  File dir = SPIFFS.open(dname);           // SPIFFS library
  File file = dir.openNextFile();          // openNextFile
  while(file)
  {
    Serial.print("file ");Serial.print(file.name());
    Serial.print("\t");
    Serial.print("size ");Serial.println(file.size());
    file = dir.openNextFile();             // openNextFile
  }
}
```

Listing 20-3 illustrates using SPIFFS for data logging applications, with the instructions file.println("123") and file.println("XYZ"), for example. SPIFFS is also available for uploading files containing HTML and AJAX code for a web page or image files. The Arduino IDE requires a separate plugin for the ESP8266 and ESP32 microcontrollers, when uploading files to SPIFFS. Instructions for installing and running the plugin are available at arduino-esp8266.readthedocs.io/en/latest/filesystem.html and github.com/me-no-dev/arduino-esp32fs-plugin, respectively. The unzipped *esp8266littlefs.jar* or *esp32fs.jar* (Java Archive) file containing the plugin must be located in the *Sketchbook location* ➤ *tools* ➤ *ESP8266LittleFS* ➤ *tool* or *Sketchbook location* ➤ *tools* ➤ *ESP32FS* ➤ *tool* folder, where the *Sketchbook location* folder is defined in the Arduino IDE, by selecting *File* ➤ *Preferences*. If the Arduino IDE is open, then Arduino IDE must be closed and restarted, and the *Tools* menu will then include the *ESP8266 LittleFS Data Upload* or *ESP32 Sketch Data Upload* option.

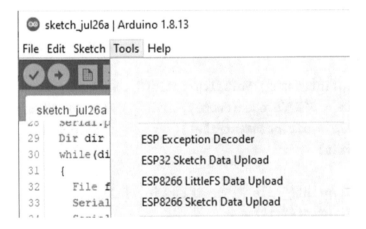

Figure 20-4. *Plugin details for uploading files to SPIFFS*

The text file containing HTML or AJAX code for a web page must be stored in the *data* folder within the sketch folder. In the Arduino IDE, select the *Sketch* menu, click *Show Sketch Folder,* and create a folder named *data*. A file *filename.txt* is referenced as */filename.txt* in the sketch. Prior to uploading the text file to the Arduino IDE, ensure that both *Board* and *Port* are selected and that the Serial Monitor is closed. In the Arduino IDE, select the *Tools* menu, and click the *ESP8266 LittleFS Data Upload* or *ESP32 Sketch Data Upload* option. Once the message *LittleFS Image Uploaded* or *SPIFFS Image Uploaded* is displayed, compile and upload the sketch.

In Chapter 8 (Updating a web page), HTML and AJAX code for a web page was included on a separate tab, *buildpage.h*, from the main sketch with the instruction `#include "buildpage.h"`. The default web page was loaded by the instruction `server.on("/", base)` referencing the *base* function to send the string *page* containing the HTML or AJAX code for the web page to the client, with the instruction `server.send (200, "text/html", page)`.

When HTML or AJAX code is included in a separate file, such as *webcode.txt*, that is uploaded to SPIFFS, then the separate tab, *buildpage.h*, is not required and the *base* function now uploads the file on SPIFFS that is then sent to the client. The *base* function is changed to

```
void base()
{
  File file = SPIFFS.open("/webcode.txt","r");   // file for webpage
  server.streamFile(file, "text/html");          // send file to server
  file.close();
}
```

Moreover, the first and last lines of the string containing the HTML or AJAX code, namely `char page[] PROGMEM = R"(`, and `)"` of the string *page* are deleted. Using the example of Listing 8-4, the first and last lines of the file *webpage.txt* are now `<!DOCTYPE html><html>` and `</body></html>`, respectively.

In Chapter 2 (Intranet camera), images are stored on the micro-SD card of the ESP32-CAM module with the instructions in Listing 2-1:

```
fs::FS & fs = SD_MMC;                      // with SD_MMC library,
File file = fs.open(filename.c_str(), FILE_WRITE);
                                           // access SD card
file.write(frame->buf, frame->len);        // save file to SD card
```

The ESP32-CAM module stores a JPEG-formatted image in SPIFFS with the instructions

```
File file = SPIFFS.open("/photo.jpg", FILE_WRITE);
                                               // access SPIFFS
file.write(frame->buf, frame->len);            // write file to SPIFFS
```

and the image size is displayed with the instructions

```
Serial.print("Image size: ");
Serial.println(String(frame->len));
```

In Chapter 2 (Intranet camera), ESP32-CAM images are uploaded to a web page from PROGMEM, as flash (or program) memory has more capacity than RAM, and uploading from PROGMEM is substantially faster than uploading from SPIFFS, which takes several seconds.

Downloading SPIFFS files

While data files containing HTML and AJAX code for a web page can remain stored in SPIFFS, data files stored in SPIFFS by a data logging sketch may require downloading to a computer or laptop for subsequent analysis by specific software. A sketch to analyze the data files, while stored in SPIFFS, is another option.

Files stored in SPIFFS are downloaded to a computer or laptop with the sketch in Listing 20-5. The *ESPAsyncWebServer* and *AsyncTCP* libraries by Hristo Gochkov are required, and *.zip* files containing the libraries are downloaded from github.com/me-no-dev/ESPAsyncWebServer and github.com/me-no-dev/AsyncTCP, respectively. The *ESPAsyncWebServer* library references the *AsyncTCP* and Wi-Fi libraries, so the instructions #include <AsyncTCP.h> and #include <WiFi.h> or #include <ESP8266WiFi.h> are not required. A directory list of the files held in SPIFFS is displayed on the Serial Monitor, and a selected file is then downloaded to the computer or laptop. The sketch includes an HTTP GET request for the file stored in SPIFFS to be downloaded. The default value of the last parameter of the request->send instruction is *false*, to indicate implementation of the file, as in a file containing HTML code, rather than downloading of the file. The user determines where the file is saved on the computer or laptop.

Listing 20-5. Downloading SPIFFS data file

```
#include <LittleFS.h>                    // include LittleFS and
#include <ESPAsyncWebServer.h>           // ESPAsyncWebServer libraries
AsyncWebServer server(80);
char ssid[] = "xxxx";                    // change xxxx to Wi-Fi ssid
char password[] = "xxxx";                // change xxxx to Wi-Fi password
String filename;                         // file to be downloaded

void setup()
{
  Serial.begin(115200);                  // define Serial Monitor baud rate
  WiFi.begin(ssid, password);            // initialise Wi-Fi
  while (WiFi.status() != WL_CONNECTED) delay(500);
  Serial.print("IP Address: ");
  Serial.println(WiFi.localIP());        // display WLAN IP address
  server.begin();                        // initialise server
  server.on("/download", HTTP_GET,
  [](AsyncWebServerRequest * request)
```

```
  { request->send(LittleFS, filename, "text/plain", true); });
  LittleFS.begin();                    // initialise SPIFFS
  dirContent("");                      // contents of main directory
  dirContent("temp");                  // content of "temp" sub-directory
  Serial.println("\nEnter directory/filename to download");
}

void loop()
{
  if(Serial.available() > 0)       // filename entered on Serial Monitor
  {
    filename = Serial.readString();            // read Serial buffer
    Serial.print("In the browser, enter ");
    Serial.print(WiFi.localIP());
    Serial.print("/download to download file: ");
    Serial.println(filename);
    Serial.println("\n\nEnter directory/filename to download");
  }
}

void dirContent(String dname)   // function to display directory content
{
  Serial.print("\nContent of directory: ");
  Serial.println(dname);
  Dir dir = LittleFS.openDir("/"+dname);
  while(dir.next())
  {
    File file = dir.openFile("r");                       // read file
    Serial.print(dname);Serial.print("/");
    Serial.print(file.name());Serial.print("\t");
    Serial.print("size ");Serial.println(file.size());
  }                                                      // filesize
}
```

Listing 20-5 is for an ESP8266 microcontroller. For an ESP32 microcontroller, the *LittleFS* library is replaced with the *SPIFFS* library; and, as with Listing 20-3, the *dirContent* function is changed to the function in Listing 20-4. In the *dirContent* function, the instruction File dir = SPIFFS.open(dname) is also changed to File dir = SPIFFS. open("/"+dname). The contents of the main and "temp" *directories* are separately displayed with the ESP8266 microcontroller, but the content of all *directories* is displayed with the instruction dirContent("") with the ESP32 microcontroller.

Saving data directly to Excel

The ESP8266 and ESP32 microcontrollers cannot emulate a USB device, such as a keyboard, to send a character or a string to a connected laptop or computer. However, the Arduino Pro Micro can emulate a USB device for automated data recording projects. For example, data collected by a sensor connected to a Pro Micro is sent to the connected laptop or computer and written directly to a Microsoft Excel file. Sensor data is plotted immediately, in contrast to the microcontroller storing data on an SD card, that is then imported to a Microsoft Excel file.

Keyboard emulation is started with the instruction Keyboard.begin(), but it is important to have a control system in place to end keyboard emulation by the Pro Micro; otherwise, the computer keyboard will not function. For example, changing the state of a GPIO pin, by pressing a switch connected to the Pro Micro, can trigger the instruction Keyboard. end() and end the Pro Micro keyboard emulation. A character or string, *str*, is sent to the attached computer with the instruction Keyboard. print(str) or Keyboard.println(str), with the latter including the

ASCII characters for a carriage return and a new line. Before loading a sketch using the keyboard emulation instructions, it is recommended to test the sketch with the `Serial.print()` or `Serial.println()` instruction and that the control system to stop the sketch operates correctly. The Pro Micro keyboard emulation will print to the open window that is currently running on the attached computer. While the sketch with the `Keyboard.print()` instructions is compiling in the Arduino IDE, the computer cursor must be positioned on a worksheet of the Microsoft Excel file.

The sketch in Listing 20-6 reads the temperature on a BMP280 sensor, measures the light intensity with a light-dependent resistor (LDR), and writes the data directly to the open Microsoft Excel worksheet. Keyboard emulation by the Pro Micro is stopped by pressing the switch with a pull-down resistor, which changes the state of the GPIO pin attached to the switch and triggers the `Keyboard.end()` instruction. In the sketch, data is written to the Microsoft Excel worksheet every five seconds. The ASCII characters for keyboard control of 9, 10, 11, and 13 for a horizontal tab, line feed, vertical tab, and carriage return are used to format data on the Microsoft Excel worksheet. For example, the tab keyboard control characters are sent to the connected laptop or computer with the instruction `Keyboard.print(char(9))`.

Listing 20-6. Saving data directly to an Excel file

```
#include <Keyboard.h>              // include Keyboard library
#include <Adafruit_Sensor.h>       // include Unified Sensor library
#include <Adafruit_BMP280.h>       // include BMP280 library
Adafruit_BMP280 bmp;               // associate bmp with BMP280
int BMPaddress = 0x76;             // I2C address of BMP280
int switchPin = A3;                // define switch and LDR pins
int LDRpin = 9;
unsigned long nowTime, lastTime = 0;
float temp, bright;
```

```
int counter = 0;

void setup()
{
  Keyboard.begin();                     // initialise Keyboard
  bmp.begin(BMPaddress);                // initialise BMP280
  header();                             // call header function
}

void loop()
{                                       // MUST BE ABLE TO STOP KEYBOARD
  if(digitalRead(switchPin) == HIGH)    // switch to stop Keyboard
  {
    Keyboard.end();                     // stop Keyboard
    while(1);                           // and do nothing else
  }
  nowTime = millis();                   // set start of time interval
  if(nowTime - lastTime > 5000)         // collect data every 5s
  {
    counter++;                          // increment counter
    temp = bmp.readTemperature();       // get BMP280 reading
    bright = analogRead(LDRpin);        // and brightness reading
    Keyboard.print(counter);            // print counter to Excel
    Keyboard.print(char(9));            // print tab character
    Keyboard.print(temp);               // print temp to Excel
    Keyboard.print(char(9));            // print bright to Excel, with
    Keyboard.println(bright);           // carriage return and new line
    lastTime = nowTime;                 // update start of time interval
  }
}
```

```
void header()                      // function to print columns headers to Excel
{
  Keyboard.print("counter");       // print "counter" to Excel
  Keyboard.print(char(9));         // print tab character
  Keyboard.print("temp");
  Keyboard.print(char(9));
  Keyboard.print("bright");
  Keyboard.print(char(13));        // print carriage return character
  Keyboard.print(char(10));        // print new line character
}
```

Connections for the Pro Micro, BMP280, and LDR are shown in Figure 20-5 and listed in Table 20-3. Note the importance of ensuring that there is a reliable control system to stop the keyboard emulation function, while the sketch is running, as otherwise keyboard control of the attached computer is compromised.

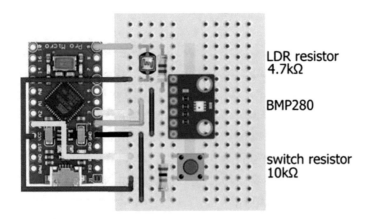

Figure 20-5. *Pro Micro with BMP280 sensor and light-dependent resistor*

Table 20-3. *Saving data directly to an Excel file*

Component	Connect to	And to
BMP280 VCC	Pro Micro 3.3V	
BMP280 GND	Pro Micro GND	
BMP280 SDI (Serial data)	Pro Micro pin 2	
BMP280 SCK (serial clock)	Pro Micro pin 3	
BMP280 CSB (chip select)	Not connected	
BMP280 SDO (serial data out)	Pro Micro GND	
LDR top leg	Pro Micro pin 9	
LDR top leg	10 kΩ resistor	Pro Micro GND
LDR bottom leg	Pro Micro 3.3V	
Switch top leg	Pro Micro pin A3	
Switch top leg	10 kΩ resistor	Pro Micro GND
Switch bottom leg	Pro Micro 3.3V	

Summary

OTA (over the air) updating is described to remotely upload a sketch to a ESP8266 or ESP32 microcontroller. The EEPROM (Electrically Erasable Programmable Read-Only Memory) and SPIFFS (Serial Peripheral Interface Flash File System) partitions of flash memory of the ESP8266 and ESP32 microcontrollers are used to save data or files or images. Saving data on the microcontroller internal EEPROM is described with an example of storing and retrieving sensor measurements. Storing files on SPIFFS is described with an example of creating, writing to, reading from, renaming, and deleting a file. A file containing HTML or AJAX code for a web page is uploaded to SPIFFS with the *Sketch Data Upload* plugin for the Arduino IDE. Data is also saved directly to a Microsoft Excel worksheet with an Arduino Pro Micro emulating a keyboard, with an example given of temperature and light intensity measurements.

Components List

- ESP8266 microcontroller: LOLIN (WeMos) D1 mini or NodeMCU board

- ESP32 microcontroller: DEVKIT DOIT or NodeMCU board

- Arduino Pro Micro

- Ultraviolet sensor

- Temperature sensor: BMP280

- Light-dependent resistor

- Tactile switch

- Resistors: 4.7 kΩ, 10 kΩ

CHAPTER 21

Microcontrollers

Several microcontrollers are used in the book, depending on the required function of the microcontroller. The LOLIN (WeMos) D1 mini board, based on the ESP8266 microcontroller, is used in applications requiring Wi-Fi connectivity. The ESP32 DEVKIT DOIT board, based on the ESP32 microcontroller, is ideal for applications requiring intense data processing with either Wi-Fi or Bluetooth connectivity. The ESP32-CAM board, which is based on the ESP32-S microcontroller, is the obvious choice for applications requiring both a camera and Wi-Fi functionality. The Arduino Pro Micro emulates a USB device, such as a keyboard, in applications that store data directly to a Microsoft Excel spreadsheet. The Arduino Uno and the smaller Arduino Nano, both based on the ATmega328P microcontroller, are appropriate for applications when Wi-Fi connectivity or high processing power is not required. Table 21-1 summarizes some of the properties of the microcontrollers, with further information available from www.arduino.cc/en/Main/Products or from www.espressif.com/en/products/devkits. The ESP8266 and ESP32 microcontrollers have significantly higher CPU frequencies, with more flash memory and RAM (random access memory) than the ATmega328P microcontroller. A sketch is stored in flash memory, while sketch variables are stored in RAM.

© Neil Cameron 2021
N. Cameron, *Electronics Projects with the ESP8266 and ESP32*,
https://doi.org/10.1007/978-1-4842-6336-5_21

Table 21-1. *Microcontroller properties*

Property	ESP32	ESP8266	ATmega328P	ATmega32U4
Development board	DEVKIT DOIT	LOLIN (WeMos) D1 mini	Arduino Uno/Nano	Arduino Pro Micro
Architecture	32-bit	32-bit	8-bit	8-bit
CPU frequency	240 MHz	160 MHz	16 MHz	16 MHz for 5V
Flash memory	4 MB	4 MB	32 kB	32 kB
(S)RAM	520 kB	<50 kB	2 kB	2.5 kB
Time for 10k primes	385 ms	1786 ms	56732 ms	57027 ms

All development boards have PWM (pulse width modulation) pins and ADC (analog to digital converter) pins. The ESP8266 and ESP32 microcontrollers both have Wi-Fi connectivity, with the ESP32 microcontroller also having both Bluetooth and Bluetooth Low Energy connectivity, DAC (digital to analog converter) pins, touch-sensitive pins, and a Hall effect sensor, (see Chapter 22 (ESP32 microcontroller features)).

The result of higher CPU frequency, flash memory, and RAM is the lower processing time for a sketch. For example, the sketch in Listing 21-1 measures the time required to determine the first 10k prime numbers. The sketch may not be optimal, in terms of minimizing processing time, but is sufficient for establishing a benchmark. The ATmega microcontroller required 57 seconds to perform the task, while the ESP8266 and ESP32 microcontrollers required under two seconds and less than half a second, respectively. The CPU frequency of the ESP32 microcontroller is changed, in the Arduino IDE, to 10, 20, 40, 80, or 160 MHz by selecting *Tools* ➤ *CPU Frequency*. As the CPU frequency doubles, the time to determine the first 10k prime numbers essentially halves from 11607 ms with 10 MHz to 5060 ms with 20 MHz, to 2403 ms with 40 MHz, to 1172 ms with 80 MHz, and to 579 ms with 160 MHz.

Listing 21-1. Determine the first 10k prime numbers

```
int Nprimes = 9999;                    // required number of primes - 1
unsigned long number = 2;              // start from number 2
int count = 1;                         // prime number counter
unsigned int start = 0;                // store processing time
unsigned long ms;
int chk, limit, mod, divid;

void setup()
{
  Serial.begin(115200);                // Serial Monitor baud rate
  while(!Serial);                      // wait for Pro Micro to connect Serial
  Serial.print("\nCPU "); Serial.println(F_CPU/1000000);
  start = millis();                    // start of processing time
}

void loop()
{
  number++;                            // increment number to check
  chk = is_prime(number);
  if (chk > 0) count++;                // increment counter when prime
  if (count > Nprimes)
  {
    ms = millis() - start;             // display results
    Serial.print("Found ");
    Serial.print(count);
    Serial.print(" primes in ");
    Serial.print(ms);
    Serial.println(" ms");
    Serial.print("Highest prime is ");
```

```
   Serial.println(number);
   delay(50000);                        // long delay when finished
  }
}

int is_prime(unsigned long num)  // function to check if prime number
{
  mod = num % 2;                       // exclude even numbers
  if (mod == 0) return 0;
  limit = sqrt(num);                   // check divisors less than square root
  for (int divid = 3; divid <= limit; divid = divid + 2)
  {
    mod = num % divid;                 // remainder after dividing
    if (mod == 0) return 0;            // not prime if zero remainder
  }
  return 1;                            // no divisor with zero remainder
}
```

The development boards have different pin layouts and installation and sketch loading requirements, so details of each development board are described separately. Information on the pin layout of a development board that is accessible with the Arduino IDE is listed in the file *pins_arduino*, which is located in the file *user* ➤ *AppData* ➤ *Local* ➤ *Arduino15* ➤ *packages* ➤ *microcontroller* ➤ *hardware* ➤ *category* ➤ *version* ➤ *variants* ➤ *board*, where *microcontroller, category, version,* and *board* correspond to the particular development board. For example, pin layout information on the LOLIN (WeMos) D1 mini board is located in the file *user* ➤ *AppData* ➤ *Local* ➤ *Arduino15* ➤ *packages* ➤ *esp8266* ➤ *hardware* ➤ *esp8266* ➤ *version* ➤ *variants* ➤ *d1_mini*.

Information on the microcontroller CPU frequency and GPIO (General-Purpose Input-Output) pins allocated to SPI (Serial Peripheral Interface) and I2C (Inter-Integrated Circuit) communication is obtained within the Arduino IDE framework. The sketch in Listing 21-2 also provides information about the sketch itself. The sketch is run with any microcontroller that is accessible by the Arduino IDE.

Listing 21-2. Microcontroller information

```
String str, adjStr;

void setup()
{
  Serial.begin(115200);            // Serial Monitor baud rate
  Serial.println();
  while(!Serial);                  // Pro Micro wait for serial port
  Serial.print("Arduino IDE version ");
  str = String(ARDUINO);           // Arduino IDE version
  adjStr = str.substring(1,str.length()-5)+".";
  adjStr = adjStr + str.substring(str.length()-4,
  str.length()-2)+".";
  adjStr = adjStr + str.substring(str.length()-2);
  Serial.println(adjStr);          // date and time sketch compiled
  Serial.print("Compiler version");
  Serial.println(__VERSION__);
  Serial.print("Compiled date"); Serial.println(__DATE__);
  Serial.print("Compiled time"); Serial.println(__TIME__);
  Serial.print("Sketch location"); Serial.println(__FILE__);
  Serial.print("CPU frequency(MHz)");      // CPU frequency
  Serial.println(F_CPU/1000000);
  Serial.print("Development board");
  Serial.println(ARDUINO_BOARD);
  #ifdef __AVR__                    // development board
    Serial.print("Microcontroller");
    Serial.println(ARDUINO_MCU);
```

```
#endif                           // microcontroller
Serial.print("SPI MOSI");Serial.println(MOSI);  // pin layout SPI
Serial.print("SPI MISO");Serial.println(MISO);
Serial.print("SPI SCK");Serial.println(SCK);
Serial.print("SPI SS");Serial.println(SS);
Serial.print("I2C SDA");Serial.println(SDA);  // pin layout I2C
Serial.print("I2C SCL");Serial.println(SCL);
#ifndef ESP32
Serial.print("LED");Serial.println(LED_BUILTIN);  // built-in LED
#endif
}

void loop()                      // nothing in loop function
{}
```

The parameters *ARDUINO_BOARD* and *ARDUINO_MCU* are generated by instructions based on line 58 of the *platform.txt* file that refers to compiling *C++* files. The line starts with *recipe.cpp.o.pattern*. The *platform. txt* file is located in *user* ➤ *AppData* ➤ *Local* ➤ *Arduino15* ➤ *packages* ➤ *arduino* ➤ *hardware* ➤ *avr* ➤ *version*. The line from the *platform.txt* file is pasted into a new file, *platform.local.txt*, with the addition of

-DARDUINO_BOARD="{build.board}" and -DARDUINO_ MCU="{build.mcu}". The file *platform.local.txt* is stored in the same folder as the *platform.txt* file. When the sketch is compiled, the two variables are accessible. The parameter *ARDUINO_BOARD* already exists for the ESP8266 and ESP32 microcontrollers, and the parameter *ARDUINO_MCU* does not need to be displayed for ESP8266 and ESP32 microcontrollers.

Listing 21-2 includes the compiler directives of *#ifdef* and *#endif,* for the compiler to determine if the microcontroller is defined as AVR based, *__AVR__*, or not defined as an ESP32 and then only incorporate the relevant instructions in the compilation process. The compiler directives of *#if, #elif,* and *#else* correspond to *if* with a condition, *else if,* and *else* in the C language. The directive *#ifndef* is equivalent to *if not defined as*. The compiler directive *#ifdef* must be followed by an *#endif* directive.

Microcontrollers are broadly grouped as AVR based (*__AVR__*), *ESP8266,* and *ESP32*. AVR may be an acronym of the inventors of the AVR architecture: **A**lf-Egil Bogen and **V**egard Wollan **R**ISC processor. Details of specific microcontroller groupings are listed in the Arduino, ESP8266, or ESP32 *boards.txt* file that is located in the same directory as the *platform. txt* file, with a grouping defined by *board.build*. Examples of specific ESP8266 or ESP32 microcontroller groupings are *ESP8266_WEMOS_ D1MINI* and *ESP8266_NODEMCU* or *ESP32_DEV* and *FEATHER_ESP32*. If a specific microcontroller grouping is used in a compiler directive, then the grouping is preceded with *ARDUINO_*, as in #ifdef ARDUINO_ESP32_DEV.

The Arduino IDE has predefined values for the constants π, e, π/180, and 180/π, defined as PI, EULER, DEG_TO_RAD, and RAD_TO_DEG, respectively. Values are located in the file *Program Files (x86)* ➤ *Arduino* ➤ *hardware* ➤ *arduino* ➤ *avr* ➤ *cores* ➤ *arduino* ➤ *Arduino*.

Arduino Uno

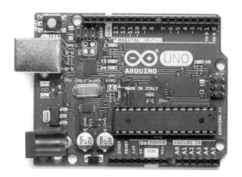

The Arduino Uno is based on the ATmega328P microcontroller, and the development board operates at 5 V, powered through a USB connection at 5 V or a DC input jack at 7–12 V. The maximum current supply from a GPIO pin is 40 mA, with a maximum current from all output pins of 200 mA. In a sketch, GPIO pins are referenced by the numbering on the development board and not by the GPIO pin numbers of the ATmega328P microcontroller. The exception is the ADC pins A0–A5 which are also referenced as pin numbers 14–19. Communication pins for I2C are A4 (SDA) and A5 (SCL)

and for SPI are 11 (MOSI), 12 (MISO), 13 (SCK), and 10 (SS). PWM pins are 3, 5, 6, 9, 10, and 11. Interrupt pins, *INT0* and *INT1*, are 2 and 3. The built-in LED is on pin 13.

Arduino Nano

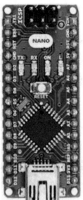

Transmit
Receive

Ground
Interrupt0
Interrupt1

Digital
inputs

SPI SS
SPI MOSI
SPI MISO

Voltage input (6-20V)
Ground

5V output
Analog input only
Analog input only
I2C SCL
I2C SDA

Analog inputs

AREF
3.3V output
SPI SCK, LED

The Arduino Nano has the same ATmega328P microcontroller as the Arduino Uno and the same pin functionality, except that pins A6 and A7 are analog input only. Digital pins are prefixed with *D* on the development board. The development board operates at 5 V and is powered through a mini-USB connection at 5 V.

In January 2018, Arduino released a new bootloader for the Arduino Nano, so the relevant processor must be selected in the Arduino IDE. In the *Tools* ➤ *Processor* menu, select either the *ATmega328P* option or the *ATmega328P (Old Bootloader)* option.

Arduino Pro Micro

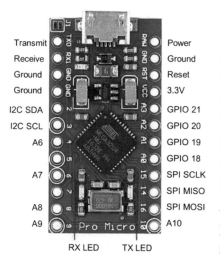

Transmit	Power
Receive	Ground
Ground	Reset
Ground	3.3V
I2C SDA	GPIO 21
I2C SCL	GPIO 20
A6	GPIO 19
	GPIO 18
A7	SPI SCLK
	SPI MISO
A8	SPI MOSI
A9	A10

RX LED   TX LED

In the Arduino IDE, the Arduino Pro Micro is referenced as the Arduino Leonardo in the *Tools* ➤ *Board* menu. The development board operates at 5 V and is powered through a mini-USB connection at 5 V. In a sketch, pins are referenced by the numbering on the development board and not by the GPIO pin numbers of the ATmega32U4 microcontroller. The ADC pins A0–A3 are also referenced as pin numbers 18–21. Pins 4, 6, 8, 9, and 10 correspond to the ADC pins A6–A10.

Communication pins for I2C are 2 (SDA) and 3 (SCL) and for SPI are 16 (MOSI), 14 (MISO), and 15 (SCK). PWM pins are 3, 5, 6, 9, and 10. Interrupt pins, *INT0, INT1, INT2, INT3,* and *INT6,* are 3, 2, 0 (RX), 1 (TX), and 7. The built-in RX and TX LEDs are on pins 17 and 30, which are active *LOW,* and are automatically defined as *OUTPUT* pins. The TX LED is turned off or on with the built-in macro *TXLED0* or *TXLED1*, respectively (see Listing 21-3). When the *TXLED0* and *TXLED1* macros are not utilized, then the *TXLED* pin must be defined.

Listing 21-3. Controlling Pro Micro LEDs

```
int RXLED = 17;            // define RXLED pin
//int TXLED = 30;          // required if not using macros

void setup()
{}                         // nothing in setup function
```

```
void loop()
{
  digitalWrite(RXLED, HIGH);      // turn off RXLED
// digitalWrite(TXLED, HIGH);      // turn off TXLED
  TXLED0;                          // macro to turn off TXLED
  delay(1000);
  digitalWrite(RXLED, LOW);       // turn on RXLED
// digitalWrite(TXLED, LOW);       // turn on TXLED
  TXLED1;                          // macro to turn on TXLED
  delay(1000);
}
```

When a sketch uploads, the ATmega32U4 bootloader Serial port opens and then closes after the sketch is uploaded. The ATmega32U4 Serial port then opens, so the COM port may change after a sketch is loaded. The instruction while(!Serial) waits until the Serial connection is established. The ATmega32U4 microcontroller does not reset when a COM port is opened, unlike ATmega328P of the Arduino Uno.

The Arduino Pro Micro microcontroller is reset by connecting the reset (RST) pin, which has a pull-up resistor, to GND twice to put the Arduino Pro Micro microcontroller into bootloader mode for an eight-second period, before a sketch is started. The ATmega32U4 microcontroller may become un-programmable or *bricked* if a problem occurs when uploading a sketch that uses the *Keyboard* library or with an incorrectly defined microcontroller, such as a 16 MHz/5 V microcontroller defined as 8 MHz/3.3 V. The bootloader may have to be reinstalled, and the *Atmega_Board_Programmer* by Nick Gammon is recommended, which is downloaded from githib.com/nickgammon/arduino_sketches.

ESP8266 development board

The LOLIN (WeMos) D1 mini development board (see Figure 21-1) is based on the ESP-8266EX microcontroller and has Wi-Fi functionality. The development board operates at 3.3 V and is powered through a micro-USB connection at 5 V, through the 3.3 V voltage regulator, or directly on the 3.3 V pin, but the former connection is recommended. The pins are not 5 V tolerant, and the maximum current supply from a pin is 12 mA.

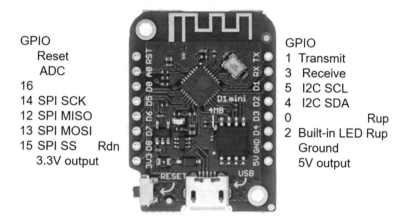

Figure 21-1. *LOLIN (WeMos) D1 mini development board*

In a sketch, pins are referenced by either the numbering on the development board prefixed by the letter *D* for digital pins or by the ESP-8266EX microcontroller GPIO numbers. The ADC pin is A0 and has 10-bit resolution. Pins for I2C communication are D2 or GPIO 4 (SDA) and D1 or GPIO 5 (SCL) and for SPI communication are D7 or GPIO 13 (MOSI), D6 or GPIO 12 (MISO), D5 or GPIO 14 (SCK), and D8 or GPIO 15 (SS). The four digital pins, D2, D6, D5, and D8 or GPIO 4, GPIO 12, GPIO 14, and GPIO 15, have 10-bit PWM resolution and interrupt functionality. The built-in LED on pin D4 or GPIO 2 is active *LOW*. Note that pins D3 or GPIO 0 and D4 or GPIO 2 have built-in pull-up resistors, while pin D8 or GPIO 15 has a built-in pull-down resistor. When uploading a sketch, pins D3 and D4 must not be pulled *LOW,* and similarly pin D8 must not be pulled *HIGH*. In Figures 21-1 and 21-2, a built-in pull-up or pull-down resistor is indicated by *Rup* or *Rdn*.

The CH340G USB to UART (Universal Asynchronous Receiver-Transmitter) driver for the LOLIN (WeMos) D1 mini is downloaded from docs.wemos.cc/en/latest/ch340_driver.html. Save the *CH341SER_WIN_3.5* zip file on the Desktop, right-click *Extract All,* and in the extracted folder *CH341SER_WIN_3.5* right-click the *SETUP* application, select *Run as administrator,* and install the driver *CH341S64.SYS*. Drivers are located in the *C:* ➤ *Windows* ➤ *System32* ➤ *drivers* folder.

The NodeMCU ESP8266 development board (see Figure 21-2) has the same effective functionality as the LOLIN (WeMos) D1 mini development board. The NodeMCU ESP8266 development board has three 3.3V pins and four GND pins for connecting to other devices and two built-in LEDs on pins D4 or GPIO 2 and D0 or GPIO 16, which are active *LOW*. The ESP8266 microcontroller stores a sketch in an external flash memory chip and communicates with the flash chip over an SDIO (Secure Digital Input-Output) interface. The NodeMCU ESP8266 development board GPIO 6–11 pins correspond to the SDIO interface pins labeled CLK, SD0, SD1, SD2, SD3, and CMD.

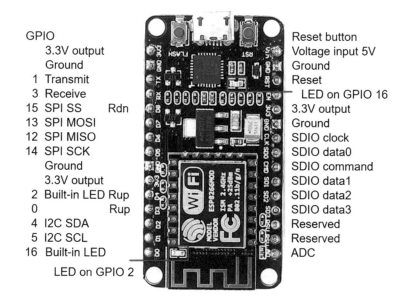

GPIO					
	3.3V output				Reset button
	Ground				Voltage input 5V
1	Transmit				Ground
3	Receive				Reset
15	SPI SS	Rdn			LED on GPIO 16
13	SPI MOSI				3.3V output
12	SPI MISO				Ground
14	SPI SCK				SDIO clock
	Ground				SDIO data0
	3.3V output				SDIO command
2	Built-in LED	Rup			SDIO data1
0		Rup			SDIO data2
4	I2C SDA				SDIO data3
5	I2C SCL				Reserved
16	Built-in LED				Reserved
	LED on GPIO 2				ADC

Figure 21-2. *NodeMCU ESP8266 development board*

The *CP210x USB to UART Bridge* driver for the NodeMCU ESP8266 development board is downloaded from www.silabs.com/products/ development-tools/software/usb-to-uart-bridge-vcp-drivers. Save the *CP210x_Universal_Windows_Driver* zip file on the Desktop and right-click *Extract All*. In the extracted folder *CHP210x_Universal_Windows_ Driver*, right-click either the *x64* or *x86* version of the *CP210xVCPInstaller* application for a 64-bit or a 32-bit operating system, respectively. To determine if a computer has a 64-bit or a 32-bit operating system, select *Control Panel* ➤ *System and Security* ➤ *System*, and the system type is displayed. Select *Run as administrator* and install the driver *silabser.sys*. Drivers are located in the *C:* ➤ *Windows* ➤ *System32* ➤ *Drivers* folder. The computer may need to be restarted to complete the driver installation.

For both the LOLIN (WeMos) D1 mini and NodeMCU ESP8266 development boards, select *File* ➤ *Preferences* in the Arduino IDE and enter the URL `http://arduino.esp8266.com/stable/package_esp8266com_index.json` in the *Additional Boards Manager URLs* box. If there is already a URL in the box, then separate the URLs with a comma.

ESP8266 libraries are installed in the Arduino IDE by selecting *Tools* ➤ *Board* ➤ *Boards Manager*, entering *8266* in the *Filter* option to display *esp8266* by *ESP8266 Community,* and clicking *Install.* In the *Tools* ➤ *Board* drop-down list, select *LOLIN(WEMOS) D1 R2 & mini,* as listed in the *ESP8266 Boards* section. In *Tools* ➤ *CPU Frequency,* select 160 MHz; and in *Tools* ➤ *Port,* select the relevant COM port.

Reference documentation for the ESP8266 microcontroller is available at `arduino-esp8266.readthedocs.io/en/latest/index.html`.

ESP8266 analog input

The ESP8266 microcontroller 10-bit analog to digital converter (ADC) functionality converts a voltage, between 0 and 3.2 V, on the analog input pin *A0* to a digital value between 0 and 1023. The instruction `analogRead(A0)` reads the voltage on the analog input pin *A0*. The reference voltage of the ESP8266 microcontroller ADC is 1 volt; and an internal voltage divider, consisting of 100 kΩ and 220 kΩ resistors (see Figure 21-3), increases the maximum voltage on the analog input pin to 3.2 V. Given a voltage, V_{IN}, on the ESP8266 development board analog input pin, the corresponding ADC value is $V_{IN} \times \dfrac{100\,k\Omega}{(220+100)\,k\Omega} \times 1024$.

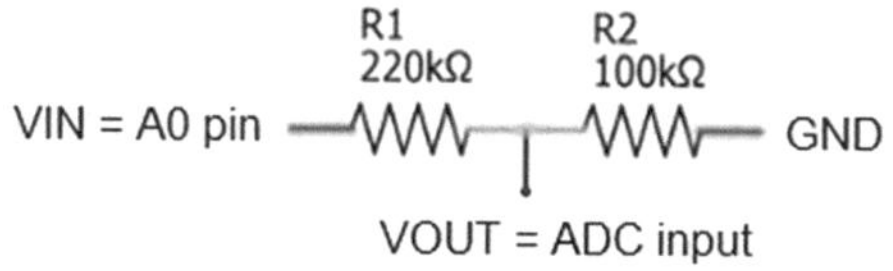

R1
220kΩ

R2
100kΩ

VIN = A0 pin ──/\/\/\──┬──/\/\/\── GND

VOUT = ADC input

Figure 21-3. *Analog to digital converter*

ADC values for input voltages between 3.2 V and 3.3 V are constrained to 1023. A 10 kΩ resistor connected between the input voltage and the ESP8266 development board analog input pin increases the limit of 3.2 V on the analog input pin to 3.3V.

ESP8266 interrupts

An interrupt is attached to a pin on the ESP8266 development board, such as pins D1–D7 of the LOLIN (WeMos) D1 mini, with the instruction `attach Interrupt(digitalPinToInterrupt(switchPin), change, FALLING)` (see Figure 21-4, left side). The switch is connected to GND and the switch pin on the ESP8266 development board. The instruction `pinMode(switchPin, INPUT_PULLUP)` activates the internal pull-up resistor on the switch pin, so the switch pin state is *HIGH*. When the switch is pressed, the switch pin is connected to GND, changing the switch pin state to *LOW*, with the *FALLING* state activating the interrupt. The ESP8266 microcontroller stores compiled code in internal RAM (IRAM), rather than in the slower flash memory, by prefixing sketch instructions with the *IRAM_ATTR* attribute. The interrupt ISR is defined as `IRAM_ATTR void ISR()` rather than void `ISR()`. If the interrupt ISR is defined before the sketch *setup* function, then the ISR definition instruction is changed to `void IRAM_ATTR ISR()`.

In contrast, if the switch pin is D8, then the switch is connected to 3.3V and the switch pin on the development board (see Figure 21-4, right side). Pin D8 has a built-in pull-down resistor, so the pin state is *LOW*. The interrupt is attached to pin D8 with the instruction `attachInterrupt` (`digitalPinToInterrupt(switchPin)`, `change`, `RISING`). When the switch pin is pressed, the switch pin state changes to *HIGH*, with the *RISING* state activating the interrupt. The *RISING* interrupt with pin D8 as the switch pin is less susceptible to switch bouncing than the *FALLING* interrupt on pins D1–D7. Note that the difference between the two circuits in Figure 21-4 is the switch pin is connected to pins D7 and GND or the switch pin is connected to D8 and 3.3V.

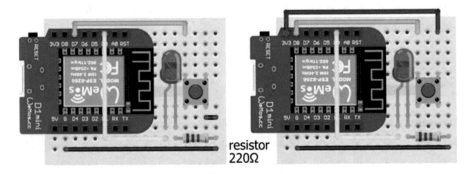

resistor
220Ω

Figure 21-4. *Interrupts with LOLIN (WeMos) D1 mini*

The sketch in Listing 21-4 illustrates the difference between interrupts attached to ESP8266 development board pins D7 and D8. When the interrupt is attached to pin D7, the pin is defined as `INPUT_PULLUP` to activate the built-in pull-up resistor, and the interrupt is activated on a *FALLING* signal. If the interrupt is attached to pin D8, then a *RISING* signal activates the interrupt.

Listing 21-4. Interrupts with the ESP8266 development board

```
int LEDpin = D0;                          // define LED pin
int switchPin = D7;                       // define switch pin
volatile int LEDstate = LOW;              // initial LED state
                                          // volatile as LEDstate in ISR
void setup()
{
  Serial.begin(115200);                   // Serial Monitor baud rate
  pinMode(LEDpin, OUTPUT);                // define LEDpin as OUTPUT
  pinMode(switchPin, INPUT_PULLUP);  // when switch pin is D1 to D7
  attachInterrupt(digitalPinToInterrupt(switchPin), change,
  FALLING);                              // when switch pin is D8
// attachInterrupt(digitalPinToInterrupt(switchPin), change,
// RISING);
}

void loop()
{
  Serial.println(digitalRead(switchPin)); // display switch pin state
  delay(1000);
}

IRAM_ATTR void change()                   // interrupt service routine (ISR)
{
  LEDstate = 1-LEDstate;                  // change LED state
  digitalWrite(LEDpin, LEDstate);         // turn LED on or off
}
```

ESP8266 watchdog timer

If an ESP8266 microcontroller is prevented from performing background tasks by a long period of inactivity during a sketch, then the watchdog timer may initiate a software reset. Background tasks include maintaining a Wi-Fi connection or managing the TCP/IP (Transmission Control Protocol/Internet Protocol) Internet connection. A software reset is indicated by the messages *Soft WDT reset* and *rst cause:2, boot mode:(3,6)*. Including the instruction delay(1) or yield() in the sketch at the point of inactivity may resolve the software reset. The yield() instruction allows completion of background tasks.

The sketch location of the software reset by the watchdog timer is determined with the *ESP Exception Decoder*. Instructions for installing and running the *ESP Exception Decoder* are outlined at arduino-esp8266. readthedocs.io/en/latest/faq/a02-my-esp-crashes.html. The *ESP Exception Decoder* is downloaded from github.com/me-no-dev/ EspExceptionDecoder. The unzipped *EspExceptionDecoder.jar* (Java Archive) file containing the *ESP Exception Decoder* must be located in the *Sketchbook location* ➤ *tools* ➤ *EspExceptionDecoder* ➤ *tool* folder, where the *Sketchbook location* folder is defined in the Arduino IDE, by selecting *File* ➤ *Preferences*.

A hardware reset by the watchdog timer is indicated with the messages *wdt reset* and *rst cause:4, boot mode:(3,6)*. The location of the hardware reset in a sketch is not determined with the *ESP Exception Decoder*, so a series of Serial.println() instructions is used to determine the last successful instruction before the hardware reset.

ESP32 development board

The ESP32 development board, such as the ESP32 DEVKIT DOIT, is based on the ESP32 microcontroller and has both Wi-Fi and Bluetooth functionality. The development board operates at 3.3 V and is powered through a micro-USB connection at 5 V or directly on the 3.3V *VIN* pin, but the former connection is recommended. The GPIO pins are not 5 V tolerant, and the maximum current supply from a pin is 12 mA.

In a sketch, pins are referenced by ESP32 microcontroller GPIO numbers. There are six ADC pins (GPIO 32, GPIO 33, GPIO 34, GPIO 35, GPIO 36, and GPIO 39) with 12-bit resolution and two DAC (digital to analog converter) pins (GPIO 25 and GPIO 26) with 8-bit resolution. Communication pins for I2C are GPIO 21 (SDA) and GPIO 22 (SCL) and for SPI are GPIO 23 (MOSI), GPIO 19 (MISO), GPIO 18 (CLK), and GPIO 5 (CS). All GPIO pins, except the input-only pins (GPIO 34, GPIO 35, GPIO 36, and GPIO 39), are PWM pins; and all GPIO pins have interrupt functionality. There are nine capacitive touch pins (GPIO 2, GPIO 4, GPIO 12, GPIO 13, GPIO 14, GPIO 15, GPIO 27, GPIO 32, and GPIO 33). The built-in LED is on GPIO 2, and the LED is active *HIGH*. Several pins are available to the real-time clock to trigger the ESP32 microcontroller from sleep mode. Internal pull-up resistors are connected to GPIO pins 0, 5, 14, and 15 with pull-down resistors on GPIO pins 2,4, and 12. The ESP32 microcontroller contains a Hall effect sensor. Pin layouts of the ESP32 DEVKIT DOIT and NodeMCU development boards with 30 and 38 pins are shown in Figures 21-5 and 21-6, respectively, to illustrate development board differences. Pin functions are coded as *A#*, analog input; *T#*, capacitive touch; *input*, input only; *RTC*, real-time clock; *Rup*, built-in pull-up resistor; and *Rdn*, built-in pull-down resistor. GPIO 6–11 pins of the NodeMCU development board are connected to the integrated flash memory, and use of the pins is not recommended.

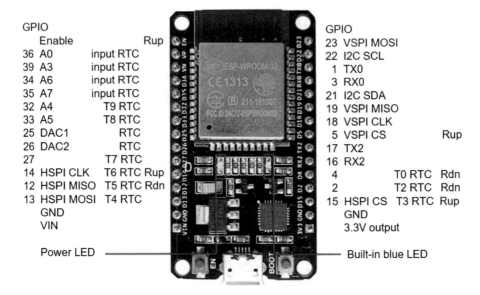

Figure 21-5. *ESP32 DEVKIT DOIT 30-pin layout*

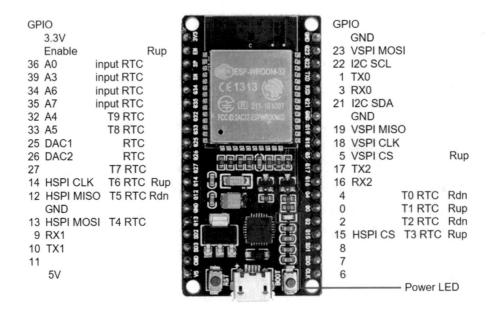

Figure 21-6. *ESP32 NodeMCU 36-pin layout*

The *CP210x USB to UART Bridge* driver for the ESP32 development board is downloaded from `www.silabs.com/products/development-tools/software/usb-to-uart-bridge-vcp-drivers`. Save the *CP210x_Universal_Windows_Driver* zip file on the Desktop and right-click *Extract All*. In the extracted folder *CP210x_Universal_Windows_Driver*, right-click either the *x64* or *x86* version of the *CP210xVCPInstaller* application for a 64-bit or a 32-bit operating system, respectively. To determine if a computer has a 64-bit or a 32-bit operating system, select *Control Panel ➤ System and Security ➤ System,* and the system type is displayed. Select *Run as administrator* and install the driver *silabser.sys*. Drivers are located in the *C: ➤ Windows ➤ System32 ➤ Drivers* folder. The computer may need to be restarted to complete the driver installation.

In the Arduino IDE, select *File ➤ Preferences* and enter the URL `https://dl.espressif.com/dl/package_esp32_index.json` in the *Additional Boards Manager URLs* box. If there is already a URL in the box, then separate the URLs with a comma.

ESP32 libraries are installed in the Arduino IDE by selecting *Tools ➤ Board ➤ Boards Manager*, entering *ESP32* in the *Filter* option to display *esp32* by *Espressif Systems,* and clicking *Install*. In the *Tools ➤ Board* drop-down list, select *ESP32 Dev Board* or your specific ESP32 development board as listed in the *ESP32 Boards* section. In *Tools ➤ Upload Speed, CPU Frequency, Flash Frequency, Flash Mode, Flash Size,* and *Partition Scheme*, select *921600, 240MHz (WiFI/BT), 80MHz, DIO, 4MB (32Mb),* and *Default 4MB with spiffs*, respectively. The SPI Flash Mode setting of *QIO* (Quad Input/Output) is faster than the *DIO* (Dual Input/Output) setting, but not all settings are available to each device. After loading a sketch, the message *rst:0x3 (SW_RESET),boot:0x13 (SPI_FAST_FLASH_BOOT)* is displayed if the *QIO* setting is unsupported. Further details are available at `github.com/espressif/esptool/wiki/SPI-Flash-Modes`. Finally, in *Tools ➤ Port,* select the relevant COM port.

Reference documentation for the ESP32 microcontroller is available at docs.espressif.com/projects/esp-idf/en/latest/esp32/index.html, particularly the *API Reference* section.

The ESP32 microcontroller includes several features that are specific to the ESP32 microcontroller, which are described in Chapter 22 (ESP32 microcontroller features). Sketch instructions for an ESP32 development board differ in several ways from programming a board containing an ATmega328P or ESP8266 microcontroller. The following examples illustrate programming an ESP32 development board to access features that are available to the ATmega328P or ESP8266 microcontroller.

ESP32 digital input

To read the state of a GPIO pin, the pin is defined with the instruction `pinMode(pin, INPUT)`. If a GPIO pin is to be held *LOW*, then the internal pull-down resistor on the GPIO pin is activated with the instruction `pinMode(pin, INPUT_PULLDOWN)`. Similarly, the instruction `pinMode(pin, INPUT_PULLUP)` activates the internal pull-up resistor on the GPIO pin, which is also available on the ATmega328P or ESP8266 microcontroller. Scenarios for activating the pull-up or pull-down resistor on a GPIO pin are to maintain the default state of a switch to *HIGH* or *LOW*, respectively, or for triggering an interrupt with a *FALLING* or *RISING* signal, respectively.

ESP32 analog input

The 12-bit analog to digital converter (ADC) functionality converts a voltage, between 0 and 3.3 V, on an analog input pin to a digital value between 0 and 4095. The instruction `analogRead(ADCpin)` reads the voltage on the *ADCpin*, with the *ADCpin* defined as either the GPIO number 32, 33, 34, 35, 36 (pin VP), or 39 (pin VN) or by A4, A5, A6, A7, A0, or A3, respectively. The mapping of voltage to digital value is linear for input voltages of between 0.5 V and 2.5 V with increments of 0.8 mV. The ESP32 microcontroller incorporates more pins with ADC functionality, but the pins are not available on the ESP32 DEVKIT DOIT or NodeMCU development board.

The ADC resolution on an *ADC pin* is increased using the instruction analogSetPinAttenuation(ADCpin, attenuation) with attenuation values of *ADC_11dB* (default), *ADC_6dB, ADC_2_5dB,* or *ADC_0d.* The input voltage, V_{IN}, on an ADC pin is reduced to $V_{IN} / \sqrt{10^{(dB/10)}}$ for a given decibel value. For example, the 2.5 dB attenuation reduces an input voltage of 1 V to 0.75 V resulting in an ADC value of 3072 = 4096*0.75, while the default 11 dB setting results in an ADC value of 1154. The sketch in Listing 21-5 changes the attenuation setting of an ADC pin.

Listing 21-5. Analog to digital conversion

```
int ADCpin = 36;                          // define ADC pin

void setup()
{
  Serial.begin(115200);                   // Serial Monitor baud rate
  Serial.println();
  analogSetPinAttenuation(ADCpin, ADC_11db);
                                          // default setting of 11dB
  Serial.println(analogRead(ADCpin));     // read ADC pin
  analogSetPinAttenuation(ADCpin, ADC_6db);
                                          // change setting to 6dB
  Serial.println(analogRead(ADCpin));
  analogSetPinAttenuation(ADCpin, ADC_2_5db);
  Serial.println(analogRead(ADCpin));
  analogSetPinAttenuation(ADCpin, ADC_0db);
```

```
  Serial.println(analogRead(ADCpin));
}

void loop()
{}                                          // nothing in loop function
```

ESP32 pulse width modulation

All GPIO pins, except the input-only pins (GPIO 34, GPIO 35, GPIO 36, and GPIO 39), are PWM pins and can generate a square wave with variable duty cycle. Three instructions are required for PWM

```
ledcAttachPin(wavePin, channel)
ledcSetup(channel, freq, resolution)
ledcWrite(channel, duty)
```

with the parameters PWM output channel (*channel*), GPIO pin to output square wave (*wavePin*), square wave frequency (*freq*), PWM resolution (*resolution*), and duty cycle (*duty*). The ESP32 microcontroller uses 8, 10, 12, or 15-bit resolution for PWM, providing ranges from 0 to 255, 1023, 4095, or 32767, respectively. In comparison, the Arduino Uno ATmega328P and ESP8266 microcontrollers use 8-bit and 10-bit resolution, respectively. The maximum square wave frequency is equal to $80 \text{ MHz}/2^{resolution}$. For example, with 8-bit or 15-bit resolution, the maximum square wave frequency is 312.5 kHz or 2.44 kHz, with a trade-off between the number of PWM levels, which is the resolution, and the maximum square wave frequency. The sketch in Listing 21-6 increases and then decreases the brightness of an LED by changing the 5 kHz square wave duty cycle.

Listing 21-6. PWM signal

```
int channel = 0;                        // define PWM output channel
int wavePin = 25;                       // square wave output pin
int freq = 5000;                        // square wave frequency
int resolution = 8;                     // PWM resolution
int bright = 0;
int increm = 5;                         // increment in duty cycle
int lag = 25;                           // time between PWM changes

void setup()
{
  pinMode(wavePin, OUTPUT);             // square wave pin as output
  ledcAttachPin(wavePin, channel);      // attached channel to pin
  ledcSetup(channel, freq, resolution);
}

void loop()
{
  ledcWrite(channel, bright);           // set channel duty cycle
  delay(lag);
  bright = bright + increm;             // increment duty cycle
  if(bright <= 0 || bright >= 255) increm = - increm;
}                                       // reverse duty cycle increment
```

ESP32 serial input

The ESP32 DEVKIT DOIT 30-pin development board has two Serial ports with the *Serial* transmit and receive pins on GPIO 1 (TX0) and GPIO 3 (RX0) and the *Serial2* transmit and receive pins on GPIO 17 (TX2) and GPIO 16 (RX2). In Chapter 12 (GPS tracking app with Google Maps), the ESP8266 microcontroller sketch to update positional information of a u-blox NEO-7M GPS module required the *SoftwareSerial* library for Serial communication. Similarily, in Chapter 5 (MP3 player), the *SoftwareSerial* library was required for Serial communication with the MP3 player. The ESP32 development board Serial ports enable Serial communication with more than one device, without having to utilize libraries to provide the Serial communication functionality. The instruction `Serial2.begin(baud, SERIAL_8N1, RXD2, TXD2)` establishes Serial communication on the second Serial port on pins *RXD2* and *TXD2*, with the baud rate defined by the parameter *baud*.

The ESP32 NodeMCU 36-pin development board has three Serial ports with the *Serial1* transmit and receive pins on GPIO 10 (TX1) and GPIO 9 (RX1). The instruction `Serial1.begin(baud, SERIAL_8N1, RXD1, TXD1)` establishes Serial communication on the Serial port on pins *RXD1* and *TXD1*, with a baud rate defined by the parameter *baud*.

Wi-Fi communication and web server

Several projects in the book require Wi-Fi communication with web server functionality. For the ESP8266 microcontroller, the required instructions are

```
#include <ESP8266WiFi.h>
#include <ESP8266WebServer.h>
ESP8266WebServer server
```

For the ESP32 microcontroller, the corresponding instructions are

```
#include <WiFi.h>
#include <WebServer.h>
WebServer server(80)
```

noting that a port number must be specifically defined for the ESP32 microcontroller. The *ESP8266WebServer* and *WebServer* libraries reference the corresponding Wi-Fi library, so the `#include <ESP8266WiFi.h>` or `#include <WiFi.h>` instructions are not required.

ESP8266 and ESP32 interrupts

Interrupts are attached with the instruction attachInterrupt(digitalP inToInterrupt(switchPin), ISR, state change) with the parameters defining the *switchPin* attached to the interrupt, the interrupt service routine (ISR), and the change in the switch state, *state change*, equal to either *CHANGE, FALLING, RISING, HIGH,* or *LOW.* The ESP8266 and ESP32 microcontrollers store compiled code in internal RAM (IRAM), rather than in the slower flash memory, by prefixing code with the *IRAM_ATTR* attribute. The interrupt ISR is defined as IRAM_ATTR void ISR() rather than void ISR(). If the interrupt ISR is defined before the *setup* function, then the ISR definition instruction is changed to void IRAM_ATTR ISR().

ESP8266 and ESP32 and an OLED screen

The *Wire* library is required when using the *Adafruit SSD1306* library to display images on an OLED screen, with the OLED I2C pins connected to an ESP8266 or ESP32 development board. The *Adafruit SSD1306* library references the *Adafruit GFX* and *Wire* libraries, so the #include <Adafruit_GFX.h> and #include <Wire.h> instructions are not required. The OLED screen size, pixel *width* and *height,* is defined in the instruction Adafruit_SSD1306 oled(width, height, &Wire, -1) with the *-1* indicating that a reset pin is not defined for the OLED screen. The *width, height,* and *&Wire* parameters are not explicitly defined when using an OLED screen with an ATmega328P microcontroller.

ESP32 and servo motors

The ESP32 development board requires an ESP32-specific servo library, rather than the Arduino IDE built-in *Servo* library. The *ESP32Servo* library by Kevin Harrington and John K. Bennett is recommended, and the library is available in the Arduino IDE. The built-in *Servo* library instructions

```
#include <Servo.h>                 // include Servo library
servoFB.attach(FBpin)              // initialise servo motor to FBpin
```

are replaced with the *ESP32Servo* library instructions

```
#include <ESP32Servo.h>
servoFB.setPeriodHertz(F)              // define servo frequency (F)
servoFB.attach(FBpin, minPW, maxPW)  // initialise servo motor to FBpin
```

There is no change to the following instructions:

```
Servo servoFB                      // associate servoFB with servo lib
servoFB.writeMicroseconds(T)       // move to position mapped to Tμs
servoFb.write(N)                   // move to angle N°
```

In the `servoFB.attach(FBpin, minPW, maxPW)` instruction, the *minPW* and *maxPW* parameters refer to the pulse width, in microseconds, of a square wave to move the servo motor to 0° and 180°, respectively. Default values for the *minPW* and *maxPW* parameters are 1000 μs and 2000 μs, with values of 500 μs and 2500 μs for the Tower Pro SG90 servo. The square wave frequency, *F*, is included in the instruction `servoFB.setPeriodHertz(F)`, which is generally 50 Hz. A sketch to calibrate a servo motor is given in Chapter 9 (WebSocket).

Summary

Properties of the ESP8266 and ESP32 microcontrollers are described, with examples to illustrate several features. Specific ESP32 microcontroller instructions are required for several properties available to the ESP8266 microcontroller, and the instruction differences are highlighted. Attaching interrupts to an ESP8266 development board and resolving timeout issues with the watchdog timer are discussed. The Arduino Uno, Nano, and Pro Micro are briefly described as the microcontrollers are used in several sketches.

Components List

- ESP8266 microcontroller: LOLIN (WeMos) D1 mini or NodeMCU board

- ESP32 microcontroller: DEVKIT DOIT or NodeMCU board

- LED: 1×

- Resistor: 220 Ω

- Tactile switch

CHAPTER 22

ESP32 microcontroller features

Features specific to the ESP32 microcontroller are described in this chapter. In Chapter 21 (Microcontrollers), differences in instructions for ESP8266 and ESP32 microcontrollers regarding features that are available to both microcontrollers were described. The ESP32 microcontroller has two cores, which are managed independently, Bluetooth communication and Bluetooth Low Energy (BLE) communication, four independent timers, a digital to analog converter (DAC) with capacitive touch sensors, and a Hall effect sensor. The ESP32 DEVKIT DOIT development board is illustrated in Figure 22-1.

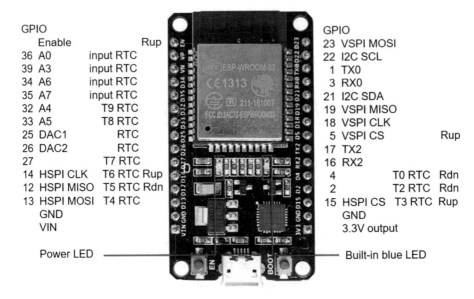

GPIO
Enable		Rup
36 A0	input RTC	
39 A3	input RTC	
34 A6	input RTC	
35 A7	input RTC	
32 A4	T9 RTC	
33 A5	T8 RTC	
25 DAC1	RTC	
26 DAC2	RTC	
27	T7 RTC	
14 HSPI CLK	T6 RTC Rup	
12 HSPI MISO	T5 RTC Rdn	
13 HSPI MOSI	T4 RTC	
GND		
VIN		

Power LED

GPIO
23 VSPI MOSI		
22 I2C SCL		
1 TX0		
3 RX0		
21 I2C SDA		
19 VSPI MISO		
18 VSPI CLK		
5 VSPI CS		Rup
17 TX2		
16 RX2		
4	T0 RTC	Rdn
2	T2 RTC	Rdn
15 HSPI CS	T3 RTC	Rup
GND		
3.3V output		

Built-in blue LED

Figure 22-1.   *ESP32 DEVKIT DOIT development board*

Microcontroller CPU and memory

The CPU frequency of the ESP32 microcontroller is changed, in the Arduino IDE, to 10, 20, 40, 80, 160, or 240 MHz by selecting *Tools* ➤ *CPU Frequency*. The impact of different CPU frequencies is determined by measuring the time taken to calculate the first 10k prime numbers (see Chapter 21 (Microcontrollers)). As the CPU frequency doubles, the time to determine the first 10k prime numbers essentially halves from 11607 ms with 10 MHz to 5060 ms with 20 MHz, to 2403 ms with 40 MHz, to 1172 ms with 80 MHz, and 579 ms with 160 MHz. The time taken with a CPU frequency of 240 MHz was only 385 ms.

The ESP32 microcontroller 4 MB flash memory is partitioned to non-volatile storage (NVS), over the air (OTA) updates, applications, SPIFFS, and EEPROM (see Chapter 20 (OTA and saving data to EEPROM, SPIFFS, and Excel)), which are adjusted within the Arduino IDE depending on the memory requirements of a sketch. Select the *Tools* menu and *Partition scheme* for various combinations of application, SPIFFS, and OTA memory allocation. For example, the default allocation is base, 36 kB where 1 kB is 1024 byte; NVS, 20 kB; OTA, 8 kB; protocol and application cores, 2 × 1280 kB; and SPIFFS, 1472 kB.

ESP32 cores

The ESP32 microcontroller includes two cores, each with a Tensilica Xtensa 32-bit LX6 microprocessor, in contrast to the ESP8266 microcontroller with one Tensilica L106 32-bit processor. The protocol core, *PRO_CPU,* manages Wi-Fi, Bluetooth, SPI, and I2C communication, while the application core, *APP_CPU,* is for application development. The two cores are managed by the ESP-IDF (Espressif IoT Development Framework) FreeRTOS (Real-Time Operating System), which is a modification of FreeRTOS, with details available at `www.freertos.org/a00106.html`. The Arduino IDE implementation of the ESP32 incorporates ESP-IDF *FreeRTOS.* The *FreeRTOS* library by Richard Barry that is available in the Arduino IDE is compatible with the ATmega328P and ATmega32U4 microcontrollers of the Arduino Uno, Nano, and Pro Micro, but there is currently no *FreeRTOS* library for the ESP8266 microcontroller.

Tasks are allocated to a specific core with the instruction

```
xTaskCreatePinnedToCore(code, "detail", 1000, NULL, pr,
&TaskName, core);
```

where *code* is the function containing the task instructions, *detail* is a string describing the task, *pr* is the task priority from 0 (lowest priority) to 24, *&TaskName* is a pointer to the task handle, and *core* is the core number, *0* or *1* for the protocol or application core. The *1000* value is the default memory allocation in bytes, and the *NULL* value indicates that no parameters are passed. Confirmation that a task is allocated to a core is obtained with the parameter xPortGetCoreID(). The task handle is defined with the instruction TaskHandle_t TaskName, but is only required to delete a task with the instruction vTaskDelete(TaskName). The term &TaskName is replaced with *NULL* in the xTaskCreatePinnedToCore() instruction.

Task instructions are bracketed by

```
void code(void * parameter)     // code function
{
  for(;;)                       // equivalent to a for instruction
  {
    Task instructions           // task instructions
  }
}
```

The instruction for(;;) has the same format as for(int i=0; i<max; i++), but without the parameters, and effectively runs the task instructions in an infinite loop.

The timing of tasks is based on the number of clock *ticks*, with a *tick* equal to 1 ms in the ESP-IDF *FreeRTOS*, as defined by the parameter *portTICK_PERIOD_MS*. The instruction vTaskDelay(xOneSec) represents a one-second delay, with the variable *xOneSec*, which is a *TickType_t* object, defined as xOneSec = 1000/portTICK_PERIOD_MS. A time interval is measured as the number of elapsed *ticks*, with the instructions

```
int tickTime = xTaskGetTickCount();       // tick count at start
vTaskDelay(xOneSec);                       // time interval
int tick = xTaskGetTickCount() - tickTime; // change in tick count
```

The sketch in Listing 22-1 simultaneously turns on or off two LEDs at different time intervals, with the tasks controlling the LEDs allocated to different ESP32 cores. A task is allocated to an ESP32 core with the xTaskCreatePinnedToCore instruction. For comparison, the *codeRed* function uses ESP-IDF *FreeRTOS* time instructions, while the *codeBlue* function uses standard Arduino IDE instructions. In the *loop* function, the instruction vTaskDelay(NULL) prevents processor time being allocated to the function.

Listing 22-1. A task on each core

```
int redLED = 26;                          // define LED pins
int blueLED = 27;
TickType_t xOneSec;                       // create time delay variable

void setup()
{
  Serial.begin(115200);                   // Serial Monitor baud rate
  pinMode(redLED, OUTPUT);                // set LED pins as output
  pinMode(blueLED, OUTPUT);
  xOneSec = 1000 / portTICK_PERIOD_MS; // define number of ticks
  xTaskCreatePinnedToCore(codeRed, "red LED one sec",
1000, NULL, 2, NULL, 0);                  // allocate tasks to cores
  xTaskCreatePinnedToCore(codeBlue, "blue LED quarter sec",
1000, NULL, 1, NULL, 1);
}

void codeRed(void * parameter)            // function for red LED
{
  for (;;)
  {
    int tickTime = xTaskGetTickCount(); // tick count at start
    digitalWrite(redLED, HIGH);         // turn on or off LED
    vTaskDelay(xOneSec);                // task delay for one second
    digitalWrite(redLED, LOW);
```

```
    vTaskDelay(xOneSec);
    int tick = xTaskGetTickCount() - tickTime;   // change in tick
                                                  // count
    Serial.print("Core ");Serial.print(xPortGetCoreID());
    Serial.print(" red ");Serial.println(tick);
  }
}

void codeBlue(void * parameter)        // similar task with 250ms delay
{
  for (;;)
  {
    unsigned long start = millis(); // time at start
    digitalWrite(blueLED, HIGH);
    delay(250);                             // task delay of 250ms
    digitalWrite(blueLED, LOW);
    delay(250);
    start = millis() - start;
    Serial.print("Core ");Serial.print(xPortGetCoreID());
    Serial.print(" blue ");Serial.println(start);
  }
}

void loop()
{                                       // no instructions in loop function
  vTaskDelay(NULL);                     // other than zero delay
}
```

Turning on or off two LEDs with a 32-bit microcontroller operating at 240 MHz is trivial, but the sketch demonstrates using both ESP32 cores simultaneously. The sketch in Listing 22-2 determines the first 5k and 10k primes simultaneously, with each task allocated to a different ESP32 core.

Allocation of tasks to different cores effectively doubles task output relative to performing a task on one ESP32 core. The last instruction, vTaskDelay(1), of each task prevents the watchdog timer from resetting the ESP32 microcontroller. The task to determine 10k prime numbers takes 334 ms to complete, but when the instruction vTaskDelay(NULL) is deleted, the task takes 662 ms to complete. The *loop* function is allocated to the application core, and the instruction vTaskDelay(NULL) prevents the use of processor time unnecessarily.

Listing 22-2. Simultaneous determination of the first 5k and 10k prime numbers

```
unsigned long num5k = 2, num10k = 2;        // start from number 2
int count5k = 1, count10k = 1;              // prime number counters
unsigned int start5k = 0, start10k = 0;     // processing times

void setup()
{
  Serial.begin(115200);                     // Serial Monitor baud rate
  xTaskCreatePinnedToCore(code5k, "5k", 1000, NULL, 1, NULL, 0);
  xTaskCreatePinnedToCore(code10k, "10k", 1000, NULL, 1, NULL, 1);
}

void code5k(void * parameter)       // function for 5k primes
{
  for (;;)
  {
    num5k++;                        // increment number to check
    int chk = is_prime(num5k);      // call function to test for prime
    if (chk > 0) count5k++;         // increment counter when prime
    if (count5k > 4999)             // count up to 5k numbers
```

```
    {
      printLine(start5k, count5k, num5k);
                                            // function to display results

      num5k = 2;
      count5k = 1;                         // reset parameters
      start5k = millis();
      vTaskDelay(1);                       // delay for watchdog timer
    }
  }
}

void code10k(void * parameter)      // function for 10k primes
{
  for (;;)
  {
    num10k++;
    int chk = is_prime(num10k);
    if (chk > 0) count10k++;
    if (count10k > 9999)
    {
      printLine(start10k, count10k, num10k);
      num10k = 2;
      count10k = 1;
      start10k = millis();
      vTaskDelay(1);
    }
  }
}

void printLine(unsigned long start, int count, unsigned long number)
{
  int ms = millis() - start;
```

```
  Serial.print("Core ");Serial.print(xPortGetCoreID());
  Serial.print(" Found ");Serial.print(count);
  Serial.print(" primes in "); Serial.print(ms);
  Serial.print(" ms");
  Serial.print(" highest prime is ");Serial.println(number);

}

int is_prime(unsigned long num) // function to check if prime number
{
  int mod = num % 2;                    // exclude even numbers
  if (mod == 0) return 0;
  int limit = sqrt(num);        // check divisors less than square root
  for (int divid = 3; divid <= limit; divid = divid + 2)
  {
    mod = num % divid;                  // remainder after dividing
    if (mod == 0) return 0;             // not prime if zero remainder
  }
  return 1;                             // no divisor with zero remainder
}

void loop()
{
  vTaskDelay(NULL);
}
```

Information is passed between tasks operating on either the same ESP32 core or different ESP32 cores using either a semaphore or a queue to control information transfer. The semaphore method is analogous, to an extent, to a relay race in which one runner passes a baton to a second runner to allow the second runner to start running. However, with the

semaphore method, the first runner keeps running! The instructions
`SemaphoreHandle_t baton` and `baton = xSemaphoreCreateMutex()`
create a semaphore variable, *baton*, with the semaphore given by one task
and taken by the other task with the instructions `xSemaphoreGive(baton)`
and `xSemaphoreTake(baton, portMAX_DELAY)`, respectively. The position
of the `xSemaphoreGive(baton)` instruction in the first task instructions
determines when the second task is initiated. With the semaphore method,
any information required to complete the second task is contained in
a global variable, which is defined with the instruction `volatile type`
`variable`.

The queue method is analogous to a manager allocating work items
to a worker, with the worker completing the work items on a first-in
first-out basis. The instructions `QueueHandle_t queue` and `queue =`
`xQueueCreate(N, sizeof(int))` create the queue variable, *queue*, with
up to *N* work items. A work item is added or removed to or from the queue
with the instructions `xQueueSend(queue, &work, portMAX_DELAY)` or
`xQueueReceive(queue, &work, portMAX_DELAY)`, respectively, where
`&work` is the pointer to the work item.

The difference between the semaphore and queue methods for
transferring information between tasks is the use of global variables
by the semaphore method. The instructions in Table 22-1 illustrate the
similarities and differences between the semaphore and queue methods.
Differences between the semaphore and queue methods are highlighted
in bold. In the sketch, the task allocated to ESP32 protocol core turns on
the red LED for one second and off for a random time period, *redOff*. The
task allocated to ESP32 application core turns on the blue LED for the
time period that the red LED is off. The `delay(1)` instruction following the
instruction to allocate a value to the variable *redOff* allows for processing
time.

With the semaphore method, the variable *redOff* is a global variable
that is accessible to the task controlling the blue LED. With the queue

method, the variable *redOff* is added to the queue by the task controlling the red LED and read from the queue, as the variable *blueOn*, by the task controlling the blue LED. For both methods, when the xSemaphoreGive() or xQueueSend() instruction precedes the instruction to turn on the red LED, the two LEDs are turned on simultaneously. In contrast, the two LEDs turn on alternately, when the xSemaphoreGive() or xQueueSend() instruction precedes the instruction to turn off the red LED. The sketch illustrates timing two tasks to commence simultaneously or alternately.

Table 22-1. *Semaphore and queue methods*

Semaphore	Queue
int redLED = 26;	int redLED = 26;
int blueLED= 27;	int blueLED = 27;
SemaphoreHandle_t baton;	**QueueHandle_t queue;**
volatile int redOff;	
void setup() {	void setup() {
pinMode(redLED, OUTPUT);	pinMode(redLED, OUTPUT);
pinMode(blueLED, OUTPUT);	pinMode(blueLED, OUTPUT);
xTaskCreatePinnedToCore(codeRed,	xTaskCreatePinnedToCore(codeRed,
"red LED ", 1000, NULL, 1, NULL, 0);	"red LED ", 1000, NULL, 1, NULL, 0);
xTaskCreatePinnedToCore(codeBlu,	xTaskCreatePinnedToCore(codeBlue,
"blue LED", 1000, NULL, 1, NULL, 1);	"blue LED", 1000, NULL, 1, NULL, 1);
baton = xSemaphoreCreateMutex();	**queue = xQueueCreate(1,**
	sizeof(int));
}	}

(continued)

Table 22-1. (*continued*)

Semaphore	Queue

void codeRed(void * parameter) {
for (;;) {
redOff = random(500, 2000);
delay(1);
xSemaphoreGive(baton);
 	
digitalWrite(redLED, HIGH);
delay(1000);
digitalWrite(redLED, LOW);
delay(redOff);
} }
	void codeRed(void * parameter) {
	for (;;) {
	int redOff = random(500, 2000);
	delay(1);
	**xQueueSend(queue, &redOff,
	portMAX_DELAY);**
	digitalWrite(redLED, HIGH);
	delay(1000);
	digitalWrite(redLED, LOW);
	delay(redOff);
	} }

void codeBlu(void * parameter) {
for (;;)
{
 	
**xSemaphoreTake(baton,
portMAX_DELAY);**
digitalWrite(blueLED, HIGH);
delay(redOff);
digitalWrite(blueLED, LOW);
} }
	void codeBlue(void * parameter) {
	for (;;)
	{
	int blueOn;
	**xQueueReceive(queue, &blueOn,
	portMAX_DELAY);**
	digitalWrite(blueLED, HIGH);
	delay(blueOn);
	digitalWrite(blueLED, LOW);
	} }

void loop() { vTaskDelay(NULL); }	void loop() { vTaskDelay(NULL); }

Bluetooth communication

The ESP32 microcontroller operates both Bluetooth and Bluetooth Low Energy communication protocols. Bluetooth communication requires a Serial Bluetooth connection, which is established with the instructions

```
#include <BluetoothSerial.h>          // include Bluetooth library
BluetoothSerial SerialBT;             // associate SerialBT with library
SerialBT.begin("ESP32 Bluetooth");    // identify Bluetooth
```

Serial Bluetooth communicates by sending one character at a time. Text entered on the Serial Monitor is sent with either SerialBT.write(Serial.read()) or SerialBT.write(c) for the character *c*. The sketch in Listing 22-3 establishes a Serial Bluetooth connection and displays the received message from the Bluetooth device on the Serial Monitor. The Serial.write() instruction converts the ASCII code to display alphanumeric characters, while Serial.print() displays the ASCII code for each character in the received message. To both transmit a message to the Bluetooth device and display the transmitted message on the Serial Monitor, each character of the message is transmitted individually as the Serial buffer is not read twice.

Listing 22-3. Bluetooth communication

```
#include <BluetoothSerial.h>      // include Bluetooth library
BluetoothSerial SerialBT;         // associate SerialBT with library
String str;
int strLen;
char c;
```

```
void setup()
{
  Serial.begin(115200);                      // Serial Monitor baud rate
  SerialBT.begin("ESP32 Bluetooth");   // identify Bluetooth device
}

void loop()
{                                            // received message from Bluetooth device
  if(SerialBT.available()) Serial.write(SerialBT.read());
  if(Serial.available())                     // message to transmit
  {
    str = Serial.readString();               // read and display
    Serial.print("\t\t\t\t");Serial.println(str);   // Serial buffer
    strLen = str.length();
    for (int i=0; i<strLen; i++)
    {
      c = str[i];                            // for each message character
      SerialBT.write(c);                     // transmit to Bluetooth device
    }
    SerialBT.write('\n');                    // add new line character
  }
  delay(50);
}
```

There are several Bluetooth communication applications to download from *Google Play Store* for an Android tablet to communicate with the ESP32 Bluetooth. The *Bluetooth Terminal HC-05* app, by mightyIT, is recommended. After opening the *Bluetooth Terminal HC-05* app, the client scans for the required device (see Figure 22-2) and establishes a connection to the server.

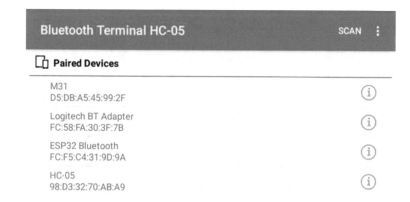

Figure 22-2. *Client scanning for Bluetooth server*

Once the client-server connection is established, Bluetooth communication between the two devices enables transmission of alphanumeric text, as shown in Figure 22-3.

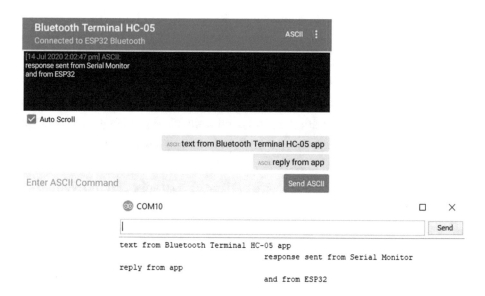

Figure 22-3. *Bluetooth communication of text messages*

Bluetooth Low Energy communication

Bluetooth Low Energy (BLE) communicates on the same 2.4 GHz as Bluetooth, over a similar transmission range, but with reduced power consumption. With BLE, data is transmitted only when a connection is established with the client and the client has requested notification of updated data values. The server advertises its existence, the client scans devices, and when the client detects the required device, the client establishes a connection with the server. For example, the ESP32 microcontroller is the server, and the Android tablet or mobile phone is the client, which is point-to-point communication. The broadcast and mesh network topologies are for one–to–many and many-to-many device communication. This chapter focuses on point-to-point communication.

BLE is used to periodically transmit small amounts of data, such as in environmental monitoring sensors, home automation appliances, and health and sports equipment, such as in heart rate and blood pressure monitors on a smart watch. Data transmitted with BLE has a defined format, depending on the category of data that is transmitted, with the format termed the Generic ATTribute (GATT) profile, which is used by appliances communicating with BLE. A data category consists of a BLE service, such as *Environmental Sensing*, which includes characteristics, such as temperature or humidity, with both the service and each characteristic having a specific UUID (Universal Unique IDentifier). Details of the GATT services and characteristics are available at `www.bluetooth.com/specifications/gatt/services`. For example, the UUIDs of *Environmental Sensing* and *temperature* are *0x181A* and *0x2A63*, respectively, with *temperature* formatted as *uint16_t* with two decimal points.

The sketch in Listing 22-10 illustrates the ESP32 microcontroller transmitting three Environmental Sensing characteristics with BLE communication. The three characteristics, *temperature, heat index,* and *UV (ultraviolet) index,* are formatted for BLE as *uint16_t* with 2DP, *uint8_t* with 0DP, and *uint8_t* with 0DP, respectively. To illustrate formatting sensor data for BLE, the *heat index* characteristic is derived from the real number *temp*, with the *UV index* derived from the integer *UV*. Note that there are limitations on the possible values of characteristics, such as the *battery level* characteristic, *0x2A19*, which is a percentage between 0 and 100.

The *ESP32 BLE Arduino* library by Neil Kolban is automatically incorporated in the Arduino IDE when the ESP32 Board Manager is installed. Listings 22-10 and 22-11 are based on sketches in the *ESP32 BLE Arduino* library and of Andreas Spiess (`github.com/SensorsIot/Bluetooth-BLE-on-Arduino-IDE`).

The first section of the sketch in Listing 22-4 installs the BLE libraries and defines the UUIDs for the service and the three characteristics. The characteristic UUIDs and required formats are available at `www.bluetooth.com/specifications/gatt/characteristics`. Each characteristic has up to four properties, `PROPERTY_READ`, `PROPERTY_WRITE`, `PROPERTY_NOTIFY`, and `PROPERTY_INDICATE`, with the `PROPERTY_NOTIFY` property allocated to characteristics transmitted by the server to a client. The *ServerConnect* class determines if a client has established a connection with the server. In the *setup* function, the BLE server and service are defined, with each characteristic defined and added to the BLE service.

In the `loop` function, if the client has established a connection with the server, then the client is notified of the updated characteristic values. In the example, the *temp* and *UV* values are converted to the required BLE formats for the *temperature, heat index,* and *UV index* characteristics. The *temperature* characteristic is *uint16-t* formatted by allocating the upper and lower bytes of the real number *temp* to the *tempData* array with two elements, with the upper byte obtained by bit shifting out the lower byte of the real number. The *heat index* characteristic is *uint8_t* formatted by changing the format of the real number, which is termed *casting*. The *UV index* characteristic is obtained with the instruction (`uint8_t*)&UV`, which points (*) to the address (&) of the integer *UV*. Chapter 14 (ESP-NOW and LoRa communication) describes variable pointers and addresses.

When each characteristic is formatted for BLE communication, the characteristic value is updated and the client notified, with the instructions setValue() and notify(). The *BLEUtils* and *BLEServer* libraries are referenced by the *BLEDevice* library, so the instructions #include <BLEUtils.h> and #include <BLEServer.h> are not explicitly required.

Listing 22-4. BLE communication as a server

```
#include <BLEDevice.h>                          // include BLE libraries
#include <BLE2902.h>
BLEServer * pServer;                            // define BLE server,
BLEService * pService;                          // BLE service and
BLECharacteristic * pChar;                      // BLE Characteristic
int devConnect = 0;
#define SERVICE_UUID BLEUUID((uint16_t)0x181A)
                                                // environmental service
BLECharacteristic tempChar(BLEUUID((uint16_t)0x2A6E),
   BLECharacteristic::PROPERTY_NOTIFY);
BLECharacteristic UVChar  (BLEUUID((uint16_t)0x2A76),
   BLECharacteristic::PROPERTY_NOTIFY);
BLECharacteristic heatChar(BLEUUID((uint16_t)0x2A7A),
   BLECharacteristic::PROPERTY_NOTIFY);
class ServerConnect: public BLEServerCallbacks
{                                               // to check if connected
   void onConnect(BLEServer * pServer) {devConnect = 1;}
   void onDisconnect(BLEServer * pServer) {devConnect = 0;}
};

float temp = 0;
uint8_t tempData[2];
uint16_t tempValue;
int UV = 0, heat;
```

```
void setup()
{
  Serial.begin(115200);                      // Serial monitor baud rate
  BLEDevice::init("ESP32");                        // define BLE device
  pServer = BLEDevice::createServer();             // define BLE server
  pServer->setCallbacks(new ServerConnect());
                                                   // check if connected
  pService = pServer->createService(SERVICE_UUID);
                                                   //define BLE service
  pService->addCharacteristic(&tempChar);     // define temperature
  tempChar.addDescriptor(new BLE2902());      //  characteristic
  pService->addCharacteristic(&UVChar);       // define UV index
  UVChar.addDescriptor(new BLE2902());        //  characteristic
  pService->addCharacteristic(&heatChar);     // define heat index
  heatChar.addDescriptor(new BLE2902());      //  characteristic
  pServer->getAdvertising()->addServiceUUID(SERVICE_UUID);
  pService->start();                               // start service
  pServer->getAdvertising()->start();              // advertise service
  Serial.println("Waiting for client to connect");
}

void loop()
{
  if(devConnect == 1)                        // if the client is connected
  {
    temp = temp + 1.11;
    tempValue = (uint16_t)(temp*100);  // convert to uint16_t with 2DP
    tempData[0]= tempValue;                  // LSB (least significant byte)
    tempData[1]= tempValue >> 8;             // MSB (most significant byte)
    tempChar.setValue(tempData, 2);          // update characteristic
```

```
tempChar.notify();                      // notify client
heat = (uint8_t)temp;                   // convert to uint8_t with 0DP
heatChar.setValue(heat);
heatChar.notify();
UV = UV + 1;
UVChar.setValue((uint8_t*)&UV, 4);  // point to address of UV
UVChar.notify();
Serial.print(temp);Serial.print("\t");
                                        // display values on Monitor
Serial.print(heat);Serial.print("\t");
Serial.println(UV);
delay(1000);                            // delay between sensor readings
}
}
```

The *nRF Connect* and *nRF Toolbox* apps by Nordic Semiconductor are recommended for BLE communication and are available to download from *Google Play Store* for an Android tablet or mobile phone. After opening the *nRF Connect* app, the client scans for the required device (see Figure 22-4) and establishes a connection to the server.

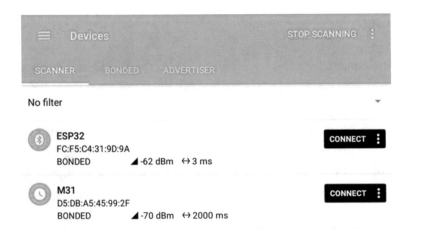

Figure 22-4. *Client scanning for BLE server*

The *Environmental Sensing* service is displayed with updated values of the *temperature, heat index,* and *UV index* characteristics (see Figure 22-5). Clicking the BLE characteristic arrows (circled in Figure 22-5) enables or disables display of updated characteristic values by the app, but only in the context of the sketch in Listing 22-4. Note that updating the *heat index* characteristic is currently disabled in Figure 22-5.

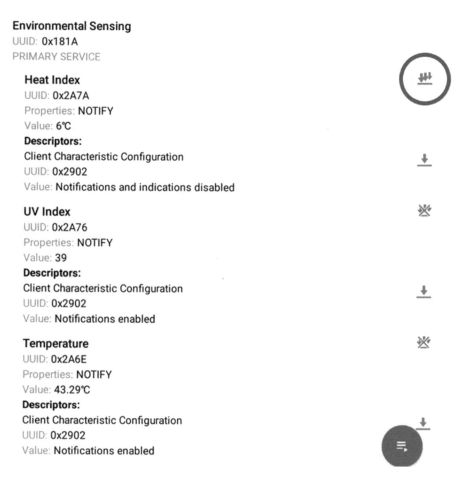

Figure 22-5. *BLE Environmental Sensing service*

Both data transmission and reception by the server and client are demonstrated with the sketch in Listing 22-5. The server transmits updated characteristic values to the client, as in Listing 22-4; but in Listing 22-5, the client transmits alphanumeric text to the server and also notifies the server if updated characteristic values are required by the client. To illustrate the server responding to alphanumeric text received from the client, an LED attached to the ESP32 development board is turned on or off when the client transmits the text *LED*.

The first section of Listing 22-5 installs BLE libraries, as in Listing 22-4, but the UART service is not defined as a GATT BLE service, so UUIDs for the UART service and the transmit and receive characteristics are defined explicitly, rather than implicitly as in Listing 22-4. The three UUIDs are the default UUIDs used by Nordic Semiconductor for UART transmission. The *RXCallback* class manages data reception by the server, with the string *RXstr* containing the received alphanumeric text. The *NotifyCallback* class sets the value of the *devNotify* variable, which determines whether or not the server transmits updated characteristic values to the client. In the *setup* function, the transmit (TX) and receive (RX) characteristics are defined with PROPERTY_NOTIFY and PROPERTY_WRITE, respectively, with the *NotifyCallback* and *RXCallback* classes attached to the TX description and RX characteristic, respectively (see Figure 22-6).

In the *loop* function, the server transmits updated characteristic values, but only if the client both has established a connection and has requested the updated characteristic values. The C instruction *dtostrf* is a method of formatting a real number as a character array, with the required BLE format. The instruction dtostrf(value, 8, 1, valueStr) converts the real number *value* to a character array, of length eight, representing *value* with 1DP.

Listing 22-5. Transmit and receive with BLE communication

```
#include <BLEDevice.h>              // include BLE libraries
#include <BLE2902.h>
BLEServer * pServer;                // define BLE server,
BLEService * pService;              // BLE service,
BLECharacteristic * pTXChar;        // BLE transmit and
BLECharacteristic * pRXChar;        // receive characteristics,
BLEDescriptor * pTXDesc;            // transmit descriptor
int devConnect = 0;
int devNotify = 0;
int LEDpin = 25;
int LEDstate = 0;
float value;
char valueStr[8];
char SERVICE_UUID[] = "6E400001-B5A3-F393-E0A9-E50E24DCCA9E";
                                    // UUIDs
char RXChar_UUID[] =  "6E400002-B5A3-F393-E0A9-E50E24DCCA9E";
char TXChar_UUID[] =  "6E400003-B5A3-F393-E0A9-E50E24DCCA9E";

void changeLED()                    // function to change LED state
{
  LEDstate = 1 - LEDstate;          // turn on or off LED
  digitalWrite(LEDpin, LEDstate);
}
class ServerConnect: public BLEServerCallbacks
{                                   // to check if connected
  void onConnect(BLEServer * pServer) {devConnect = 1;}
  void onDisconnect(BLEServer * pServer) {devConnect = 0;}
};
```

```
class RXCallback: public BLECharacteristicCallbacks
{                                       // receive client data
  void onWrite(BLECharacteristic * pCharacteristic)
  {
    std::string RXstr = pCharacteristic->getValue();
    if (RXstr.length() > 0)             // client data available
    {
      Serial.print("Received: ");       // read client data
      for (int i=0; i<RXstr.length(); i++) Serial.
      print(RXstr[i]);
      Serial.println();
      if(RXstr == "LED") changeLED();   // call changeLED function
    }
  }
};

class NotifyCallback: public BLEDescriptorCallbacks
{                                       // client data notification
  void onWrite(BLEDescriptor * pDescriptor)
  {                                     // obtain TX descriptor
    uint8_t * TXvalue = pDescriptor->getValue();
    devNotify = 0;
    if (pDescriptor->getLength() > 0)   // client data available
    {
      if(TXvalue[0] == 1) devNotify = 1; // update data notification
      Serial.print("Notify: ");Serial.println(devNotify);
    }
  }
};
```

```
void setup()
{
  Serial.begin(115200);                      // Serial monitor baud rate
  pinMode(LEDpin, OUTPUT);
  BLEDevice::init("ESP32");                  // define BLE device
  pServer = BLEDevice::createServer();       // define BLE server
  pServer->setCallbacks(new ServerConnect());
                                             // check if connected
  pService = pServer->createService(SERVICE_UUID);
                                             // define BLE service
                                             // define TX characteristic
  pTXChar = pService->createCharacteristic(
  TXChar_UUID, BLECharacteristic::PROPERTY_NOTIFY);
  pTXDesc = new BLE2902();                   // define TX descriptor
  pTXDesc->setCallbacks(new NotifyCallback());
                                             // attach notify callback
  pTXChar->addDescriptor(pTXDesc);
                                             // define RX characteristic
  pRXChar = pService->createCharacteristic(
  RXChar_UUID, BLECharacteristic::PROPERTY_WRITE);
  pRXChar->setCallbacks(new RXCallback());   // attach RX callback
  pService->start();                         // start service
  pServer->getAdvertising()->start();        // advertise service
  Serial.println("Waiting for client to connect");
}

void loop()
{                                            // if the client is connected and
  if(devConnect == 1 && devNotify == 1) // requests data notification
  {
    value = random(10, 200)*1.5;      // generate real number
```

```
    dtostrf(value, 8, 1, valueStr);  // convert 8-char string with 1DP
    pTXChar->setValue(valueStr);      // update characteristic
    pTXChar->notify();                // notify client
    Serial.print(value);Serial.print("\t");Serial.
    println(valueStr);
    delay(3000);                      // delay between updates
  }
}
```

After opening the *nRF Connect* app, scanning for the required device, and establishing a connection to the server, the Nordic UART Service is displayed. Updating of the *TX* characteristic (see Figure 22-6) by the server is enabled or disabled by clicking the BLE arrows (see Figure 22-5). When the single BLE arrow opposite *RX characteristic* is clicked, a pop-up window for entering alphanumeric text appears, and the entered text is displayed as the *RX characteristic* value (see Figure 22-6). Entering the text *LED* results in the ESP32 microcontroller turning on or off the LED connected to the ESP32 development board.

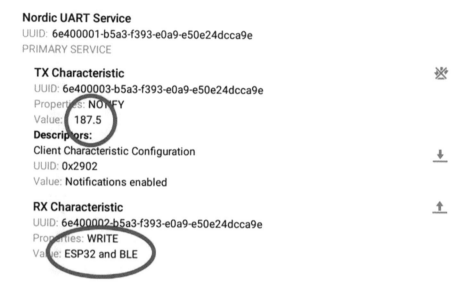

Nordic UART Service
UUID: 6e400001-b5a3-f393-e0a9-e50e24dcca9e
PRIMARY SERVICE

TX Characteristic
UUID: 6e400003-b5a3-f393-e0a9-e50e24dcca9e
Properties: NOTIFY
Value: 187.5
Descriptors:
Client Characteristic Configuration
UUID: 0x2902
Value: Notifications enabled

RX Characteristic
UUID: 6e400002-b5a3-f393-e0a9-e50e24dcca9e
Properties: WRITE
Value: ESP32 and BLE

Figure 22-6. *Transmission and reception with BLE communication*

The *nRF Toolbox* app has a keypad function for transmitting alphanumeric text with BLE communication to the server. On opening the *nRF Toolbox* app, select the UART button and click the *CONNECT* button to display available devices (see Figure 22-7). Select the required device or select *SCAN* to detect more devices.

Figure 22-7.   nRF Toolbox app

The displayed keypad (see Figure 22-8) is configured by selecting *EDIT*, clicking the relevant keypad button, entering alphanumeric text to be transmitted when the keypad button is clicked, and selecting a symbol to be displayed on the keypad button. In the context of Listing 22-5, the text *LED* was allocated to the center keypad button.

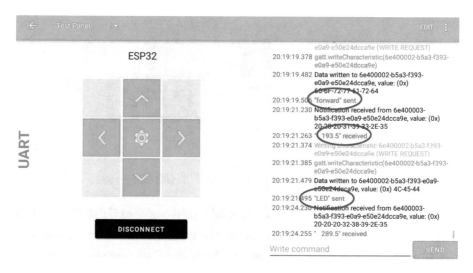

Figure 22-8. *Keypad function in nRF Toolbox app*

For a sketch using BLE communication to control motors attached to the remote ESP32 development board, the keypad buttons would be allocated the text *forward, backward, left,* and *right* or *fast* and *slow* (see Figure 22-8). The text received by the ESP32 microcontroller is interpreted in a similar manner to the *LED* text in the *RXCallback* class in Listing 22-5 with the corresponding functions called to control the motors or other devices.

In another BLE example, the ESP32 microcontroller, acting as the client, scans advertising BLE devices and turns on an LED when a particular BLE device is detected (see Figure 22-9). The ESP32 microcontroller could turn on a relay, rather than just an LED, to activate an appliance when the BLE device, such as your smart watch, is identified. The BLE address of your smart watch is available on the watch or is determined by a BLE scanning app, such as the *nRF Connect* and *nRF Toolbox* apps by Nordic Semiconductor. For the sketch, the BLE address of the watch must be changed to lowercase, for example, from *D5:DB:A5:45:99:2F* to *d5:db:a5:45:99:2f.*

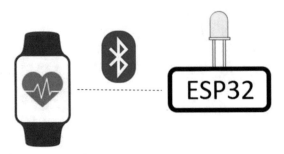

Figure 22-9. *Scanning for a particular BLE device*

The sketch in Listing 22-6 scans for BLE devices; and if the BLE address of the device, such as your smart watch, matches the defined BLE address, then the *paired* variable is set to one by the *watchCallback* class. If none of the scanned devices pair with the ESP32 microcontroller, the BLE client, then the *paired* variable is set to zero. Occasionally, the BLE scan incorrectly does not detect a BLE device, so non-detection of the defined BLE device is required for two consecutive scans before the LED is turned off. The *BLEAdvertisedDevice* library is referenced by the *BLEScan* library, so the instruction #include <BLEAdvertisedDevice.h> is not explicitly required.

Listing 22-6. BLE watch control

```
#include <BLEDevice.h>              // include BLE library
BLEScan * pBLEScan;                 // pointer to BLE scanner
BLEAddress * pAddress;              //  and to BLE address
BLEScanResults devices;
String watch = "d5:db:a5:45:99:2f"; // change upper to lower case
String scan;
int scanTime = 3;                   // scan devices for 3s
int paired = 0, lastPair = 0;
int LEDpin = 25;                    // define LED pin
```

```
class watchCallback: public BLEAdvertisedDeviceCallbacks
{                                      // BLE advertising devices
  void onResult(BLEAdvertisedDevice advertised)
  {                                      // option to display device data
// Serial.printf("found device: %s \n",
// advertised.toString().c_str());
    pAddress = new BLEAddress(advertised.getAddress());
                                         // BLE address
    scan = pAddress->toString().c_str();        // convert to string
    if(scan == watch) paired = 1;   // device matches watch address
  }
};

void setup()
{
  Serial.begin(115200);              // Serial Monitor baud rate
  pinMode(LEDpin, OUTPUT);           // LED pin as output
  BLEDevice::init("");               // initialise BLE client
  pBLEScan = BLEDevice::getScan(); //create new scan
  pBLEScan->setAdvertisedDeviceCallbacks(new watchCallback());
  pBLEScan->setActiveScan(true);
}

void loop()
{
  devices = pBLEScan->start(scanTime, false);   // start scanning
// Serial.print("scanned devices ");
// Serial.print(devices.getCount());
  digitalWrite(LEDpin, paired);         // turn on or off LED
  if(paired == 0 && lastPair == 1) digitalWrite(LEDpin, 1);
```

```
lastPair = paired;          // 2 consecutive non-pairings to turn off
paired = 0;                 // reset paired variable
pBLEScan->clearResults();   // delete scan results
}
```

Timers

The ESP32 microcontroller has four independent timers, *timer0–timer3*, and a timer frequency of 80 MHz, such that each timer *tick* lasts 0.0125 µs. The 16-bit timer pre-scaler determines the number of timer *ticks* included in one count of the timer register. For example, a pre-scaler of 80 results in the timer register incrementing every microsecond (80 × 0.0125) and the timer counting to one million every second. An interrupt is attached to a timer to trigger an event. Four instructions are required to define the timer properties

```
timer = timerBegin(0, 80, true);         // timer0, pre-scalar of 80
timerAttachInterrupt(timer, &timerISR, true);
                                          // attach interrupt ISR
timerAlarmWrite(timer, 1000000, true);   // alarm count = 10⁶
timerAlarmEnable(timer);                  // enable the timer alarm
```

with the *timer* variable defined by the instruction hw_timer_t * timer = NULL and the interrupt service routine (ISR) equal to *timerISR*. If *timer0* is to count down, the first instruction is timerBegin(0, 80, false). The ISR is triggered when the value in the timer register equals the alarm count, which is 10^6 in the example. The first and last instructions of the ISR are equal to

```
portENTER_CRITICAL_ISR(&timerMux)
portEXIT_CRITICAL_ISR(&timerMux)
```

with the variable *timerMux* defined by the instruction

```
portMUX_TYPE timerMux = portMUX_INITIALIZER_UNLOCKED
```

If the real number variable *value* is accessed in an ISR and is incremented in the *loop* function, then *value* is defined with the instruction volatile float value and in the *loop* function is bracketed with the instructions

```
portENTER_CRITICAL(&timerMux)
value = value + 1
portEXIT_CRITICAL(&timerMux)
```

Wi-Fi and Bluetooth communication may impact the timing of interrupts. The communication functionality is stopped with the instructions WiFi.mode(WIFI_OFF) and btStop(), respectively.

To illustrate use of timers, two LEDs are turned on and off at different intervals, with the intervals controlled by two timers (see Figure 22-10 and Listing 22-7).

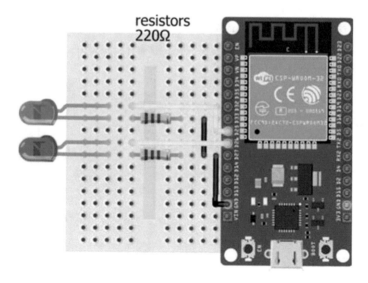

Figure 22-10. *ESP32 timers*

Listing 22-7. Timer control of two independent events

```
hw_timer_t * timer1 = NULL;                   // define timer1
portMUX_TYPE timer1Mux = portMUX_INITIALIZER_UNLOCKED;
hw_timer_t * timer2 = NULL;                   // define timer2
portMUX_TYPE timer2Mux = portMUX_INITIALIZER_UNLOCKED;
int LED1pin = 25;
int LED2pin = 26;                             // define LED pins

void setup()
{
  Serial.begin(115200);
  pinMode(LED1pin, OUTPUT);
  pinMode(LED2pin, OUTPUT);
  timer1 = timerBegin(1, 80, true);          // set timer1 properties
  timerAttachInterrupt(timer1, &timer1ISR, true);
  timerAlarmWrite(timer1, 250000, true);   // interval of 0.25s
  timerAlarmEnable(timer1);
  timer2 = timerBegin(2, 80, true);          // set timer2 properties
  timerAttachInterrupt(timer2, &timer2ISR, true);
  timerAlarmWrite(timer2, 1000000, true);  // interval of 1s
  timerAlarmEnable(timer2);
}

void loop()
{
  vTaskDelay(NULL);
}

IRAM_ATTR void timer1ISR()                    // ISR for timer1
{
  portENTER_CRITICAL_ISR(&timer1Mux);
  digitalWrite(LED1pin, !digitalRead(LED1pin));
```

```
  portEXIT_CRITICAL_ISR(&timer1Mux);
}

IRAM_ATTR void timer2ISR()                    // ISR for timer 2
{
  portENTER_CRITICAL_ISR(&timer2Mux);
  digitalWrite(LED2pin, !digitalRead(LED2pin));
  portEXIT_CRITICAL_ISR(&timer2Mux);
}
```

Real-time clock and sleep mode

Several GPIO pins are accessible by the real-time clock (RTC) input-output (*rtc_io*) library to trigger the ESP32 microcontroller from sleep mode. The *rtc-io* library is included in the ESP32 libraries within the Arduino IDE. The instruction esp_sleep_enable_ext0_wakeup(pin, state) wakes the ESP32 microcontroller from sleep mode, when the state of the *pin* is equal to *state*. For example, if pressing a switch connected to GPIO 32 is to wake the ESP32 microcontroller from sleep mode, the parameter *pin* is defined as *GPIO_NUM_32* or as *(gpio_num_t)switchPin*, given the pin definition instruction int switchPin = 32 (see Figure 22-11). The value of *state* is zero or one if the switch has a pull-up or pull-down resistor, respectively. ESP32 microcontroller pull-up and pull-down resistors are disabled during sleep, so the instruction rtc_gpio_pullup_en(pin) or rtc_gpio_pulldown_en(pin) enables a pull-up or pull-down resistor on the GPIO pin connected to a switch, if required for the switch. Details of sleep modes and wake-up options are available at docs.espressif.com/projects/esp-idf/en/latest/esp32/api-reference/system/sleep_modes.html.

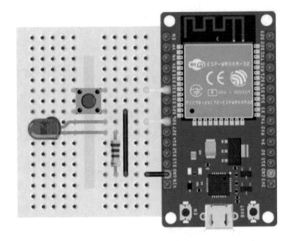

Figure 22-11. *ESP RTC and sleep mode*

Note that a pin is pulled up or pulled down, for use with a switch, with the instruction pinMode(pin, INPUT_PULLUP) or pinMode(pin, INPUT_PULLDOWN), respectively. The sketch in Listing 22-8 enables the switch on pin 32 to wake the ESP32 from sleep mode, flashes both an LED and the built-in LED, and then returns the ESP32 to sleep mode.

Listing 22-8. RTC and sleep mode

```
#include <driver/rtc_io.h>          // include rtc input-output library
int switchPin = 32;                 // define switch pin
int LEDpin = 26;                    // and LED pin
int builtinLED = 2;

void setup()
{
  Serial.begin(115200);             // Serial Monitor baud rate
  pinMode(LEDpin, OUTPUT);          // LED pins as output
  pinMode(builtinLED, OUTPUT);
  flash();                          // call flash function
  rtc_gpio_pullup_en((gpio_num_t)switchPin);  // pull-up switch pin
```

```
  esp_sleep_enable_ext0_wakeup((gpio_num_t)switchPin, 0);
}                              // wakeup on switch pin with state 0

void loop()
{
  Serial.print("sleep mode on pin ");Serial.println(switchPin);
  esp_deep_sleep_start();         // ESP32 in sleep mode
}

void flash()
{
  for (int i=0; i<3; i++)            // flash LEDs three times
  {
    digitalWrite(LEDpin, HIGH);             // LED on pin
    digitalWrite(builtinLED, HIGH);         // and built-in LED
    delay(200);
    digitalWrite(LEDpin, LOW);
    digitalWrite(builtinLED, LOW);
    delay(100);
  }
}
```

The ESP32 RTC wakes the ESP32 microcontroller from sleep mode after a period of time has elapsed, with the instruction esp_sleep_enable_timer_wakeup(N), where N is the required number of microseconds.

In sleep mode, the ESP32 RTC memory functions, while the ESP32 microcontroller CPU and memory are disabled. If information is to be retained in sleep mode, then data is stored in RTC memory by including *RTC_DATA_ATTR* in the data definition instruction. For example, if the integer variable *var* is to be retained during sleep mode, the variable is defined as RTC_DATA_ATTR int var.

The sketch in Listing 22-9 defines a counter to be stored in RTC memory, prints the incremented value, and puts the microcontroller into sleep mode, to be woken with the RTC timer after 5 seconds.

Listing 22-9. RTC timer and sleep mode

```
RTC_DATA_ATTR int count = 0;              // store count in RTC memory
unsigned long micro = 5000000;            // time interval in µs

void setup()
{
  Serial.begin(115200);                   // Serial Monitor baud rate
  esp_sleep_enable_timer_wakeup(micro);   // RTC timer interval in µs
}

void loop()
{
  count++;                                // increment and print count
  Serial.print("count ");Serial.println(count);
  esp_deep_sleep_start();
}                                         // microcontroller in sleep mode
```

Digital to analog converter

The 8-bit digital to analog converter (DAC) functionality converts a digital value, between 0 and 255, to a voltage between 0 and 3.3 V on a DAC pin. With an 8-bit DAC, there are 256 voltage classes with levels 0–255; and for a reference voltage of 3.3 V, a DAC voltage class spans 12.9 mV. The instruction dacWrite(DACpin, N) outputs a voltage on the *DACpin*, with the *DACpin* defined as either the GPIO 25 or 26 or by the term *DAC1* or *DAC2*, respectively. The sketch in Listing 22-10 generates a range of voltages between 0.5 V and 3 V.

Listing 22-10. Digital to analog converter

```
int DACpin = DAC1;                    // define DAC pin

void setup()
{}                                    // nothing in setup function

void loop()
{
  for (int i=0; i<255; i=i+39)
  {
    dacWrite(DACpin, i);              // output voltage 0.5V, 1V...
    delay(2000);
  }
}
```

Capacitive touch sensor

The capacitive touch sensors detect changes in capacitance on a touch pin, for use of a touch pin instead of a switch. When a wire connected to a touch pin is pressed, the touch pin value falls. The instruction touchRead(touchPin) reads the *touchPin* value, with the *touchPin* defined as either the GPIO number 2, 4, 12, 13, 14, 15, 27, 32, or 33 or by T2, T0, T5, T4, T6, T3, T7, T9, or T8, respectively. An interrupt is attached to the touch pin with the interrupt triggered when the touch pin value falls below a threshold. The instruction touchAttachInterrupt(touchPin, ISR, threshold) defines the touch pin, the interrupt service routine (ISR), and the threshold below which the interrupt is triggered. To prevent the touch pin repeatedly triggering the interrupt, when the touch pin is pressed, a time interval must elapse since the touch pin was touched before the interrupt is triggered. The sketch in Listing 22-11 turns on or off an LED when a wire connected to a touch pin is pressed. Note that the touch interrupt ISR *change* does not have to be defined as *IRAM_ATTR*.

Listing 22-11. Capacitive touch sensor

```
int touchPin = T7;                           // define touch pin
int LEDpin = 32;                             // and LED pin
int threshold = 50;                          // limit for touch pin
volatile unsigned long lastTouch = 0;        // time touch pin pressed

void setup()
{
  pinMode(LEDpin, OUTPUT);                    // LED pin as output
  touchAttachInterrupt(touchPin, change, threshold);
}                                            // define interrupt

void change()                                // ISR
{                                            // touch pin recently pressed
  if (millis() - lastTouch < 1000) return;
  lastTouch = millis();                      // update touch time
  digitalWrite(LEDpin, 1 - digitalRead(LEDpin));
}                                            // change LED state

void loop()                                  // nothing in loop function
{}
```

Hall effect sensor

The ESP32 microcontroller contains a Hall effect sensor, which is activated by a magnetic field. The instruction hallRead() returns the Hall Effect value, with high absolute values indicating the strength of the magnetic field and positive or negative values indicating the direction of the magnetic field. The Hall effect sensor is also used to measure rotational speed of a wheel or shaft with an attached magnet. The sketch in Listing 22-12 turns on or off an LED when the magnetic field is detected by the ESP32 Hall effect sensor.

Listing 22-12. Hall effect sensor

```
int LEDpin = 32;                      // define LED pin
unsigned long lastHall = 0;           // time Hall value changed

void setup()
{
  pinMode(LEDpin, OUTPUT);            // LED pin as output
}

void loop()
{
  if(abs(hallRead()) > 30) change();  // call change function
}                                     // when magnetic field detected

void change()
{
  if(millis() - lastHall < 1000) return; // check time last change
  lastHall = millis();                    // update change time
  digitalWrite(LEDpin, 1 - digitalRead(LEDpin));
}                                         // change LED state
```

Summary

The ESP32 microcontroller has two cores, each with a Tensilica Xtensa 32-bit LX6 microprocessor, and allocation of tasks to different cores effectively doubles task output relative to performing a task on one ESP32 core. The ESP32 microcontroller has Wi-Fi communication, SPI and I2C communication, analog to digital conversion, pulse width modulation, and interrupt functions. Several features are specific to the ESP32 microcontroller, which include Bluetooth and Bluetooth Low Energy communication, four independent timers for controlling events, a real-time clock to trigger the ESP32 microcontroller from sleep mode, digital to analog converter functionality, capacitive touch sensors for use of a touch pin instead of a switch, and a Hall effect sensor, which is activated by a magnetic field. Examples illustrate use of the ESP32 comprehensive features.

Components List

- ESP32 microcontroller: DEVKIT DOIT or NodeMCU board

- LED: 2×

- Resistor: 2× 220 Ω

- Tactile switch

APPENDIX

Libraries

The majority of the required libraries are uploaded within the Arduino IDE with other libraries available through GitHub, `www.github.com`, or specific websites as listed in Table A-1. Example sketches, within each library, are accessed in the Arduino IDE by selecting *File* ➤ *Example* ➤ *library name*. A library is included in a sketch with the instruction `#include` `<libraryname.h>`, which references the library located in the Arduino IDE libraries folder. To determine the location of the Arduino IDE libraries folder, select *File* ➤ *Preferences* in the Arduino IDE, and the libraries folder is located in the sketchbook location, for example, *C:\Users\user\ Documents\Arduino*.

When a library is included in a sketch, a variable is generally associated with the library, which is termed *creating an instance of the class*, where *class* is the library. The variable has the properties of the library, in a similar way that a variable defined as an integer has the properties of an integer. Instructions specific to a library are prefixed with the variable name. For example, the *ESP8266WebServer* library is installed with the instruction `#include <ESP8266WebServer.h>`, and the instruction `ESP8266WebServer server` associates the *server* variable with the library. An *ESP8266WebServer* library-specific instruction is prefixed with `server.` as in `server.handleClient()`.

© Neil Cameron 2021
N. Cameron, *Electronics Projects with the ESP8266 and ESP32*,
https://doi.org/10.1007/978-1-4842-6336-5

There are three methods to install a library:

1. Use the Library Manager.

    Open the Arduino IDE, select the *Sketch* menu and select *Include Library* ➤ *Manage Libraries*. In the *Library Manager* window, use the *Filter your search* option to locate the required library. Select the library version number and click *Install*. The *More info* option provides access to GitHub for library documentation and updates.

2. Import a zip file.

    Download the library in a *.zip* file and store the *.zip* file on your computer or laptop. In the Arduino IDE, select the *Sketch* menu and select *Include Library* ➤ *Add .ZIP library*. Select the location where the *.zip* file was saved, select the *.zip* file, and click *Open*.

3. Manual install.

    Download the library in a *.zip* file, and extract the contents of the *.zip* file to the default library folder, such as *C:\Users\user\Documents\Arduino*. The Arduino IDE must be restarted before the library is listed in the Arduino IDE, using the *Sketch* ➤ *Include Library* option.

Table A-1. *Libraries with details on source and author*

Library	Author and Source if Not Available in the Arduino IDE
Adafruit BMP280	Adafruit
Adafruit GFX	Adafruit
Adafruit ILI9341	Adafruit
Adafruit ILI9341 esp	NailBuster Software nailbuster.com/?page_id=341
Adafruit INA219	Adafruit
Adafruit MCP4725	Adafruit
Adafruit NeoPixel	Adafruit
Adafruit SSD1306	Adafruit
Adafruit S7735 and ST7789	Adafruit
Adafruit Unified Sensor	Adafruit
ArduinoJson	Benoit Blanchon
ArduinoOTA	Built-in
AsyncTCP	Hristo Gochkov github.com/me-no-dev/AsyncTCP
BLEDevice	Built-in with ESP32
BLEScan	Built-in with ESP32
BLEServer	Built-in with ESP32
BLEUtils	Built-in with ESP32
BLE2902	Built-in with ESP32
BluetoothSerial	Built-in with ESP32 Espressif Systems

(*continued*)

Table A-1. (*continued*)

Library	Author and Source if Not Available in the Arduino IDE
CayenneMQTT	Cayenne
EEPROM	David Mellis
ESP IDF FreeRTOS	Built-in with ESP32 Espressif Systems
esp_camera	Built-in with ESP32 Espressif Systems
esp_http_server	Built-in with ESP32 Espressif Systems
ESP32 BLE Arduino	Neil Kolban, built-in with ESP32 installation
ESP32 vs1053 ext	Wolle github.com/schreibfaul1/ESP32-vs1053_ext
ESP32Servo	Kevin Harrington and John K. Bennett
ESPAsyncWebServer	Hristo Gochkov github.com/me-no-dev/ESPAsyncWebServer
ESPmDNS	Built-in with ESP32 Espressif Systems
ESP-NOW	Built-in with ESP8266 and ESP32 Espressif Systems
ESP8266mDNS	Built-in with ESP8266
ESP8266WebServer	Built-in with ESP8266
ESP8266WiFi	Built-in with ESP8266
FS	Built-in with ESP8266
IRremote	Ken Shirriff github.com/z3t0/Arduino-IRremote
IRremoteESP8266	David Conran, Sebastien Warin, Mark Szabo, and Ken Shirriff

(*continued*)

Table A-1. (*continued*)

Library	Author and Source if Not Available in the Arduino IDE
Keyboard	Built-in
LittleFS	Built-in with ESP8266
LoRa	Sandeep Mistry
MD_AD9833	Marco Colli, MajicDesigns
MD_DS3231	Marco Colli, MajicDesigns
NeoGPS	Slash Devin
NewPing	Tim Eckel
NewPingESP8266	Tim Eckel and Jordan Shaw github.com/jshaw/NewPingESP8266
NTPtimeESP	Andreas Spiess github.com/Sensorslot/NTPtimeESP
printf	Included in RF24
rc-switch	Saut Özgür
RF24	James Coliz
RH_ASK	Mike McCauley www.airspayce.com/mikem/arduino/ RadioHead
rtc-io	Built-in with ESP32
RunningMedian	Rob Tillaart
SD	Built-in
SD_MMC	Built-in with ESP32 Espressif Systems
Servo	Built-in, Michael Margolis

(*continued*)

Table A-1. (*continued*)

Library	Author and Source if Not Available in the Arduino IDE
SoftwareSerial	Built-in
SPI	Built-in
SPIFFS	Built-in with ESP32 Espressif Systems
TFT_eSPI	Bodmer
Ticker	Built-in with ESP8266
Time	Michael Margolis
VS1053	Ed Smallenburg and James Coliz github.com/baldram/ESP_VS1053_Library
WebServer	Built-in with ESP32 Espressif Systems
WebSocketsServer	Markus Sattler
WiFi	Built-in with ESP32 Espressif Systems
WiFiUdp	Built-in with ESP8266 and ESP32 Espressif Systems
Wire	Built-in, Nicholas Zambetti
XPT2046	Spiros Papadimitriou github.com/spapadim/XPT2046

Index

© Neil Cameron 2021
N. Cameron, *Electronics Projects with the ESP8266 and ESP32*,
https://doi.org/10.1007/978-1-4842-6336-5

Printed in the United States
By Bookmasters